"R4R is a wonderful book. Written by renowned experts it oozes compassion, hope, humanity, humour and lashings of clinical wisdom whilst at the same time being scholarly and grounded in the latest evidence. Its approach to multi-family treatment of anorexia nervosa views this illness through a theoretically informed relational lens as a disorder of intra- and interpersonal disconnection and uses education and skills building to repair these relationship ruptures and facilitate growth of the individual and the people close to them. The case stories and therapeutic dialogue are detailed and realistic: individual characters leap off the page and their struggles and dilemmas always ring true. I learnt so much from this book. An absolute gem. This is a must-read for any clinician working with people with anorexia nervosa and their families."
Ulrike Schmidt, MD, PhD, FRCPsych, FAED, professor of Eating Disorders, King's College London and consultant psychiatrist, Maudsley Hospital; National Institute of Health Research senior investigator

"Congratulations to Tantillo, McGraw and Le Grange for this exceptional, must read book for providers of young adults with anorexia nervosa and their caregivers. R4R MFTG consists of 16-sessions grounded in well known theoretical frameworks, particularly Relational-Cultural theory. In each chapter, the authors provide a step-by-step guide of the structure and processes of delivering R4R MFTG in a variety of different contexts. Through detailed examples, analogies, metaphors, and handouts, providers will be well prepared to deliver this intervention to young adults with AN and their families. This book not only acknowledges the intense emotions experienced by the young adult with AN, but also the tumultuous emotions experienced by caregivers. The authors empower providers to use an optimistic healing and recovery approach that supports all involved in battling against the anorexia nervosa. By honouring and giving a voice to the experiences of young adults with AN and their families, those impacted by AN will become more powerful and resilient than the eating disorder."
Gina Dimitropoulos, MSW, PhD, associate professor of Social Work, University of Calgary and research lead for the Calgary Eating Disorder Program

"A beautifully written, innovative tour de force, a good read, and an inspiring contribution based on a multi-family therapy group approach to the complex, challenge of treating anorexia nervosa. The authors provide an elegant description of the biopsychosocial nature and associated treatment of anorexia nervosa developed in concert with the participating young adults and their families. From the biology of anorexia nervosa to problems with emotion, and internal and external disconnection, the authors provide unusual insight into human function and dysfunction. We can all benefit from their empathy and their wisdom. While termed a manual, this book is much more. Grounded in theory, it adds a relational/family lens to effective individual approaches, reports the evidence supporting this multi-family therapy group method, AND it provides an eminently practical manual describing the treatment in detail. *Multifamily Therapy Group for Young Adults with Anorexia Nervosa* is a MUST read for any therapist working with young adults, as it provides invaluable insight into the importance of families as crucibles for the development of self, identity, and a meaningful life. Tantillo, McGraw and Le Grange show us how to take a group of struggling families and create a community that supports young adults' recovery from anorexia nervosa and associated suffering. This approach, Reconnecting for Recovery, is simply brilliant!"

Susan H McDaniel, PhD, ABPP, Dr Laurie Sands distinguished professor of Families & Health, vice chair, Department of Family Medicine, University of Rochester Medical Center

"I am delighted to provide an endorsement for this much needed treatment manual. Whilst carers of children and adolescents are now routinely included in their loved ones' treatment programmes, I regularly meet carers of young adults who despair that they are being excluded because their child has reached a magical age of 18. This manual will fill a huge void and empower eating disorder specialist teams around the world to offer a programme to families of young people aged between 18 and 40, in a multifamily group setting. This model draws on the well-researched motivational Interviewing principles and stages of change theory and then goes a step further to include Relational-Cultural Theory, which asserts that AN is characterized by a number of internal and interpersonal disconnections that can obstruct collaborative caregiving and recovery. Participants are guided to explore in detail all aspects of internal and interpersonal disconnection that can be caused by anorexia nervosa. Acknowledging and discussing these in the group setting then empowers the family to work as a team to rebuild connections, potentially to avoid further disconnections, and disempower the eating disorder. In turn the young adult can then mature and grow in a healthy, happy and age appropriate manner. The manual guides the therapy team through a clearly set out programme of 16 sessions, with an array of useful handouts and clinical vignettes, whilst also allowing the therapists to pace with the needs of the participants of their multifamily group."

Jenny Langley, Author of *The New Maudsley Training Manual, Boys Get Anorexia Too* and New Maudsley Carer Skills Workshop facilitator and trainer

"This ground-breaking book completely reverses once-standard negative and judgmental dogma about families and eating disorders. Dr. Tantillo and her colleagues present brilliant insights into the inherent need for affected families to move from the inter- and intra-personnel disconnections caused by an eating disorder toward creating, repairing or strengthening connections at various levels. Clearly detailed are the 'how-to-steps' for families to forge powerful healing connections. By actively addressing the misunderstanding, shame, blame and guilt that often separate individuals in a family into units of 'I' or 'You' when the disorder is active, multi-family group therapy facilitates movement toward a collective 'WE' in recovery. Moreover, multi-family therapy groups allow mutual support and practical advice to be shared across affected family units."

Richard E. Kreipe, MD, FAAP, FSAHM, FAED, professor emeritus, Division of Adolescent Medicine, Department of Pediatrics, Golisano Children's Hospital, University of Rochester Medical Center

"This is an important contribution to the field of eating disorders written by well respected, experienced clinicians in the field. This treatment manual covers the Relational/Motivational multifamily therapy group approach for young adults with anorexia nervosa developed from clinical experience and in collaboration with families. This book gives excellent insight into the challenging fields of adolescent and young adult mental health, and will provide useful guidance for clinicians, researchers, students and trainees. Involving families in the treatment is hugely important in our field and the practical aspects of knowing how to do so will help colleagues implement this important work in their clinical services."

Kate Tchanturia, PhD, FAED, FBPS, FHEA, consultant clinical psychologist, Eating Disorders, professor of Psychological Medicine, King's College London

"Reconnecting for Recovery (R4R) is a user-friendly manual that helps clinicians learn a multi-family approach for the treatment of young adults with anorexia nervosa. The treatment is unique and well matched to the needs of individuals with anorexia nervosa whose illness often leads to isolation from family, friends, and school or professional life. The authors offer a model of eating disorders as illnesses characterized by internal and social disconnections, and a set of strategies that help affected families work together to help their loved ones achieve recovery. Tantillo and her team of authors have brought together impressive clinical expertise, recommendations from stakeholders, and the evidence base relevant to family-based treatment to provide a practical book chock-full of skill-building exercises for families."

Evelyn Attia, MD, professor of Psychiatry, Columbia University Irving Medical Center; director, Center for Eating Disorders, New York-Presbyterian Hospital

"Tantillo, Sanftner and Le Grange coherently provide clinicians with a rationale and method to comprehensively take a multifamily therapy group framework and feature a motivational and relational approach for young adults with anorexia nervosa, Reconnecting for Recovery (R4R). The authors step into a complex illness with a well-structured treatment that brings severed facets of the illness together by reconnecting multiple dimensions to move recovery forward. The manual is practical and easy to follow. It takes what is hard to do therapeutically and makes it doable."

Laura Hill, PhD, International Eating Disorder Consultant

Multifamily Therapy Group for Young Adults with Anorexia Nervosa

Multifamily Therapy Group for Young Adults with Anorexia Nervosa describes a new and innovative family-centered outpatient Multifamily Therapy Group (MFTG) approach called Reconnecting for Recovery (R4R) for young adults with anorexia nervosa that is based on a relational reframing of eating disorders.

Developed in concert with young adults and their families and informed by clinical observations, theory, and research, R4R is designed to help young adults and family members learn the emotional and relational skills required to avoid or repair relationship ruptures for continued collaboration in recovery. The book begins with an overview of anorexia nervosa, MFTG treatment approaches, and the development of R4R and moves into a session by session review of R4R including session goals, exercises and handouts. Protocols, case vignettes, and other materials help translate the theory and research underlying this multifamily therapy group model into practice.

This treatment manual provides readers with explicit guidance in how to develop and conduct an outpatient R4R MFTG and a deeper understanding of the nature, purposes, and processes that characterize one.

Mary Tantillo, PhD, PMHCNS-BC, CGP, FAED, is professor of clinical nursing at University of Rochester School of Nursing, director of the Western New York Comprehensive Care Center for Eating Disorders, and founder of The Healing Connection Inc.

Jennifer Sanftner McGraw, PhD, is professor of psychology and department chair at Slippery Rock University and founder and director of the Slippery Rock chapter of the Reflections Body Image Program.

Daniel Le Grange, PhD, holds a distinguished professorship in the department of psychiatry at the University of California, San Francisco and is director of the eating disorders program in the Division of Child and Adolescent Psychiatry.

Caruana Santo, Artist and young adult in recovery from an eating disorder.

Bieber Marie, RD, CSP, CDN, Registered dietitian specializing in eating disorders in private practice and on the Western New York Comprehensive Care Center for Eating Disorders Project ECHO[TM] team.

Multifamily Therapy Group for Young Adults with Anorexia Nervosa
Reconnecting for Recovery

Mary Tantillo, Jennifer Sanftner McGraw, and Daniel Le Grange

Illustrations by Santo Caruana and Marie Bieber RD, CSP, CDN

NEW YORK AND LONDON

First published 2021
by Routledge
52 Vanderbilt Avenue, New York, NY 10017

and by Routledge
2 Park Square, Milton Park, Abingdon, Oxon, OX14 4RN

Routledge is an imprint of the Taylor & Francis Group, an informa business

© 2021 Taylor & Francis

The right of Mary Tantillo, Jennifer Sanftner McGraw, and Daniel Le Grange to be identified as authors of this work has been asserted by them in accordance with sections 77 and 78 of the Copyright, Designs and Patents Act 1988.

All rights reserved. No part of this book may be reprinted or reproduced or utilised in any form or by any electronic, mechanical, or other means, now known or hereafter invented, including photocopying and recording, or in any information storage or retrieval system, without permission in writing from the publishers.

Trademark notice: Product or corporate names may be trademarks or registered trademarks, and are used only for identification and explanation without intent to infringe.

Library of Congress Cataloging-in-Publication Data
Names: Tantillo, Mary, author. | Sanftner McGraw, Jennifer, author. |
Le Grange, Daniel, author.
Title: Multifamily therapy group for young adults with anorexia nervosa :
reconnecting for recovery / Mary Tantillo, Jennifer Sanftner McGraw, Daniel
Le Grange.
Description: First edition. | New York : Routledge, 2020. | Includes
bibliographical references and index. | Summary: "Multifamily Therapy Group
for Young Adults with Anorexia Nervosa describes a new and innovative family-
centered outpatient Multifamily Therapy Group (MFTG) approach called
Reconnecting for Recovery (R4R) for young adults with anorexia nervosa that is
based on a relational reframing of eating disorders. Developed in concert with
young adults and their families and informed by clinical observations, theory, and
research, R4R is designed to help young adults and family members learn the
emotional and relational skills required to avoid or repair relationship ruptures for
continued collaboration in recovery. The book begins with an overview of anorexia
nervosa, MFTG treatment approaches, and the development of R4R and moves
into a session by session review of R4R including session goals, exercises and
handouts. Protocols, case vignettes, and other materials help translate the theory
and research underlying this multifamily therapy group model into practice. This
treatment manual provides readers with explicit guidance in how to develop and
conduct an outpatient R4R MFTG and a deeper understanding of the nature,
purposes, and processes that characterize one"-- Provided by publisher.
Identifiers: LCCN 2020024926 (print) | LCCN 2020024927 (ebook) | ISBN
9781138624900 (paperback) | ISBN 9781138624894 (hardback) | ISBN
9780429460364 (ebook)
Subjects: LCSH: Eating disorders in adolescence--Treatment. | Anorexia in
adolescence--Treatment. | Family psychotherapy.
Classification: LCC RC552.E18 T37 2020 (print) | LCC RC552.E18 (ebook) |
DDC 616.85/2600835--dc23
LC record available at https://lccn.loc.gov/2020024926
LC ebook record available at https://lccn.loc.gov/2020024927

ISBN: 978-1-138-62489-4 (hbk)
ISBN: 978-1-138-62490-0 (pbk)
ISBN: 978-0-429-46036-4 (ebk)

Typeset in Baskerville
by MPS Limited, Dehradun

This book is dedicated to all the patients and families we have been privileged to serve. And to The Spirit that moves within each of us, inviting us to ever more authentically connect with ourselves and with others in therapy and in life.

Contents

List of Figures	xiv
List of Tables	xv
Foreword by Janet Treasure	xvi
Foreword by June Alexander	xviii
Acknowledgments	xxii
List of Contributors	xxiv

1   Reconnecting for Recovery (R4R): A Relational/
Motivational Multifamily Therapy Group for
Young Adults with Anorexia Nervosa   1

2   The Promise of Multifamily Therapy Group for
Young Adults with Anorexia Nervosa   22

3   Development of the Reconnecting for Recovery
(R4R) MFTG Approach and This Manual   41

4   Getting Ready: Group Structure, Co-Facilitation,
Recruitment, and Initial Phone Screening   62

5   Session 1: Engaging and Evaluating Young Adults
with Anorexia Nervosa and Their Families:
Assessment, Joining, and Orientation   67

6   Session 2: Engaging and Evaluating Young Adults
with Anorexia Nervosa and Their Families:
Assessment, Joining, and Orientation (Continued)   87

xii   *Contents*

7   Session 3: Anorexia Nervosa—A Disease of
    Disconnection—Introduction, Recovery Process,
    Motivational Interviewing Principles, and the
    Spiral of Change   98

8   Session 4: Anorexia Nervosa—A Disease of
    Disconnection—Introduction, Recovery Process,
    Motivational Interviewing Principles, and the
    Spiral of Change (Continued)   114

9   Session 5: Biopsychosocial Factors for Anorexia
    Nervosa and Co-morbidity   126

10 Session 6: Biopsychosocial Factors (Continued),
    Disconnection and Functional Analysis Skills   138

11 Session 7: Strategies to Promote Mutual Connection 152

12 Session 8: Anorexia Nervosa and the Family
    Context: Rules and Relationships   158

13 Session 9: Identifying Points of Tension and
    Disconnections Related to Anorexia Nervosa,
    Recovery, and Relationships   173

14 Session 10: Nourishing and Empowering the "We"
    in Relationships   194

15 Session 11: Waging Good Conflict in Connection   207

16 Session 12: Moving from Disconnection to
    Connection: Building Strong Connections to Work
    through Tension and Disconnections Related to
    Adulthood and Recovery   217

17 Session 13: Relapse Prevention and Maintaining
    Good Connection   235

18 Session 14: Relapse Prevention (Continued) and
    Preparing for Termination   256

Contents xiii

19 Session 15: Relapse Prevention (Continued),
Termination, and Next Steps for Continued
Connections in Recovery 266

20 Session 16: Relapse Prevention (Continued),
Termination, and Next Steps for Continued
Connections in Recovery 273

21 What Is Next? Training, Dissemination, Clinical
Practice, and Research 280

Index 294

List of Figures

5.1	Disconnection	69
5.2	Disconnection	70
5.3	Mutual Relationships	74
5.4	The Five Good Things	77
5.5	Animal Caregiver Styles	79
7.1	Spiral of Change	108
7.2	How Do You Feel Today?	111
10.1	The Interactions Among Patient Internal Disconnections, Interpersonal Disconnections with Loved Ones, Negative Relational Images and Meanings, and Anorexia Nervosa Thoughts, Attitudes and Behaviors	140
13.1	Recovery Plate	192
14.1	Forces that Perpetuate Interpersonal Disconnections and Anorexia Nervosa	195

List of Tables

3.1	Disconnections Experienced by 8-week MFTG Alumni Patients and Family Members	43
3.2	Reconnecting for Recovery Goals	55
3.3	Reconnecting for Recovery Multifamily Therapy Group Sessions and Topics	56
4.1	R4R MFTG Inclusion and Exclusion Criteria	63
6.1	Reconnecting for Recovery Syllabus (R4R)	95
7.1	Process of Change and Interventions to Promote Eating Disorder Recovery	110
9.1	Phenomena Involving Intrapersonal Processes of Disconnection	127
9.2	Phenomena Involving Interpersonal Processes of Disconnection	127
9.3	Interpersonal Disconnections with Close Others	128
10.1	Functional Analysis Example—Rhinoceros and Dolphin Caregiver Responses	147
10.2	Functional Analysis Worksheet	149
12.1	Strategies to Promote Mutual Connections and Recovery	159
12.2	Implicit and Explicit Rules Regarding the Eating Disorder, Recovery, and Relationships	164
12.3	Rules and Relationships: The Family Context of Eating Disorders	170
13.1	Points of Tension and Disconnections Related to Anorexia Nervosa, Recovery and Relationships	175
13.2	Moving Through Disconnection to Better Connection: Learning a New Relational Language and Process	183
13.3	Mealtime Guidelines and Support Strategies for Recovery	186
13.4	Coaching and Mealtime Assistance	189
17.1	Animal Metaphors for Caregiving Styles: Caregiver and Patient Responses and Impact on Recovery	242

Foreword by Janet Treasure, PhD, FRCP, FRCPsych

Professor of Psychiatry, IOPPN, King's College London

The Reconnecting for Recovery Multifamily Therapy Group described in this treatment manual reframes anorexia nervosa as a disease of disconnection and places connection at the heart of recovery. The voices of individuals in recovery and their caregivers need to inform our understanding of these internal and interpersonal disconnections and the best ways in which to reconnect young adults to themselves and those who care for them. Therefore, In the spirit of connection June and I are jointly writing the foreword to this manual.

As I write this foreword, I am living through the strange scenario of international self-isolation from COVID 19. This strategy has been used many times over time in the human battle with disease. For example, I am isolated with my family in Derbyshire. In 1665 the Derbyshire village of Eyam put itself into isolation when the plague was brought from London in a consignment of second-hand clothes. Although the death rate in the village was high, this strategy limited the spread of this disease.

Now we have all experienced to some degree the pain and discomfort that social isolation brings, although this has been buffered by the technological wizardry of social media. However, we need to remember that a doctor describing her personal experience with anorexia nervosa stated isolation was the one word that summarised the impact of the illness (McKnight & Boughton, 2009). We also have June's vivid testimony. These descriptions of lived experience illustrate why this book with its focus on connection is an invaluable asset to all interested in the management of these conditions.

The clinical features of the illness with a median onset at 15 years and an average illness duration of 10 years signposts the need to consider how the critical developmental stage of transition from care within the family of birth to the family of choice may be blighted by the illness. It seems ironic to me that treatment is often scaffolded around structures that are constructed around standard developmental milestones rather than individualised needs. Thus, an individual with an early onset that stunts development may be fast forwarded to a system that expects adult level autonomy with disconnection from the family just because the eighteenth birthday or some arbitrary marker has been passed. This book describes how a microenvironment of care from friends, family and professionals can be used in order to nurture growth into recovery.

A predisposition to problems in social emotional functioning increases the risk of developing anorexia nervosa (Caglar-Nazali et al. 2014). Also, there may be a differential sensitivity to punishment and reward. These biological and psychological factors can underpin the perfect storm that triggers the onset of anorexia nervosa. Vicarious learning from social structures can play an important role in modifying inborn and acquired traits. Learning and support from the experience of the family and close others can make the challenge of transitioning into new structures more customised rather than the one size fits all approach that many current systems deliver.

Individuals who are sensitive to ranking and the judgments of others and who fear making mistakes are at risk of developing an eating disorder. However, if and when, these potential talents are channelled and supported by social moderators such as those exemplified in this book, then they can contribute to the formation of a committed citizen (as June's health story exemplifies). The approach taken in this book offers a developmentally sensitive and informed approach connected with state-of-the-art professional knowledge of the illness. As EM Forster said "**only connect**! ..., and human love will be seen at its height. Live in fragments no longer." This book can help put this into practice and overcome the strong strangulating strictures of the eating disorder voice.

Janet Treasure, OBE, PhD, FRCP, FRCPsych, is an award-winning researcher and clinician with over 35 years specialising in eating disorder treatment. Janet has been the author of over 500 published papers, held the Chief Medical Advisor position at Beat, the UK's primary eating disorder charity, and currently works in the academic section of the Eating Disorder Unit at King's College London and the clinical section of the South London and Maudsley. She is the author of multiple self-help materials designed for, and with, patients and carers of individuals with eating disorders, and textbooks that stand as fundamental guidelines for treatment worldwide.

References

Caglar-Nazali, H. P., Corfield, F., Cardi, V., Ambwani, S., Leppanen, J., Olabintan, O., Deriziotis, S., Hadjimichalis, A., Scognamiglio, P., Eshkevari, E., & Micali, N. A. (2014). Systematic review and meta-analysis of 'Systems for Social Processes' in eating disorders. *Neuroscience & Biobehavioral Reviews*. *42*:55-92. https://doi.org/10.1016/j.neubiorev.2013.12.002

McKnight, R., & Boughton N. (2009). Anorexia nervosa. *British Medical Journal, 24*

Foreword by June Alexander, PhD

Author and memoir-writing mentor, Australia

My life with Anorexia Nervosa (AN) has been a story of disconnections and connections.

I will celebrate my 70th birthday at the end of this year. I am no longer battling the AN that developed at age 11, but I am still trying to hold the hand of the Little June that got lost in the illness at that time, and to show and reassure her that Healthy Adult June can take care of her so that she feels safe, and secure. Today, stories like mine can be avoided.

Reconnecting Adult June with Little June has been difficult. For decades I had nobody to explain what is known today and revealed in this treatment manual – that AN is characterized by internal and interpersonal disconnections and that recovery is very much about connections with self and others. As a teenager and young adult, I wondered, "Do other people think the same way as I do?" I had no answer. My experience was limited to my own mind, which was very busy, with multiple thoughts bombarding and exploding all day long, largely keeping me in a world of my own. Feeling carefree was a foreign concept.

I was 56 years old when able to eat three meals and three snacks daily without feeling guilty. Today, decisions about everything to do with life don't depend on how I am coping or not coping with calorie counting; I don't care what size clothing I wear; I can arrive late for a meeting without feeling ashamed; I exercise daily with my puppy Maisie because I want to, not because I am compelled to; I don't have rigid rules about what I must do, and must not do, as a means of getting through the day. I have learned to love the color gray for it is a sponge, a filter, a bridge, between black and white. Life is good.

However, the events of my 11th year continue to shape my life. That was the year when AN embedded itself in my brain and set about disconnecting me from my healthy self and from everyone I loved. I experienced what is described in this manual – that AN is a disease of disconnection.

My family of origin and I missed out on the critical need to develop relational skills that would promote unity and understanding. By the time I healed and reconnected with my healthy self, my family had created a life without me.

Foreword by June Alexander xix

As a child with AN in the early 1960s in rural Australia, there was no help available. Growing up, I missed out on learning relational skills that would foster a sense of connection, not only within my family of origin but also with friends at school, in the workplace and in the wider community. Much of my maturity was stunted, leading to perceived inadequacy, failure and low self-efficacy. In many ways I was a textbook case of the illness – low body weight due to restriction of intake and excessive exercise, fear of weight gain, poor body image.

Between the age of 20 and 30, suicidal thoughts were frequent. Married to my childhood sweetheart at 20, with four children by the age of 25, by age 27, my increasing self-harm was making me aware that I needed help, but I feared that if I told a doctor about my inner story, they would declare me an incredibly weak-minded person, or worse, that I was insane and needed to be locked up away from my children. Death beckoned. Luckily, my love for my children won out, and after 16 years of private hell, and another night of self-harm, I sobbed my story out to a local general practitioner (GP). By this time, the illness had created many distressing disconnections for myself and others.

For years, I feared that if I was authentic with others about my inner torment and insistent, demanding thoughts, the disconnection would increase. The few times I tried to speak with my family, they had said, "Pull up your socks" and, "You think about yourself too much." The insinuation was that I was weak for not coping. Such responses increased my sense of disconnection and personal failure, and I withdrew even more. This painful relational dilemma became progressively desperate until my love for my children, aged two to six, won out – enabling me to connect by a thin thread to myself and to dare to be honest with the GP. The line between life and death was extremely fine – death would have been the ultimate disconnection that AN could serve up when chronically cut off from myself and others.

Six years of misdiagnosis followed my initial outpouring to the GP. They were difficult years. At age 33, I met a psychiatrist who won my trust but flatly said that my chances were 'fair.' He diagnosed chronic AN, chronic anxiety and chronic depression.

The anxiety had developed before the AN, and would continue beyond my recovery from AN.

There was no quick fix. For decades, the AN had affected every decision and hampered my ability to form friendships and to feel good about myself. My mother's plaintive comment, "Why can't you be like the other girls?" pierced my soul. I didn't know how school friends could eat a salad roll and a cream bun for lunch and not feel terribly guilty. If I dared to eat what they ate, to try and appear 'normal,' I would have to undergo a punishing exercise routine and food deprivation that night, causing a fresh tirade from my mother ("how dare you waste this food"). This was a regular painful relational dilemma – do what AN says and forfeit relationships with loved ones or do what loved ones ask and undergo self-punishment. This led to uncharacteristic deceitful behavior – for instance, giving my packed school lunch to others, or

xx *Foreword by June Alexander*

tossing it in a bin, rather than risking my mother's ire. As a teenager, young wife and mother, I wanted to be like the others, but I didn't know how. I felt different in a negative way, always on the periphery of social interaction. I didn't know how to be carefree. I didn't belong.

So, when I met the psychiatrist who saved my life, I was prescribed medications, which helped to numb my brain, but some of the drugs had gruelling side-effects and are now banned. I was a guinea pig. In my 30s and 40s I did not know who I was; my identity was shredded, lost; I didn't know if a thought was a healthy-me thought, or was borne of the AN, or was shaped by the medication, and this affected all areas of life. Disconnection was rife.

The losses were heart-breaking.

I lost my marriage and became progressively alienated from my family of origin (my parents, and sister). I was considered unreliable, irresponsible and self-centered. These were characteristics of my illness, but my family thought they were real 'me' and made decisions accordingly.

In the 1980s, my youngest child, a daughter, lived with her dad from the age of eight. I was terrified she would 'catch' my illness. Sacrifices were great. The AN had a mantra. Isolate and conquer.

The illness almost killed me, but not quite. The psychiatrist who won my trust and for the most part was not fooled by my powerful AN, worked patiently with me over 25 years. He kept his door open and encouraged me to keep trying. My psychiatrist, together with several other health professionals and a church minister, believed in me when I was unable to believe in, or connect with my healthy self. Gradually, by daring to trust in my treatment team more than my AN, I was guided over the line in reconnecting with 51 per cent 'me.' Thereafter, recovery became easier to strengthen and sustain as the 'voice' of my healthy self had more sway.

I am fortunate. The father of my children came from a stable, secure and safe family and provided a supportive rock and steadying influence for both our children and me during the difficult decades of my treatment and recovery. As the children grew into young adults, they joined their father in 'being there' as carers when I needed a boost in support. My family today comprises my ex-husband as a friend, my four children, their partners and five grandchildren. We gather for birthdays and special occasions like Christmas and my heart sings.

Sadly, my illness occurred during a time when partners were shut out of treatment sessions, leading to an exacerbation of disconnection. AN loved this. However, while AN ruined my marriage, for three is a crowd, it did not destroy the friendship and early connection that my husband and I had forged in our teenage years. For this I am grateful.

Two other factors have contributed to my survival and sustained freedom. One factor is a passion for writing – a passion that was budding and blooming before the age of 11. A Christmas gift of a diary in the same year that AN developed set me on a path of diary-writing which continues to this day. The ravaging disintegration of self is documented, as is the slow but persistent reconnection with healthy self. This documentation has been helpful in accepting what happened, allowing me to grieve for the little girl lost, and move forward. The other factor is engagement in the eating disorder field – upon escaping my AN prison after 44 years, and writing my memoir, *A Girl Called Tim*, I became aware that there were others like me. I began learning about my illness through attending eating disorder conferences and listening to our wonderful researchers in the field, which helped me to accept, in my 60s, that I was not a weak or bad person after all; I was someone who had an illness called AN. I became involved in advocacy, promoting a message of 'recovery at every age,' and became part of a global 'family of choice' which has contributed to an invaluable sense of acceptance, belonging and connectedness.

Life is good. But a disconnect remains. Little June has yet to master the skill of being able to be vulnerable and allow herself to be cared for in a safe, loving and happy relationship, first and foremost with myself. Safe and 'nice' men have been pushed away, while men who have a nature like AN, have at times entered a relationship and, like AN, have been very difficult to eliminate. A patient psychologist is working with me to overcome self-doubt and to strengthen self-respect. Damage was done to my thought and behavioral processes when AN developed at age 11, and I need to go back there to establish a healthy reconnection.

I remain hopeful of one day being in a healthy relationship not only with myself but with someone who is attracted to Healthy Adult June. I have come so far. I deserve the full cherry of life experiences, as does every child who develops AN. Any small accomplishment that nurtures self-esteem and self-belief is a major achievement.

I hope you can see, as noted in this treatment manual, that this difficult illness is about disconnectedness and connectedness with self and others, more than it is about weight or size. This illness is in the brain. This illness affects relationships and every part of life. I would not wish my experience on anyone.

AN is easier to treat successfully as soon as possible after diagnosis, and when the entire family – mother, father, siblings and the child with the illness – is involved in treatment. I am delighted to be invited to contribute to this Foreword for *Multifamily Therapy Group for Young Adults with Anorexia Nervosa: Reconnecting for Recovery*. With this evidence-based therapy, families of children who develop AN today, can look forward to their youngster getting their life back on track quickly, with family relationships strengthened rather than destroyed. Nothing is more important than this.

Dr. June Alexander is author, co-author and co-editor of nine non-fiction books, including her memoir. All are about eating disorders. June is a life skills and story-writing peer mentor. Her PhD explored the use of diary writing in eating disorder recovery. Her website The Diary Healer informs and encourages people in eating disorder recovery, while also promoting life writing and diary-writing as a self-help and creative tool. Websites: www.thediaryhealer.com and www.lifestoriesmentor.com.au

Acknowledgments

This treatment manual emphasizes the importance of healing and growth in connection with others in therapy and life. The birth and development of this manual also occurred within many loving and supportive connections. We would like to take a moment to express our appreciation for the technical and emotional support we received throughout the development of this manual.

We are grateful for Routledge's belief in our ability to publish written work that would be helpful to clinicians, young adults with anorexia nervosa, and their family members. We are thankful for the patience and good counsel of the editorial staff including Amanda Devine and Grace McDonnell. Their encouragement was especially appreciated because Dr. Tantillo experienced a house fire during the development of this manual. The kind emails of support from Routledge staff and countless family members, friends, colleagues, patients and families meant a great deal. Their messages of love emboldened her to persevere with manual development. And like the phoenix that rose from the ashes, so did this manual and her new home.

We would also like to thank our colleagues and friends at the University of Rochester School of Nursing (URSON) (especially the research support staff involved in the Reconnecting for Recovery [R4R] pilot study and Alexandra Wilkosz and Susan Reynolds, our two study interventionists), the Western New York Comprehensive Care Center for Eating Disorders and The Healing Connection. They would often ask how the writing was coming and were some of our best cheerleaders. Dr. Tantillo would like to thank Dr. Richard Kreipe and Dr. Kathy Rideout for their encouragement and support of her work leading up to and including this manual. Additionally, she would like to thank her long-time academic mentor, Dr. Susan McDaniel, for her support and wisdom. She has been instrumental in Dr. Tantillo's professional development and scholarship leading to the development of this manual. We are also thankful for funding from the NY State Department of Health, Hilda and Preston David Foundation, and the URSON and Dr. Pamela Klainer (Jeremy A. Klainer Dean's Discretionary Award) that allowed us to develop R4R over the years, complete the R4R pilot study, and publish this treatment manual.

Dr. Tantillo sends an extra special thanks to her family who supported her throughout the development of this manual. They understood that they would eventually see her at holidays and family events "once she had written for a little while." She is also thankful for the support of her stepchildren, Katie and Paul, whose attentive listening and good humor allowed her to persist on challenging days. And she is very thankful to her son, Eddie, who lights up her life. His boundless energy, free spirit, soulfulness, compassion and perseverance are a constant source of inspiration. She would also like to express her deep appreciation to her husband, best friend and soulmate – Odysseus. He, more than anyone else, directly experienced the impact of what it is like to be married to someone who works her normal job by day and writes by night and weekends. He would often see Dr. Tantillo leave in the morning and know he would not see her till late into the evening. Living up to his name, he accompanied her on this writing voyage and regardless of the challenges, remained a source of encouragement till the end of the journey. Long before she began writing this manual, he would say to her, "You should write a book!" So, she finally did this in concert with two of her gifted colleagues, Dr. Jennifer McGraw and Dr. Daniel Le Grange. She is very grateful for her connections with them because this manual would not have evolved into the cogent and creative work it is without the two of them.

Dr. McGraw wishes to acknowledge the love and support of her husband and soul mate – Bob – during this process. It was his encouragement and belief in us that buoyed her spirits, especially during the times of intensity, when there were also many other demands at play. He understood that it was a labor of love for us and a long time in coming. In the final stages of preparing the manuscript, it was many hours at the computer on evenings and weekends that got us to the finish line. She is grateful for his patience with her in seeing it through.

And of course, many thanks to patients and families who inspire us every day and who have provided feedback about the development of R4R Multifamily Therapy Group through the years. This group emerged within and because of the connections with all of you.

And finally, we want to thank The Spirit who guided us during the writing of this manual. We thank Him/Her for helping us write about the disconnections characterizing AN and the ways to transform those disconnections into reconnections and new connections with self and others as an antidote. No one treatment approach will "cure" AN, but we hope this treatment manual will bring us one step closer to what will promote healing and wholeness for patients and families, allowing them to reclaim their health and their lives.

List of Contributors

Dr. Mary Tantillo is a professor of Clinical Nursing at the University of Rochester School of Nursing and a clinical professor in the Department of Psychiatry at the University of Rochester School of Medicine and Dentistry. She has devoted over 35 years to working with adolescents and adults with eating disorders and their families in a variety of clinical and community settings. She is the founder of The Healing Connection, a free-standing nonprofit eating disorder facility for adolescents and adults in Rochester, New York, as well as the director of the Western New York Comprehensive Care Center for Eating Disorders, one of three state centers funded by the New York state Department of Health. She is also a fellow of the Academy for Eating Disorders. Dr. Tantillo's research interests focus on the application of Relational Cultural Theory in understanding the etiology and treatment of eating disorders, especially group, family, and multifamily treatments.

Dr. Jennifer Sanftner McGraw is professor of psychology and department chair at Slippery Rock University. She is a clinical psychologist, who has been teaching and conducting research in body image and eating disorders throughout her career. She is founder and director of the Reflections Body Image Program on the Slippery Rock University Campus. Her research interests focus on application of Relational Cultural Theory to understanding the etiology and treatment of eating disorders, and the use of intervention programs to prevent disordered eating in college students, including women, men, and those with diverse sexualities and gender identities.

Dr. Daniel Le Grange holds a distinguished professorship at the University of California, San Francisco (UCSF), where he is a Benioff UCSF professor in Children's Health in the Department of Psychiatry UCSF Weill Institute for Neurosciences, and director of the Eating Disorders Program in the Division of Child and Adolescent Psychiatry. Dr. Le Grange also is emeritus professor of Psychiatry and Behavioral Neuroscience at The University of Chicago. He received his doctoral education at the Institute of Psychiatry and the Maudsley Hospital, the

University of London, and completed postdoctoral training at Stanford University School of Medicine, California. Dr. Le Grange's research interests focus primarily on treatment studies for adolescents and transition aged youth with eating disorders. This focused scholarship has been translated into nine languages. Dr. Le Grange is a Fellow of the Academy for Eating Disorders, and a member of the Eating Disorders Research Society.

1 Reconnecting for Recovery (R4R)

A Relational/Motivational Multifamily Therapy Group for Young Adults with Anorexia Nervosa

Mary Tantillo, Jennifer Sanftner McGraw, and Daniel Le Grange

Introduction and Purpose of This Book

In his book, *Persuasion and Healing*, Jerome Frank (1991) noted that all psychotherapies are characterized by a "conceptual scheme or myth" that provides a credible explanation for patient symptoms and a prescribed approach believed to resolve these symptoms and restore health (pp. 42–43). Identifying a credible framework for understanding the symptoms and experiences of young adults with anorexia nervosa (AN) and their families is critical because making sense of events transpiring in recovery and life are as essential as "the need for food and water" (Frank & Frank, 1991, p. 24). This need is amplified in AN because the disorder obstructs young adults' abilities to accurately *make sense* of their own internal and interpersonal experiences, while also preventing them from taking in the needed energy required for recovery and continued growth and development. AN also challenges caregiver sensibilities, because their young adult loved ones either do not recognize they are ill or are unable to articulate what is transpiring within. A credible explanation or "conceptual frame" for the symptoms and experiences of young adults with AN and their families must be heavily informed by patient and family lived experience, along with clinical observations, theory, and research for it to be meaningful and acceptable. It must be compelling enough to keep the therapist, young adult with AN, and family members connected and actively participating in the prescribed treatment throughout the hardships of treatment and joys of recovery.

This treatment manual describes a new and innovative multifamily therapy group (MFTG) approach (*Reconnecting for Recovery, R4R*) for young adults with AN that is based on a *relational reframing* of eating disorders as *Diseases of Disconnection*. This new conceptual frame was developed in concert with young adults and their families over the last decade (Tantillo, 2006; Tantillo, McGraw, Hauenstein, & Groth, 2015; Tantillo & Sanftner, 2010a) and is also informed by clinical observations, theory, and research (Tantillo, 2010; Tantillo,

McGraw, Lavigne, Brasch, & Le Grange, 2019; Tantillo & Sanftner, 2010b; Tantillo, Sanftner, & Hauenstein, 2013). Although the R4R approach integrates Motivational Interviewing (MI) principles (Miller & Rollnick, 2013) and Stages of Change Theory (Prochaska, Norcross, & DiClemente, 1994), it is heavily informed by Relational-Cultural Theory (R-CT) (Jordan, 2018; Miller & Stiver, 1997; Tantillo & Sanftner, 2010a). The latter asserts that *intrapersonal (biological and psychological) and interpersonal (affective and behavioral) processes of disconnection* occurring in concert with other biopsychosocial risk factors can increase risk for development and maintenance of eating disorders and other mental and physical health problems. Examples of intrapersonal processes of disconnections include alexithymia and poor interoceptive awareness, which obstruct a patient's ability to name and express internal emotional and bodily states. Examples of interpersonal processes of disconnection include self-silencing and avoidance, which prevent communication of feelings and needs and increase isolation and conflict with family members. It is the interplay of intra- and interpersonal processes of disconnection that contributes to the *interpersonal disconnections* experienced by young adults with AN and their families. Interpersonal disconnections are marked by a lack of communication or high expressed emotion (e.g., emotional over-involvement, hostility, and criticism [Butzlaff & Hooley, 1998; Leff & Vaughn, 1985; Le Grange, Eisler, Dare, & Hodes, 1992; Le Grange, Hoste, Lock, & Bryson, 2010; van Furth, van Strien, Martina, van Son, Hendrickx, & van Engeland, 1996]) due to a neural and relational misalignment (Stephens, Silbert, & Hasson, 2010) between patient and family. Thus, the young adult with AN and family members are not accurately reading each other's emotions and needs, and caregivers have difficulty developing accurate empathy and responding effectively. These experiences can perpetuate illness, because young adults with AN are often psychosocially challenged, do not cope well with intense emotion, and frequently end up using AN symptoms to manage intense affect and interpersonal stress.

In the R4R MFTG approach, AN is externalized and viewed as the force that creates and maintains disconnections. Patients and family members are often reminded that AN does this to continue its exclusive "relationship" with the patient. They are taught that AN not only creates disconnections but also offers itself as a solution to these disconnections. Although R4R MFTG affirms the importance of nutritional rehabilitation and mealtime assistance to target the disconnections related to malnutrition and starvation (e.g., numbing of emotions), it predominantly focuses on building group member emotional and relational skills that are required to identify the disconnections characterizing AN and to foster mutual relationships for recovery. Qualitative and quantitative empirical findings, patient and family narratives, and clinical observations support the notion that improved connections with self and others are essential for recovery from AN (Bell, 2011; Berkman, Lohr, & Bulik, 2007; Federici & Kaplan, 2008; Lowe, Zipfel, Buchholz, Dupont, Reas, & Herzog., 2001; Tozzi, Sullivan, Fear,

McKenzie, & Bulik, 2003; Wright & Hacking, 2012). Relational-Cultural Theory (Jordan, 2018; Miller & Stiver, 1997; Tantillo & Sanftner, 2010a), at the heart of R4R, emphasizes that a mutual sense of perceived understanding, empathy, and empowerment (perceived mutuality) in relationships is what moves patients and families toward new and better connections and continues forward momentum in treatment and recovery.

If we adopt the relational reframe that AN is a disease of disconnection, then helping young adults with AN and their family members to develop relational skills that promote perceived mutuality is critical. Clinical observation, patient and family subjective accounts, and empirical work (Frey, 2013; Lenz, 2016; Jordan, 2018; Tantillo, 2006; Tantillo, 2010; Tantillo, Anson, Lavigne, & Wilkosz, 2019; Tantillo, McGraw, Hauenstein, & Groth, 2015; Tantillo, McGraw, Lavigne, Brasch, & Le Grange, 2019; Tantillo, Sanftner, & Hauenstein, 2013) lend support to the notion that promoting perceived mutuality among young adults with AN and their family members is an essential evidence-based practice. Relational skills that foster a sense of perceived mutuality are also especially important for young adults who developmentally are supposed to be refining connections with their families of origin while building additional connections with others outside the family at school, work, and in the broader community. Poor psychosocial functioning predicts outcome in AN (Bell, 2011; Berkman, Lohr, & Bulik, 2007; Federici & Kaplan, 2008; Lowe, Zipfel, Buchholz, Dupont, Reas, & Herzog, 2001; Tozzi, Sullivan, Fear, McKenzie, & Bulik, 2003; Wright & Hacking, 2012). The inability to build and sustain mutual connections can hinder a young adult's ability to navigate the myriad transitions that characterize this developmental period. Perceived failure and low self-efficacy can lead to increased use of AN symptoms to cope with stress and loss, contributing to illness maintenance (Schmidt & Treasure, 2006).

Although individual therapy, family therapy, and group therapy can all assist in promoting reconnection with self and others (Byrne et al., 2017; Grenon, Schwartze, Hammond, Ivanova, Proulx, & Tasca, 2017; Jewell, Blessit, Stewart, Simic, & Eisler, 2016; Jordan, 2018), R4R MFTG leverages the combined strengths, resources, and coping strategies of a number of patients and families. MFTG becomes a therapeutic village in which group members experience a strong sense of universality and purpose. Patients and families can try out new ways of thinking, explore new values and goals, and experiment with new behaviors.

The R4R MFTG approach puts connection and collaboration at the heart of therapeutic work and teaches patients and family members to view disconnection (in R-CT) and dissonance (in MI) as signals to re-examine what is happening in relationships. Our integrated Relational/Motivational R4R MFTG approach views the experience of dissonance or disconnection as an opportunity to strengthen relationships versus allow AN to take advantage of the disconnection, damage relationships, perpetuate illness, and obstruct recovery.

The R4R treatment manual begins with a concise overview of AN in young adults; the promise of MFTG for treating AN; and the Relational/Motivational theory, principles, and research informing the R4R treatment approach. This information allows readers to understand the rationale behind group goals, structure, content, and processes. The manual outlines 16 weekly outpatient sessions over 26 weeks, beginning with two sessions emphasizing joining, assessment, and orientation, and continuing with the description of eight weekly, four biweekly, and two monthly group treatment sessions. Each session describes group goals, content, exercises, and materials, as well as relevant therapist interventions. The manual includes protocols, case vignettes, and other materials that translate patient lived experience, theory, and research underlying this multifamily therapy group model into practice. Because the R4R approach was developed in partnership with patients and families, this manual clearly conveys the power of family work and the resources families bring to bear upon treatment and recovery. The manual reminds us of the importance of caring communities including families of origin and families of choice (partners, friends, sponsors, and mentors) in the treatment of young adults with AN.

Overview of Anorexia Nervosa

AN is a serious psychiatric disorder that predominantly affects females and is characterized by low body weight due to restriction of intake, fear of weight gain, and persistent behaviors that obstruct weight gain. Individuals with AN commonly experience disturbances in body image. Their self-evaluation is heavily influenced by their body weight and shape, rendering them unable to recognize the seriousness of their low body weight (American Psychiatric Association [APA], 2013). According to epidemiological estimates, the lifetime prevalence of AN in females using DSM IV (APA, 1994) criteria ranges from 1.2% to 2.2%. When expanded criteria that more closely match the DSM-5 criteria are used (APA, 2013; Swanson, Crow, Le Grange, Swendsen, & Merikangas, 2011), the estimates are higher, near 4.3% (Smink, van Hoeken, & Hoek, 2012). Lifetime prevalence is estimated at 0.24% for males (Smink, van Hoeken, & Hoek, 2012). The typical age of onset is mid to late adolescence (Arcelus, Mitchell, Wales, & Nielsen, 2011). AN has the highest mortality rate of any mental illness at between 5% and 20% (Smink, van Hoeken, & Hoek, 2012). Females between the ages of 15 and 24 with AN have 12 times the death rate as those with other psychiatric disorders (Sullivan, 1995). Mortality peaks between the ages of 20 and 30, with 20% of deaths being the result of suicide (Arcelus, Mitchell, Wales, & Nielsen, 2011; Crow, 2013; Papadopoulos, Ekbom, Brandt, & Ekselius, 2009).

Comorbidity studies indicate that the most common psychiatric disorders accompanying AN are anxiety disorders (over 50%; the most frequent being generalized anxiety disorder, obsessive-compulsive disorder, and social phobia, with the anxiety disorder typically preceding the onset of AN), depressive disorders (estimates range from 20% to 80%), obsessive-compulsive personality disorder (35%) (Bulik, 2002a; O'Brien & Vincent, 2003), and substance use disorders, particularly alcohol use disorder (17.2% for illicit drugs; 22.4% for alcohol) (Baker, Mitchell, Neale, & Kendler, 2010). Approximately 70% of people diagnosed with an eating disorder have a comorbid condition (Keski-Rahkonen & Mustelin, 2016). Older adolescents and young adults present with more comorbidity compared to younger adolescents (Fischer & Le Grange, 2007; Le Grange, Lock, Agras, Moye, Bryson, Jo, & Kraemer, 2012). For example, the median onset age of mood disorders is 25, whereas that for substance use disorders is 20 (Jones, 2013; Kessler, Amminger, Aguilar-Gaxiola, Alonso, Lee, & Ustun, 2007; Kessler, Berglund, Demler, Jin, Merikangas, & Walters, 2005). Morbidity and mortality risks peak during the emerging adult years (18 to 29; Jones, 2013; Kessler, Amminger, Aguilar-Gaxiola, Alonso, Lee, & Ustun, 2008; Merikangas, He, Brody, Fisher, Bourdon, & Koretz, 2010).

Physiological complications of AN can be life threatening and include disorders of the cardiovascular, endocrine, gastrointestinal, integumentary, and hematological systems (Watson & Bulik, 2013). The global burden of AN can be seen in terms of Disability Adjusted Life Years (DALY), wherein each DALY is equivalent to the loss of one year of healthy functioning (Erskine, Whiteford, & Pike, 2016). AN in women and men accounts for a total of 470,000 DALYs, indicating the disorder is responsible for substantially reduced quality of life (Erskine, Whiteford, & Pike, 2016). In addition to the high burden of illness shouldered by patients with AN, caregiving burden is also high and similar to that experienced by caregivers of individuals with psychotic disorders (Treasure, Murphy, Szmukler, Todd, Gavan, & Joyce, 2001). Costs for treatment of AN and bulimia nervosa (BN) are comparable to the cost of treatment for schizophrenia (Striegel-Moore, Leslie, Petrill, Garvin, & Rosenheck, 2000).

Risk Factors

Few clearly established risk factors for AN have been identified (Striegel-Moore & Bulik, 2007). Body dissatisfaction and dieting have long been associated with AN. However, longitudinal research has not yet clearly established these as risk factors for AN. Other potential risk factors include temperamental (perfectionism), psychological (low self-esteem, negative affect, and negative self-evaluation), and familial (family discord; high parental demands; parental overprotectiveness; negative comments related to weight, eating, and/or appearance from family; and parental eating disorders) (Fairburn, Cooper, Doll, & Welch, 1999; Pike, Hilbert, Wilfley, Fairburn, Dohm, Walsh, & Striegel-Moore, 2008; Walters & Kendler, 1995) factors. In addition, some studies (Lindberg & Hjern, 2003; McClelland & Crisp, 2001) have highlighted high socioeconomic status as a risk factor, although it is possible this is due to bias in diagnosis and/or treatment availability for those of higher socioeconomic status.

At least one prospective study suggests that AN risk is elevated by a low, rather than a high incidence of dieting, in addition to low body mass index (BMI), high negative affect, and poor psychosocial functioning (Stice, Gau, Rohde, & Shaw, 2017). These authors postulate that adolescents and young adult females with lower BMI and/or a tendency to undereat for a variety of reasons, but not due to dieting, and who have negative affect and difficulty getting along with family members and peers are at risk to develop AN. Alternatively, undereating could cause or exacerbate negative affect and interpersonal conflicts leading to greater risk of AN onset (Stice, Gau, Rohde, & Shaw, 2017). These findings are supported by data indicating that low birth weight, being small for gestational age, and perinatal obstetric complications (Cnattinguis, Hultman, Dahl, & Sparen, 1999; Favaro, Tenconi, & Santonastaso, 2006), along with a history of struggles and conflicts around eating and meals (Kotler, Cohen, Davies, Pine, & Walsh, 2001), are associated with development of AN.

Theories of Etiology and Maintenance

Theories of the etiology of AN exist in all major theoretical paradigms (for an overview, c.f., Watkins, 2011). While there is some support for each model, no one model can provide the comprehensive explanation needed to account for the range of psychopathology seen in AN.

Sociocultural Theories

Sociocultural theories of AN have been emphasized historically. These theories focus on perceived cultural pressure to match a thin ideal, which is internalized in the context of the general cultural objectification of the female body. Over time, internalization of the objectified thin ideal creates body dissatisfaction, leading to dieting and the emergence of eating disorders, including AN (c.f., Striegel-Moore & Bulik, 2007; Watkins, 2011). Although research supports the links between the objectified thin ideal and the development of body dissatisfaction and subsequent disordered eating in general, including models for BN (e.g., McKnight Investigators, 2003; Stice & Shaw, 2002; Stice & Van Ryzen, 2018), it is unclear whether AN specifically develops due to this process. Another major limitation of the basic sociocultural model is that it does not explain why only some individuals develop eating disorders, given that most women, especially, albeit not limited to the western world, are exposed to cultural ideals of thinness (Striegel-Moore & Bulik, 2007). In order to address this limitation, psychosocial variables, such as social pressure to be thin, high socioeconomic status, and social anxiety, are added to explain individual vulnerability, along with certain biological predispositions, such as elevated weight, perfectionism, impulsivity, and individual differences in responses to starvation (Striegel-Moore & Bulik, 2007). Other limitations to the sociocultural theories of AN include the fact that AN has existed, and continues to exist, outside of cultures that value the thin ideal (Watkins, 2011). This model also confounds risk with symptomatology in that body dissatisfaction and dieting are each both a risk factor and an element of the disorder (Striegel-Moore & Bulik, 2007).

Cognitive and Cognitive Behavioral Models

Cognitive and cognitive behavioral models have consistently featured prominently in understanding AN, and etiological models have considerable overlap with illness maintenance models (Shafran & de Silva, 2003). These cognitive and cognitive behavioral models emphasize the behaviors of dieting and restriction as a means of control, achievement, and stress management (e.g., Pike, Carter, & Olmsted, 2010; Pike, Walsh, Vitousek, Wilson, & Bauer, 2003; Shafran & de Silva, 2003; Slade, 1982). Weight loss is positively reinforced by peers and family members, in terms of initial praise received, subsequent attention and concern for low weight, and feelings of moral superiority and success. Food restriction is negatively reinforced by the avoidance of the perception of being fat, and dieting is seen as a way to achieve virtue and compensate for a self that is viewed as unworthy. Within this model, starvation itself is seen to cause concrete thinking, which in turn perpetuates the behavior (Shafran & de Silva, 2003).

In another cognitive behavioral model, Fairburn, Shafran, and Cooper (1999), emphasize the need for self-control, which is achieved primarily through dietary restriction. Food restriction is reinforced by the physiological effects of starvation, which cause discomfort after eating even small amounts of food. This restriction is further reinforced by Western culture's overvaluation of shape and weight, which equates shape and weight with self-worth and self-control (Fairburn, Shafran, & Cooper, 1999). More recently, Fairburn and colleagues have developed the transdiagnostic model, which theorizes the same maintenance pathway for all DSM eating disorders. This model posits that perfectionism, low self-esteem, difficulty tolerating intense negative moods, and interpersonal difficulties interact to perpetuate eating disorders within an individual who places disproportionate emphasis on shape and weight as markers of self-worth (Fairburn, Cooper, & Shafran, 2003).

Neurobiological Models

Several neurobiological models have been proposed that integrate biological, pre- and perinatal influences, and developmental impacts (c.f., Rose & Frampton, 2011 for a summary of seven leading models). These models include aspects of both the pathogenesis and maintenance of AN in terms of structure and function. Although a comprehensive summary is beyond the scope of this chapter, some prominent features are worth noting. Overall, there is decreased brain volume in both gray and white matter. This specifically occurs in areas of the hypothalamus and basal ganglia and results in changes in connectivity in regions related to body perception and motivated survival behaviors such as feeding (Gaudio, Dakanalis, Fariello, & Riva, 2018). There has also been much focus on the role of the insula, which has been shown to be differentially activated in patients with AN and is associated with difficulty with the integration of information from cognitive, affective, and physiological systems.

8 *Mary Tantillo, Jennifer Sanftner McGraw, and Daniel Le Grange*

The differential activation of the insula may be related to the observed symptoms and clinical features of body image disturbances, difficulty in emotion regulation, cognitive rigidity, and motor agitation, among others (Nunn, Frampton, Gordon, & Lask, 2008). Another brain area in which there may be different functioning is the cortico-striato-thalamo-cortical network (Marsh, Maia, & Peterson, 2009). Differences in this network cause an inability to control thoughts (such as those about weight and shape) and behaviors (e.g., ritualistic eating and dieting) and impair reward circuitry, reducing the capacity of food to be rewarding. The hypothalamic-pituitary-axis is another brain system thought to be associated with AN (Connan, Campbell, Katzman, Lightman, & Treasure, 2003; Southgate, Tchanturia, & Treasure, 2005). Here, it is argued that deficits in this system lead to chronic stress and maladaptive emotional and cognitive responses to stress, as well as poor social functioning.

Other Models Incorporating Biology and Environment

Several models incorporate various underlying biological mechanisms that are well supported by research (Rose & Frampton, 2011). These include genetic predispositions, including those to specific personality traits, such as a tendency to worry about and anticipate consequences, attention to detail, the drive to accomplish, perfectionism, and harm-avoidance (Kaye, Fudge, & Paulus, 2009). Neurotransmitter dysfunction, primarily in the serotonin and dopamine systems, results in anxiety, behavioral inhibition, and dysfunctional reward responding (Kaye, Fudge, & Paulus, 2009). Norepinepherine has also been implicated, as it causes increased sympathetic nervous system arousal, inhibition of cerebral blood flow to the insula, and impaired neuroplasticity (Nunn, Lask, & Frampton, 2011).

Several models emphasize experiences of traumatic stress and/or challenging early attachment experiences (Connan, Campbell, Katzman, Lightman, & Treasure, 2003; Nunn, Lask, & Frampton, 2011; Southgate, Tchanturia, & Treasure, 2005) that combine and interact with other variables to create biological vulnerabilities in social, emotional, and cognitive functioning. Other processes include biological changes during puberty, such as synaptic pruning and myelination that reorganize the brain, redistribution of fat mass, and changes in social expectations. These processes interact to affect behavioral and affective responses (Connan, Campbell, Katzman, Lightman, & Treasure, 2003; Nunn, Lask, & Frampton, 2011; Southgate, Tchanturia, & Treasure, 2005), leading to AN symptoms and clinical presentation.

In a model integrating biological vulnerabilities with environmentally mediated processes, Schmidt & Treasure (2006) describe the intra- and interpersonal processes that serve to maintain AN. The Cognitive-Interpersonal Model emphasizes dietary restraint as being reinforced by intrapersonal (e.g., improved mood and well-being) and interpersonal (e.g., positive attention from peers) factors. This process is moderated by neurotransmitter dysfunction. Once dieting leads to a feeling of mastery and self-control, the person begins to develop positive beliefs about extreme dieting and its ability to make them feel in control. With starvation come physiological changes that affect appetite and produce feelings of discomfort in response to eating. This experience causes eating to be associated with negative physical and emotional sensations. Emotional numbness through starvation becomes an aspect of AN that patients appreciate because it buffers them from dealing with anxiety, fear, and other painful emotions.

Although attention from others due to weight loss is initially positive, over time attention evolves into a more negative form, wherein friends and family members express concern and distress over the person's low weight and restrictive behaviors. This concern may be perceived as positive in that the person feels the care and concern of others without having to communicate their needs directly. Or, it may be perceived as negative when friends and family members begin to feel guilty, burdened, and/or helpless, and express either overt or covert criticism and/or conflict. Underlying patient traits, such as perfectionism and avoidance, contribute to the process, which then results in the person seeking distance from others, becoming intolerant of negative emotions, and developing sensitivity to criticism (Schmidt & Treasure, 2006). The patient may engage in AN behaviors to cope with negative interactions with others and, thus, AN is maintained.

Treatment of Anorexia Nervosa in Young Adults

There is no research that supports a definitive treatment for adults with AN. Clinical practice guidelines have been published by the American Psychiatric Association (APA, 3rd Edition; Yager, Devlin, Halmi, Herzog, Mitchell, Powers, & Zerbe, 2012), the Royal Australian and New Zealand College of Psychiatrists (RANZCP; Hay et al., 2014), and the United Kingdom's National Institute for Health and Care Excellence (NICE, 2017). Psychotherapy is strongly recommended as part of treatment for AN, particularly once eating and nutrition are stabilized. However, for adults with AN, no one modality of therapy is consistently recommended from among all of the options (Byrne et al., 2017; Zipfel et al., 2014). The NICE guidelines recommend individual eating disorder–focused cognitive behavioral therapy (CBT-ED), Maudsley anorexia nervosa treatment for adults (MANTRA), specialist supportive clinical management (SSCM), or eating disorder–focused focal psychodynamic therapy (FPT). The Australian and US guidelines do not specifically recommend any particular modality due to the limited number of randomized controlled trials focusing on adults with AN, small sample sizes utilizing mixed populations of patients with eating disorders, high dropout rates, short duration, and lack of long-term follow-up on studies that do exist (Yager, Devlin, Halmi, Herzog, Mitchell, Powers, & Zerbe, 2012; Hay et al., 2014).

Psychotropic medication options for AN are limited (Davis & Attia, 2017; Hay & Claudino, 2012; Milano, De Rosa, Milano, Riccio, Sanseverino, &

Capasso, 2013; Walsh et al., 2006), and some practice guidelines suggest that medication not be used as the sole means of treatment (NICE, 2017). Pharmacology research is plagued by many of the same methodological limitations as the psychotherapy research and has produced mixed results (Yager, Devlin, Halmi, Herzog, Mitchell, Powers, & Zerbe, 2012). Low dose antipsychotic medications offer promise as a component of treatment, as some studies have demonstrated they can improve weight gain and reduce depression, anxiety, and eating disorder pathology (Davis & Attia, 2017; Himmerich & Treasure, 2018). However, to date, evidence is inconsistent, with some studies showing improvement over placebo and others not. In addition, adverse effects are reported by some, including rising levels of glucose, insulin, thyroid stimulating hormone, and prolactin (Attia et al., 2019; Hay & Claudino, 2012; Marzola, Desedime, Giovannone, Amianto, Fassino, & Abbate-Daga, 2015; McKnight & Park, 2010). There is no support for use of antidepressants in treatment of AN (Marvanova & Gramith, 2018; Walsh et al., 2006; Yager, Devlin, Halmi, Herzog, Mitchell, Powers, & Zerbe, 2012). Medications prescribed with the goal of minimizing loss of bone density are also not supported (Hay et al., 2014; Mehler & MacKenzie, 2009; Misra, Golden, & Katzman, 2016; Teng, 2011; Yager, Devlin, Halmi, Herzog, Mitchell, Powers, & Zerbe, 2012). In terms of use of antipsychotics for comorbid conditions or symptoms, caution is advised until it can be determined that the symptoms are not due to starvation (Hay & Claudino, 2012; Hay et al., 2014).

Although family therapy is strongly recommended for children and adolescents with AN (Eisler, Wallis, & Dodge, 2015; Lock & Le Grange, 2013), evidence is not robust enough at present to recommend it for adults. There are only a few available studies with small sample sizes and potential biases (Yager, Devlin, Halmi, Herzog, Mitchell, Powers, & Zerbe, 2012). However, several studies suggest family therapy is a promising avenue to pursue for young adults or transition age youth with AN, given the lack of consensus on psychotherapeutic approaches for adults (Chen, Weissman, Zeffiro, Yiu, Eneva, Arlt, & Swantek, 2016; Dimitropoulos, Lock, Le Grange, & Anderson, 2015; Dimitropoulos et al., 2018).

The first controlled family therapy trial evaluating the Maudsley family therapy for AN (FT-AN) included younger adolescents and young adults (n = 57), and was conducted by Russell, Szmukler, Dare, and Eisler (1987). Study patients were hospitalized in order to achieve weight restoration and, upon discharge, were randomly assigned to one year of either family therapy or individual supportive therapy, which served as a control treatment. The family members participating in family therapy consisted of the patient's household members at the time. The results indicated that family therapy was superior for patients whose illness began at a relatively younger age (i.e., before age 18) and was not considered chronic (Russell, Szmukler, Dare, & Eisler, 1987). The outcomes were body weight along with the Morgan and Russell Outcome Scales (Morgan & Hayward, 1988), which assess nutritional status, menstrual functioning, mental state, psychosexual adjustment, and socioeconomic functioning. The family therapy group reported improved weight status and better scores than the individual therapy group on all of the Morgan and Russell scales, except mental state (Russell, Szmukler, Dare, & Eisler, 1987). Additional studies have supported family therapy approaches for adolescents over the past 30 years (e.g., Agras et al., 2014; Le Grange, Hughes, Court, Yeo, Crosby, & Sawyer, 2016; Lock, Le Grange, Agras, Moye, Bryson, & Jo, 2010). Specifically, a derivative of the original Maudsley approach, called family-based treatment (FBT), consists of 10 to 20 sessions that puts parents in charge of their child's nutritional rehabilitation. It focuses on symptom interruption and restoration of health during the first phase, returns control of intake to adolescents in the second phase, and focuses on adolescent stressors that could lead to relapse in the third phase (Lock & Le Grange, 2013).

Another earlier psychotherapy trial that evaluated a combined family and individual psychotherapy approach for adolescents and adults (ages 13 to 27) was conducted by Hall and Crisp (1987). This intervention was flexibly applied based on clinician judgment and was compared with dietary advice in a sample of 30 outpatients with AN. The findings indicated that weight and global adjustment increased for both groups, and the psychotherapy group alone showed significant improvement on social and sexual adjustment (Hall & Crisp, 1987).

Crisp, Norton, Gowers, Halek, Bowyer, Yeldham, Levett, and Bhat (1991) compared several inpatient and outpatient treatment options, including some components of family therapy, in a sample of 90 young adult outpatients. At the one-year follow-up, all groups showed significant weight gain, but only participants in the two groups that involved direct work with families gained significantly more than the no treatment group. Significant improvement of menstrual status and nutrition and socioeconomic adjustment were also reported for participants receiving some amount of family therapy (Crisp et al., 1991).

Later, in 2001, Dare and colleagues compared family therapy (one year) with focal psychoanalytic psychotherapy (one year), cognitive-analytic therapy (seven months), and routine treatment, which served as a control. Randomization was stratified to control for several variables (e.g., age of onset, duration of illness) in this sample of 84 patients, who presented for outpatient treatment. For the family therapy condition, participants were seen with either their parents or their spouse. Differences were not observed for the Morgan and Russell scales. However, patients in both the family therapy and focal psychoanalytic psychotherapy groups showed significantly greater weight gain than those in the routine treatment condition. The authors of this study note that this sample of patients came into the study with a relatively poor prognosis due to later age of onset, longer duration of illness, and historically unsuccessful treatments (Dare, Eisler, Russell, Treasure, & Dodge, 2001).

In 2004, Ball and Mitchell compared behavioral family therapy with cognitive behavior therapy in a sample of 25 women with AN between the ages of 13 and 23, all of whom were living with their family of origin. Outcome measures included physical status (weight and menses), eating disorder symptoms, self-esteem, depression, and state anxiety. Results indicated gains were made on all of the outcome measures, but neither treatment approach was superior to the other (Ball & Mitchell, 2004).

A recently published case series of family therapy with young adults with AN included 22 primarily female participants, who completed 18 to 20 sessions of outpatient family therapy (Chen, Weissman, Zeffiro, Yiu, Eneva, Arlt, & Swantek, 2016). The treatment was adapted from FBT for adolescents (Dimitropoulos, Lock, Le Grange, & Anderson, 2015; Lock & Le Grange, 2013), with three primary differences. First, patients were given their choice of which support adult to include (e.g., partner, close friend, family member). Second, the approach was more collaborative than would typically be the case with family therapy with adolescents. For example, with the primary goal being weight gain, patients were supported in making developmentally appropriate behavioral and psychological changes that promoted recovery, such as learning to prepare and consume food and manage independence. Throughout treatment they were encouraged to develop autonomy in basic life decisions. However, if participants were not gaining weight, some decision making was taken over by the support adult. The third adaptation was the focus placed on developmental transitions appropriate to young adults.

Outcome measures at the end of the adapted FBT, and a one-year follow-up, included BMI, eating disorder symptoms, global functioning (GAF score), and perceptions of suitability of the treatment approach for the population. Results indicated that participants found the treatment to be acceptable. Young adult participants also reported sustained weight gain and improvement in eating disorder symptoms and behaviors (Chen, Weissman, Zeffiro, Yiu, Eneva, Arlt, & Swantek, 2016). (See also Chen, Le Grange, Doyle, Zaitsoff, Doyle, Roehrig, and Washington [2010] for a case series describing this treatment with patients with AN reporting similar outcomes.)

Most recently, Dimitropoulos et al. (2018) examined the feasibility and acceptability of an adaptation of FBT for transition age youth (FBT-TAY). Preliminary results showed that this intervention was acceptable and feasible to all study therapists as evidenced by their fidelity to the model. FBT-TAY was also a feasible and acceptable intervention to transition age youth, given only 27.27% chose treatment as usual over FBT-TAY. Participants presented significant improvement at the end of treatment and three months post-treatment from baseline on eating disorder psychopathology. Participants also achieved and maintained weight restoration at the end of treatment and three months post-treatment when compared to baseline.

Because a family therapy approach with young adults may involve partners, it is relevant to also report on a recently published study examining a 26-week couple-based intervention for 20 patients with AN (Baucom, Kirby, Fischer, Baucom, Hamer, & Bulik, 2017). Participants engaged in the couples treatment in addition to individual CBT in this open trial. Outcome measures, including BMI and eating disorder symptoms, as well as depression, anxiety, and interpersonal functioning, were assessed at the end of treatment and at three-month follow-up. Patients made significant improvements in BMI, anxiety, depression, and dyadic adjustment by the end of treatment and in eating disorder symptoms by the follow-up assessment (Baucom, Kirby, Fischer, Baucom, Hamer, & Bulik, 2017).

In summary, AN, if not identified and treated early, can become a chronic illness, with considerable comorbidity, a high likelihood of medical complications, and relatively high mortality. Although excellent work is being done in order to identify the most relevant risk factors and refine models of etiology, much remains to be learned about this illness. The treatment literature on AN is limited, and consensus has not been reached on the best ways to treat the illness, especially for adult presentations. Overall, less than half of patients fully recover, and although another third improve, as many as 20% remain chronically ill or die from the illness (Steinhausen, 2002). Family therapy has demonstrated much success in the treatment of adolescents with AN, but its efficacy in young adults is less clear. Nevertheless, a handful of studies suggest adaptations can be made to family therapy that make it relevant to treatment for young adult populations.

References

No DOI

Agras, W. D., Lock, J., Brandt, H., Bryson, S. W., Dodge, E., Halmi, K. A., Jo, B., Johnson, C., Kaye, W., Wilfley, D., & Woodside, B. (2014). Comparison of 2 family therapies for adolescent anorexia nervosa: A randomized parallel trial. *JAMA Psychiatry 71*(11), 1279–1286. https://dx.doi.org/10.1001/jamapsychiatry.2014.1025.

Arcelus, J., Mitchell, A. J., Wales, J., & Nielsen, S. (2011). Mortality rates in patients with anorexia nervosa and other eating disorders: A meta-analysis of 36 studies. *Archives of General Psychiatry, 68*(7), 724–731. http://dx.doi.org./10.1001/archgenpsychiatry.2011.74.

*American Psychiatric Association (1994). *Diagnostic and statistical manual of mental disorders* (4th ed.). Author.

*American Psychiatric Association (2013). *Diagnostic and statistical manual of mental disorders* (3rd ed.). Author.

Attia, E., Steinglass, J. E., Walsh, B. T., Wang, Y., We, P., Schreyer, C., Wildes, J., Yilmaz, Z., Guarda, A. S., Kaplan, A. S., & Marcus, M. D. (2019). Olanzapine versus placebo in adult outpatient with anorexia nervosa: A randomized clinical trial. *The American Journal of Psychiatry, 176*(6), 449–456. https://doi.org/10.1176/appi.ajp.2018.18101125.

Baker, J. H., Mitchell, K. S., Neale, M. C., & Kendler, K. S. (2010). Eating disorder symptomatology and substance use disorders: Prevalence and shared risk in a population based twin sample. *International Journal of Eating Disorders, 43*(7), 648–658. http://dx.doi.org/10.1002/eat.20856.

Ball, J., & Mitchell, P. (2004). A randomized controlled study of cognitive behavior therapy and behavioral family therapy for anorexia nervosa patients. *Eating Disorders, 12*, 303–314. https://dx.doi.org/10.1080/10640260490521389.

Baucom, D. H., Kirby, J. S., Fischer, M. S., Baucom, B. R., Hamer, R., & Bulik, C. M. (2017). Findings from a couple-based open trial for adult anorexia nervosa. *Journal of Family Psychology, 31*(5), 584–591. http://dx.doi.org/10.1037/fam0000273.

Bell, L. (2011). What can we learn from consumer studies and qualitative research in the treatment of eating disorder? *Eating and Weight Disorders, 8*(3), 181–187. https://dx.doi.org/10.1007/BF03325011.

Berkman, N. D., Lohr, K. N., & Bulik, C. M. (2007). Outcomes of eating disorders: A systematic review of the literature. *International Journal of Eating Disorders, 40*, 293–309. https://dx.doi.org/10.1002/eat.20369.

*Bulik, C. M. (2002a). Anxiety, depression, and eating disorders. In C. G. Fairburn & K. D. Brownell (Eds.), *Eating disorders and obesity* (pp. 193–198). Guilford Press.

Butzlaff, R. L., & Hooley, J. M. (1998). Expressed emotion and psychiatric relapse: A meta-analysis. *Archives of General Psychiatry, 55*, 547–552. https://dx.doi.org/10.1001/archpsyc.55.6.547.

Byrne, S., Wade, T., Hay, P., Touyz, S., Fairburn, C. G., Treasure, J., Schmidt, U., McIntosh, V., Allen, K., Fursland, A., & Crosby, R. D. (2017). A randomized controlled trial of three psychological treatments for anorexia nervosa. *Psychological Medicine, 16*, 2823–2833. http://dx.doi.org/10.1017/S0033291717001349.

Chen, E. Y., Le Grange, D., Doyle, A. C., Zaitsoff, S., Doyle, P., Roehrig, J. P., & Washington, B. (2010). A case series of family-based therapy for weight restoration in young adults with anorexia nervosa. *Journal of Contemporary Psychotherapy, 40*(4), 219–224. https://dx.doi.org/10.1007/s10879-010-9146-0.

Chen, E. Y., Weissman, J. A., Zeffiro, T. A., Yiu, A., Eneva, K. T., Arlt, J. M., & Swantek, M. J. (2016). Family-based therapy for young adults with anorexia nervosa restores weight. *International Journal of Eating Disorders, 49*(7), 701–707. https://dx.doi.org/10.1002/eat.22513.

Cnattingius, S., Hultman, C. M., Dahl, M., & Sparen, P. (1999). Very preterm birth, birth trauma, and the risk of anorexia nervosa among girls. *Archives of General Psychiatry, 56*, 634–638. http://dx.doi.org/10.1001/archpsyc.56.7.634.

Connan, F., Campbell, I. C., Katzman, M., Lightman, L, & Treasure, J. (2003). A neurodevelopmental model for anorexia nervosa. *Physiology and Behavior, 79*, 13–24. https://dx.doi.org/10.1016/S0031-9384(03)00101-X.

Crisp, A. H., Norton, K., Gowers, S., Halek, C., Bowyer, C., Yeldham, D., Levett, G., & Bhat, A. (1991). A controlled study of the effect of therapies aimed at adolescent and family psychopathology in anorexia nervosa. *British Journal of Psychiatry, 159*, 325–333. http://dx.doi.org/10.1192/bjp.159.3.325.

Crow, S. (2013). Eating disorders and risk of death. [Editorial]. *American Journal of Psychiatry, 170*(8), 824–825. https://dx.doi.org/10.1176/appi.ajp.2013.13050654.

Dare, C., Eisler, I., Russell, G., Treasure, J., & Dodge, L. (2001). Psychological therapies for adults with anorexia nervosa: Randomised controlled trial of out-patient treatments. *British Journal of Psychiatry, 178*, 216–221. http://dx.doi.org/10.1192/bjp.178.3.216.

Davis, H., & Attia, E. (2017). Pharmacotherapy of eating disorders. *Current Opinion in Psychiatry, 30*, 452–457. https://dx.doi.org/10.1097/YCO.0000000000000358.

*Dimitropoulos, G., Lock, J., Le Grange, D., & Anderson, K. (2015). Family therapy for transition youth. In K. Loeb, D. Le Grange, & J. Lock (Eds.), *Family therapy for* *adolescent eating and weight disorders: New applications* (pp. 230–255). Routledge/Taylor & Francis Group.

Dimitropoulos, G., Landers, A. L., Freeman, V. E., Novick, J., Cullen, O., Engleberg, M., Steinegger, C., & Le Grange, D. (2018). Family-based treatment for transition age youth: Parental self-efficacy and caregiver accommodation. *Journal of Eating disorders, 6*(13), 2–11. https://dx.doi.org/10.1186/s40337-018-0196-0.

Eisler, I, Wallis, A & Dodge, E. (2015). What's new is old and what's old is new: The origins and evolution of eating disorders family therapy. In K. Loeb, D. Le Grange, & J. Lock (Eds.), *Family therapy for adolescent eating and weight disorders: New applications* (pp. 6–42). Taylor and Francis Inc. https://dx.doi.org/10.4324/9781315882444.

Erskine, H. E., Whiteford, H. A., & Pike, K. M. (2016). The global burden of eating disorders. *Current Opinion in Psychiatry, 29*, 346–353. https://dx.doi.org/10.1097/YCO.0000000000000276.

Fairburn, C. G., Cooper, Z., Doll, H. A., & Welch, S. L. (1999). Risk factors for anorexia nervosa. *Archives of General Psychiatry, 56*, 468–476. http://dx.doi.org/10.1001/archpsyc.56.5.468.

Fairburn, C. G., Cooper, Z., & Shafran, R. (2003). Cognitive behaviour therapy for eating disorders: A "transdiagnostic" theory and treatment. *Behaviour Research and Therapy, 41*, 509–528. http://dx.doi.org/10.1016/S0005-7967(02)00088-8.

Fairburn, C. G., Shafran, R., & Cooper, Z. (1999). A cognitive behavioural theory of anorexia nervosa. *Behaviour Research and Therapy, 37*, 1–13. http://dx.doi.org/10.1016/S0005-7967(98)00102-8.

Favaro, A., Tenconi, E., & Santonastaso, P. (2006). *Perinatal factors and the risk of developing anorexia nervosa and bulimia nervosa. Archives of General Psychiatry, 63*, 82–88. http://dx.doi.org/10.1001/archpsyc.63.1.82.

Federici, A., & Kaplan, A. S. (2008). The patient's account of relapse and recovery in anorexia nervosa: A qualitative study. *European Eating Disorder Review, 16*(1), 1–10. https://dx.doi.org/10.1002/erv.813.

Fischer, S., & Le Grange, D. (2007). Comorbidity and high-risk behaviors in treatment-seeking adolescents with bulimia nervosa. *International Journal of Eating Disorders, 40*(8), 751–753. https://dx.doi.org/10.1002/eat.20442.

Frank, J. D., & Frank, J. B. (1991). Persuasion and healing: A comparative study of psychotherapy (3rd edition). Johns Hopkins University Press.

Frey, L. (2013). Relational-cultural therapy: Theory, research, and application to counseling competencies. *Professional Psychology: Research and Practice 44*(3), 177–185. https://dx.doi.org/10.1037/a0033121.

Gaudio, S., Dakanalis, A., Fariello, G., & Riva, G. (2018). Neuroscience, brain imaging, and body image in eating and weight disorders. In M. Cuzzolaro & S. Fassino (Eds.), *Body image, eating, and weight* (pp. 97–111). Springer International Publishing. https://dx.doi.org/10.1007/978-3-319-90817-5_7.

Grenon, R., Schwartze, D., Hammond, N., Ivanova, I., Proulx, G., & Tasca, G. (2017). Group psychotherapy for eating disorders: A meta-analysis. *International Journal of Eating Disorders, 50*(9), 997–1013. http://dx.doi.org/10.1002/eat.22744.

Hall, A., & Crisp, H. (1987). Brief psychotherapy in the treatment of anorexia nervosa outcome at one year. *British Journal of Psychiatry, 151*, 185–191. http://dx.doi.org/10.1192/bjp.151.2.185.

Hay, P., Chinn, D., Forbes, D., Madden, S., Newton, R., Sugenor, L., Touyz, S., & Ward, W. (2014). Royal Australian and New Zealand College of Psychiatrists clinical practice guidelines for the treatment of eating disorders. *Australian and New Zealand Journal of Psychiatry, 48*(11), 1–62. http://dx.doi.org/10.1177/0004867414555814.

Hay, P. J., & Claudino, A. M. (2012). Clinical psychopharmacology of eating disorders: a research update. *International Journal of Neuropsychopharmacology, 15*(2), 209–222. https://dx.doi.org/10.1017/S1461145711000460.

Himmerich, H., & Treasure, J. (2018). Psychopharmacological advances in eating disorders. *Expert Review of Clinical Pharmacology, 11*(1), 95–108. https://dx.doi.org/10.1080/17512433.2018.1383895.

Jewell, T., Blessit, E., Stewart, C., & Simic, M., & Eisler, I. (2016). Family therapy for child and adolescent eating disorders: A critical review. *Family Process, 55*(3), 577–594. http://dx.doi.org/10.1111/famp.12242.

Jones, P. B. (2013). Adult mental health disorders and their age at onset. *The British Journal of Psychiatry, 202*(s5–s10). https://dx.doi.org/10.1192/bjp.bp.112.119164.

Jordan, J. (2018). *Relational-cultural therapy* (2nd ed.). American Psychological Association. https://dx.doi.org/10.1037/0000063-001.

Kaye, W. H., Fudge, J. L., & Paulus, M. (2009). New insights into symptoms and neurocircuit function of anorexia nervosa. *Nature Reviews Neuroscience, 10*(8), 573–584. https://dx.doi.org/10.1038/nrn2682.

Keski-Rahkonen, & Mustelin, L. (2016). Epidemiology of eating disorders in Europe: Prevalence, incidence, comorbidity, course, consequences, and risk factors. *Current Opinion in Psychiatry, 29*(6), 340–345. https://dx.doi.org/10.1097/YCO.0000000000000278.

Kessler, R. C., Amminger, P., Aguilar-Gaxiola, S., Alonso, J., Lee, S., & Ustun, B. (2007). Age of onset of mental disorders: A review of recent literature. *Current Opinion in Psychiatry, 20*(4), 359–364. http://dx.doi.org/10.1097/YCO.0b013e32816ebc8c.

Kessler, R. C., Berglund, P., Demler, O., Jin, R., Merikangas, K. R., & Walters, E. E. (2005). Lifetime prevalence and age-of-onset distributions of DSM-IV disorders in the national comorbidity survey replication. *Archives of General Psychiatry, 62*, 593–602. http://dx.doi.org/10.1001/archpsyc.62.6.593.

Kotler, L. A., Cohen, P., Davies, M., Pine, D. S., & Walsh, B. T. (2001). Longitudinal relationships between childhood, adolescent, and adult eating disorders. *Journal of the American Academy of Child and Adolescent Psychiatry, 40*(12), 1434–1440. http://dx.doi.org/10.1097/00004583-200112000-00014.

*Leff, J., & Vaughn, C. (1985). *Expressed emotion in families.* The Guilford Press.

Le Grange, D., Eisler, I., Dare, C., & Hodes, M. (1992). Family criticism and self-starvation: A study of expressed emotion. *Journal of Family Therapy, 14*, 177–192. https://dx.doi.org/10.1016/0272-7358(85)90018-2.

Le Grange, D., & Hoste, R., Lock, J., & Bryson, S. W. (2010). Parental expressed emotional of adolescents with anorexia nervosa: Outcome in family-based treatment. *International Journal of Eating Disorders, 44*, 731–734. https://dx.doi.org/10.1002/eat.20877.

Le Grange D., Hughes, E. K., Court, A., Yeo, M., Crosby, R. D., & Sawyer, S. M. (2016). Randomized clinical trial of parent-focused treatment and family-based treatment for adolescent anorexia nervosa. *Journal of the American Academy of Child and Adolescent Psychiatry, 55*, 683–692. https://dx.doi.org/10.1016/j.jaac.2016.05.007.

Le Grange, D., Lock, J., Agras, S., Moye, A., Bryson, S. W., Jo, B., & Kraemer, H. C. (2012). Moderators and mediators of remission in family-based treatment and adolescent focused therapy for anorexia nervosa. *Behavior Research and Therapy*, *50*(2), 85–92. https://dx.doi.org/10.1016/j.brat.2011.11.003.

Lenz, S. A. (2016). Relational-cultural theory: Fostering the growth of a paradigm through empirical research. *Journal of Counseling and Development*, *94*(4), 415–428. http://dx.doi.org/10.1002/jcad.12100.

Lindberg, L., & Hjern, A. (2003). Risk factors for anorexia nervosa: A national cohort study. *International Journal of Eating Disorders*, *34*, 397–408. https://dx.doi.org/10.1002/eat.10221.

Lock, J., & Le Grange, D. (2013). *Treatment manual for anorexia nervosa: A family-based approach*. The Guilford Press.

Lock, J., Le Grange, D., Agras, W. S., Moye, A., Bryson, S. W., & Jo, B. (2010). Randomised clinical trial comparing family-based treatment with adolescent-focused individual therapy for adolescents with anorexia nervosa. *Archives of General Psychiatry*, *67*(10), 1025–1032. https://dx.doi.org/10.1001/archgenpsychiatry.2010.128.

Lowe, B., Zipfel, S., Buchholz, C., Dupont, Y., Reas, D. L., & Herzog, W. (2001). Long-term outcome of anorexia nervosa in a prospective 21-year follow-up study. *Psychological Medicine*, *31*, 881–890. https://dx.doi.org/10.1017/S003329170100407X.

Marsh, R., Maia, T. V., & Peterson, B. S. (2009). Functional disturbances within frontostriatal circuits across multiple childhood psychopathologies. *American Journal of Psychiatry*, 166-664-674. https://dx.doi.org/10.1176/appi.ajp.2009.08091354.

Marvanova, M., & Gramith, K. (2018) Role of antidepressants in the treatment of adults with anorexia nervosa. *Mental Health Clinician*, *8*(3), 127–137. https://dx.doi.org/10.9740/mhc.2018.05.127.

Marzola, E., Desedime, N., Giovannone, C., Amianto, F., Fassino, S., & Abbate-Daga, G. (2015). Atypical antipsychotics as augmentation therapy in anorexia nervosa. *Plos/One*. https://dx.doi.org/10.1371/journal.pone.0125569.

McClelland, L., & Crisp, A. (2001). Anorexia nervosa and social class. *International Journal of Eating Disorders*, *29*, 150–156. http://dx.doi.org/10.1002/1098-108X(200103)29:2<150::AID-EAT1004>3.0.CO;2-I.

McKnight, R., & Park, R. J. (2010). Atypical antipsychotics and anorexia nervosa: A review. *European Eating Disorders Review* *18*(1), 10–21. https://dx.doi.org/10.1002/erv.988.

McKnight Investigators. (2003). Risk factors for the onset of eating disorders in adolescent girls: Results of the McKnight longitudinal risk factor study. *American Journal of Psychiatry*, *160*(2), 248–254. http://dx.doi.org/10.1176/appi.ajp.160.5.1024.

Mehler, P. S., & MacKenzie, T. D. (2009). Treatment of osteopenia and osteoporosis in anorexia nervosa: a systematic review of the literature. *International Journal of Eating Disorders*, *42*(3), 195–201. https://dx.doi.org/10.1002/eat.20593.

Merikangas, K. R., He, J. P., Brody, D., Fisher, P. W., Bourdon, K., & Koretz, D. S. (2010). Prevalence and treatment of mental disorders among US children in the 2001-2004 NHANES, *Pediatrics*, *125*(1), 75–81. https://dx.doi.org/10.1542/peds.2008-2598.

Milano, W., De Rosa, M., Milano, A., Riccio, B., Sanseverino, B., & Capasso, A. (2013). The pharmacological options in the treatment of eating disorders. *International Scholarly Research Notices*, *15*(2), 209–222. https://dx.doi.org/10.1155/2013/352865.

*Miller, W. R., & Rollnick, S. (2013). *Motivational interviewing: Helping people change* (3rd ed.). The Guilford Press.

*Miller, J. B., & Stiver, I. P. (1997). *The healing connection: How women form relationships in therapy and in life*. Beacon Press.

Misra, M., Golden, N. H., & Katzman, D. K. (2016). State of the art systematic review of bone disease is anorexia nervosa. *International Journal of Eating Disorders, 49*(3), 276–292. https://dx.doi.org/10.1002/eat.22451.

Morgan, H. G., & Hayward, A. E. (1988). Clinical assessment of anorexia nervosa. The Morgan-Russell outcome assessment schedule. *British Journal of Psychiatry, 152,* 367–371. https://dx.doi.org/10.1192/bjp.152.3.367.

National Institute for Health and Care Excellence. (2017, May). *Eating disorders: Recognition and treatment.* http://www.nice.org.uk/guidance/ng69.

Nunn, K., Frampton, I., Gordon, I., & Lask, I. (2008). The fault is not in her parents but in her insula: A neurobiological hypothesis of anorexia nervosa. *European Eating Disorders Review, 16*(5), 355–360. https://dx.doi.org/10.1002/erv.890.

Nunn, K., Lask, B., & Frampton, I. (2011). Towards a comprehensive, casual and explanatory neuroscience model of anorexia nervosa. In B. Lask & I. Frampton (Eds.), *Eating disorders and the brain.* John Wiley & Sons, Ltd. https://dx.doi.org/10.1002/9781119998402.ch8.

O'Brien, K. M., & Vincent, N. K. (2003). Psychiatric comorbidity in anorexia and bulimia nervosa: Nature, prevalence, and causal relationships. *Clinical Psychology Review, 23,* 57–74. http://dx.doi.org/10.1016/S0272-7358(02)00201-5.

Papadopoulos, F. C., Ekbom, A., Brandt, L, & Eskelius, L. (2009). Excess mortality, causes of death and prognostic factors in anorexia nervosa. *The British Journal of Psychiatry, 194,* 10–17. https://dx.doi.org/10.1192/bjp.bp.108.054742.

*Pike, K. M., Carter, J. C., & Olmsted, M. P. (2010). Cognitive-behavioral therapy for anorexia nervosa. In C. M. Grilo & J. E. Mitchell (Eds.), *The treatment of eating disorders: A clinical handbook* (pp. 83–107). Guilford Press.

Pike, K. M., Hilbert, A., Wilfley, D. E., Fairburn, C. G., Dohm, F. A., Walsh, B. T., & Striegel-Moore, R. (2008). Toward an understanding of risk factors for anorexia nervosa: A case-controlled study. *Psychological Medicine, 38*(10), 1443–1453. https://dx.doi.org/10.1017/S0033291707002310.

Pike, K. M., Walsh, B. T., Vitousek, K., Wilson, G. T., & Bauer, J. (2003). Cognitive behavior therapy in the posthospitalization treatment of anorexia nervosa. *American Journal of Psychiatry, 160*(11), 2046–2049. https://dx.doi.org/10.1176/appi.ajp.160.11.2046.

*Prochaska, J. O., Norcross, J. C., DiClemente, C. C. (1994). *Changing for good: A revolutionary six-stage program for overcoming bad habits and moving your life positively forward.* William Morrow.

Rose, M., & Frampton, I. (2011). Conceptual models. In B. Lask & I. Frampton (Eds.), *Eating disorders and the brain.* John Wiley & Sons, Ltd. https://dx.doi.org/10.1002/9781119998402.ch7.

Russell, G. F. M., Szmukler, G. I., Dare, C., & Eisler, I. (1987). An evaluation of family therapy in anorexia nervosa and bulimia nervosa. *Archives of General Psychiatry, 44,* 1047–1056. http://dx.doi.org/10.1001/archpsyc.1987.01800240021004.

Schmidt, U., & Treasure, J. (2006). Anorexia nervosa: Valued and visible. A cognitive-interpersonal maintenance model and its implications for research and practice. *British Journal of Clinical Psychology, 45,* 343–366. http://dx.doi.org/10.1348/014466505X53902.

Shafran, R., & de Silva, P. (2003). Cognitive-behavioural models. In J. Treasure, U. Schmidt, & E. van Furth (Eds.), *Handbook of eating disorders* (pp. 121–138). John Wiley & Sons, Ltd.

Slade, P. (1982). Towards a functional analysis of anorexia nervosa and bulimia nervosa. *British Journal of Clinical Psychology, 21*(3), 167–179. https://dx.doi.org/10.1111/j.2044-8260.1982.tb00549.x.

Smink, F. R. E., van Hoeken, D., & Hoek, H. W. (2012). Epidemiology of eating disorders: Incidence, prevalence and mortality rates. *Current Psychiatry Reports, 14*, 406–414. https://dx.doi.org/10.1007/s11920-012-0282-y.

Southgate, L., Tchanturia, K., Treasure, J. (2005). Building a model of the aetiology of eating disorders by translating experimental neuroscience into clinical practice. *Journal of Mental Health, 14*(6), 553–566. https://dx.doi.org/10.1080/09638230500347541.

Steinhausen, H. (2002). The outcome of anorexia nervosa in the 20th century. *American Journal of Psychiatry, 159*, 1284–1293. http://dx.doi.org/10.1176/appi.ajp.159.8.1284.

Stephens, G. J., Silbert, L. J., & Hasson, U. (2010). *Speaker listener neural coupling underlies successful communication. Proceedings of the National Academy of Sciences, USA, 107*(32), 11425–11460. https://doi.org/10.1073/pnas.1008662107.

Stice, E., Gau, J. M., Rohde, P., & Shaw, H. (2017). Risk factors that predict future onset of each DSM-5 eating disorder: Predictive specificity in high-risk adolescent females. *Journal of Abnormal Psychology, 126*(1), 38–51. https://dx.doi.org/10.1037/abn0000219.

Stice, E., & Shaw, H. (2002). Role of body dissatisfaction in the onset and maintenance of eating pathology: A synthesis of research findings. *Journal of Psychosomatic Research, 53*, 985–993. http://dx.doi.org/10.1016/S0022-3999(02)00488-9.

Stice, E., & Van Ryzin, M. J. (2018). A prospective test of the temporal sequencing of risk factor emergence in the dual pathway model of eating disorders. *Journal of Abnormal Psychology, 128*(2), 119–128. https://dx.doi.org/10.1037/abn0000400.

Striegel-Moore, R. H., & Bulik, C. M. (2007). Risk factors for eating disorders. *American Psychologist, 62*(3), 181–198. https://dx.doi.org/10.1037/0003-066X.62.3.181.

Striegel-Moore, R. H., Leslie. D., Petrill, S. A., Garvin, V., & Rosenheck, R. A. (2000). One-year use and cost of inpatient and outpatient services among female and male patients with an eating disorder: Evidence from a national database of health insurance claims. *International Journal of Eating disorders, 27*, 381–389. http://dx.doi.org/10.1002/(SICI)1098-108X(200005)27:4<381::AID-EAT2>3.0.CO;2-U.

Sullivan, P. F. (1995). Mortality in anorexia nervosa. *American Journal of Psychiatry, 152*(7), 1073–1074. http://dx.doi.org/10.1176/ajp.152.7.1073.

Swanson, S. A., Crow, S. J., Le Grange, D., Swendsen, J., & Merikangas, K. R. (2011). Prevalence and correlates of eating disorders in adolescents. *Archives of General Psychiatry, 68*(7), 714–723. https://dx.doi.org/10.1001/archgenpsychiatry.2011.22.

Tantillo, M. (2006). A relational approach to eating disorders multifamily therapy group: Moving from difference and disconnection to mutual connection. *Families, Systems, & Health, 23*(1), 82–102. https://dx.doi.org/10.1037/1091-7527.24.1.82.

Tantillo, M. (2010). *Eating disorders multifamilty therapy group: Outcomes and alumnae analysis.* Unpublished raw data.

Tantillo, M., Anson, E., Lavigne, H., & Wilkosz, A. (2019). *The effectiveness of a relational/motivational partial hospitalization program for eating disorders: An analysis of treatment outcomes.* Unpublished manuscript, University of Rochester School of Nursing.

Tantillo, M., McGraw, J. S., Hauenstein, E., & Groth, S. W. (2015). Partnering with patients and families to develop an innovative multifamily therapy group treatment for adults with anorexia nervosa. *Advances in Eating Disorders: Theory, Research, and Practice, 3*(3), 269–287. https://dx.doi.org/10.1080/21662630.2015.1048478.

Tantillo, M., McGraw, J. S., Lavigne, H. M., Brasch, J., & Le Grange, D. (2019). A pilot study of multifamily therapy group for young adults with anorexia nervosa: Reconnecting for recovery. *International Journal of Eating Disorders*, *52*(8), 950–955. https://dx.doi.org/10.1002/eat.23097.

Tantillo, M., & Sanftner, J. L. (2010a). Mutuality and motivation: Connecting with patients and families for change in the treatment of eating disorders. In M. Maine, D. Bunnell, & B. McGilley (Eds.), *Treatment of eating disorders: Bridging the gap between research and practice*. Elsevier. http://dx.doi.org/10.1016/B978-0-12-375668-8.10019-1.

Tantillo, M., & Sanftner, J. L. (2010b). Measuring perceived mutuality in women with eating disorders: The development of the Connection Disconnection Scale. *Journal of Nursing Measurement*, *18*, 100–119. http://dx.doi.org/10.1891/1061-3749.18.2.100.

Tantillo, M., Sanftner, J. L., & Hauenstein, E. (2013). Restoring connection in the face of disconnection: An integrative approach to understanding and treating anorexia nervosa. *Advances in Eating Disorders: Theory, Research, and Practice*, *1*, 21–38. https://dx.doi.org/10.1080/21662630.2013.742980.

Teng, K. (2011). Premenopausal osteoporosis, an overlooked consequence of anorexia nervosa. *Cleveland Clinic Journal of Medicine*, *78*(1), 50–58. https://dx.doi.org/10.3949/ccjm.78a.10023.

Tozzi, F., Sullivan, P., Fear, J., McKenzie, J., & Bulik, C. (2003). Causes and recovery in anorexia nervosa: The patient's perspective. *International Journal of Eating Disorders*, *33*(2), 143–154. https://dx.doi.org/10.1002/eat.10120.

Treasure, J., Murphy, T., Szmukler, G., Todd, G., Gavan, K., & Joyce. J. (2001). The experience of caregiving for severe mental illness: A comparison between anorexia nervosa and psychosis. *Social Psychiatry and Psychiatric Epidemiology: The International Journal for Research in Social and Genetic Epidemiology and Mental Health Services*, *36*, 343–347. https://dx.doi.org/10.1007/s001270170039.

van Furth, E. F., van Strien, D. C., Martina, L. M. L., van Son, M. J. M., Hendrickx, J. J. P., & van Engeland, H. (1996). Expressed emotion and the prediction of outcome in adolescent eating disorders. *International Journal of Eating Disorders*, *20*, 19–31. https://dx.doi.org/10.1002/(SICI)1098-108X(199607)20:1<19::AID-EAT3>3.0.CO;2-7.

Walsh, B. T., Kaplan, A. S., Attia, E., Olmsted, M., Parides, M., Carter, J. C., Pike, K. M., Devlin, M., Woodside, B., Roberto, C. A., & Rockert, W. (2006). Fluoxetine after weight restoration in anorexia nervosa: A randomized controlled trial. *JAMA*, *295*(22), 2605–2612. https://dx.doi.org/10.1001/jama.295.22.2605.

Walters, E. E., & Kendler, K. S. (1995). Anorexia nervosa and anorexic-like syndromes in a population-based female twin sample. *American Journal of Psychiatry*, *152*(1), 64–71. http://dx.doi.org/10.1176/ajp.152.1.64.

Watkins, B. (2011). Eating disorders: An overview. In B. Lask & I. Frampton (Eds.), *Eating disorders and the brain*. John Wiley & Sons, Ltd. https://dx.doi.org/10.1002/9781119998402.ch2.

Watson, H. J., & Bulik, C. M. (2013). Update on the treatment of anorexia nervosa: Review of clinical trials, practice guidelines and emerging interventions. *Psychological Medicine*, *43*, 2477–2500. https://dx.doi.org/10.1017/S0033291712002620.

Wright, K. M., & Hacking, S. (2012). An angel on my shoulder: A study of relationships between women with anorexia and health care professionals. *Journal of Psychiatric and Mental Health Nursing*, *19*(2), 107–115. https://dx.doi.org/10.1111/j.1365-2850.2011.01760.x.

Yager, J., Devlin, M. J., Halmi, K. A., Herzog, D. B., Mitchell, J. E., Powers, P., & Zerbe, K. J. (2012, August). *Guideline watch (August 2012)*. *Practice guideline for the treatment of patients with eating disorders* (3rd ed.). Washington, DC: American Psychiatric Association.

Zipfel, S., Wild, B., Grob, G., Friederich, H., Teufel, M., Schellberg, D., Giel, K., de Zwaan, M., Dinkel, A., Herpertz, S., Burgmer, M., Lowe, B., Tagay, S., von Wietersheim, J., Zeeck, A., Schade-Brittinger, C., Schauenburg, H., & Herzog, W. (2014). Focal psychodynamic therapy, cognitive behavior therapy, and optimized treatment as usual in outpatients with anorexia nervosa (ANTOP study): Randomised controlled trial. *The Lancet*, *383*, 127–137. https://dx.doi.org/10.1016/S0140-6736(13)61746-8.

2 The Promise of Multifamily Therapy Group for Young Adults with Anorexia Nervosa

Mary Tantillo, Jennifer Sanftner McGraw, and Daniel Le Grange

As noted in Chapter 1, the field has yet to identify a definitive treatment for AN in young adults. Historically, research trials examining possible psychological treatment approaches have tended to focus on individual therapies (Agras & Robinson, 2010; Byrne et al., 2017; Fairburn, 2008; McIntosh et al., 2005; Schmidt et al., 2012; Schmidt, Wade, & Treasure, 2014; Watson & Bulik, 2013) or single-family therapies (Chen, Le Grange, Doyle, Zaitsoff, Doyle, Roehrig, & Washington, 2010; Chen, Weissman, Zeffiro, Yiu, Eneva, Arlt, & Swantek, 2016; Dare, Eisler, Russell, Treasure, and Dodge, 2001; Dimitropoulos, Landers, Freeman, Novick, Garber, & Le Grange, 2018; Dimitropoulos, Lock Le Grange, & Anderson, 2015). More recently, Multifamily Therapy Group (MFTG) treatments for AN have increased in number, including in Australia (Rhodes, Baillee, Brown, & Madden., 2008; Wallis et al., 2013), Belgium (Depestele & Vandereycken, 2009; Depestele, Claes, & Lemmens, 2015), Canada (Girz, Robinson, Foroughe, Jasper, & Boachie, 2013), Denmark (Hollesen, Clausen, & Rokkedal, 2013), Germany (Scholz & Asen, 2001), the Netherlands (Fleminger, 2005), Prague (Mehl, Tomanová, Kuběna, & Papežová, 2013), United Kingdom (Dare & Eisler, 2000; Eisler et al., 2016), and the United States (Knatz, Murray, Matheson, Boutelle, Rockwell, Eisler, & Kaye, 2015; Marzola, Knatz, Murray, Rockwell, Boutelle, Eisler, & Kaye, 2015; Tantillo, 2006; Tantillo, McGraw, Hauenstein, & Groth, 2015; Tantillo, Sanftner, & Hauenstein, 2013). Before discussing Multifamily Therapy Group treatment specifically for young adults with AN, it is important to review the nature, origins, and outcomes of MFTG as related to adults with other chronic behavioral and physical health problems and adolescents with AN. This review will promote a better understanding of the promise of MFTG for young adults with AN and the MFTG treatment for young adults described in this treatment manual.

Nature, Origins, and Outcomes of Multifamily Therapy Group Treatment

MFTG is a group psychotherapy that commonly involves between five and seven patients and their respective family members meeting routinely

The Promise of Multifamily Therapy   23

(e.g., weekly or monthly) to learn about a psychological or physical health condition or disorder and effective ways to support the individual in recovery. Many MFTGs have included family of origin members, whereas others permit attendance of family of choice members such as partners, best friends, and mentors. While MFTGs are usually comprised of patients and their significant others, some MFTGs are comprised only of parents or other family caregivers (Depestele, Claes, Dierckx, Colman, Schoevaerts, & Lemmens, 2017; Uehara, Kawashima, Goto, Tasaki, & Someya, 2001).

Regardless of group composition, MFTG members become a strong and sustainable therapeutic community (i.e., supportive network for patients and family members) (Tantillo, McGraw, Hauenstein, & Groth, 2015) through the group's ability to leverage the combined resources, strengths, and adaptive coping strategies of all members (Eisler, 2005). MFTG offers multiple opportunities for healing, growth, and change that are different from what is possible in individual and single-family therapies. For example, because family members in MFTG focus on individuals with AN in other families, as well as their own loved one, they have opportunities to reflect on their lives from new and different perspectives (Asen, 2002). The ability to learn about oneself and others in this way fosters a sense of universality (feeling connected with others who share one's experience) while also reducing defensiveness, shame, and blame. Through this experience, MFTG decreases caregiver burden and distress and promotes validation and connection among patients and families (Eisler, 2005; Simic & Eisler, 2015; Tantillo, McGraw, Hauenstein, & Groth, 2015).

Since the early 1960s, MFTG has been used successfully to treat a variety of chronic psychiatric and physical health problems, including schizophrenia (Dyck et al., 2000; Laqueur, Laburt, & Morong, 1964; McFarlane, 2002), bipolar illness (Moltz & Newmark, 2002), depression (Anderson, Griffin, Rossi, Pagonis, Holder, & Treiber, 1986; Lemmens, Eisler, Buysse, Heene, & Demyttenaere, 2009; Lemmens, Eisler, Dierick, Lietaer, & Demyttenaere, 2009), substance abuse (Kaufman & Kaufmann, 1972, 1977), diabetes, asthma, and cancer (Gonzales & Steinglass, 2002; Steinglass, 1998), as well as brain injury (Couchman, McMahon, Kelly, & Ponsford, 2014). The content and format of MFTGs are developed in the context of the etiological and maintenance factors of the targeted illness, as well as protective factors that promote relapse prevention and recovery (McFarlane, 2002). For example, psychotic disorders severely impact a patient's ability to process information (McFarlane, 2002) and create high caregiving demands and high expressed emotion. The latter involves intense emotional expression between patients and caregivers, including critical or hostile comments and attitudes and/or emotional over-involvement that can adversely impact treatment outcome (Butzlaff & Hooley, 1998; Kyraicou, Treasure, & Schmidt, 2008a; Le Grange, Eisler, Dare, & Hodes, 1992; Le Grange, Hoste, Lock, & Bryson, 2010; Leff & Vaughn, 1985; Rienecke, Accurso, Lock, & Le Grange, 2016; van Furth, van Strien, Martina, van Son, Hendrickx, & van Engeland, 1996; Vaughn & Leff, 1976;

24 *Mary Tantillo, Jennifer Sanftner McGraw, and Daniel Le Grange*

Zabala, Macdonald, & Treasure, 2009). Therefore, MFTGs for schizophrenia contain not only psychoeducation about the illness but also a strong emphasis on problem-solving and communication skills (McFarlane, 2002; McFarlane, 2016).

Empirical work related to MFTGs for adults with chronic psychiatric illnesses (Detre, Sayres, Norton, & Lewis, 1961; McFarlane, 2002) have produced impressive results in terms of cost savings and patient and family outcomes. Study findings reveal that MFTG can expand the patient's and family's social network, and thereby decrease isolation, expressed emotion, vulnerability to stress, and potential health problems related to the burden of illness (Gelin, Cook-Darzens, & Hendrick, 2017; Hazel, McDonell, Short, Berry, Voss, Rodgers, & Dyck, 2004; Lyman, Braude, George, Dougherty, Daniels, Ghose, & Delphin-Rittmon, 2014; McFarlane, 2002, 2016; Penninx, Kriegsman, van Eijk, Boeke, & Deeg, 1996). MFTGs have been shown to promote symptom reduction; decrease relapse and hospital readmission rates; increase patient vocational and social functioning; enhance communication within and between families; and improve collaboration among patients, family members, and clinicians (Asen, 2002; Dyck et al., 2000; Gelin, Cook-Darzens, & Hendrick, 2017; Lemmens, Eisler, Buysse, Heene, & Demyttenaere, 2009; Lemmens, Eisler, Dierick, Lietaer, & Demyttenaere, 2009; McFarlane, 2002; Scholz, Rix, Scholz, Gantchev, & Thömke, 2005; Steinglass, 1998). Study findings have also supported the notion that MFTG may be a cost-effective alternative to individual treatments (Asen & Scholz, 2010; Asen, 2002).

MFTG capitalizes on group therapeutic processes (Yalom & Leszcz, 2005) as well as family therapy principles (Bowen, 1985; Hecker, Mims, & Boughner, 2003). (See Boxes 2.1 and 2.2.)

Box 2.1 Group Therapeutic Factors That Promote Change[1]

Instillation of hope

Universality

Imparting information

Altruism (concern with the well-being of others that increases one's sense of purpose and value)

Corrective recapitulation of the primary family group (corrective reexperiencing of early family relationships in group)

Development of socializing techniques

Imitative behavior (trying on coping skills and perspectives of others)

Interpersonal learning

Group cohesiveness (a sense of community that promotes belonging and safety)

[1]Yalom & Leszcz, 2005

The Promise of Multifamily Therapy 25

Box 2.2   Family Therapy Principles[1,2]

Systemic thinking
Understanding and appreciating the impact of relational patterns on individual and family functioning
Considering the importance of multigenerational behavioral patterns (e.g., related to anxiety management)
Normalizing family challenges
Assuming problems do not reside inside the patient or family member and can be solved within relationship
Viewing family members as resources instead of problems in the treatment process
Believing that reframing and redefining a problem situation can be helpful

[1]Bowen, 1985; [2]Hecker, Mims, & Boughner, 2003

Both group psychotherapy and family therapy also assert that the whole is bigger, different from, and more complex than the sum of its parts (Hecker, Mims, & Boughner, 2003). MFTG is able to extend and enrich the therapeutic work accomplished in individual and single-family therapy because it involves a "neighborhood of interplaying diverse perspectives" available to influence healing and growth in individual members, families, and the group as a whole. Each relationship in MFTG takes on a life of its own, as does each family system, and the overall group. The sum, the relationships among MFTG members, is greater, different, and more complex than the contribution of individual MFTG members (Connors & Caple, 2005; Hecker, Mims, & Boughner, 2003). Interdependence is valued, promoted, and used to foster growth and change (Tantillo, McGraw, Hauenstein, & Groth, 2015).

The presence of many families in the MFTG room allows for interventions and activities impossible in individual and single-family therapy. For example, the group offers opportunities for patients to support other patients and/or family members and for family members to support other family members and/or patients. It also allows for activities such as "cross-parenting" (McFarlane, 2002, p. 44), wherein a patient may feel less threatened hearing feedback from another patient's parent than from his/her own parent. Similarly, it may be easier to hear feedback from a young adult in another family than hearing it from one's daughter, son, or partner.

Additional research is needed to explore whether the patient and family changes effected by MFTG are related to MFTG's structure, its psychoeducational component, or the interplay of both elements. Outside of research study findings confirming MFTG's ability to decrease expressed emotion, MFTG mechanisms of change are still unclear (Gelin, Cook-Darzens, &

Hendrick, 2017). There is some empirical support for the notion that the MFTG format (the social interactions occurring among families), rather than its particular content (psychoeducation), may best explain MFTG's efficacy (McFarlane, 2016; Mueser, Sengupta, Schooler, Bellack, Xie, Glick, & Keith, 2001). It may be that the group's enhanced social support decreases family member distress, thereby reducing the patient's vulnerability to relapse (McFarlane, 2016). This hypothesis makes sense when considering how important caring communities have been evolutionarily to human beings. Caring communities are based on the value of connections and the belief that each person in the community has gifts to share with others (McKnight & Block, 2012). They foster a sense of abundance in the face of member distress and the perceived scarcity of resources needed to cope with adversity. MFTG promotes an abundant community for patients and families, reminding them of the strengths and resources they possess when illnesses such as eating disorders promote fear and a scarcity mentality (Tantillo, 2017). In this way, the wholeness of the patient can be restored through community wholeness (Berry, 1977) and the collaborative efforts of all.

MFTG for Adolescents with AN

Over the last 20 years there has been an increase in the clinical and empirical work related to MFTGs for adolescents with AN. MFTG for adolescents has been offered as an intensive, stand-alone, longer-term treatment (e.g., 10–20 days over 9–12 months) in concert with single-family treatment (FT-AN) (Eisler, 2005; Simic & Eisler, 2015) or without FT-AN (Asen & Scholz, 2010; Gelin, Fuso, Hendrick, Cook-Darzens, & Simon, 2015; Scholz & Asen, 2001) and as a short-term (five consecutive days) intensive stand-alone treatment (Marzola, Knatz, Murray, Rockwell, Boutelle, Eisler, & Kaye, 2015). Alternatively, it has been offered within other levels of care (e.g., partial hospitalization/day treatment programs [Tantillo, 2006], inpatient programs [Depestele, Claes, Dierckx, Colman, Schoevaerts, & Lemmens, 2017; Fleminger, 2005; Honig, 2005], and outpatient clinics [Slagerman & Yager, 1989]).

MFTG treatment for adolescents with AN (MFT-AN) was originally developed by clinicians in London (Dare & Eisler, 2000) and Dresden (Scholz & Asen, 2001) with the hope of providing a different type of intensive treatment for a sub-group of adolescents who did not respond well to FT-AN. Empirical findings revealed that 10% to 20% of adolescents receiving FT-AN required additional partial hospitalization or inpatient medical or psychiatric treatment, while 10% to 15% needed ongoing treatment into young adulthood (Eisler et al., 2016; Eisler, Le Grange, & Lock, 2015). MFT-AN integrates the principles of FT-AN (Eisler, 2005; Eisler, Le Grange, & Lock, 2015) with more general concepts of MFTG (Asen & Scholz, 2010; Simic & Eisler, 2015) as well as other cognitive, psychodynamic, and group therapy conceptualizations and interventions (Eisler et al., 2016; Eisler, Simic, Blessitt, Dodge, and team, 2016; Simic & Eisler, 2015).

Specifically, MFT-AN as developed by the Maudsley Child and Adolescent Eating Disorders Service in London is comprised of four phases, addressing (1) engagement and therapeutic alignment with patients and families; (2) challenging the eating disorder; (3) exploring individual and family developmental issues; and (4) termination, relapse prevention, and future plans (Simic & Eisler 2015). MFT-AN is delivered over 9 to 12 months and is begun with an afternoon of orientation and psychoeducation, followed by four full days of MFT-AN, and then six one-day follow-up sessions. Single FT-AN is available at a frequency based on family needs. A similar program in Dresden provides 20 days of MFT-AN beginning with five consecutive treatment days and two day-long follow-up sessions without single FT-AN outside MFT-AN sessions (Asen & Scholz, 2010; Scholz & Asen, 2001; Simic & Eisler, 2015). Both programs include coaching and mealtime support for patients and family members who consume a meal and snacks throughout each treatment day. Post-meal processing with other patients and families can provide additional strategies for successful meal completion.

Empirical work related to MFTGs for adolescents with AN has produced impressive results in terms of cost savings and patient and family outcomes (Asen, 2002; Dare & Eisler, 2000; Eisler, 2005; Scholz & Asen, 2001; Simic & Eisler, 2015). Study findings reveal that MFTG for adolescents improves AN symptoms, including stabilization of eating, reduction in binge-vomit episodes, weight gain, and return of menses from baseline to end of treatment (Dare & Eisler, 2000; Eisler et al., 2016; Gabel, Pinhas, Eisler, Katzman, & Heinmaa, 2014; Hollesen, Clausen, & Rokkedal, 2013; Marzola, Knatz, Murray, Rockwell, Boutelle, Eisler, & Kaye, 2015; Scholz & Asen, 2001). The use of MFTG is also associated with high satisfaction with and reduced dropouts from treatment (Asen, 2002; Dare & Eisler, 2000; Eisler et al., 2016; Scholz, Rix, Scholz, Gantchev, & Thömke, 2005) and contributes to decreased inpatient length of stay and less relapse (Scholz & Asen, 2001). Family outcomes from MFTG include a decrease in negative expressed emotion by family members of patients with AN, and improved family functioning (e.g., joint problem solving) and communication (Dare & Eisler, 2000; Eisler, 2005; Scholz & Asen, 2001; Voriadaki, Simic, Espiec, & Eisler, 2015). Research findings indicate that MFTG is as effective as a single-family therapy format, but is also more cost-effective (Brunaux & Cook-Darzens, 2008; Geist, Heinmaa, Stephens, Davis, & Katzman, 2000).

Results from Eisler and colleagues' (Eisler et al., 2016) recently completed multicenter randomized controlled trial (RCT) showed that both FT-AN and MFT (a combination of MFT with single FT-AN visits) produced significant improvements over time in eating disorders psychopathology and depression. Both were associated with high treatment adherence rates and moderate to high patient and parent satisfaction ratings. At 12 months (end of treatment) there were no statistically significant differences between the two treatments for percentage of median BMI (%mBMI) [i.e., 50th centile] for adolescents of the same height, age, and sex; eating disorder psychopathology; depression; or self-esteem. However, at six-month follow-up there was a significant difference in %mBMI favoring MFT-AN

(Eisler et al., 2016). The significant clinical improvements produced by MFTG with adolescents with AN and their families in the Eisler and colleagues RCT (2016) (Eisler et al., 2016), as well as other empirical studies (Asen, 2002; Dare & Eisler, 2000; Gabel, Pinhas, Eisler, Katzman, & Heinmaa, 2014; Gelin, Cook-Darzens, & Hendrick, 2017; Hollesen, Clausen, & Rokkedal, 2013; Marzola, Knatz, Murray, Rockwell, Boutelle, Eisler, & Kaye, 2015), along with the findings related to high satisfaction rates, fewer treatment dropouts and relapses, and greater cost-effectiveness of MFTG, have led clinicians and researchers to explore the potential usefulness of MFTG for young adults with AN.

MFTG for Young Adults with AN

Because MFTG has been shown to be effective for adults with a variety of chronic mental and physical health problems (Anderson, Griffin, Rossi, Pagonis, Holder, & Treiber, 1986; Dyck et al., 2000; Gonzales & Steinglass, 2002; Lemmens, Eisler, Buysse, Heene, & Demyttenaere, 2009; McFarlane, 2002), as well as for adolescents with AN (Eisler et al., 2016; Gelin, Cook-Darzens, & Hendrick, 2017; Simic & Eisler, 2015), there is reason to believe it may also offer benefits for the treatment of young adults with AN. There is sparse literature about MFTG for young adults with eating disorders (Colahan & Robinson, 2002; Slagerman & Yager, 1989; Tantillo, McGraw, Hauenstein, & Groth, 2015) or their parents (Uehara, Kawashima, Goto, Tasaki, & Someya, 2001). Some early empirical work related to an MFTG model specifically developed to treat young adults with AN (Dimitropoulos, Farquhar, Freeman, Colton, & Olmsted, 2015; Tantillo, McGraw, Hauenstein, & Groth, 2015) shows the promise of MFTG for this population. In their 2015 study examining the outcomes of single-family versus multifamily therapy interventions, Dimitropoulos, Farquhar, Freeman, Colton, and Olmsted (2015) found that inpatients or day treatment patients receiving either treatment did equally well with regard to eating disorder psychopathology, weight, and mood and family outcomes (decreased negative caregiving appraisals and expressed emotion). Qualitative findings revealed that group members found that sharing with others who understood their challenges related to AN was the most beneficial part of treatment. This finding, along with the high attendance and low dropout rate, supported the feasibility and acceptability of this treatment. Dimitropoulos, Farquhar, Freeman, Colton, and Olmsted (2015) note, however, that their study was small, did not involve random assignment or a wait list or control group, and that improvements in family functioning may also have been related to the inpatient or day treatment programming patients simultaneously received. They call for future research, including larger RCTs, data collection on other treatments received (in addition to MFTG) from end of treatment to follow-up, and self-report measures regarding patient perceived changes in family members.

Why Should We Continue Exploration of the Potential Benefits of MFTG for Young Adults?

Continued exploration of the potential benefits of MFTG for young adults and their families is essential for developmental, clinical, and relational reasons. Young adults, viewed as "transition age youth (ages 17–25)," (Dimitropoulos, Lock, Le Grange, & Anderson, 2015, p. 230) and "emerging adults" (late teens through twenties with a focus on ages 18–25) (Arnett, 2000, p. 469; 2004, 2006) are tackling many developmental milestones that can increase stress and potentially increase vulnerability to illness. They are engaged in identity exploration and development and face new roles and responsibilities in the form of college, employment, and relationships. The age of "feeling in between" (adolescent dependence on others versus adult self-sufficiency and responsibility) (Arnett, 2000, 2004) has moved into the mid to late twenties over the last several decades. For example, the median age for marriage is now 29 for men and 27 for women as compared to 22 and 20, respectively, 60 years ago (Wang & Parker, 2014). Transitioning to adulthood takes longer now than has been the case in the past, with more young adults beginning and remaining in college, experiencing repeated residential moves, and women desiring to build a career before having children. These factors can also slow economic independence. Those who had developmental challenges in adolescence may be at greater risk of additional challenges in emerging adulthood (Bulik, 2002b; Milevsky, Thudium, & Guldin, 2014). Moreover, those patients who are ethnic minorities have the extra challenge of developing their identity within the dominant culture (Phinney, 2003).

Young adults who develop AN commonly struggle with emerging adulthood tasks due to fears related to maturation, anxious temperament, poor emotion regulation and coping, and perfectionistic standards (Bulik, 2002b; Kaye, Fudge, & Paulus, 2009). The disturbed cognitions related to AN and the sequelae of starvation only amplify developmental challenges. It is in this context that MFTG provides an opportunity for young adults with AN to benefit from the universality and connection with peers who have similar developmental struggles. MFTG also offers connection with parents from other families who have witnessed the struggles of their young adult offspring and can offer validation and support in a way that may be received more readily than from one's own parents.

Continued exploration of the benefits of MFTG for young adults is also justified from a clinical perspective. Chapter 1 revealed that individuals in young adulthood are at high risk for AN, as well as comorbid illnesses such as anxiety and mood and substance use disorders. Mortality risks also peak during the emerging adult years (18–29) (Crow, Peterson, Swanson, Raymond, Specker, Eckert, & Mitchell, 2009; Jones, 2013; Kaye, Bulik, Thornton, Barbarich, & Master, 2004; Kessler, Amminger, Aguilar-Gaxiola, Alonso, Lee, & Ustun, 2008; Merikangas, He, Brody, Fisher, Bourdon, & Koretz, 2010; Steinhausen, 2002; Swanson, Crow, Le Grange, Swendsen, &

Merikangas, 2011). Despite the high risks of illness and mortality, empirical work has not yet supported a definitive treatment for AN in young adults (Bulik, Berkman, Brownley, Sedway & Lohr, 2007; Kass, Kolko, Wilfley, 2013). MFTG may hold promise as an adjunct or primary mode of treatment during this developmental period.

Additionally, approximately half of adolescents with eating disorders experience a chronic illness course (Lock, Le Grange, Agras, Moye, Bryson, & Jo, 2010; Treasure & Russell, 2011) and need to transition from pediatric to adult treatment settings (Baldock, 2010). Dimitropoulos and colleagues (Dimitropoulos, Tran, Agarwal, Sheffield, & Woodside, 2013; Dimitropoulos, Tran, Agarwal, Sheffield, & Woodside, 2012) have noted barriers to this transition, including lack of continuous and coordinated care, illness-related factors such as ambivalence regarding weight gain, and the absence of psychosocial skills required to make this transition due to the sequelae of starvation and its adverse impact on the brain and relationships with supportive others. As patients experience an increased duration of illness and proceed from early to late adolescence and into young adulthood, their chances of responding to FBT-AN and experiencing remissions are reduced (Eisler, Dare, Russell, Szmukler, Le Grange, & Dodge, 1997; Le Grange, Lock, Agras, Moye, Bryson, Jo, & Kraemer, 2012; Russell, Szmukler, Dare, & Eisler, 1987). Given the number of adolescents who continue with this diagnosis into young adulthood, as well as dwindling remission rates over time, there is an urgency to identify more effective treatments for young adults with AN. MFTG may act as a therapeutic holding environment for patients and families that can interrupt a chronic course of AN.

Finally, there are relational justifications to support exploring the benefits of MFTG. Since relationships with close others have been cited as the "driving force" in recovery (Tozzi, Sullivan, Fear, McKenzie, & Bulik, 2003), and recovery from AN is related to improvements in social functioning (Berkman, Lohr, & Bulik,, 2007; Lowe, Zipfel, Buchholz, Dupont, Reas, & Herzog, 2001; Strober, Freeman, & Morrell, 1997), it is imperative that caregivers gain knowledge and skills in how to effectively respond to patients when they experience AN symptoms during emerging adulthood. Young adults with AN often yearn for the increased autonomy and independence that are associated with the transition out of adolescence into adulthood. However, the ego-syntonic nature of AN, the possible experience of anosognosia (not recognizing that one is ill) (Vandereycken, 2006), and the ambivalence and avoidance that characterize AN obstruct the development of true autonomy and healthy self-development (Dimitropoulos, Lock, Le Grange, & Anderson, 2015; Strauss & Ryan, 1987). The less than full development of the frontal cortex before mid-twenties and the biological impact of AN on the brain can also obstruct patient comprehension of consequences and overall information processing (Giedd, 2008; Katzman, Christensen, Young & Zipursky, 2001; Keys, Brozek, Henschel, Mickelsen, & Taylor, 1950). Patient desire for, but inability to exert, true autonomy in the area related to normalization of eating

The Promise of Multifamily Therapy 31

and weight gain creates a challenge for parents who need help knowing when to allow their young adult more choice during treatment. Developing a balanced frame of reference and emotional and relational skills for how to navigate this challenge is important because empirical work has shown that perceived parental autonomy support relates positively to self-endorsed motivation and eventual BMI for patients with AN (van der Kaap-Deeder, Vansteenkiste, Soenens, Verstuyf, Boone, & Smets, 2014).

Additionally, young adults with AN who achieve a sense of control through food restriction and weight loss feel relieved when other adults, including their parents, support their recovery work (Westwood & Kendal, 2012). A shift in patient attitudes and perspectives related to behavioral change can occur over time in treatment if caregivers learn to empower the young adult and disempower the illness (Westwood & Kendal, 2012). If young adults have difficulty listening to parental feedback due to the premium they place on desired autonomy, they may be open to the feedback from other empathic and encouraging adults (e.g., another patient's parent or partner) (Asen & Scholz, 2010; Eisler, 2005). MFTG can strengthen relationships among young adults and their parents, other caregivers, and siblings when developmental forces, AN symptoms, and the associated interpersonal disconnections threaten to isolate patients from their loved ones and their support.

Parents (and other caregivers) of young adults who are ambivalent about unifying their efforts to eliminate AN also need a tremendous amount of support. Parents may respond with self-doubt and accommodation to AN in the face of a young adult in denial about his/her illness (Treasure, Smith, & Crane, 2017). The young adult patient often normalizes her/his behaviors or angrily rejects parental structure, stating that parents are unfairly depriving the young adult of independent decision making and choices about intake, exercise, and other treatment-related issues. Parents can also feel a tremendous amount of emotional distress, shame, and guilt (Highet, Thompson, & King, 2005; Kyraicou, Treasure, & Schmidt, 2008b; Zabala, Macdonald, & Treasure, 2009) because their child is not moving along the developmental trajectory they envisioned. They see their child's peers continuing with development, while their child's emotional development is arrested. Their concern can become manifested in high levels of expressed emotion (Hooley, 2007; van Furth, van Strien, Martina, van Son, Hendrickx, & van Engeland, 1996) or they can feel helpless and hopeless, isolate themselves, and disengage from the patient and recovery work (Treasure, Smith & Crane, 2017). These experiences account for why family members value the opportunity to talk with others who share the same lived experience (Dimitropoulos, Farquhar, Freeman, Colton, & Olmsted, 2015; Graap, Bleich, Herbst, Sherzinger, Trostmann, Wancata, & de Zwaan, 2008; Haigh & Treasure, 2003; Tantillo, McGraw, Hauenstein, & Groth, 2015; Whitney, Murray, Gavan, Todd, Whitaker, & Treasure, 2005). This opportunity is enriched, and the number of young adult and family member resources multiplied, in MFTG.

32   *Mary Tantillo, Jennifer Sanftner McGraw, and Daniel Le Grange*

References

*No DOI

*Agras, W. S., & Robinson, A. H. (2010). What treatment research is needed for anorexia nervosa? In C. M. Grilo & J. E. Mitchell (Eds.), *The treatment of eating disorders: A clinical handbook* (pp. 554–543). The Guilford Press.

Anderson, C. M., Griffin, S., Rossi, A., Pagonis, I., Holder, D. P., & Treiber, R. (1986). A comparative study of the impact of education vs. process groups for families of patients with affective disorders. *Family Process, 25*, 185–205. https://dx.doi.org/10.1111/j.1545-5300.1986.00185.x.

Arnett, J. J. (2000). Emerging adulthood: A theory of development from the late teens through the twenties. *American Psychologist, 55*(5), 469–480. https://dx.doi.org/10.1037/0003-066x.55.5.469.

*Arnett, J. J. (2004). *Emerging adulthood: The winding road from the late teens through the twenties.* Oxford University Press.

Arnett, J. J. (2006). *Emerging adults in America: Coming of age in the 21st century.* American Psychological Association. https://dx.doi.org/10.1037/11381-000.

Asen, E. (2002). Multiple family therapy: An overview. *Journal of Family Therapy, 24*, 3–16. https://dx.doi.org/10.1111/1467-6427.00197.

Asen, E., & Scholz, M. (2010). *Multi-family therapy: Concepts and techniques.* Routledge. https://dx.doi.org/10.1080/01609513.2011.620785.

*Baldock, E. (2010). An ethico-legal account of working with careers in eating disorders. In J. Treasure, U. Schmidt, and P. Macdonald (Eds.). *The clinician's guide to collaborative caring in eating disorders: The New Maudsley Method* (pp. 30–42). Routledge.

Berkman, N. D., Lohr, K. N., & Bulik, C. M. (2007). Outcomes of eating disorders: A systematic review of the literature. *International Journal of Eating Disorders, 40*, 293–309. https://dx.doi.org/10.1002/eat.20369.

*Berry, W. (1977). *The wild geese. Collected poems 1957–1982.* North Point Press. (FIND DOI).

*Bowen, M. (1985). *Family therapy in clinical practice.* Rowman & Littlefield Publishers. (FIND DOI).

Brunaux, F., & Cook-Darzens, S. (2008). La thérapie multifamiliale: Une alternative à la thérapie unifamiliale dans le traitement de l'anorexie mentale de l'enfant et de l'adolescent? *Thérapie Familiale, 29*, 87–102. https://dx.doi.org/10.3917/tf.081.0087.

Bulik, C. M. (2002b). Eating disorders in adolescents and young adults. *Child and Adolescent Psychiatric Clinics of North America, 11*(2), 201–218. https://dx.doi.org/10.1016/S1056-4993(01)00004-9.

Bulik, C. M., Berkman, N. D., Brownley, K. A., Sedway, J. A., & Lohr, K. N. (2007). Anorexia nervosa treatment: A systematic review of randomized controlled trials. *International Journal of Eating Disorders, 40*(4), 310–320. http://dx.doi.org/10.1002/eat.20367.

Butzlaff, R. L., & Hooley, J. M. (1998). Expressed emotion and psychiatric relapse: A meta-analysis. *Archives of General Psychiatry, 55*, 547–552. https://dx.doi.org/10.1001/archpsyc.55.6.547.

Byrne, S., Wade, T., Hay, P., Touyz, S., Fairburn, C. G., Treasure, J., Schmidt, U., McIntosh, V., Allen, K., Fursland, A., & Crosby, R. D. (2017). A randomized controlled trial of three psychological treatments for anorexia nervosa. *Psychological Medicine, 16*, 2823–2833. http://dx.doi.org/10.1017/S0033291717001349.

Chen, E. Y., Le Grange, D., Doyle, A. C., Zaitsoff, S., Doyle, P., Roehrig, J. P., & Washington, B. (2010). A case series of family-based therapy for weight restoration in young adults with anorexia nervosa. *Journal of Contemporary Psychotherapy, 40*(4), 219–224. https://dx.doi.org/10.1007/s10879-010-9146-0.

Chen, E. Y., Weissman, J. A., Zeffiro, T. A., Yiu, A., Eneva, K. T., Arlt, J. M., & Swantek, M. J. (2016). Family-based therapy for young adults with anorexia nervosa restores weight. *International Journal of Eating Disorders, 49*(7), 701–707. https://dx.doi.org/10.1002/eat.22513.

Colahan, M., & Robinson, P. H. (2002). Multi-family groups in the treatment of young adults with eating disorders. *Journal of Family Therapy, 24*(1), 17–30. https://dx.doi.org/10.1111/1467-6427.00198.

Connors, J. V., & Caple, R. B. (2005). A review of group-systems theory. *The Journal for Specialists in Group Work, 30*(2), 93–110. https://dx.doi.org/10.1080/01933920590925940.

Couchman, G., McMahon, G., Kelly, A., & Ponsford, J. (2014). New kind of normal: Qualitative accounts of multi-family group therapy for acquired brain injury. *Neuropsychological Rehabilitation: An International Journal, 24*(6), 809–832. https://dx.doi.org/10.1080/09602011.2014.912957.

Crow, S. J., Peterson, C. B., Swanson, S. A., Raymond, N. C., Specker, S., Eckert, E. D., & Mitchell, J. M. (2009). Increased mortality in bulimia nervosa and other eating disorders. *American Journal of Psychiatry, 66*(12), 1342–1346. https://dx.doi.org/10.1176/appi.ajp.2009.09020247.

Dare, C., & Eisler, I. (2000). A multi-family group day treatment programme for adolescent eating disorder. *European Eating Disorders Review, 8*(1), 4–18. https://dx.doi.org/10.1002/(SICI)1099-0968(200002)8:1<4::AID-ERV330>3.0.CO;2-P.

Dare, C., Eisler, I., Russell, G. F., Treasure, J., & Dodge, L. (2001). Psychological therapies for adults with anorexia nervosa: Randomised controlled trial of out-patient treatments. *British Journal of Psychiatry, 178*, 216–221. http://dx.doi.org/10.1192/bjp.178.3.216.

Depestele, L., Claes, L., Dierckx, E., Colman, R., Schoevaerts, K., & Lemmens, G. (2017). An adjunctive multi-family group intervention with or without patient participation during an inpatient treatment for adolescents with an eating disorder: A pilot study. *European Eating Disorders Review, 25*, 570–578. https://dx.doi.org/10.1002/erv.2556.

Depestele, C., & Claes, L., & Lemmens, G. (2015). Promotion of an autonomy-supportive parental style in a multi-family group for eating-disordered adolescents. *Journal of Family Therapy, 37*(1), 24–40. https://dx.doi.org/10.1111/1467-6427.12047.

*Depestele, L., & Vandereycken, W. (2009). Families around the table: Experiences with a multifamily approach in the treatment of eating-disordered adolescents. *International Journal of Child and Adolescent Health, 2*, 255–261.

*Detre, T., Sayres, J., Norton, N. M., & Lewis, H. C. (1961). An experimental approach to the treatment of acutely ill psychiatric patients in the general hospital. *Connecticut Medicine, 25*, 613–619.

Dimitropoulos, G., Farquhar, J. C., Freeman, V. E., Colton, P. A., & Olmsted, M. P. (2015). Pilot study comparing multi-family therapy to single family therapy for adults with anorexia nervosa in an intensive eating disorder program. *European Eating Disorders Review, 23*, 294–303. http://dx.doi.org/10.1002/erv.2359.

*Dimitropoulos, G., Landers, A. L., Freeman, V., Novick, J., Garber, A., & Le Grange, D. (2018). Open trial of family-based treatment of anorexia nervosa for transition youth. *Journal of the Canadian Academy of Child and Adolescent Psychiatry*, *27*(1), 50–61.

*Dimitropoulos, G., Lock, J., Le Grange, D., & Anderson, K. (2015). Family therapy for transition youth. In K. Loeb, D. Le Grange, & J. Lock (Eds.), *Family therapy for adolescent eating and weight disorders: New applications* (pp. 230–255). Routledge/Taylor & Francis Group.

Dimitropoulos, G., Tran, A. F., Agarwal, P., Sheffield, B., & Woodside, B. (2012). Navigating the transition from pediatric to adult eating disorder programs: Perspective of service providers. *International Journal of Eating Disorders*, *45*(6), 759–767. https://dx.doi.org/10.1002/eat.22017.

Dimitropoulos, G., Tran, A. F., Agarwal, P., Sheffield, B., & Woodside, B. (2013). Challenges in making the transition between pediatric and adult eating disorder programs: A qualitative study from the perspective of service providers. *Eating Disorders: The Journal of Treatment and Prevention*, *21*(1), 1–15. https://dx.doi.org/10.1080/10640266.2013.741964.

Dyck, D. G., Short, R. A., Hendryx, M. S., Norell, D., Myers, M., Patterson, T., McDonell, M. G., Voss, W. D., & McFarlane, W. R. (2000). Management of negative symptoms among patients with schizophrenia attending multiple-family groups. *Psychiatric Services*, *51*, 513–519. https://dx.doi.org/10.1176/appi.ps.51.4.513.

Eisler, I. (2005). The empirical and theoretical base of family therapy and multiple family day therapy for adolescent anorexia nervosa. *Journal of Family Therapy*, *27*, 104–131. https://dx.doi.org/10.1111/j.1467-6427.2005.00303.x.

Eisler, I., Dare, C., Russell, G. F., Szmukler, G., Le Grange, D., & Dodge, E. (1997). Family and individual therapy in anorexia nervosa: A five-year follow-up. *Archives of General Psychiatry*, *54*, 1025–1030. http://dx.doi:10.1001/archpsyc.1997.01830230063008.

*Eisler, I., Le Grange, D., & Lock, J. (2015). Family therapy for adolescent eating disorders. In T. Sexton & J. Lebow (Eds.), *Handbook of family therapy* (4th ed.) (pp. 387–406). Routledge.

Eisler, I., Simic, M., Blessitt, E., Dodge, L., and team. (2016). *Maudsley Service Manual for Child and Adolescent Eating Disorders*. [Child and Adolescent Eating Disorders Service, South London and Maudsley NHS Foundation Trust, 2016]. https://www.national.slam.nhs.uk/wp-content/uploads/2011/11/Maudsley-Service-Manual-for-Child-and-Adolescent-Eating-Disorders-July-2016.pdf.

Eisler, I., Simic, M., Hodsoll, J., Asen, E., Berelowitz, M., Connan, F., Ellis, G., Hugo, P., Schmidt, U., Treasure, J., Yi, I., & Landau, S. (2016). A pragmatic randomized multi-centre trial of multifamily and single family therapy for adolescent anorexia nervosa. *BMC Psychiatry*, *16*(1), 522–435. https://dx.doi.org/10.1186/s12888-016-1129-6.

*Fairburn, C. G. (2008). *Cognitive behavior therapy and eating disorders*. The Guilford Press.

Fleminger, S. (2005). A model for treatment of eating disorders in adolescents in a specialized centre in The Netherlands. *Journal of Family Therapy*, *27*, 147–157. https://dx.doi.org/10.1111/j.1467-6427.2005.00307.x.

*Gabel, K., Pinhas, L., Eisler, I., Katzman, D., & Heinmaa, M. (2014). The effect of multiple family therapy on weight gain in adolescents with anorexia nervosa: Pilot data. *Journal of the Canadian Academy of Child and Adolescent Psychiatry*, *23*(3), 196–199.

Geist, R., Heinmaa, M., Stephens, D., Davis, R., & Katzman, D. K. (2000). Comparison of family therapy and family group psychoeduction in adolescents with anorexia nervosa. *Canadian Journal of Psychiatry*, *45*, 173–178. https://dx.doi.org/10.1177/070674370004500208.

Gelin, Z., Cook-Darzens, S., & Hendrick, S. (2017). The evidence base for multiple family therapy in psychiatric disorders: A review (part 1). *Journal of Family Therapy*, *40*(3), 302–325. https://dx.doi.org/10.1111/1467-6427.12178.

Gelin, Z., Fuso, S., Hendrick, S., Cook-Darzens, S., & Simon, Y. (2015). The effects of a multiple family therapy on adolescents with eating disorders: An outcome study. *Family Process*, *54*, 160–172. https://dx.doi.org/10.1111/famp.12103.

Giedd, J. N. (2008). The teen brain: Insights from neuroimaging. *Journal of Adolescent Health*, *42*(4), 335–343. https://dx.doi.org/10.1016/j.jadohealth.2008.01.007.

Girz, L., Robinson, A. L., Foroughe, M., Jasper, K., & Boachie, A. (2013). Adapting family-based therapy to a day hospital programme for adolescents with eating disorders: Preliminary outcomes and trajectories of change. *Journal of Family Therapy*, *35*(S1), 102–120. https://dx.doi.org/10.1111/j.1467-6427.2012.00618.x.

*Gonzales, S., & Steinglass, P. (2002). Application of multifamily groups in chronic medical disorders. In W. R. McFarlane (Ed.) *Multifamily groups in the treatment of severe psychiatric disorders* (pp. 315–340). The Guilford Press. (FIND DOI).

Graap, H., Bleich, S., Herbst, F., Sherzinger, C., Trostmann, Y., Wancata, J., & de Zwaan, M. (2008). The needs of carers: A comparison between eating disorders and schizophrenia. *Social Psychiatry and Psychiatric Epidemiology*, *43*(10), 800–807. https://dx.doi.org/10.1007/s00127-008-0364-7.

Haigh, R., & Treasure, J. (2003). Investigating the needs of carers in the area of eating disorders: Development of the Carers' Needs Assessment Measure (CaNAM). *European Eating Disorders Review*, *11*, 125–141. https://dx.doi.org/10.1002/erv.487.

Hazel, N. A., McDonell, M. G., Short, R. A., Berry, C. M., Voss, W. D., Rodgers, M. L., & Dyck, D. G. (2004). Impact of multiple-family groups for outpatients with schizophrenia on caregivers' distress and resources. *Psychiatric Services*, *55*, 35–51. https://dx.doi.org/10.1521/ijgp.2009.59.3.435.

*Hecker, L. L., Mims, G. A., & Boughner, S. R. (2003). General systems theory, cybernetics and family therapy. In J. L. Wetchler & L. L. Hecker (Eds.), *An introduction to marriage and family therapy* (pp. 39–62). Routledge.

Highet, N., Thompson, M., & King, R. M. (2005). The experience of living with a person with an eating disorder: The impact of the carers. *Eating Disorders: The Journal of Treatment and Prevention*, *13*(4), 327–344. https://dx.doi.org/10.1080/10640260591005227.

Hoing, P. (2005). A multi-family group programme as part of an inpatient service for adolescents with a diagnosis of anorexia nervosa. *Clinical Child Psychology and Psychiatry*, *10*, 465–475. https://dx.doi.org/10.1177/1359104505056309.

Hollesen, A., Clausen, L., & Rokkedal, K. (2013). Multiple family therapy for adolescents with anorexia nervosa: A pilot study of eating disorder symptoms and interpersonal functioning. *Journal of Family Therapy*, *35*(S1), 53–67. https://dx.doi.org/10.1111/1467-6427.12000.

Jones, P. B. (2013). Adult mental health disorders and their age at onset. *The British Journal of Psychiatry*, *202*, s5–s10. https://dx.doi.org/10.1192/bjp.bp.112.119164.

Hooley, J. M. (2007). Expressed emotion and relapse of psychopathology. *Annual Review of Clinical Psychology*, *3*, 329–352. https://dx.doi.org/10.1146/annurev.clinpsy.2.022305.095236.

Kass, A. E., Kolko, R. P., & Wilfley, D. E. (2013). Psychological treatments for eating disorders. *Current Opinion in Psychiatry*, *26*(6), 549–555. https://dx.doi.org/10.1097/YCO.0b013e328365a30e.

Katzman, D. K., Christensen, B., Young, A. R., & Zipursky, R. B. (2001). Starving the brain: Structural abnormalities and cognitive impairment in adolescents with anorexia nervosa. *Seminars in Clinical Neuropsychiatry*, *6*(2), 146–152. https://dx.doi.org/10.1053/scnp.2001.22263.

*Kaufman, E., & Kaufman, P. (1972). *Family therapy of drug and alcohol abuse* (2nd ed.). Allyn and Bacon.

Kaufman, E., & Kaufman, P. (1977). Multiple family therapy: A new direction in the treatment of drug abusers. *The American Journal of Drug and Alcohol Abuse*, *4*, 467–478. https://dx/doi.org/10.3109/00952997709007004.

Kaye, W. H., Bulik, C. M., Thornton, L., Barbarich, N., & Master, K. (2004). Comorbidity of anxiety disorders with anorexia bulimia nervosa. *American Journal of Psychiatry*, *161*, 2215–2221. https://dx.doi.org/10.1176/appi.ajp.161.12.2215.

Kaye, W. H., Fudge, J. L., & Paulus, M. (2009). New insights into symptoms and neurocircuit function of anorexia nervosa. *Nature Reviews Neuroscience*, *10*(8), 573–584. https://dx.doi.org/10.1038/nrn2682.

Kessler, R. C., Amminger, P., Aguilar-Gaxiola, S., Alonso, J., Lee, S., & Ustun, B. (2008). Age of onset of mental disorders: A review of recent literature. *Current Opinion in Psychiatry*, *20*(4), 359–364. http://dx.doi.org/10.1097/YCO.0b013e32816ebc8c.

*Keys, A., Brozek, J., Henschel, A., Mickelsen, O., & Taylor, H. L. (1950). *The biology of human starvation*. University of Minnesota Press.

Knatz, S., Murray, S. B., Matheson, B., Boutelle, K., Rockwell, R. E., Eisler, I., & Kaye, W. H. (2015). A brief, intensive application of multi-family-based treatment for eating disorders. *Eating Disorders*, *23*(4), 1–10. http://dx.doi.org/10.1080/10640266.2015.1042318.

Kyraicou, O., Treasure, J., & Schmidt, U. (2008a). Expressed emotion in eating disorders assessed via self-report: An examination of factors associated with expressed emotion in carers of people with anorexia nervosa in comparison to control families. *International Journal of Eating Disorders*, *41*(1), 37–46. https://dx.doi.org/10.1002/eat.20469.

Kyraicou, O., Treasure, J., & Schmidt, U. (2008b). Understanding how parents cope with living with someone with anorexia nervosa: Modelling the factors that are associated with carer distress. *International Journal of Eating Disorders*, *41*(4), 233–242. https://dx.doi.org/10.1002/eat.20488.

*Laqueur, H. P., Laburt, H. A., & Morong, E. (1964). Multiple family therapy: Further developments. *International Journal of Social Psychiatry*, *10*, 69–80.

*Leff, J., & Vaughn, C. (1985). *Expressed emotion in families*. The Guilford Press.

Le Grange, D., Eisler, I., Dare, C., & Hodes, M. (1992). Family criticism and self-starvation: A study of expressed emotion. *Journal of Family Therapy*, *14*, 177–192. https://dx.doi.org/10.1046/j..1992.00451.x.

Le Grange, D., & Hoste, R., Lock, J., & Bryson, S. W. (2010). Parental expressed emotional of adolescents with anorexia nervosa: Outcome in family-based treatment. *International Journal of Eating Disorders*, *44*, 731–734. https://dx.doi.org/10.1002/eat.20877.

The Promise of Multifamily Therapy   37

Le Grange, D., Lock, J., Agras, W. S., Moye, A., Bryson, S. W., Jo, B., & Kraemer, H. C. (2012). Moderators and mediators of remission in family-based treatment and adolescent focused therapy for anorexia nervosa. *Behavior Research and Therapy, 50*(2), 85–92. https://dx.doi.org/10.1016/j.brat.2011.11.003.

Lemmens, G. M. D., Eisler, I., Buysse, A., Heene, E., & Demyttenaere, K. (2009). The effects of mood on adjunctive single-family and multi-family group therapy in the treatment of hospitalized patients with major depression. *Psychotherapy and Psychosomatics, 79*, 98–105. https://dx.doi.org/10.1159/000201935.

Lemmens, G. M. D., Eisler, I., Dierick, P., Lietaer, G., & Demyttenaere, K. (2009). Therapeutic factors in a systemic multi-family group treatment for major depression: Patients' and partners' perspectives. *Journal of Family Therapy, 31*, 250–269. https://dx.doi.org/10.1111/j.1467-6427.2009.00465.x.

Lock, J., Le Grange, D., Agras, W. S., Moye, A., Bryson, S. W., & Jo, B. (2010). Randomised clinical trial comparing family-based treatment with adolescent-focused individual therapy for adolescents with anorexia nervosa. *Archives of General Psychiatry, 67*(10), 1025–1032. https://dx.doi.org/10.1001/archgenpsychiatry.2010.128.

Lowe, B., Zipfel, S., Buchholz, C., Dupont, Y., Reas, D. L., & Herzog, W. (2001). Long-term outcome of anorexia nervosa in a prospective 21-year follow-up study. *Psychological Medicine, 31*, 881–890. https://dx.doi.org/10.1017/s003329170100407x.

Lyman, D. R., Braude, L., George, P., Dougherty, R. H., Daniels, A. S., Ghose, S. S., & Delphin-Rittmon, M. E. (2014) Consumer and family psychoeducation: Assessing the evidence. *Psychiatric Services, 65*(4), 416–428. https://dx.doi.org/10.1176/appi.ps.201300266.

Marzola, E., Knatz, S., Murray, S. B., Rockwell, R., Boutelle, K., Eisler, I., & Kaye, W. H. (2015). Short-term intensive family therapy for adolescent eating disorders: 30-month outcome. *European Eating Disorders Review, 23*(3), 210–218. https://dx.doi.org/10.1002/erv.2353.

*McFarlane, W. R. (2002). *Multifamily groups in the treatment of severe psychiatric disorders.* The Guilford Press.

McFarlane, W. R. (2016). Family interventions for schizophrenia and the psychoses: a family review. *Family Process, 55*(3), 460–482. https://dx.doi.org/10.1111/famp.12235.

McIntosh, V. V. W., Jordan, J., Carter, F., Luty, S. E., McKenzie, J. M., Bulik, C. M., Frampton, C. M. A., & Joyce, P. R. (2005). Three psychotherapies for anorexia nervosa: A randomized controlled trial. *American Journal of Psychiatry, 162*(4), 741–747. https://dx.doi.org/10.1176/appi.ajp.162.4.741.

*McKnight, J., & Block, P. (2012). *The abundant community: Awakening the power of families and neighborhoods.* Berrett-Koehler Publishers, Inc.

Mehl, A., Tomanová, J., Kuběna, A., & Papežová, H. (2013). Adapting multifamily therapy to families who care for a loved one with an eating disorder in the Czech Republic combined with follow-up pilot study of efficacy. *Journal of Family Therapy, 35*(S1), 82–101. https://dx.doi.org/10.1111/j.1467-6427.2011.00579.x.

Merikangas, K. R., He, J. P., Brody, D., Fisher, P. W., Bourdon, K., & Koretz, D. S. (2010). Prevalence and treatment of mental disorders among US children in the 2001–2004 NHANES, *Pediatrics, 125*(1), 75–81. https://dx.doi.org/10.1542/peds.2008-2598.

Milevsky, A., Thudium, K., & Guldin, J. (2014). *The transitory nature of parent, sibling and romantic partner relationships in emerging adulthood.* Springer. https://dx.doi.org/10.1007/978-3-319-06638-7.

*Moltz, D. A., & Newmark, M. (2002). Multifamily groups for bipolar illness. In W. R. McFarlane (Ed.), *Multifamily therapy groups in the treatment of severe psychiatric disorders* (pp. 220–243). The Guilford Press.

Mueser, K. T., Sengupta, A., Schooler, N. R., Bellack, A. S., Xie, H., Glick, I. D., & Keith, S. J. (2001). Family treatment and medication dosage reduction in schizophrenia: Effects on patient social functioning, family attitudes, and burden. *Journal of Consulting and Clinical Psychology, 69*(1), 3–12. https://dx.doi.org/10.1037/0022-006X.69.1.3.

Penninx, B. W. J. H., Kriegsman, D. M. W., van Eijk, J. T. M., Boeke, A. J. P., & Deeg, D. H. H. (1996). Differential effects of social support on the course of chronic disease: A criterion-based literature review. *Families, Systems, & Health, 14*, 223–244. https://dx.doi.org/10.1037/h0089816.

Phinney, J. (2003). Ethnic identity and acculturation. In K. M. Chun, P. B. Organista, & G. Martin (Eds.), *Acculturation: Advances in theory, measurement, and applied research* (pp. 63–81). American Psychological Association. https://dx.doi.org/10.1037/10472-006.

Rhodes, P., Baillee, A., Brown, J., & Madden, S. (2008). Can parent-to-parent consultation improve the effectiveness of the Maudsley model of family-based treatment for anorexia nervosa? A randomized control trial. *Journal of Family Therapy, 30*(1), 96–108. https://dx.doi.org/10.1111/j.1467-6427.2008.00418.x.

Rienecke, R. D., Accurso, E. C., Lock, J., & Le Grange, D. (2016). Expressed emotion, family functioning and treatment outcome for adolescents with anorexia nervosa. *European Eating Disorders Review, 24*(1), 43–51. https://dx.doi.org/10.1002/erv.2389.

Russell, G. F. Szmukler, G. I., Dare, C., & Eisler, I. (1987). An evaluation of family therapy in anorexia nervosa and bulimia nervosa. *Archives of General Psychiatry, 44*, 1047–1056. http://dx.doi.org/10.1001/archpsyc.1987.01800240021004.

Schmidt, U., Oldershaw, A., Jichi, F., Sternheim, L., Startup., H., McIntosh, V., Jordan, J., Tchanturia, K., Wolff, G., Rooney, M., Landau, S., & Treasure, J. (2012). Outpatient psychological therapies for adults with anorexia nervosa: Randomised controlled trial. *British Journal of Psychiatry, 5*, 392–399. http://dx.doi.org/10.1192/bjp.bp.112.112078.

Schmidt, U., Wade, T. D., & Treasure, J. L. (2014). The Maudsley Model of anorexia nervosa treatment of adults (MANTRA): Development, key features, and preliminary evidence. *Journal of Cognitive Psychotherapy, 28*(1), 48–71. http://dx.doi.org/10.1891/0889-8391.28.1.48.

Scholz, M., & Asen, E. (2001). Multiple family therapy with eating disordered adolescents: Concepts and preliminary results. *European Eating Disorders Review, 9*, 33–42. https://dx.doi.org/10.1002/erv.364.

Scholz, M., Rix, M., Scholz, K., Gantchev, K., & Thömke, V. (2005). Multiple family therapy for anorexia nervosa: Concepts, experiences and results. *Journal of Family Therapy, 27*, 132–141. https://dx.doi.org/10.1111/j.1467-6427.2005.00304.x.

*Simic, M., & Eisler, I. (2015). Multi-family therapy. In I. Eisler, A. Wallis, E. Dodge, K. L. Loeb, D. Le Grange, & J. Lock (Eds.), *Family Therapy for Adolescent Eating and Weight Disorders* (pp. 110–138). Routledge.

*Slagerman, M., & Yager, J. (1989). Multiple family group treatment for eating disorders: A short term program. *Psychiatric Medicine, 7*, 269–283.

Steinglass, P. (1998). Multiple family discussion groups for persons with chronic medical illness. *Families, Systems and Health, 16*, 55–70. https://dx.doi.org/10.1111%2Fj.1545-5300.2011.01359.x.

The Promise of Multifamily Therapy   39

Steinhausen, H. (2002). The outcome of anorexia nervosa in the 20th century. *American Journal of Psychiatry, 159*, 1284–1293. http://dx.doi.org/10.1176/appi.ajp.159.8.1284.

Strauss, J., & Ryan, R. (1987). Autonomy disturbances in subtypes of anorexia nervosa. *Journal of Abnormal Psychology, 96*(3), 254–258. https://dx.doi.org/10.1037//0021-843X.96.3.254.

Strober, M., Freeman, R., & Morrell, W. (1997). The long-term course of severe anorexia nervosa in adolescents: Survival analysis of recovery, relapse, and outcome predictors over 10-15 years in a prospective study. *International Journal of Eating Disorders, 22*(4), 339–360. https://dx.doi.org/10.1002/(sici)1098-108x(199712)22:4%3C339::aid-eat1%3E3.0.co;2-n.

Swanson, S. A., Crow, S. J., Le Grange, D., Swendsen, J., & Merikangas, K. R. (2011). Prevalence and correlates of eating disorders in adolescents. *Archives of General Psychiatry, 68*(7), 714–723. https://dx.doi.org/10.1001/archgenpsychiatry.2011.22.

Tantillo, M. (2006). A relational approach to eating disorders multifamily therapy group: Moving from difference and disconnection to mutual connection. *Families, Systems, & Health, 23*(1), 82–102. https://dx.doi.org/10.1037/1091-7527.24.1.82.

Tantillo, M. (2017). *Reconnecting for recovery multifamily therapy group: Capitalizing on connection and community in the treatment of adults with anorexia nervosa.* Gurze/Salcore Eating Disorders Resource Catalogue. https://www.edcatalogue.com/reconnecting-recovery-multifamily-therapy-group capitalizing-connection-community-treatment-adults-anorexia-nervosa/.

Tantillo, M., McGraw, J. S., Hauenstein, E., & Groth, S. W. (2015). Partnering with patients and families to develop an innovative multifamily therapy group treatment for adults with anorexia nervosa. *Advances in Eating Disorders: Theory, Research, and Practice, 3*(3), 269–287. https://dx.doi.org/10.1080/21662630.2015.1048478.

Tantillo, M., Sanftner, J. L., & Hauenstein, E. (2013). Restoring connection in the face of disconnection: An integrative approach to understanding and treating anorexia nervosa. *Advances in Eating Disorders: Theory, Research, and Practice, 1*, 21–38. https://dx.doi.org/10.1080/21662630.2013.742980.

Tozzi, F., Sullivan, P., Fear, J., McKenzie, J., & Bulik, C. (2003). Causes and recovery in anorexia nervosa: The patient's perspective. *International Journal of Eating Disorders, 33*(2), 143–154. https://dx.doi.org/10.1002/eat.10120|.

Treasure, J., & Russell, G. F. (2011). The case for early intervention in anorexia nervosa: Theoretical exploration of maintaining factors. *The British Journal of Psychiatry, 199*(1), 5–7. https://dx.doi.org/10.1192/bjp.bp.110.087585.

Treasure, J., Smith, G., & Crane, A. (2017). *Skills-based learning for caring for a loved one with an eating disorder* (2nd ed.). Routledge. https://dx.doi.org/10.4324/9781315735610.

Uehara, T., Kawashima, Y., Goto, M., Tasaki, S., & Someya, T. (2001). Psychoeducation for the families of patients with eating disorders and changes in expressed emotion: A preliminary study. *Comprehensive Psychiatry, 42*(2), 132–138. https://dx.doi.org/10.1053/comp.2001.21215.

Vandereycken, W. (2006). Denial of illness in anorexia nervosa—a conceptual review: Part 2 different forms and meanings. *European Eating Disorders Review, 14*(5), 352–368. https://dx.doi.org/10.1002/erv.722.

Van der Kaap-Deeder, J., Vansteenkiste, M., Soenens, B., Verstuyf, J., Boone, L., & Smets, J. (2014). Fostering self-endorsed motivation to change in patients with an eating disorder: The role of perceived autonomy and psychological need satisfaction. *International Journal of Eating Disorders, 47*, 585–600. https://dx.doi.org/10.1002/eat.22266.

van Furth, E. F., van Strien, D. C., Martina, L. M. L., van Son, M. J. M., Hendrickx, J. J. P., & van Engeland, H. (1996). Expressed emotion and the prediction of outcome in adolescent eating disorders. *International Journal of Eating Disorders*, *20*, 19–31. https://dx.doi.org/10.1002/(SICI)1098-108X(199607)20:1<19::AID-EAT3>3.0. CO;2-7.

Vaughn, C. E., & Leff, J. P. (1976). The measurement of expressed emotion in the families of psychiatric patients. *British Journal of Social and Clinical Psychology*, *15*, 157–165. https://dx.doi.org/10.1111/j.2044-8260.1976.tb00021.x.

Voriadaki, T., Simic, M., Espiec, J., & Eisler, I. (2015). Intensive multi-family therapy for adolescent anorexia nervosa: Adolescents' and parents' day-to-day experiences. *Journal of Family Therapy*, *37*, 5–23. https://dx.doi.org/10.1111/1467-6427.12067.

Wallis, A., Alford, C., Baudinet, J., Cook, A., Robertson, A., Cubitt, A., Madden, S., & Kohn, M. (2013). Innovations in Maudsley family based treatment for anorexia nervosa at the Children's Hospital at Westmead: A family admission programme. *Journal of Family Therapy*, *35*(S1), 68–81. https://dx.doi.org/10.1111/j.1467-6427. 2012.00604.x.

Wang, W., & Parker, K. (September 24, 2014). *Record share of Americans have never married.* Pew Research Center. https://www.pewsocialtrends.org/2014/09/24/record-share-of-americans-have-never-married/.

Watson, H. J., & Bulik, C. M. (2013). Update on the treatment of anorexia nervosa: Review of clinical trials, practice guidelines and emerging interventions. *Psychological Medicine*, *43*(12), 2477–2500. https://dx.doi.org/10.1017/S0033291712002620.

Westwood, L. M., & Kendal, S. E. (2012). Adolescent client views towards the treatment of anorexia nervosa: A review of the literature. *Journal of Psychiatric Mental Health Nursing*, *19*(6), 500–508. https://dx.doi.org/10.1111/j.1365-2850.2011. 01819.x.

Whitney, J., Murray, J., Gavan, K., Todd, G., Whitaker, W., & Treasure, J. (2005). Experience of caring for someone with anorexia nervosa: Qualitative study. *The British Journal of Psychiatry*, *187*, 444–449. https://dx.doi.org/10.1192/bjp.187. 5.444.

*Yalom, I., & Leszcz, M. (2005). *The theory and practice of group psychotherapy* (5th ed.). Basic Books.

Zabala, M. J., Macdonald, P., & Treasure, J. (2009). Appraisal of the caregiving burden, expressed emotion, and psychological distress in families of people with eating disorders: A systematic review. *European Eating Disorders Review*, *17*(5), 338–349. https://dx.doi.org/10.1002/erv.925.

3 Development of the Reconnecting for Recovery (R4R) MFTG Approach and This Manual

Mary Tantillo, Jennifer Sanftner McGraw, and Daniel Le Grange

In Chapter 2, we outlined the nature, origins, and outcomes of MFTG treatment, including a review of the empirical work, clinical observations, and theory underlying its development and effectiveness for adolescents and adults with AN and other behavioral and physical health conditions. We also discussed the potential usefulness of MFTG for young adults given their developmental challenges, the high risk of developing AN and comorbid illnesses and increased mortality during young adulthood, as well as caregiver needs for support and education to promote patient autonomy while not enabling AN.

In Chapter 3, we will discuss the theory, clinical observation, patient and family member lived experience, and empirical work that contributed to the development of the R4R MFTG approach and manual. We will also review how R4R MFTG is different from other MFTGs, why clinicians should use the R4R MFTG manual, who is qualified to use the treatment manual, and the importance of working closely with other treatment team members when conducting R4R. We end the chapter with a review of R4R MFTG goals, group sessions, and topics.

The Birth of R4R

Reconnecting for Recovery (R4R) is a Relational/Motivational MFTG approach that was borne out of more than a decade of planning and early development in partnership and close coordination with patients and families (Tantillo & Sanftner, 2010a, 2010b; Tantillo, 2010, 2011; Tantillo, McGraw, Hauenstein, & Groth, 2015; Tantillo, Sanftner, & Hauenstein, 2013). Early work included clinical observation, review of theory and research to create the intervention and the model informing it, and development of a psychometrically tested measure (Connection-Disconnection Scale) to assess perceived mutuality (PM) in relationships, which is postulated to be R4R's central healing factor (Tantillo & Sanftner, 2010b). Preliminary empirical work examining the relationships between PM and eating disorder symptoms, as well as the effectiveness of a Relational/Motivational approach to understanding and treating eating disorders, has been reviewed elsewhere (Tantillo &

Sanftner, 2010a, 2010b; Tantillo, Sanftner, & Hauenstein, 2013). A manuscript reporting favorable outcomes for patients attending a Relational/Motivational Eating Disorder Partial Hospitalization Program (which includes an MFTG) is being prepared for manuscript submission (Tantillo, Anson, Lavigne, & Wilkosz, 2019). Findings revealed statistically and clinically significant improvements from baseline to discharge in eating disorder symptoms, mood, PM, and quality of life. Additionally, there was an inverse relationship between levels of PM at discharge with both parents and eating disorder psychopathology, depression, and higher levels of quality of life.

In regard to research findings specifically examining the helpfulness of a Relational/Motivational MFTG approach, previous program evaluation (2008–2010) findings of the first iteration of R4R, a close-ended outpatient eight-week (90-minute session) group, supported its effectiveness (Tantillo, 2006; Tantillo, 2010, 2011). Findings specifically showed that patients in the original eight-week Relational/Motivational MFTG treatment had fewer eating disorder symptoms from baseline to end of treatment (with an especially favorable influence on level of restraint [Eating Disorder Examination Questionnaire 4] and drive for thinness [Eating Disorder Inventory 3]), an increased patient and parent PM from baseline to end of group, and high patient and family satisfaction at end of treatment (Tantillo, 2010). Also, the patients' experience of PM with parents and eating disorder symptoms were negatively correlated, indicating that a decrease in eating disorder symptoms was associated with an increase in PM (Tantillo, 2010). By end of treatment, fathers' experiences of PM with their young adult or adolescent child showed meaningful clinical improvements. The majority of mothers also experienced increases in PM by end of treatment, but three of ten experienced drops in PM. This finding underscored the possible need for more time in MFTG. This notion was supported in a follow-up focus group wherein alumni members of the eight-week groups (seen in the outpatient MFTGs between 2008 and 2010) voiced the desire for a 16-week group. Alumni provided focus group feedback on benefits and limitations of the group and how to enrich and extend the eight-week group format to develop R4R's 16-session, 26-week group cycle format targeting AN in young adults (Tantillo, 2010; Tantillo, McGraw, Hauenstein, & Groth, 2015).

Specifically, content analysis of focus group feedback revealed that recovery from AN is "long, arduous, and marked by disconnections and intense emotions" (p. 8) (including those related to parenting an ill young adult and receiving help as a young adult) (see Table 3.1), and that the eight-week MFTG improved communication, the quality of connections, and identification and expression of emotions, and indirectly helped AN symptoms (Tantillo, McGraw, Hauenstein, & Groth, 2015).

Throughout the focus groups, alumni MFTG members discussed how strengthened connections among patients and family members helped them unite against and externalize AN and jointly name and repair the disconnections it created for everyone. An MFTG alumna mother and patient express this as follows.

Development of the Reconnecting for Recovery   43

Table 3.1 Disconnections Experienced by Eight-Week MFTG Alumni Patients and Family Members

---

- Patient's disconnection from emotions (e.g., starvation helps numb fear)
- Disconnection from each another (e.g., due to parental guilt or blame related to "causing AN" and patients' self-silencing to protect parents from disappointment)
- Family members not knowing what to say to patients
- Conflict avoidance
- Parents and patients ascribing different meanings to the same word
- Diminished engagement related to exhaustion
- Patient and family member disconnection from others outside the family

---

So, what's the normal child growing up and (what's this other thing getting in the way) … the (disconnection part of it just spreads) so much because it … impacts the child and the family. Then it spreads out even more … I (wouldn't get together with friends) … I was (disconnecting from him [husband] and from her [patient]). … So by starting to (rebuild all those relationships), I was able to help her more. And just to me, it [rebuilding relationships] was the (biggest part of it).

(Mother) (Tantillo, McGraw, Hauenstein, & Groth, 2015, p. 11)[1]

I think it helps when you focus on the (disconnection). … Then you can focus on it as a disease. … So I think we reframe it in a way that takes the guilt and the blame off of people. Like it's not any person's fault. … When we (focus on connecting more) it really (does make a difference).

(Female Patient) (Tantillo, McGraw, Hauenstein, & Groth, 2015, p. 11)[1]

Overall, content analysis findings supported the idea that alumni did experience changes in the emotional, relational, and behavioral areas targeted by the eight-week MFTG, including a greater ability to identify and repair disconnections related to AN and develop better or new connections with one another. One female patient articulately stated how MFTG's emphasis on connections with self and others can indirectly affect intake and weight gain. She noted the favorable impact of MFTG on her self-concept and self-worth, as well as her relationship with her mother. She described how changes in these factors and her attribution of meanings and perception of her mother's mealtime support efforts influenced her ability to stabilize her eating and weight.

Group affected the way (I thought about myself) … (took away … the embarrassment and the shame and negativity that I felt towards myself) … [MFTG] is where I really started (feeling better about myself) … starting to like (love myself again). Like when you (feel good about yourself), I think you're (less likely to restrict). … I wouldn't say it would cause weight gain, but I would say it'd definitely be (correlated with weight gain). … During MFTG … I started to (trust my mom more), and see that (her relationship with me) and my ED was more of (her wanting me to be healthy rather than her sabotaging what was familiar to me). ... I started to (let her serve me meals). ... I (felt more safe with eating) ... when you are (more open to eating), you're (not completely refusing every meal) and (weight gain may happen).

(Female Patient) (Tantillo, McGraw, Hauenstein, & Groth, 2015, p. 12)[1]

Program evaluation and qualitative content findings related to the eight-week MFTG allowed the authors to apply and receive grant funding from the Hilda and Preston Davis Foundation from 2014 to 2018 to conduct a pilot investigation on the extended 16-session, 26-week group cycle (Tantillo, McGraw, Lavigne, Brash, & Le Grange, 2019). Two R4R group cycles were conducted (total n = 10 patients and 14 family members [four fathers, five mothers, two partners and three friends]) with outcomes examined from baseline (BL) to end of treatment (EOT) and six-month follow-up (6MFU). Findings revealed that the R4R MFTG was feasible and acceptable to patients and families. Eating disorder psychopathology (measured by the Eating Disorder Examination [Cooper & Fairburn, 1987]) and Lack of Emotional Awareness (ability to attend to and acknowledge emotions measured by the Difficulties in Emotion Regulation Scale [Gratz & Roemer, 2004]) improved significantly from BL to EOT and BL to 6MFU with moderate to large effect sizes. Limited Access to Emotion Regulation Strategies (LAERS–the belief that one can access effective emotion regulation strategies to manage situations, also measured by the DERS) improved significantly from BL to 6MFU with a moderate effect size. Improvements in LAERS from BL to EOT and weight from BL to EOT and BL to 6MFU were not significant.

Study findings provided preliminary support for R4R's ability to greatly reduce AN symptoms during and after treatment, as well as assist patients with emotion regulation so they can connect with their authentic feelings. Over time, R4R also seems to increase patient beliefs that they can access emotion regulation strategies to manage situations. Changes in weight were smaller throughout the study, but these findings were in line with BMI improvements occurring in other outpatient treatments (Byrne et al., 2017). Also, R4R focuses more on development of emotional and relational processing skills than nutritional rehabilitation.

What Is the R4R Approach and What Makes R4R Different from Other Multifamily Therapy Groups?

R4R MFTG is similar to other MFTGs because it maximizes the resources, strengths, adaptive coping strategies, and problem-solving skills of a number of families (Eisler, 2005; McFarlane, 2002; Simic & Eisler, 2015). It is more similar to the relationally focused MFTGs for adolescents with AN (Asen & Sholz, 2010; Depestele, Claes, & Lemmens, 2015; Eisler et al., 2016; Eisler, Lock, & Le Grange, 2010), Lemmens et al.'s MFTG for depression (Lemmens, Eisler, Buysse, Heene, & Demyttenaere, 2009; Lemmens, Eisler, Dierick, Lietaer, & Demyttenaere, 2009; Lemmens, Eisler, Migerode, Heireman, & Demyttenaere,

Development of the Reconnecting for Recovery   45

2007), and Couchman and colleagues' (Couchman, McMahon, Kelly, & Ponsford, 2014) MFTG for acquired brain injury because these MFTG models externalize the illness, understand it within a relational context, promote self-awareness through interpersonal learning, and foster new and different perspectives through mutual support and feedback.

At the same time, R4R is different from other MFTGs. R4R leverages patient and family resources and strengths specifically through the use of an integrated treatment model that is informed by Motivational Interviewing principles (Miller & Rollnick, 2013), Stages of Change Theory (McConnaughy, DiClemente, Prochaska, Velicer, 1989; Prochaska, Norcross, & DiClemente, 1994), and, most importantly, Relational-Cultural Theory (Tantillo & Sanftner, 2010a; Tantillo, Sanftner, & Hauenstein, 2013). This integrated Relational/Motivational approach focuses more predominantly on the development of emotional and relational processing skills required to prevent or repair disconnections associated with AN (Tantillo & Sanftner, 2010a; Tantillo, McGraw, Hauenstein, & Groth, 2015).

When patients begin R4R, the therapist's assessment of stage of change allows for an accurate matching of interventions with the patient's readiness for change (Geller, Cockell, & Drab, 2001; Geller, Drab-Hudson, Wisenhunt, & Srikameswaran, 2004; Prochaska, Norcross, & DiClemente, 1994; Rieger & Touyz, 2006). Use of Motivational Interviewing (MI) principles allows the therapist to respond to the patient in a way that acknowledges the important functions of an eating disorder to the patient, while creating discrepancy between the patient's life goals and values and AN's adverse impact on these goals and values. Motivational Interviewing reduces patient ambivalence about change and solicits change talk (e.g., statements that indicate the patient desires change, is capable of making changes, sees the reasons or necessity for change, is committing to make the change, or has taken action toward making change) and behavior (Miller & Rollnick, 2013; Tantillo & Sanftner, 2010a).

Whereas R4R is rooted in Stages of Change Theory and Motivational Interviewing principles, R4R's theoretical grounding in Relational-Cultural Theory (R-CT) is what is at the heart of R4R and led to R4R's innovative relational reframing of AN as a *"disease of disconnection."* This conceptual scheme emphasizes the disconnections that characterize AN and foster disconnection from the self (e.g., one's genuine thoughts, feelings, and needs), body, and others (Tantillo, Sanftner, & Hauenstein, 2013). More recent biopsychosocial integrative models emphasizing neurodevelopmental and interpersonal factors related to the etiology and maintenance of AN support the existence of these disconnections (Connan, Campbell, Katzman, Lightman, & Treasure, 2003; Lask & Frampton, 2011; Nunn, Frampton, & Lask, 2012; Southgate, Tchanturia, & Treasure, 2005).

Specifically, R4R's new relational reframe asserts that there are *intrapersonal (biological and psychological) processes of disconnection* contributing to, for example, a patient's difficulties with awareness of internal psychological and bodily states and regulation of emotions (Garner, 2004; Jansch, Harmer, & Cooper, 2009;

Keys, Brozek, Henschel, Mickelsen, & Taylor, 1950; Kucharska-Pietura, Nikolaou, Masiak, & Treasure, 2004; Nunn, Frampton, & Lask, 2012; Pollatos, Herbert, Schandry, & Gramann, 2008; Troop, Schmidt, & Treasure, 1995) and *interpersonal (affective and behavioral) processes of disconnection* contributing to, for example, a patient's self-silencing, minimizing of experience, and avoidance of conflict in relationships (Geller, Cockell, Hewitt, Goldner, & Flett, 2000; Schmidt & Treasure, 2006; Haynos & Fruzzetti, 2011; Kaye, Fudge, & Paulus, 2009). This relationally informed conceptual scheme further asserts that the interplay of these intra- and interpersonal processes of disconnection can lead to *interpersonal disconnections from loved ones*. For example, because a patient with AN may have more difficulty accurately identifying feelings and needs and reading others' facial expressions (Jansch, Harmer, & Cooper, 2009; Pollatos, Herbert, Schandry, & Gramann, 2008; Zonnevijlle-Bendere, van Goozen, Cohen-Kennenis, van Elburgh, & van Engeland, 2002) (*intrapersonal process of disconnection*), and will tend to isolate or avoid others in the face of conflict (*interpersonal process of disconnection*), he/she can have difficulty conveying internal experiences and needs to others, especially in the face of tension and intense emotion. At the same time, caregivers, who also experience distress in response to their loved one's AN, may be more emotionally challenged and be less able to empathize, encourage, and empower their loved one at certain times, especially in the face of intense emotion (Butzlaff & Hooley, 1998; Treasure, Smith, & Crane, 2017; van Furth, van Strien, Martina, van Son, Hendrickx, & van Engeland, 1996). The interplay of these processes can contribute to *interpersonal disconnections* characterized by overprotectiveness, pseudo-mutuality, conflict avoidance, and little space for the patient's and/or caregiver's authentic feelings and needs or relationships that involve conflict, tension, too much space, and no shared understanding of each person's experience. Patient and family relationships can include both kinds of disconnections in the face of AN.

The *interpersonal disconnections* patients and family members experience because of AN can compromise continued joint work in recovery. Patients with eating disorders have reported worse family functioning than other family members (Ciao, Accurso, Fitzsimmons-Craft, Lock, & Le Grange, 2015), and caregivers of patients with eating disorders have reported significantly more negative caregiving experiences (e.g., shame or self-blame) compared with parents of healthy controls (Kyraicou, Treasure, & Schmidt, 2008b). Over time, AN can more easily trigger interpersonal disconnections when there is no relational repair and patient and family members chronically experience a diminishing sense of perceived mutuality (i.e., mutual trust, respect, and understanding). When patients with AN feel misunderstood, confused, and overwhelmed with intense emotion, they may turn to AN to cope with these experiences. It is known that repeated and chronic disconnections can serve as maintaining factors in eating disorders (Tantillo & Sanftner, 2010a, 2010b; Tantillo, Sanftner, & Hauenstein, 2013; Tantillo, McGraw, Hauenstein, & Groth, 2015).

The R4R relational reframing of AN views PM as the central healing factor that remedies the disconnections associated with AN. Perceived mutuality paves

Development of the Reconnecting for Recovery   47

the way toward healing, growth, and recovery. The experience of PM restores a bidirectional sense of trust, empathy, empowerment, self-worth, understanding, and desire for more connection (Genero, Miller, Surrey, & Baldwin, 1992; Jordan, 2018; Miller & Stiver, 1997). Where there is PM, there is a greater chance for reconnection with the self, one's body, and others. Reconnecting for Recovery MFTG assists families to identify and repair disconnections that maintain AN and restores a sense of connection with oneself and others. It accomplishes this task through teaching MFTG members the importance of naming disconnections caused by AN and equipping them with the emotional and relational skills to do relational repair and foster PM in relationships.

Central to PM is the simultaneous ability to be open to the influence of others while also being aware of how one influences others. Perceived mutuality requires individuals to be emotionally vulnerable and engaged in a constantly changing pattern of responding to and affecting the other's state (Jordan, 2018). In R4R MFTG members develop PM by practicing being "different-in-connection." This means that they practice being open to and embracing others' differences (i.e., different perspectives, feelings and needs) while remaining in connection with themselves and others (Genero, Miller, Surrey, & Baldwin, 1992; Tantillo, 2006).

In the R4R approach group facilitators teach about and model PM by also sharing how they are influenced by patient and family feelings, thoughts, and behaviors. This intervention can be especially helpful if members feel stuck as they identify disconnections and employ strategies to repair relational ruptures. Therapist self-disclosure is one way in which the therapist authentically represents herself in the relationship with group members to promote their authenticity and self-empathy, perceived mutuality, healing, and growth in relationships (Tantillo, 2004). The group facilitators emphasize how everyone, including the therapists, are changed through naming and repairing disconnections related to AN and the experience of PM (Tantillo, 2006; Tantillo & Sanftner, 2010a; Tantillo, Sanftner, & Hauenstein, 2013). This approach demystifies therapy and the role of the facilitators and promotes collaboration and patient and family empowerment. (See Tantillo, 2004 for a more detailed explanation of appropriate and therapeutic use of self-disclosure in R-CT.) See Box 3.1 for factors to consider before engaging in therapist self-disclosure and Box 3.2 for the possible uses and examples of therapist self-disclosure in R4R.

Box 3.1   Factors to Consider Before Using Therapist Self-Disclosure in R4R Group

Patient and family member needs, vulnerabilities, and strengths:
Will therapist self-disclosure meet patient or family member needs or is it meeting an unconscious/unresolved or conscious therapist need such as

a desire for validation or acceptance? What is the group member's readiness for, comfort with, and ability to respond to therapist self-disclosure? Will the group member experience therapist self-disclosure as an invitation to deepen authenticity and mutual connection or as an overwhelming or threatening event that will create disconnection and obstruct relational growth?

Patient and family clinical history:
Patient's presenting history of illness and past patient and family psychiatric treatment history, family member relational histories, R4R goals, and points of tension and disconnections experienced by family members.

Therapist's intended clinical goal:
Is the therapist self-disclosing to foster perceived mutuality, deepen rapport, and invite group members to bring more of themselves into relationship? Or is the therapist's disclosure a strategy for disconnection in which the therapist is coping with his/her own intense emotions and unconscious needs and obstructing opportunities for patients and families to connect with themselves and others?

Timing:
Should the therapist help the patient(s)/family member(s) articulate their experiences first?

History of your relationship with group members:
How have tension and disconnections previously been handled between you and each member, as well as with the group as a whole?

Will self-disclosure assist members in naming and processing a disconnection?

Will self-disclosure foster authenticity, self-empathy, and perceived mutuality?

Will self-disclosure demystify therapy and the role of the therapist?

Stage of therapy.

Patient and therapist strategies for disconnection.
Therapist ability and time to manage what follows a disclosure.

Therapist willingness to discuss disclosures in the future (once disclosed, they become grist for the mill in an ongoing way).

Adequacy of therapist self-understanding, self-care, and stressors.

Box 3.2 Uses and Examples of Therapist Self-Disclosure within R4R Multifamily Therapy Group

Offer validation: I can hear how painful it was for you to not get accepted into your college of choice. You were so excited to go. It feels like a big let-down. At the same time, I am worried you are being very hard on yourself. I remember when I did not get accepted into my first choice. I initially felt so disappointed and like a failure. I had to talk with my family and friends for a while to work through all that. They helped me see how hard I was being on myself.

Foster authenticity, self-empathy, and perceived mutuality: You are telling us that it is fine that your husband is late from work and can't eat dinner with you. I am worried about that word "fine." It is probably very hard to share any negative feelings about his lateness. You know how hard he works, that he can't always control his work demands, and that he loves you. I remember when I was newly married to my husband. We had different approaches to winding down after work. He wanted to chill in front of the TV, and I wanted to talk about my day. I understood his need to do this and that he loves me, but also felt lonely and unsupported on the return home, especially during stressful days. I eventually had to share my experience because it was hurting my relationship with him. Your husband is asking for you to let him know what you need. I am wondering what you are feeling about being alone at dinner sometimes and what would be helpful?

Promote universality: I hear family members talking a lot today about the sadness and frustration that comes with watching someone you love struggle with something you can't fix. And I hear the patients saying that this often leads to more questions and hovering over them. I do not know what it is like to have a child with an eating disorder, but I do know what it is like to watch my son struggling with things I can't fix for him. I feel sad, frustrated, and helpless and get more preoccupied with thoughts of what I should do differently to help because I love him. It is during these times he tells me I act like a helicopter parent. It is hard to be a parent and it is hard to be a child who sometimes feels like they are loved too much by their parents.

Normalize (instead of pathologize) experiences: So, when we are trying to make a change like letting go of eating disorder behaviors, it is important to notice how the eating disorder gets in our way and how we might get in our own way. If I went around the room right now, each of us would be able to state one way they might get in their own way when feeling anxious about making a change. We aren't always aware of when we are using these coping strategies. So, for example, when I am stressed about making a change, I might rationalize and intellectualize things—give myself lots of reasons I should not do something a different way, when I really need to make the change. These thoughts and rationalizations help me avoid the anxiety or fear I have about making the change, but in the end, they help me avoid the change I need to make. Others of us might procrastinate or do other things in the face of a change. The patients are not the only ones who experience challenges with making a change. We all do.

Share similar experiences to empower group members: I hear you (mother of a patient) blaming yourself for not knowing that you should have checked on her again in her room last night; that she really wanted you to come back upstairs, even though the eating disorder did not want that. I don't know what it is like to have a child with an eating disorder, but I do know what it is like when I somehow feel I have failed my daughter. Like as her mother, I am supposed to somehow be able to just know how to respond in all situations. It is easy to feel like a failure because I missed the mark with her. Disconnections like these are painful and at the same time can be moments of great growth. You are acknówledging your desire to be more helpful going forward. Hindsight is always 20/20. What matters is what we can learn from the disconnection that happened the other night. You can ask your daughter now what else you could have done differently, and she can practice telling you without the eating disorder getting in the way.

Use humor to teach a therapeutic lesson: At the start of group a very perfectionistic patient tells the group leader that she never received the materials the therapist promised to send her before the group. She repeats twice that it is OK because she knows how busy the therapist is. The therapist decides to use humor to leverage this situation to teach a therapeutic lesson about imperfection. She has been able to be playful with the patient in the past as well.

Therapist (Mary):	So, somehow it is OK that I forgot these materials that I promised to send you TWICE last week? It does NOT feel OK to me (smiling). I SHOULD have remembered. A GOOD therapist would have remembered.
Patient:	OK, I know where you are going with this, Mary (chuckling).
Therapist:	Yes, somehow it's OK that I am not perfect, but it's not OK for you to not be perfect.
Patient:	Got it.

Demonstrate flexibility and openness to change and difference: So, you have shared with us how you believe you will not be triggered by your friend's food restriction at the party this weekend. And I hear your partner and others in the group voicing concern about time spent with her. I, too, am feeling a little anxious about this. At the same time, it sounds like you would like to try this out and you agreed to call your partner if you start feeling triggered. Sounds like you want to be a scientist and collect data on how things will go now that you have been in recovery for a little while. I feel more confident about your self-care plan this weekend because you are allowing others to support you. I wonder if others are feeling the same or different from what I am experiencing?

Share both sides of a relational dilemma: I wanted to share with you something I experienced during group today. You were very quiet today and said you did not feel like saying much. So, I decided to let that go until now. I wanted you to know that I felt a bit conflicted about this decision. Part of me wanted to honor your request and give you some space because I worried if I didn't, you would experience me as intrusive, pushy or controlling like you have experienced in other relationships. At the same time the other part of me worried that because I was not pushing a bit more on you to talk, you might think I don't care about you. I know you have felt that way in relationships too. I am wondering what you are thinking about what I have shared? I am also curious about what others think.

Help members move through disconnection while staying connected: The therapist notices that there is a disconnection between a patient (Samantha) and her best friend (Lauren) and the patient is having difficulty naming it and sharing the associated thoughts and feelings. The therapist attempts to help the patient address the distress she feels about her friend telling the college residence assistant (RA) (out of concern) about her eating disorder. However, Samantha is silent and shakes her head. The therapist then invokes the help of Lauren and other patients in the group who may have had similar experiences. They try to help the patient name what she may be experiencing, but she says, "She is fine and what happened is in the past."

Therapist: Samantha, it does not seem like you are fine. I want to share with you how heavy my heart feels watching you hold in what are probably pretty intense emotions. I feel sad and frustrated for you because it seems like you are trying to be a good friend and not upset Lauren with how you feel about what happened. At the same time, good friendship is based on honesty. You both said you value that about each other. What is the worst thing that will happen if you share what you felt when Lauren spoke with the RA?

Samantha:	I don't want to lose another friend.
Lauren:	You are not going to lose me by telling me how you feel. You are probably super annoyed with me. But I was so worried about you.
Therapist:	Samantha, are you feeling super annoyed like Lauren says or something different?
Samantha:	I just felt betrayed and upset because you told. But I did not want to tell you this because you could get angry with me and decide not to be my friend. I already lost so many other friends at school.

Acknowledge mistakes or limitations and apologize for contributing to disconnections: A patient becomes quiet at group's end and is looking down at the floor. The therapist notices this and gently reflects back the change in the patient's demeanor.

Patient:	I am fine.
Therapist:	It does not seem like you are fine. Something happened. Can you share what is going on inside?
Patient:	I'm just tired of everyone thinking that everything I think or do has to do with the eating disorder. I feel the way I do sometimes just because I am me, not because of the eating disorder. Sometimes I just want time to myself because it helps me calm down and feel less stimulated. It's not just because the eating disorder wants me to isolate.
Therapist:	I am wondering if I am part of the "everyone" who helped you feel this way. Was it because I started asking you questions about whether you felt triggered before you went up to your room over the weekend?
Patient:	Yes, it just seemed like you and my parents automatically assumed it was because of the eating disorder. This time it wasn't.
Therapist:	I am sorry for leaving you with the impression that I automatically assumed it was the eating disorder at work. It sounds like what I said left you feeling pretty frustrated and ganged up on. My goal is to help you find your voice, not silence it. It probably would have been better to first encourage you to share more about what you experienced before you headed upstairs to your room. This is what I would ask your parents to do as well. Then we have a more accurate understanding of what you are experiencing and how to help.

Development of the Reconnecting for Recovery   53

R4R's theoretically informed relational lens and language for how to address the adverse influence of AN on patients and families allows them to quickly externalize the illness and engage in the identification and repair of disconnections associated with AN (Miller & Stiver, 1997; Tantillo, 2006; Tantillo & Sanftner, 2010a, 2010b) without feeling a sense of shame or blame (Tantillo et al., 2013, 2015). The experience of PM and the relational repair it fosters are essential for young adults with AN and their families, since time to recovery is increased significantly among patients with disturbances in family relationships (Strober, Freeman, & Morrell, 1997). The patient's experience of family support, compassion, understanding and appropriate involvement are critical during treatment and recovery (Van der Kaap-Deeder, Vansteenkiste, Soenens, Verstuyf, Boone, & Smets, 2014; Kelly, Carter, & Borairi, 2014).

Additional Differences from Other MFTG Approaches

There are a few additional differences between R4R and other MFTGs. R4R MFTG moves beyond the traditional cognitive-behavioral model of eating disorders treatment for adults (Clark, 1995; Fairburn, 2008; Garner, Vitousek, & Pike, 1997; Pike, Walsh, Vitousek, Wilson, & Bauer, 2003) because it does not have a strong focus on refeeding and weight. While R4R acknowledges and provides some education about the importance of stabilizing eating and weight, it does not include family meals. This difference is supported by others (Schmidt & Treasure, 2006) who have commented on preliminary evidence showing that interventions focused exclusively on normalization of eating and stabilization of weight are less effective in achieving sustained change than psychological treatments that promote emotional processing (Pike, Walsh, Vitousek, Wilson, & Bauer, 2003; Serfaty, 1999). Additionally, feedback from patients treated in earlier iterations of R4R included a recommendation that MFTG focus primarily on communication and connections versus nutritional rehabilitation. They felt the latter issue could be addressed by their dietitians and/or individual or single-family therapists (Tantillo, 2011; Tantillo, McGraw, Hauenstein, & Groth, 2015).

R4R is also different from many other MFTG's because it includes family of origin members as well as other trusted adults (e.g., partners, best friends, sponsors, mentors, and coaches) who are considered 'family of choice' members with an emotional investment in the patient's recovery. Inclusion of family of choice is more developmentally appropriate for adults who spend more time outside their families of origin establishing relationships with others in work, school, religious and recreational venues (Arnett, 2000, 2004, 2006; Erikson, 1950; Rumbaut, 2004).

Finally, R4R is different from the majority of MFTG's for individuals with AN because it is a 16-session, close-ended, 90-minute outpatient group offered weekly, then every two weeks, then monthly over a 26-week period. The majority of MFTG's occur within day treatment or inpatient treatment settings or are offered as intensive short-term (five days) or longer-term (9–12 months) interventions (Marzola, Knatz, Murray, Rockwell, Boutelle, Eisler, & Kaye, 2015; Simic & Eisler, 2015). The R4R MFTG may potentially produce cost-savings because it occurs in the outpatient setting, often as an adjunct to individual or single-family therapy.

Why Use the R4R Treatment Manual?

This treatment manual contains information on how to conduct the 16-session, 26-week R4R MFTG informed by the most recent pilot study findings. We believe a manual-based approach provides the structure required to deliver R4R in a way that is more likely to lead to the positive outcomes obtained in our previous clinical and pilot study work. A manual-based approach also fosters replicability of this treatment framework. After reviewing the theory informing R4R in this chapter and the manual-based treatment approach in the following chapters, you will have a clearer understanding of the R4R MFTG and the rationale for why you would use certain interventions in each group session.

Who Is Qualified to Use the R4R Treatment Manual?

This treatment manual is intended for use by mental health clinicians (e.g., those with graduate degrees in counseling, social work, family therapy, and psychology, as well as psychiatric nurse practitioners and psychiatrists) who have received training in the assessment and treatment of eating disorders in young adults. (For the USA and Canada these clinicians would be licensed mental health providers.) Therapists receiving eating disorder training under the guidance of expert eating disorder MFTG therapists may also use this manual. We strongly suggest that therapists in training should have already received instruction in and conducted single-family and/or group therapies with patients with AN and their family members before using this manual and conducting R4R. The understanding of a MFTG approach may be clearer and its delivery more facile when the clinician has had the benefits of having been trained in and conducting these other systemically-oriented treatments. Also, R4R should be conducted with appropriate, routine consultation or supervision and involvement of professionals on the patient's health care team.

Working with Other Health Care Team Members

Since R4R is often an outpatient adjunct treatment, it is important that the R4R therapist obtain consent to talk with the patient's other health care team members before starting group. If the patient and family are requesting R4R, but the patient is not in individual and/or single-family therapy and/or being followed medically, it is wise to create a larger health care team including a primary care provider, an individual and/or family

Development of the Reconnecting for Recovery   55

therapist, and dietitian. Initial assessment can inform the recommended treatments, e.g., individual and/or single-family. If the patient declines individual or single-family therapy, and initial assessment reveals it is safe to progress with R4R, then it is advisable to ask that the patient at least be followed routinely by a primary care clinician during R4R (preferably one with eating disorder training and experience). Consent to speak with the primary care clinician would be obtained before group begins. If as group progresses, it is clear that the patient would benefit from individual and/or single-family therapy, then this would be discussed with the patient and family. Also, if the patient experiences increased psychiatric or physical health symptoms that threaten their safety or require a higher level of care, they should be referred to more intense treatment. The patient may return to MFTG after discharge depending on group norms. It can be very helpful for family members to continue in MFTG when their loved one is moved into a more intense level of care. This decision, again, depends on group norms. In our clinical experience R4R in combination with individual and/or single-family therapy and nutritional counseling can help obviate the need for partial hospitalization, inpatient or residential treatments. More research is needed to systematically explore the effectiveness of R4R in combination with other treatments.

Involvement of the R4R therapist with other health care providers on the team is essential because what the therapist learns about the patient and their family members in the R4R MFTG can enrich the team's overall understanding of the patient and family, their strengths and needs, and treatment planning. Similarly, other team members can offer information gleaned from individual, group, and single-family treatments, as well as nutritional and medical treatments, that can assist the R4R MFTG therapists in their work. Together, in connection, the R4R MFTG therapists,

Table 3.2 Reconnecting for Recovery Goals

Reduce anorexia nervosa (AN) symptoms through:

- Increase understanding regarding how AN promotes disconnection in relationships with others and obstructs recovery
- Increase understanding regarding the impact of disconnections on AN symptoms and recovery
- Increase perceived mutuality among patients and families
- Practice new emotional and relational skills that promote recovery
- Increase understanding regarding the illness and stages and processes of change so families can interact in ways that promote motivation for ongoing treatment and recovery
- Promote a sense of hopefulness and positive, healing energy that enables patients and families to remain connected and engaged in their recovery work
- Decrease isolation and expand families' and patients' social networks

56 *Mary Tantillo, Jennifer Sanftner McGraw, and Daniel Le Grange*

Table 3.3 Reconnecting for Recovery Multifamily Therapy Group Sessions and Topics

Session	Frequency	Topic
1 & 2	Weekly (Single-family assessment sessions)	Assessment, Joining, and Orientation
3	Weekly (Group sessions begin.)	Anorexia nervosa: A Disease of Disconnection—Introduction, Recovery Process, Motivational Interviewing Principles, and the Spiral of Change
4	Weekly	Anorexia nervosa: A Disease of Disconnection: Recovery Process, the Spiral of Change, and Motivational Interviewing Principles (Continued)
5	Weekly	Biopsychosocial Risk Factors for anorexia nervosa and Comorbidity
6	Weekly	Biopsychosocial Risk Factors (Continued), Disconnections, and Functional Analysis Skills
7	Weekly	Strategies to Promote Mutual Connections
8	Weekly	Anorexia nervosa and the Family Context: Rules and Relationships
9	Weekly	Identifying Points of Tension and Disconnections Related to Anorexia Nervosa, Recovery, and Relationships
10	Weekly	Nourishing and Empowering the "We" in Relationships
11	Biweekly (every two weeks)	Waging Good Conflict in Connection
12	Biweekly	Moving from Disconnection to Connection: Building Strong Connections to Work through Tension and Disconnections Related to Adulthood and Recovery
13	Biweekly	Relapse Prevention and Maintaining Good Connection
14	Biweekly	Relapse Prevention (Continued) and Preparing for Termination
15 & 16	Monthly	Relapse Prevention (Continued), Termination, and Next Steps for Continued Connections in Recovery

other health care team members, the young adult patient, and their family members work together to foster the patient's reconnection with self and others and ongoing recovery.

Summary

Over a decade of clinical observation, patient and family feedback, and preliminary research support R4R's promise as a MFTG treatment for young

Development of the Reconnecting for Recovery 57

adults with AN. R4R combines the benefits of family and group therapy and is rooted in relational and motivational theories that can foster healing, psychological change, and ongoing recovery. It is based on a new and innovative conceptual scheme (AN as a disease of disconnection) that provides a credible explanation for AN symptoms and offers a prescribed approach believed to resolve these symptoms and restore health. R4R aims to create a therapeutic community of healing that allows patients and families to view disconnections associated with AN as opportunities to strengthen their relationships and resolve for recovery. R4R's overall goals are listed in Table 3.2. Additionally, we share an outline of R4R group sessions (see Table 3.3) to enable the therapist to see all 16 sessions and the flow of group topics across the 26-week treatment period.

Note

1 Quotations. Reprinted from "Partnering with patients and families to develop an innovative multifamily therapy group treatment for adults with Anorexia Nervosa," by M. Tantillo, J. S. McGraw, E. J., Hauenstein, & S. W. Groth, 2015, *Advances in Eating Disorders: Theory, Research and Practice*, 3, pp. 11–12. Copyright 2015 by Taylor & Francis Ltd., http://www.tandfonline.com. Reprinted by permission of Taylor and Francis Ltd.

References

*No DOI

Arnett, J. J. (2000). Emerging adulthood: A theory of development from the late teens through the twenties. *American Psychologist*, *55*(5), 469–480. https://dx.doi.org/10.1037/0003-066x.55.5.469.

*Arnett, J. J. (2004). *Emerging adulthood: The winding road from the late teens through the twenties*. Oxford University Press.

Arnett, J. J. (2006). *Emerging adults in America: Coming of age in the 21st century*. American Psychological Association. https://dx.doi.org/10.1037/11381-000.

Asen, E., & Scholz, M. (2010). *Multi-family therapy: Concepts and techniques*. Routledge. https://doi.org/10.1080/01609513.2011.620785.

Butzlaff, R. L., & Hooley, J. M. (1998). Expressed emotion and psychiatric relapse: A meta-analysis. *Archives of General Psychiatry*, *55*, 547–552. https://dx.doi.org/10.1001/archpsyc.55.6.547.

Byrne, S., Wade, T., Hay, P., Touyz, S., Fairburn, C. G., Treasure, J., Schmidt, U., McIntosh, V., Allen, K., Fursland, A., & Crosby, R. D. (2017). A randomized controlled trial of three psychological treatments for anorexia nervosa. *Psychological Medicine*, *16*, 2823–2833. http://dx.doi.org/10.1017/S0033291717001349.

Ciao, A. C., Accurso, E. C., Fitzsimmons-Craft, E. E., Lock, J., & Le Grange, D. (2015). Family functioning in two treatments for adolescent anorexia nervosa. *International Journal of Eating Disorders*, *48*(1), 81–90. https://dx.doi.org/10.1002/eat.22314.

*Clark, D. A. (1995). Perceived limitations of standard cognitive therapy: A consideration of efforts to revise Beck's theory and therapy. *Journal of Cognitive Psychotherapy: An International Quarterly*, *9*(3), 153–172.

Connan, F., Campbell, I. C., Katzman, M., Lightman, L., & Treasure, J. (2003). A neurodevelopmental model for anorexia nervosa. *Physiology and Behavior, 79*, 13–24. https://dx.doi.org/10.1016/S0031-9384(03)00101-X.

Cooper, Z., & Fairburn, C. (1987). The eating disorder examination: A semi-structured interview for the assessment of the specific psychopathology of eating disorders. *International Journal of Eating Disorders, 6*(1), 1–8. https://doi.org/10.1002/1098-108X(198701)6:1<1::AID-EAT2260060102>3.0.CO;2-9.

Couchman, G., McMahon, G., Kelly, A., & Ponsford, J. (2014). New kind of normal: Qualitative accounts of multi-family group therapy for acquired brain injury. *Neuropsychological Rehabilitation: An International Journal, 24*(6), 809–832. https://dx.doi.org/10.1080/09602011.2014.912957.

Depestele, C., & Claes, L., & Lemmens, G. (2015). Promotion of an autonomy-supportive parental style in a multi-family group for eating-disordered adolescents. *Journal of Family Therapy, 37*(1), 24–40. https://dx.doi.org/10.1111/1467-6427.12047.

Eisler, I. (2005). The empirical and theoretical base of family therapy and multiple family day therapy for adolescent anorexia nervosa. *Journal of Family Therapy, 27*, 104–131. https://dx.doi.org/10.1111/j.1467-6427.2005.00303.x.

*Eisler, I., Lock, J., & Le Grange, D. (2010). Family-based treatments for adolescents with anorexia nervosa: Single-family and multifamily approaches. In C. M. Grilo & J. E. Mitchell (Eds.), *The treatment of eating disorders* (pp. 150–174). The Guilford Press.

Eisler, I., Simic, M., Hodsoll, J., Asen, E., Berelowitz, M., Connan, F., Ellis, G., Hugo, P., Schmidt, U., Treasure, J., Yi, I., & Landau, S. (2016). A pragmatic randomized multi-centre trial of multifamily and single family therapy for adolescent anorexia nervosa. *BMC Psychiatry, 16*(1), 522–435. https://dx.doi.org/10.1186/s12888-016-1129-6.

*Erikson, E. H. (1950). *Childhood and society.* Norton.

*Fairburn, C. G. (2008). *Cognitive behavior therapy and eating disorders.* The Guilford Press.

*Garner, D. (2004). *EDI-3 professional manual.* Psychological Assessment Resources.

*Garner, D. M., Vitousek, K. M., & Pike, K. M. (1997). Cognitive-behavioral therapy for anorexia nervosa. In D. M. Garner & P. E. Garfinkel (Eds.), *Handbook of treatment for eating disorders* (2nd ed.) (pp. 94–144). The Guilford Press.

Geller, J., Cockell, S. J., & Drab, D. L. (2001). Assessing readiness for change in the eating disorders: The psychometric properties of the Readiness and Motivation Interview. *Psychological Assessment, 13*(2), 189–198. https://dx.doi.org/10.1037/1040-3590.13.2.189.

Geller, J., Cockell, S. J., Hewitt, P. L., Goldner, E. M., & Flett, G. L. (2000). Inhibited expression of negative emotions and interpersonal orientation in anorexia nervosa. *International Journal of Eating Disorders, 28*, 8–19. https://doi.org/10.1002/1098-108X(200007)28:1%3C8::AID-EAT2%3E3.0.CO;2-U.

Geller, J., Drab-Hudson, D. L., Whisenhunt, B. L., & Srikameswaran, S. (2004). Readiness to change dietary restriction predicts outcomes in the eating disorders. *Eating Disorders, 12*(3), 209–224. https://doi.org/10.1080/10640260490490438.

Genero, N. P., Miller, J. B., Surrey, J., & Baldwin, L. M. (1992). Measuring perceived mutuality in close relationships: Validation of the Mutual Psychological Development Questionnaire. *Journal of Family Psychology, 6*, 36–48. https://dx.doi.org/10.1037/0893-3200.6.1.36.

Gratz, K. L., & Roemer, L. (2004). Multidimensional assessment of emotion regulation and dysregulation: Development, factor structure, and initial validation of the

Development of the Reconnecting for Recovery 59

Difficulties in Emotion Regulation Scale. *Journal of Psychopathology & Behavioral Assessment, 26*(1), 41–54. https://dx.doi.org/10.1023/B:JOBA.0000007455.08539.94.

Haynos, A. F., & Fruzzetti, A. E. (2011). Anorexia as a disorder of emotion dysregulation: Evidence and treatment implications. *Clinical Psychology: Science and Practice, 18*(3), 183–202. https://dx.doi.org/10.1111/j.1468-2850.2011.01250.x.

Jansch, C., Harmer, C., & Cooper, M. J. (2009). Emotional processing in women with anorexia nervosa and in healthy volunteers. *Eating Behaviors, 10*(3), 184–191. https://dx.doi.org/10.1037/0000063-001.

Jordan, J. (2018). *Relational-cultural therapy* (2nd ed). American Psychological Association. https://dx.doi.org/10.1037/0000063-001.

Kaye, W. H., Fudge, J. L., & Paulus, M. (2009). New insights into symptoms and neurocircuit function of anorexia nervosa. *Nature Reviews Neuroscience, 10*(8), 573–584. https://dx.doi.org/10.1038/nrn2682.

Kelly, A. C., Carter, J. C., & Borairi, S. (2014). Are improvements in shame and self-compassion early in eating disorders treatment associated with better patient outcomes? *International Journal of Eating Disorders, 47*(1), 54–64. https://dx.doi.org/10.1002/eat.22196.

*Keys, A., Brozek, J., Henschel, A., Mickelsen, O., & Taylor, H. L. (1950). *The biology of human starvation*. University of Minnesota Press.

Kucharska-Pietura, K., Nikolaou, V., Masiak, M., & Treasure, J. (2004). The recognition of emotion in the faces and voice of anorexia nervosa. *International Journal of Eating Disorders, 35*(1), 42–47. https://dx.doi.org/10.1002/eat.10219.

Kyraicou, O., Treasure, J., & Schmidt, U. (2008b). Understanding how parents cope with living with someone with anorexia nervosa: Modelling the factors that are associated with carer distress. *International Journal of Eating Disorders, 41*(4), 233–242. https://dx.doi.org/10.1002/eat.20488.

*Lask, B., & Frampton, I. (2011). *Eating disorders and the brain*. Wiley-Blackwell.

Lemmens, G. M. D., Eisler, I., Buysse, A., Heene, E., & Demyttenaere, K. (2009). The effects of mood on adjunctive single-family and multi-family group therapy in the treatment of hospitalized patients with major depression. *Psychotherapy and Psychosomatics, 79*, 98–105. https://dx.doi.org/10.1159/000201935.

Lemmens, G. M. D., Eisler, I., Dierick, P., Lietaer, G., & Demyttenaere, K. (2009). Therapeutic factors in a systemic multi-family group treatment for major depression: Patients' and partners' perspectives. *Journal of Family Therapy, 31*, 250–269. https://dx.doi.org/10.1111/j.1467-6427.2009.00465.x.

Lemmens, G. M., Eisler, I., Migerode, L., Heireman, M., & Demyttenaere, K. (2007). Family discussion group therapy for major depression: A brief systematic multi-family group intervention for hospitalized patients and their family members. *Journal of Family Therapy, 29*(1), 49–68. https://dx.doi.org/10.1111/j.1467-6427.2007.00369.x.

Marzola, E., Knatz, S., Murray, S. B., Rockwell, R., Boutelle, K., Eisler, I., & Kaye, W. H. (2015). Short-term intensive family therapy for adolescent eating disorders: 30-month outcome. *European Eating Disorders Review, 23*(3), 210–218. https://dx.doi.org/10.1002/erv.2353.

McConnaughy, E. A., DiClemente, C. C., Prochaska, J. O., & Velicer, W. F. (1989). Stages of change in psychotherapy: A follow-up report. *Psychotherapy, 26*(4), 494–503. https://dx.doi.org/10.1037/h0085468.

*McFarlane, W. R. (2002). *Multifamily groups in the treatment of severe psychiatric disorders*. The Guilford Press.

60 *Mary Tantillo, Jennifer Sanftner McGraw, and Daniel Le Grange*

*Miller, J. B., & Stiver, I. P. (1997). *The healing connection: How women form relationships in therapy and in life.* Beacon Press.

*Miller, W. R., & Rollnick, S. (2013). *Motivational interviewing: Helping people change* (3rd ed). The Guilford Press.

Nunn, K., Frampton, I., & Lask, B. (2012). Anorexia nervosa – A noradrenergic dysregulation hypothesis. *Medical Hypothesis, 78,* 580–584. https://dx.doi.org/10.1016/j.mehy.2012.01.033.

Pike, K. M., Walsh, B. T., Vitousek, K., Wilson, G. T., & Bauer, J. (2003). Cognitive behavior therapy in the posthospitalization treatment of anorexia nervosa. *American Journal of Psychiatry, 160*(11), 2046–2049. https://dx.doi.org/10.1176/appi.ajp.160.11.2046.

Pollatos, O., Herbert, B. M., Schandry, R., & Gramann K. (2008). Impaired central processing of emotional faces in anorexia nervosa. *Psychosomatic Medicine, 70*(6), 701–708. https://dx.doi.org/10.1097/PSY.0b013e31817e41e6.

*Prochaska, J. O., Norcross, J. C., DiClemente, C. C. (1994). *Changing for good: A revolutionary six-stage program for overcoming bad habits and moving your life positively forward.* William Morrow.

Rieger, E., & Touyz, S. (2006). An investigation of the factorial structure of motivation to recover in anorexia nervosa using the Anorexia Nervosa Stages of Change Questionnaire. *European Eating Disorders Review, 14,* 269–275. https://dx.doi.org/10.1002/erv.684.

*Rumbaut, R. G. (2004). Ages, life stages, and generational cohorts: Decomposing the immigrant first and second generations in the United States. *International Migration Review, 38*(3), 1160–1205.

Schmidt, U., & Treasure, J. (2006). Anorexia nervosa: Valued and visible. A cognitive-interpersonal maintenance model and its implications for research and practice. *British Journal of Clinical Psychology, 45,* 343–366. http://dx.doi.org/10.1348/014466505X53902.

Serfaty, M. A. (1999). Cognitive therapy versus dietary counseling in the outpatient treatment of anorexia nervosa: Effects of the treatment phase. *European Eating Disorders Review, 7,* 334–350. https://dx.doi.org/10.1002/(SICI)1099-0968(199911)7:5%3C334::AID-ERV311%3E3.0.CO;2-H.

*Simic, M., & Eisler, I. (2015). Multi-family therapy. In I. Eisler, A. Wallis, E. Dodge, K. L. Loeb, D. Le Grange, & J. Lock (Eds.), *Family Therapy for Adolescent Eating and Weight Disorders* (pp. 110–138). Routledge.

Southgate, L., Tchanturia, K., Treasure, J. (2005). Building a model of the aetiology of eating disorders by translating experimental neuroscience into clinical practice. *Journal of Mental Health, 14*(6), 553–566. https://dx.doi.org/10.1080/09638230500347541.

Strober, M., Freeman, R., & Morrell, W. (1997). The long-term course of severe anorexia nervosa in adolescents: Survival analysis of recovery, relapse, and outcome predictors over 10-15 years in a prospective study. *International Journal of Eating Disorders, 22*(4), 339–360. https://dx.doi.org/10.1002/(sici)1098-108x(199712)22:4%3C339::aid-eat1%3E3.0.co;2-n.

Tantillo, M. D. (2004). The therapist's use of self-disclosure in a Relational Therapy approach for eating disorders. *Eating Disorders: Journal of Treatment and Prevention, 12,* 51–73. https://dx.doi.org/10.1080/10640260490267760.

Tantillo, M. (2006). A relational approach to eating disorders multifamily therapy group: Moving from difference and disconnection to mutual connection. *Families, Systems, & Health, 23*(1), 82–102. https://dx.doi.org/10.1037/1091-7527.24.1.82.

Development of the Reconnecting for Recovery 61

*Tantillo, M. (2010). *Eating disorders multifamily therapy group: Outcomes and alumnae analysis.* Unpublished raw data.

*Tantillo, M. (2011). *Eating Disorders multifamily therapy group: Analysis of alumnae focus groups.* Unpublished raw data.

*Tantillo, M., Anson, E., Lavigne, H., & Wilkosz, A. (2019). *The effectiveness of a relational/motivational partial hospitalization program for eating disorders: An analysis of treatment outcomes.* Unpublished manuscript, University of Rochester School of Nursing.

Tantillo, M., McGraw, J. S., Hauenstein, E., & Groth, S. W. (2015). Partnering with patients and families to develop an innovative multifamily therapy group treatment for adults with anorexia nervosa. *Advances in Eating Disorders: Theory, Research, and Practice, 3*(3), 269–287. https://dx.doi.org/10.1080/21662630.2015.1048478.

Tantillo, M., McGraw, J. S., Lavigne, H. M., Brasch, J., & Le Grange, D. (2019). A pilot study of multifamily therapy group for young adults with anorexia nervosa: Reconnecting for recovery. *International Journal of Eating Disorders, 52*(8), 950–955. https://dx.doi.org/10.1002/eat.23097.

Tantillo, M., & Sanftner, J. L. (2010a). Mutuality and motivation: Connecting with patients and families for change in the treatment of eating disorders. In M. Maine, D. Bunnell, & B. McGilley (Eds.), *Treatment of eating disorders: Bridging the gap between research and practice.* Elsevier. http://dx.doi.org/10.1016/B978-0-12-375668-8.10019-1.

Tantillo, M., & Sanftner, J. L. (2010b). Measuring perceived mutuality in women with eating disorders: The development of the Connection Disconnection Scale. *Journal of Nursing Measurement, 18,* 100–119. http://dx.doi.org/10.1891/1061-3749.18.2.100.

Tantillo, M., Sanftner, J. L., & Hauenstein, E. (2013). Restoring connection in the face of disconnection: An integrative approach to understanding and treating anorexia nervosa. *Advances in Eating Disorders: Theory, Research, and Practice, 1,* 21–38. https://dx.doi.org/10.1080/21662630.2013.742980.

Treasure, J., Smith, G., & Crane, A. (2017). *Skills-based learning for caring for a loved one with an eating disorder* (2nd ed.). Routledge. https://dx.doi.org/10.4324/9781315735610.

Troop, N. A., Schmidt, U. H., & Treasure, J. L. (1995). Feelings and fantasy in eating disorders: A factor analysis of the Toronto Alexithymia Scale. *International Journal of Eating Disorders, 18*(2), 151–157. https://dx.doi.org/10.1002/1098-108x(199509) 18:2%3C151::aid-eat2260180207%3E3.0.co;2-e.

Van der Kaap-Deeder, J., Vansteenkiste, M., Soenens, B., Verstuyf, J., Boone, L., & Smets, J. (2014). Fostering self-endorsed motivation to change in patients with an eating disorder: The role of perceived autonomy and psychological need satisfaction. *International Journal of Eating Disorders, 47,* 585–600. https://dx.doi.org/10.1002/eat.22266.

van Furth, E. F., van Strien, D. C., Martina, L. M. L., van Son, M. J. M., Hendrickx, J. J. P., & van Engeland, H. (1996). Expressed emotion and the prediction of outcome in adolescent eating disorders. *International Journal of Eating Disorders, 20,* 19–31. https://dx.doi.org/10.1002/(SICI)1098-108X(199607)20:1<19::AID-EAT3>3.0.CO;2-7.

Zonnevijlle-Bender, M. J., van Goozen, S. H., Cohen-Kettenis, P. T., van Elburg, A., & van Engeland, H. (2002). Do adolescent anorexia nervosa patients have deficits in emotional functioning? *European Child & Adolescent Psychiatry, 11*(1), 38–42. https://dx.doi.org/10.1007/s007870200006.

4 Getting Ready

Group Structure, Co-Facilitation, Recruitment, and Initial Phone Screening

Mary Tantillo, Jennifer Sanftner McGraw, and Daniel Le Grange

As noted in the previous chapter, R4R is a 16-session MFTG conducted over 26 weeks. R4R MFTGs are commonly comprised of five to seven patients and their family of origin or "family of choice" members (i.e., those who are emotionally invested in the patient and her/his recovery and willing to consistently participate in R4R). The latter may include partners, close friends, mentors, sponsors, coaches, and clergy. Each R4R session is 90 minutes long and co-led by two trained MFTG therapists. It is helpful if the two therapists have co-facilitated groups together or worked with each other in the past, so they are knowledgeable about one another's clinical training and experience, strengths, potential countertransference reactions, and what Relational-Cultural Therapy (R-CT) would label as "strategies of disconnection" (Cooper & Knox, 2018; Jordan, 2017). These strategies are patterns of behavior (often unwittingly) used to protect ourselves from anxiety and other intense emotions in relationships with others (e.g., intellectualizing, changing the subject, talking a great deal, emotionally withdrawing). Because the R4R therapist's job is to help patients and families connect with themselves and others and identify and decrease their use of strategies of disconnection, it is essential that the therapists be aware of their own strategies. When co-facilitating R4R, it is important that both therapists monitor for their use of these strategies and use their own emotions as a barometer for what may be occurring in relationships between them, between them and group members, among group members, or for the group as a whole (Yalom & Leszcz, 2005).

Recruitment and R4R Phone Screening

Before beginning recruitment for group, it is important that both R4R therapists meet to discuss their recruitment strategies (e.g., soliciting referrals from primary care, behavioral health, college clinicians, or others) and agree on group inclusion and exclusion criteria when screening patients and families for R4R MFTG. Some suggested inclusion and exclusion criteria are in Table 4.1. Since R4R MFTG is designed for young adults, patient age is

Getting Ready 63

Table 4.1 R4R MFTG Inclusion and Exclusion Criteria

Patient Inclusion Criteria:

- Age (18–30 [age criteria can be extended to 40 if this is clinically indicated]).
- Gender (individuals who identify as male, female, transgender, gender nonbinary, or other).
- Diagnosis (meeting DSM-5 criteria[1] for anorexia nervosa or other specified feeding and eating disorders—restricting features).
- BMI ≥ 16 (based on DSM-5 work group discussions regarding cut-off for full threshold AN).[2]
- Medically stable.
- Ability to engage in group work.
- May be in other eating disorder treatments and must be agreeable to providing consent for R4R therapists to speak with other treatment team providers.
- Availability of at least one adult member from one's family of origin or "family of choice" willing to consistently attend R4R.

Patient Exclusion Criteria:

- Existing or previous physical or mental health conditions requiring a higher level of care (e.g., partial hospitalization, inpatient or residential). Patients with chronic suicidal ideation may participate in R4R if it is clinically indicated after careful evaluation. However, those who are acutely suicidal should be referred for emergency evaluation and potentially to a higher level of care if they require additional treatment to stabilize.
- Disorders or disabilities (e.g., developmental disabilities, cognitive impairments, behavioral difficulties, or current dependence on drugs or alcohol) that can adversely affect group participation and disrupt group work.
- Unwillingness to provide consent to speak with other treatment team providers about R4R MFTG work.

Family Member Inclusion Criteria:

- Availability of at least one adult member from one's family of origin or "family of choice" willing to consistently attend R4R.
- Additional younger family members can attend (e.g., siblings) but should be age 12 or older to be able to actively participate and obtain benefit. Depending on space constraints and the total number of families recruited, a limit of additional family members may need to be identified (e.g., up to four family members per patient).
- Ability to engage in group work.
- May be engaged in other family-based treatments and must be agreeable to providing consent for R4R therapists to speak with other treatment team providers.

(*Continued*)

64 *Mary Tantillo, Jennifer Sanftner McGraw, and Daniel Le Grange*

Table 4.1 (Continued)

Family Member Exclusion Criteria:

- Disorders or disabilities (e.g., developmental disabilities, cognitive impairments, behavioral difficulties, or current dependence on drugs or alcohol) that can adversely affect group participation and disrupt group work.
- Inability to commit to consistent attendance at R4R MFTG.
- Unwillingness to provide consent to speak with other treatment team providers about R4R MFTG work.

Notes
1 American Psychiatric Association. (2013). *Diagnostic and statistical manual of mental disorders* (5th ed.). Washington, DC.
2 Ross Crosby, personal communication, 5/26/11.

commonly between 18 and 30. An older patient (e.g., up to age 40) may be accepted if clinically indicated and the patient is still dealing with young adult developmental challenges.

Box 4.1 Description of Reconnecting for Recovery (R4R) Multifamily Therapy Group (MFTG)

R4R MFTG is a treatment for anorexia nervosa (AN) that includes education and the opportunity to build skills that effectively support patients in recovery. R4R MFTG capitalizes on the wisdom, strengths, coping strategies, and resources of all the patients and family members in the group. R4R usually includes five to seven patients and their family members. The family members can be people in your family of origin (e.g., parents and siblings) or can be family of choice members (e.g., your partner, close friends, mentors, sponsors, coaches, or clergy). R4R meets for 16 sessions over a 26-week period of time, first weekly for 10 sessions, then biweekly for four sessions, and then monthly for the last two sessions.

In R4R we view AN as a disease of disconnection. What that means is that AN will do whatever it can to disconnect the patient from his or her own genuine thoughts, feelings, and needs, as well as from loved ones. In R4R we spend time discussing the different points of tension and disconnections that AN can cause and find ways to avoid or repair these disconnections and resolve challenges that block recovery. R4R MFTG teaches the emotional and relational skills required to do this work. By doing this work together, patients and families experience more mutual understanding, empathy, trust, and respect with one another. As patients experience this mutuality in relationships with loved ones, they are better able to deal with uncomfortable intense emotions and try new coping strategies instead of relying on AN to help them cope. They are more willing to try anxiety-provoking activities such as eating more healthfully, decreasing compulsive exercise, interrupting binging or purging, and trying out new self-care strategies.

R4R MFTG is able to create a strong community of healing or therapeutic family that encourages recovery. It can help decrease the isolation that patients and family members often experience. Patients and families who have attended R4R have said that it increases a sense of connection and feeling understood by others. This experience helps patients and families feel like they are partners in the recovery process. The experience of connections with others is very important in recovery from AN because research has shown that recovery is related to the patient's quality of relationships with others. Adult patients with AN report that empathic relationships with close others have been the "driving force" in their recovery. In R4R the patient's connection with AN lessens over time as the patient feels more connected with and can make better sense of what is going on inside of themselves and with others inside and outside the group. This experience helps patients maintain ongoing motivation for recovery despite AN's efforts to hold them back.

The R4R therapists can decide whether one or both will conduct initial phone screenings. During the initial phone screening, the therapist should (a) provide a brief overview of R4R including its goals, frequency, and duration and the fact that R4R includes five to seven patients and their family members; (b) assess whether the patient meets group inclusion criteria and has at least one adult family member of origin or choice who can attend R4R; (c) obtain consent to contact the patient's primary care provider to obtain clinical documentation verifying medical stability, including weight, lab work, and physical examination findings; (d) obtain consent to speak with and obtain written clinical information from the patient's individual and/or family therapist and dietitian, if they are in other treatments; and (e) schedule the two R4R face-to-face assessment, joining, and orientation sessions. The therapist should provide a brief statement about the purpose of these sessions (e.g., they include orientation to R4R MFTG, assessment of patient and family needs related to education and skills essential for recovery, and discussion about patient and family member goals). See Box 4.1 for a description of R4R that can be conveyed to patients and families.

If after the phone screening the patient seems appropriate for R4R, the R4R therapist obtains permission to contact the identified participating family members to discuss R4R. This discussion includes R4R goals, frequency, and duration and the fact that R4R includes five to seven patients and their family members. The therapist will assess whether family members meet group inclusion criteria (see Table 4.1) and also ask for consent from family members to speak with and obtain clinical documentation from treatment providers with whom they are working if they are in other treatments with the patient. The phone call to family members should be orchestrated so that the patient first has an opportunity to speak with them about R4R MFTG and discuss the possible dates for two future assessment, joining, and orientation sessions.

The Need for a Psychiatric Evaluation

If the R4R therapist is already familiar with the patient (e.g., is seeing the patient in individual and/or family therapy or receives a referral, clinical information from a colleague who has already evaluated the patient) the therapist can decide whether a psychiatric intake evaluation is necessary before scheduling the patient and family members for the R4R assessment, joining, and orientation sessions. If the patient is new to the R4R therapist (e.g., the R4R therapist is not following them or has not received the referral and clinical information from another therapist) or if after the initial phone screening, the R4R therapist is still uncertain about the appropriateness of the patient for R4R, the therapist should conduct a face-to-face psychiatric intake evaluation session before scheduling the patient and family members for the two R4R assessment, joining, and orientation sessions. The psychiatric intake evaluation can help the therapist develop a fuller clinical picture of the patient's presenting symptoms; psychiatric history; mental status; and the nature, duration, and severity of the eating disorder. It can also reveal the patient's coping strategies, strengths, and the patient's level of comfort and ability related to group work. If the patient seems appropriate for R4R after the psychiatric intake evaluation, then the R4R therapist can contact the identified family members and schedule the two assessment, joining, and orientation sessions. If the patient needs additional or more intensive treatment before engaging in R4R MFTG, the therapist provides these recommendations.

The Need for Medical Follow-Up

Patients attending R4R should be followed medically to ensure continued medical stabilization during the group. If the patient is not being followed medically by a primary care practitioner, they should be informed that medical follow-up is necessary in order to participate in group. Emphasize that medical follow-up helps ensure patient safety and is an essential component of treatment and recovery. After establishing that the patient is medically and psychiatrically stable to begin R4R and contacting their family members, the patient and family are ready for R4R Session 1 and 2 assessment, joining, and orientation sessions.

References

*No DOI

Cooper, M., & Knox, R. (2018). Therapists' self-reported chronic strategies of disconnection in everyday life and in counselling and psychotherapy: An exploratory study. *British Journal of Guidance and Counselling, 46*(2), 185–200. https://dx.doi.org/10.1080/03069885.2017.1343457.

Jordan, J. (2017). *Relational-cultural therapy* (2nd ed.). American Psychological Association. https://dx.doi.org/10.1037/0000063-001.

*Yalom, I., & Leszcz, M. (2005). *The theory and practice of group psychotherapy* (5th ed.). Basic Books.

5 Session 1: Engaging and Evaluating Young Adults with Anorexia Nervosa and Their Families

Assessment, Joining, and Orientation

Mary Tantillo, Jennifer Sanftner McGraw, and Daniel Le Grange

Nature, Rationale, and Overall Aim of Session 1

Session 1 of R4R MFTG involves a beginning orientation to group and patient and family assessment that lasts approximately 90 minutes. A more extensive orientation to group will occur in Session 2. Session 1 orientation aims include:

- Describing the nature and goals of R4R MFTG
- Reframing eating disorders as *Diseases of Disconnection*
- Emphasizing the importance of mutual relationships in recovery

Patient and family assessments include identifying the purposes/meanings of AN and an assessment of perceived points of tension and disconnections related to AN, level of perceived mutuality, and relational patterns. The R4R therapists emphasize that the group promotes connections with self and others for recovery.

During Session 1 each patient with her/his identified family members is seen as a single family. It is ideal if the two R4R therapists can divide up the group assessments so that each therapist conducts Sessions 1 and 2 with half of the recruited families. The R4R therapist can begin with a description of R4R MFTG as seen in Box 5.1. This description is similar to that in Chapter 4 with a few additional details and can be distributed as a handout as well.

Box 5.1 Description of Reconnecting for Recovery (R4R) Multifamily Therapy Group (MFTG)

Multifamily Therapy has been around since the 1960s and has been very effective for patients with a variety of mental and physical health conditions, including addictions. MFTG capitalizes on the wisdom, strengths, coping strategies, and resources of all the patients and family members in the group. MFTGs usually include five to seven patients and their family members. The family members can be people in your family of origin (e.g., parents and siblings) or family of choice members (e.g., your partner, close friends, mentors, sponsors, coaches, or clergy).

R4R MFTG is a treatment for anorexia nervosa (AN) that includes education and the opportunity to build skills that effectively support patients in recovery. The group meets for 16 sessions over a 26-week period of time; first weekly for ten sessions, then biweekly for four sessions, and then monthly for the last two sessions. In R4R we view AN as a disease of disconnection because AN can create and maintain a number of disconnections inside the patient and between the patient and others. It does this so it can maintain its relationship with the patient. For example, an individual with AN experiences disconnection from their own genuine thoughts, feelings, and needs, which can make it difficult to identify, make sense of, and manage emotions and to feel in control of one's life. AN also involves disconnection from one's body, which makes it difficult to accurately perceive and make sense of what is going on in the body and one's bodily needs. These internal disconnections can make it increasingly challenging to make sense of and communicate one's experience to others. While AN burdens the patient with tremendous anxiety, and challenges the patient's ability to make sense of internal and interpersonal information, it also creates distress for family members through creating intense emotions, fatigue, and confusion, which prevents them from helping the patient in recovery. The combination of the patient's internal disconnections and the interpersonal disconnections patients and families experience can obstruct treatment and ongoing recovery. AN will do whatever it can to continue this pattern and perpetuate itself.

In R4R we spend time discussing the different points of tension and disconnections that AN can cause and find ways to avoid or repair these disconnections and resolve challenges that block recovery. R4R MFTG teaches the emotional and relational skills required to do this work. By doing this work together, patients and families experience more mutual understanding, empathy, trust, and respect with one another. As patients experience this mutuality in relationships with loved ones, they are better able to deal with uncomfortable, intense emotions and try new coping strategies, instead of relying on AN to help them cope. They are more willing to try anxiety-provoking activities such as eating more healthfully, decreasing compulsive exercise, interrupting binging or purging, and trying out new self-care strategies.

R4R MFTG is able to create a strong community of healing, a therapeutic family that encourages recovery. It can help decrease the isolation that patients and family members often experience. Patients and families who have attended R4R have said that it increases a sense of connection and a feeling of being understood by others. This experience helps patients and families feel like they are partners in the recovery process. The experience of connections with others is very important in recovery from AN because research has shown that recovery is related to the patient's quality of relationships with others. Adult patients with AN report that empathic relationships with close others have been the "driving force" in their recovery. In R4R, the patient's connection with AN lessens over time as the patient feels more connected with and can make better sense of what is going on inside of themselves and with close others. This experience helps patients maintain ongoing motivation for recovery despite AN's efforts to hold them back.

Reframing Eating Disorders as Diseases of Disconnection

The R4R therapist then reviews the disconnections characterizing AN. The diagrams in Figures 5.1 and 5.2 can be shown to the patient and family to visually depict the main kinds of disconnections that can occur due to AN. The therapist can point to the first diagram (Figure 5.1) and explain how it represents disconnections that involve separation and isolation. There is an "I" and a "You" but no "We." In this kind of disconnection, there is no communication or there is frequent miscommunication.

The therapist can then point to the second diagram (Figure 5.2) and explain how it represents disconnections that involve "over-involvement and over-closeness." There is little or no distinction between the "I" and the "You" and there is an absence of a healthy differentiated "We." In this kind of disconnection the patient and family may interact in a "pseudo-mutual" way. To an outside observer it may appear that patient and family relationships are fine. In reality, though, the patient and family members are likely "walking on eggshells." They may feel too anxious to voice different feelings, thoughts, or needs with one another. For example, they may have difficulty disagreeing with one another or encouraging a different way to see or respond to an event

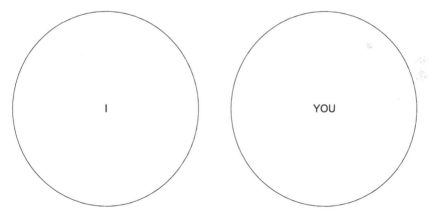

People are completely separated from each other. There are misunderstandings, miscommunication, and/or no communication. The Eating Disorder has created isolation.

Figure 5.1 Reprinted from "Reconnecting for Recovery Multifamily Therapy Group: Capitalizing on connection and community in the treatment of adults with Anorexia Nervosa," by M. Tantillo, January 31, 2017, Gürze-Salucore Eating Disorders Resource Catalogue. Copyright 2017 by Gürze-Salucore. Reprinted with permission.

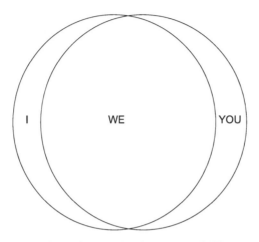

There is no space for each person's uniqueness and differences. The "we" is built only on similarities and is "pseudomutual." People "walk on eggshells" and can't be real because they fear the loss of the small amount of connection they still have.

Figure 5.2 Reprinted from "Reconnecting for Recovery Multifamily Therapy Group: Capitalizing on connection and community in the treatment of adults with Anorexia Nervosa," by M. Tantillo, January 31, 2017, Gürze-Salucore Eating Disorders Resource Catalogue. Copyright 2017 by Gürze-Salucore. Reprinted with permission.

for fear that the last shred of connection they have with one another will be lost.

As the therapist describes these disconnections, she/he takes time to ask if this concept about disconnections makes sense to the patient and family members. Usually patients and family members begin to nod in affirmation when hearing this description of the disconnections characterizing AN. The therapist can reflect this back and ask if they have an example of a disconnection they have experienced. Common examples include, but are not limited to, conflict about mealtimes, feeling invalidated or misunderstood by others, not wanting to rock the boat by suggesting new strategies in recovery, and feeling bullied by the eating disorder. It is important during this discussion about disconnections that the therapist separates the patient from the AN, so family members can begin to see that patient responses are very much mediated by the illness. Additionally, the therapist offers support to family members by acknowledging that their responses are also negatively influenced by AN. The disconnections that patients experience intrapersonally and that patients and families experience interpersonally are

Session 1: Engaging and Evaluating Young Adults   71

attributed to the adverse impact of AN on all concerned. The therapist should note how disconnections from self and others can perpetuate AN, as well as other psychological and physical health problems. For example, if the patient and family members are unable to identify and work through disconnections, AN will offer itself to the patient as a solution to managing intense emotions and will encourage more isolation. Here is an example of what one patient and family described during Session 1 and the therapist's response:

Therapist: *Mom, I saw that while I was describing the circles representing disconnections that you were nodding. Were you thinking of a particular example you wanted to share?*

Mom: *Yes, (looking hesitantly at her daughter). Every time I encourage Susan to leave the kitchen while I prepare her food, she gets very frustrated with me. She says she is an adult and has the right to see what I am doing. She **is** an adult, but she is also highly anxious during mealtimes, and I think being in the kitchen makes it worse. The tension mounts and then we can end up yelling at each other or not talking. This does not help her at mealtimes, and I end up feeling like I failed her.*

Therapist: *What you are describing can be so hard for you and for Susan. Many families and young adult patients describe a similar challenge. Susan would you agree or disagree with mom? You may have a similar or different experience.*

Susan: *Yes, it is true I feel the need to be in the kitchen. I just don't trust she is going to stay with what the meal plan says. Like she might add more butter or oil to what she is making for me. When she asks me to go read or watch TV or listen to music while she cooks, I get more frustrated with her and feel like this means she really does want to get rid of me, so she can add more calories.*

Therapist: *Are frustration and mistrust your main feelings or are there other feelings too?*

Susan: *I guess I am super anxious. I am so afraid that she will make me gain a ton of weight fast.*

Therapist: *So, mom, did you know this is what Susan experiences when you ask her to leave the kitchen?*

Mom: *I was not sure, but worried that this is what she might be thinking. Susan, I do not intend to do anything different than what your meal plan says. What can I do to help convince you?*

Therapist: *Mom, before we get to solving the disconnection, it is important to be sure we name all the feelings going on related to it. We know that Susan feels frustrated, mistrusting, and highly anxious at these times. What are you feeling while you hear her describe what she feels during the interactions in the kitchen?.*

Mom: *Well, I feel anxious too because I love her and want to do the right thing. And I don't want her to suffer more by watching me prepare food. I feel sad that she does not trust me.*

Therapist: *Her AN does not trust you, Mom. I am guessing it would be easier for her to trust you if she did not have AN shouting at her about not trusting you.*

72 Mary Tantillo, Jennifer Sanftner McGraw, and Daniel Le Grange

Susan: *I do have that voice in my head telling me not to trust. I know my mom loves me and is trying to help. Maybe we can figure out a compromise, but we have to do it before we are actually in the kitchen. I can't think then.*

Therapist: *Susan, that makes very good sense—problem-solving together a compromise that considers your feelings and needs and those of your mom's before you are in the situation. This is an excellent disconnection for us to tackle in group. And I bet other patients and families have similar challenges. I am confident that with everyone's combined wisdom we can figure out an alternative. And the most important first step in repairing disconnections is to name them and the feelings associated with them. You guys just did that. Excellent work. AN has less power over both of you and can't capitalize on your disconnection when you both are aware of what you feel and can communicate these feelings to one another.*

In this scenario the R4R therapist stops using a more didactic group orientation approach and moves to a more process-based approach that orients the patient and family members about how things will be handled in group when a disconnection is discovered. This is the therapist's first opportunity to model how to name and begin to work through disconnections using a real-life example specific to this particular family. The therapist is careful to begin with validation of the patient and the mother (a skill she wants family members to also begin with when interacting with patients during a disconnection). She deliberately asks the patient if her experience is *similar to or different from* her mother's experience to introduce the idea that they can remain connected regardless of whether they have similar or different feelings, thoughts, or needs. This intervention provides the opportunity for those with "overly close relationships" (Figure 5.2) to identify different experiences and those with little connection in relationships (Figure 5.1) to practice naming in an assertive (vs. a passive, aggressive, or passive-aggressive) way what they each experience. The therapist's validation of mother and daughter and question about similar or different experiences communicates the importance of a "both/and" approach. This intervention also begins to promote mutuality between mother and daughter through asking both of them to name and clarify their feelings. It encourages them to connect with themselves (i.e., their genuine thoughts, feelings, and needs) because this activity will help them better empathize with, understand, and connect with each other. This emotional and relational work will allow for more constructive and effective joint problem solving in the end.

Further into the conversation, the therapist also separates the patient from AN by reminding the mother that her daughter might be able to trust her more if she did not have AN. This statement helps the mother remember that her daughter does not intend to give her a hard time. The illness does. The patient responds to the mutual exchange of feelings and needs by acknowledging that the AN voice does get loud when she is in the kitchen, and she invites mom to make a compromise with her. The patient was able to advocate for herself and consider a compromise after feeling heard and validated, having a better understanding of her mother's and her own

Session 1: Engaging and Evaluating Young Adults 73

intentions and emotions, and being able to distinguish these intentions and emotions from AN thoughts. The therapist's statements throughout the conversation were informed by Relational-Cultural theoretical principles (Jordan, 2018; Miller & Stiver, 1997; Tantillo & Sanftner, 2010) that promote perceived mutuality, as well as Motivational Interviewing principles, including encouraging empathy, avoiding argumentation, rolling with resistance, and promoting young adult self-efficacy (Miller & Rollnick, 2013). The therapist's work here is a kind of foreshadowing for future group sessions.

Emphasizing the Importance of Mutual Relationships for Recovery

After reviewing the main kinds of disconnection that characterize AN, the therapist then discusses the main goal of R4R, i.e., reconnections with self and others. The therapist reinforces how our sense of self grows within connections with others and that connections with others are influenced by how connected we feel with ourselves (Miller & Stiver, 1997). The therapist can visually display what mutually empathic and empowering relationships look like by showing the patient and family members the diagram in Figure 5.3.

The R4R therapist emphasizes that mutual relationships (the experience of "perceived mutuality" according to Relational-Cultural Theory) foster psychological change, motivation for change, and ongoing recovery (Banks & Hirschman, 2016; Genero, Miller, Surrey, & Baldwin, 1992; Jordan, 2018; Miller & Stiver, 1997; Tantillo & Sanftner, 2010). The therapist should describe mutual relationships as those characterized by a bidirectional experience of trust, empathy, and understanding. Mutual relationships allow individuals to be emotionally vulnerable with one another, and each person in the relationship recognizes how they influence others and allows others to influence them. The therapist should review the "five good things" (Jordan, 2018; Miller and Stiver, 1997) associated with mutual relationships. These elements are listed in and can be shown to the patient and family members.

The five good things associated with mutual relationships are:

- Increased self-worth
- Clearer understanding about self, others, and the relationship
- Increased feelings of empowerment to advocate for self, others, and the relationship
- Increased experience of positive energy or "zest"
- Increased desire for more connection with others

When discussing mutual relationships, the R4R therapist should emphasize that mutual relationships include times of disconnection and that what makes mutual relationships different from non-mutual ones is the commitment by all involved to honor each person in the relationship, as well as the relationship.

MUTUAL RELATIONSHIPS

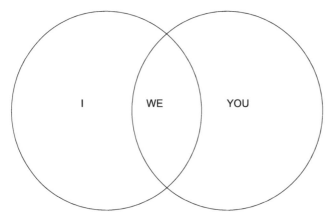

Mutual relationships honor the *integrity of the connection* between people <u>and</u> *space for each person* in the connection. Mutual relationships allow for <u>difference in connection.</u>

Figure 5.3 Reprinted from "Reconnecting for Recovery MultifamilyTherapy Group: Capitalizing on connection and community in the treatment of adults with Anorexia Nervosa," by M. Tantillo, January 31, 2017, Gürze-Salucore Eating Disorders Resource Catalogue. Copyright 2017 by Gürze-Salucore. Reprinted with permission.

(The therapist can point to Figure 5.3 again during this discussion.) This means that individuals are willing to consider the uniqueness of and differences (different feelings, thoughts, and needs) voiced by each person in the relationship as well as similarities in experiences. Individuals in mutual relationships consider the needs of each person, as well as the "We," the relationship between people. When disconnections occur in mutual relationships, individuals return to the table to identify and work through points of tension and disconnections. Disconnections are unpleasant, but much growth and change can come from them if they are repaired. What is toxic is when disconnections go repeatedly unnamed and unrepaired. These experiences can contribute to development and maintenance of AN and other mental and physical health problems (Banks & Hirschman, 2016; Eisenberger & Cole, 2012; Eisenberger, 2012; Jordan, 2018; Holt-Lunstad, Smith, Baker, Harris, & Stephenson, 2015; Nakash, Williams, & Jordan, 2004; Tantillo, Sanftner, & Hauenstein, 2013).

After completing the beginning orientation to group, the R4R therapist tells the family that she would like to separately see the patient first and then the family for a short period of time. The therapist states she will use this time to do a brief assessment of the patient's experience of AN and obtain everyone's ideas about what disconnections AN has created for them. Tell the patient and family members that you will see everyone back together quickly at the end of today's session to discuss the focus for Session 2. If the patient desires to be with the family after the brief assessment of their experience of AN, in order to name disconnections together, then this should be permitted. The therapist initially asks to see patient and family separately in case it may be difficult for patient and/or family members to identify disconnections created by AN.

Patient Assessments

Assessment of the Patient's Experience of AN

When conducting the assessment of AN, the R4R therapist asks questions regarding:

- Onset and duration of illness
- Current symptom frequency and severity
- Alleviating and aggravating factors/triggers
- Associated meanings and purposes of AN

When asking about meanings associated with AN and purposes served by AN, the therapist should normalize these questions. For example, the therapist can begin by asking about the importance of AN and how it helps the patient. If the patient is unsure about the answer or reticent to respond, the therapist can remind the patient that we maintain behaviors because they usually serve an important purpose. The therapist can also give examples of what other patients have noted, e.g., "AN helps me feel unique, in control, helps turn down intense emotions, or allows me to feel I can accomplish something." The therapist can acknowledge that we do not always know initially the purposes AN serves or what it means to us, but understanding these purposes and meanings becomes an important part of recovery.

The assessment of the patient's experience of AN may not be necessary if the R4R therapist has already worked clinically with the patient or if the therapist conducted a full psychiatric evaluation intake before the R4R assessment, joining and orientation sessions. This assessment of the eating disorder can also be briefer if the R4R therapist received substantive information from a referring clinician. The therapist can then confirm and clarify what is known thus far about the patient's eating disorder.

Assessment of the Impact of AN on the Patient: Patient Perceptions of Disconnections and Points of Tension Related to AN

Next in the individual session with the patient, the R4R therapist discusses the impact of AN on her/him, especially the points of tension and disconnections it has created for the patient. This assessment includes identification of *intra- and interpersonal processes of disconnection* (i.e., **processes promoting internal disconnections from self and one's body and disconnections from others**). These processes include disconnection from one's genuine feelings, needs, values, and interests; not being able to discern bodily needs such as knowing when one is hungry, full, or fatigued; and emotionally or behaviorally responding to others in ways that reinforce avoidance of conflict or intense emotion and silence or minimize the self). The assessment also includes identification of **interpersonal disconnections with family members and friends** that can result from the interplay of the intra- and interpersonal processes of disconnection in the face of caregiver burden and distress.

When beginning the assessment regarding **internal disconnections**, tell the patient the following:

> *The goal of an eating disorder is to ensure that the only connection we have is with IT. It creates disconnections that keep us separated from our genuine thoughts, feelings, and emotional and physical needs. We feel farther and farther away from what we really feel, think, and need and, instead, focus on food, weight, exercise, and the eating disorder and how it can help us. The eating disorder can make it difficult to accurately identify and make sense of what we experience on the inside. For example, it makes it difficult to know exactly what we feel and makes it difficult to tell the difference between emotional and physical hunger or fullness. Have you experienced any of these disconnections inside?*

When beginning the assessment of **interpersonal disconnections**, tell the patient:

> *The eating disorder also creates tension and disconnections in our relationships with others. How do you think the eating disorder has affected your relationships with others, including family members you brought to R4R? Think about the circles of disconnection we discussed earlier (see* Figures 5.1 and 5.2*). Do you feel you are too close or too far away from loved ones as a consequence of AN? Or maybe it is a combination of both experiences?*

Begin with a discussion about interpersonal disconnections with family members attending R4R and then move into a discussion about relationships with others. Interpersonal disconnections are often marked by tension, intense emotion, avoidance, or isolation. Patients often note arguments with or criticism from family members, feeling left out of family events, experiencing more isolation and aloneness, various losses of relationships with friends, and severe social anxiety and/or concerns about food that prevent them from leaving the house to go out with close friends or meet new people.

Assessment of the Patient's Level of Perceived Mutuality in Relationships with Family Members

Assess the patient's level of perceived mutuality (PM) in relationships with family members (i.e., level of mutual trust, empathy, understanding, and

empowerment with the other person). Begin with a discussion about family members attending R4R and then continue with a discussion about PM in relationships with others. It is helpful to obtain information about relationships with parents, siblings, partners, and at least one close friend. Here are some questions the therapist can use as needed when asking about each
relationship and exploring perceived mutuality:

- Does the patient feel there is a back and forth flow of thoughts, feelings, and activity with the other person?
- Is the patient able to be emotionally vulnerable with the other person?
- Does the patient feel the other person is respectful of and emotionally open to the patient's different feelings, thoughts, and needs?
- Does the patient believe that their feelings, perspectives, and needs influence the other person? (For example, what they feel, value, and need matters to others.)
- Does the patient allow the other person to influence them? (For example, do they let the other person get emotionally close to them and allow them to affect their emotions, perspectives, decisions, and behaviors?)
- Does the patient experience the Five Good Things (see page 73 and Figure 5.4) characterizing mutual relationships with the other person?

Figure 5.4 The Five Good Things as illustrated by Santo Caruana.

- Does the patient feel the relationship with the other person resembles the diagram in Figure 5.3 depicting a mutual relationship? If not, why not?
- Can the patient name and repair disconnections with the other person?
- Other questions that can help the R4R therapist assess the level of PM in relationships include:
- When you think about your relationship with _____ what do you value most about it?
- If you could change one thing about the relationship, what would it be?
- When there is conflict, how do you two respond? Do you try to resolve it? If yes, how? If not, what happens?
- Do you express love or caring for each other? If yes, how? (Normalize that families have different ways of expressing love and caring, e.g., in words, physical touch, gifts, time, and acts of service [Chapman, 2015, 2016]).
- Has any of what you have shared about the relationship with your _____ changed because of the eating disorder?

Assessment of Patient's Perception of Relational Patterns Related to AN's Impact on the Family

The R4R therapist should also assess the patient's perception of the relational patterns that have evolved due to AN's impact on family members. Relational patterns include caregiver styles, such as responding like a kangaroo (emotional over-involvement), ostrich (avoidance), jellyfish (emotional dysregulation), terrier (criticism), rhinoceros (authoritarian/aggressive), dolphin or St. Bernard (inspirational, collaborative, and mutual) (Treasure, Smith & Crane, 2017) (see Figure 5.5). It is sometimes easier for patients and families to discuss relational patterns by reflecting on these caregiving animal metaphors first. (See Session 13 in Chapter 17 for a more detailed discussion of animal caregiving metaphors.)

The therapist should show the patient these animal figures when inquiring about relational patterns. We have also purchased stuffed animals representing all these animals and point to them in the office. This brings some levity to the interview, and the therapist can normalize the idea that we all respond like certain animals when we want to help our family members but also feel stressed due to the eating disorder. Ask the patient to give you specific examples of how loved ones respond to their eating disorder in order to identify relational patterns. For example, a patient's mother may tend to reassure and protect the patient from trying new things that would make the patient anxious. This relational pattern most resembles a kangaroo caregiving style. Alternatively, a patient may perceive that her partner is unsupportive because he gets angry and yells at her when she wants to eat "safer foods" repeatedly at meals. This relational pattern resembles a rhinoceros caregiving style. The therapist may already have a fairly good sense of relational patterns based on information already gleaned from

Session 1: Engaging and Evaluating Young Adults 79

Figure 5.5 Animal Caregiver Styles: Dolphin, St. Bernard, Rhinoceros, Kangaroo, Ostrich, Jellyfish, Terrier as illustrated by Santo Caruana.

assessing the internal and interpersonal disconnections and level of perceived mutuality in relationships. It is good to check out impressions and assess the patient's insight into these relational patterns. It is also important to solicit any helpful relational patterns the patient experiences with family members. For example, a patient may experience his aunt as validating while also encouraging him to try a new food. It is important to identify "dolphins" and "St. Bernards" in the patient's life and to explicitly discuss what they say and do, as their actions promote PM, healing, and recovery.

Assessment of the patient's response to relational patterns with family members

The individual time with the patient concludes with assessment of the patient's response to the perceived relational patterns with family members. These responses likely include many of the internal and interpersonal disconnections previously noted by the patient. In response to the perceived relational patterns and associated emotions, patients may, for example, become argumentative, increase isolation or avoidance, and eventually engage in eating disorder behaviors to cope with internal and interpersonal disconnections they experience. This pattern can perpetuate illness and obstruct recovery. Also, solicit how the patient responds to any positive and mutual relational patterns and caregiving styles. It is important to make explicit what is happening in interactions with others when the patient is able to avoid engaging in AN symptoms.

Family Member Assessments

The assessments initially conducted with the patient are repeated with family members to assess their perceptions of disconnections and points of tension created by AN, the level of perceived mutuality among family members, relational patterns related to AN's impact on the family, and their perception of the patient's response to these patterns.

Assessment of the Impact of AN on the Family: Family Member Perceptions of Disconnections and Points of Tension Related to AN

This first assessment includes assessment of family member perceptions of **the interpersonal disconnections** created by AN, as well as their perceptions of the **internal disconnections** experienced by the patient due to AN. Begin the assessment by reminding family members that the patient is separate from AN. Then discuss the impact of AN on each family member. Help them identify the points of tension and disconnections it has created in relationships with the patient and with each other. For example, AN may have created tension and conflict in the relationship with the patient and

Session 1: Engaging and Evaluating Young Adults   81

in the relationship between the patient's parents, siblings, or close friends because they do not have an accurate understanding of AN and/or have divergent understandings about support strategies. When beginning this assessment of **interpersonal disconnections**, tell the family:

> *The eating disorder creates tension and disconnections in our relationships with others. How do you think the eating disorder has affected your relationships with the patient as well as the other family members here? Think about the circles of disconnection we discussed earlier (see* Figures 5.1 *and* 5.2 *on page 70–71). Do you feel you are too close or too far away from the patient as a consequence of AN? Or maybe it is a combination of both experiences? Which of these circles might also apply to how family members respond to other family members because of AN?*

Begin with a discussion about interpersonal disconnections with family members attending R4R and then follow-up as indicated with a discussion about relationships with others who are not attending group. Interpersonal disconnections are often marked by tension, intense emotion, avoidance, or isolation. Family members often note arguments with the patient, avoidance of certain topics for fear of more tension or conflict, or feeling very protective and not pushing the patient to try new foods or activities. With each other, family members may experience criticism or conflict because of different views on how to support the patient. They may also experience increased isolation, decreased communication and aloneness, as well as rejection. They can experience high levels of anxiety about what might happen if they bring the patient to social events due to the patient's eating disorder. This experience can contribute to isolation from extended family and previous peer supports and obstruct establishment of new supportive relationships.

Next, explore family members' perceptions of the patient's **internal disconnections from self and their body due to AN**. When beginning the assessment regarding internal disconnections, tell the family members the following:

> *The goal of an eating disorder is to ensure that the only connection the patient has is with IT. AN creates internal disconnections that keep the patient separated from their genuine thoughts, feelings, and emotional and physical needs. The patient feels farther and farther away from what they really feel, think, and need, and, instead, the patient focuses on food, weight, exercise, and the eating disorder and how AN can help them. The eating disorder can make it difficult to accurately identify and make sense of what the patient experiences on the inside. For example, it makes it difficult to know exactly what the patient feels and makes it difficult to tell the difference between emotional and physical hunger or fullness. Have you noticed your loved one responding in ways indicative of these internal kinds of disconnections?*

Family members may not have previously understood how AN creates internal disconnections that impair the patient's ability to accurately process

82 *Mary Tantillo, Jennifer Sanftner McGraw, and Daniel Le Grange*

information. This information can help family members understand that AN is not a volitional illness and help them make better sense of why their loved one responds in certain ways.

Assessment of Family Members' Levels of Perceived Mutuality in Relationships with the Patient and Each Other

Assess each family member's level of perceived mutuality (PM) in relationships with the patient and other family members (i.e., level of mutual trust, empathy, understanding, and empowerment with the other person). Use the questions initially posed to the patient when exploring the level of perceived mutuality with family members (see pages 12–13). Reframe them with the family members in mind. For example, ask, "Does the family member feel there is a back and forth flow of thoughts, feelings, and activity with the patient? With other family members? When you think about your relationship with _____ what do you value most about it?" Explore family members' relationships with the patient first and then explore their relationships with each other. It is essential to get a sense of PM in relationships for all family members living with, spending the most time with, or closest to the patient, because these individuals likely have a greater influence on ongoing recovery. Therefore, when indicated, also explore family member perceptions of PM in relationships with others who are not attending group.

It is helpful for the therapist to understand how family members view the quality of the connections they have with the patient, since their perceptions may differ from those of the patient. Note the disparity between the patient's and family members' perceptions of perceived mutuality in relationships. This information foreshadows the kind of emotional and relational skills work they will need to do in future group sessions. Generally, the greater the disparity between these perceptions, the greater the chance that patient and family members experience points of tension and disconnections related to AN.

Assessment of Family Members' Perceptions of Relational Patterns Related to AN's Impact on the Family

Next the R4R therapist assesses family members' perceptions of the relational patterns that have evolved due to AN's impact on the patient and family members. As discussed previously, these patterns include caregiver styles such as responding like a kangaroo (emotional over-involvement), ostrich (avoidance), jellyfish (emotional dysregulation), terrier (criticism), rhinoceros (authoritarian/aggressive), dolphin or St. Bernard (inspirational and mutual) (Treasure, Smith & Crane, 2017).

As described in the patient assessment, show the family members the animal figures when inquiring about relational patterns (e.g., refer to Figure 5.5

on page 79 or distribute stuffed animals to them). The therapist should normalize the idea that we all respond like certain animals when caring for our family members due to the caregiving burden imposed by the eating disorder. Ask family members for specific examples of how they respond to AN in order to identify relational patterns. For example, a patient's father or partner may become a "rhinoceros" and respond in an angry way, demanding the patient stop eating disorder behaviors due to underlying feelings of anxiety and helplessness.

The therapist may have a fairly good sense of relational patterns based on information already gleaned from assessing the internal and interpersonal disconnections and level of perceived mutuality in relationships. It is good to check out impressions and assess family member insight into these relational patterns and caregiving styles. Note the disparity between patient and family member perceptions of relational patterns and caregiving styles, as this information will inform the needed emotional and relational skills work in future group sessions. This assessment may be the first opportunity wherein family members recognize and explicitly state relational patterns and caregiving styles. Also note positive and mutual relational patterns that involve "dolphin or St. Bernard" caregiving responses. It is important to point out to family members what they are doing well versus focusing solely on the challenges and missteps we all experience in recovery.

Assessment of Family Member Perceptions of Patient Response to Relational Patterns with Family Members

The individual time with family members ends with an assessment of family member perceptions of patient response to relational patterns with family members. These responses commonly include many of the internal and interpersonal disconnections previously noted by the patient and family. In response to the perceived relational patterns and associated emotions, family members may recognize that patients become defensive, silent, or avoidant and that they eventually engage in symptoms. At this juncture it is important to offer education on how a turn toward eating disorder thoughts and behaviors is not a conscious choice. It is unconscious and mediated by intense emotions like fear, anxiety, shame, worthlessness, helplessness, and hopelessness. It is important to reinforce that patients engage in eating disorder behaviors to cope with internal and interpersonal disconnections and that this pattern unwittingly perpetuates the illness. Also solicit how the patient responds to any positive and mutual relational patterns and caregiving styles. It is important to make explicit what is happening in interactions with family members when the patient is able to avoid engaging in AN symptoms. This intervention promotes a sense of empowerment, identifies actions that promote PM, and positively reinforces effective support strategies.

Wrapping Up Session 1

After completing the final family assessment, the therapist invites the patient back into the office. The therapist tells the patient and family that she/he will collate the information gathered today and share everyone's perceptions about disconnections created by AN during Session 2. The therapist tells the patient and family that they do not need to compare notes on what they shared today, but that they will have more time to discuss what they shared during the next session. They are assigned homework to think about goals for the R4R MFTG based on what they shared and learned in Session 1. The therapist thanks the patient and family for all their hard work and notes how much she/he looks forward to the next session where they will also receive more orientation to R4R MFTG sessions and set their group goals.

The assessments conducted during Session 1 with the patient and family members will assist them in understanding particular points of tension and disconnections created by AN, as well as helpful strategies for connection they already use. Session 1 assessment information helps patients and families to set group goals in Session 2 and provides data for future group work. For example, the feedback collected during these assessments helps the patient, family, and R4R therapists construct a functional analysis of what transpires interpersonally among patients and family members when AN is on the scene creating tension and disconnection. (See Session 6 in Chapter 10 for more details about conducting a functional analysis.) Patient and family members can learn new emotional and relational skills that allow them to respond more effectively to one another, thus fostering collaborative caring and continued recovery. See Box 5.2 for goals, materials, and handouts for Session 1. Handouts for Session 1 and other R4R sessions are available upon request from the first author, MT.

Box 5.2   Session 1: Engaging and Evaluating Young Adults with AN and Their Families: Assessment, Joining, and Orientation

Goals

Orient Patient and Family to R4R MFTG

- Describe R4R MFTG
- Reframe eating disorders as *Diseases of Disconnection*
- Outline R4R goals—promotes connections with self and others for recovery
- Discuss the importance of mutual relationships

Patient Assessment

- Eating disorder
- Impact of AN on the patient: Patient perceptions of disconnections and points of tension related to AN
- Patient's level of perceived mutuality with family members and others
- Patient's perception of relational patterns with family members
- Patient's response to relational patterns with family members

Family Assessment

- Impact of AN on the family: Family member perceptions of disconnections and points of tension related to AN
- Family members' levels of perceived mutuality with patient and each other
- Family members' perceptions of relational patterns
- Family members' perceptions of patient response to relational patterns

Wrapping up

- Homework: Reflect on group goals

Materials

- Pictures of circles and Venn diagram showing disconnections and mutual connection
- Picture of the Five Good Things
- Pictures of animals representative of caregiving styles (or use stuffed animals)

Handouts

- Description of R4R Multifamily Therapy Group

References

*No DOI

*Banks, A., & Hirschman, L. A. (2016). *Wired to connect: The surprising link between brain science and strong, healthy relationships*. Jeremy P. Tarcher/Penguin.

*Chapman, G. (2015). *The five love languages: The secret to love that lasts*. Chicago, IL: Northfield Publishing.

*Chapman, G. (2016). *The five love languages of teenagers*. Chicago, IL: Northfield Publishing.

Eisenberger, N. I. (2012). The pain of social disconnection: Examining the shared neural underpinnings of physical and social pain. *Nature Reviews Neuroscience, 13*(6), 421–434. https://dx.doi.org/10.1038/nrn3231.

Eisenberger, N. I., & Cole, S. W. (2012). Social neuroscience and health: Neurophysiological mechanisms linking social ties with physical health. *Nature Reviews Neuroscience, 15*(5), 699–674. https://dx.doi.org/10.1038/nn.3086.

Genero, N. P., Miller, J. B., Surrey, J., & Baldwin, L. M. (1992). Measuring perceived mutuality in close relationships: Validation of the Mutual Psychological Development Questionnaire. *Journal of Family Psychology, 6*, 36–48. https://dx.doi.org/10.1037/0893-3200.6.1.36.

Holt-Lunstad, J., Smith, T. B., Baker, M., Harris, T., & Stephenson, D. (2015). Loneliness and social isolation as risk factors for mortality: A meta-analytic review. *Perspectives of Psychological Science, 10*(2), 227–237. https://dx.doi.org/10.1177/1745691614568352.

Jordan, J. (2018). *Relational-cultural therapy* (2nd ed.). American Psychological Association. https://dx.doi.org/10.1037/0000063-001.

*Miller, J. B., & Stiver, I. P. (1997). *The healing connection: How women form relationships in therapy and in life.* Beacon Press.

*Miller, W. R., & Rollnick, S. (2013). *Motivational interviewing: Helping people change* (3rd ed.). The Guilford Press.

*Nakash, O., Williams, L. M., & Jordan, J. V. (2004). *Relational-cultural theory, body image, and physical health.* Wellesley Center for Women, Working Paper No. 416, Wellesley, MA: Stone Center, Wellesley Center for Women.

Tantillo, M., & Sanftner, J. L. (2010). Mutuality and motivation: Connecting with patients and families for change in the treatment of eating disorders. In M. Maine, D. Bunnell, & B. McGilley (Eds.), *Treatment of eating disorders: Bridging the gap between research and practice.* Elsevier. http://dx.doi.org/10.1016/B978-0-12-375668-8.10019-1.

Tantillo, M., Sanftner, J. L., & Hauenstein, E. (2013). Restoring connection in the face of disconnection: An integrative approach to understanding and treating anorexia nervosa. *Advances in Eating Disorders: Theory, Research, and Practice, 1*, 21–38. https://dx.doi.org/10.1080/21662630.2013.742980.

Treasure, J., Smith, G., & Crane, A. (2017). *Skills-based learning for caring for a loved one with an eating disorder* (2nd ed.). Routledge. https://dx.doi.org/10.4324/9781315735610.

6 Session 2: Engaging and Evaluating Young Adults with Anorexia Nervosa and Their Families

Assessment, Joining, and Orientation (Continued)

Mary Tantillo, Jennifer Sanftner McGraw, and Daniel Le Grange

Nature, Rationale, and Overall Aim of Session 2

Session 2 of R4R MFTG is a conjoint family session that lasts approximately 90 minutes and involves several components including:

- A review of patient and family member points of tension and perceptions of disconnections related to AN discussed during Session 1
- Development of patient and family group goals
- Completion of orientation to R4R MFTG

While the therapist engages the patient and family in each of these components, the overall aim is to strengthen a sense of "we" that allows patient, family, and therapist(s) to begin group in a collaborative fashion. The therapist looks for opportunities to promote perceived mutuality among patient, family members, and the therapist in this and all other group sessions. This work involves promoting the "five good things" in relationships (Miller & Stiver, 1997; see Chapter 5, Figure 5.4) by helping patients and families become more open and emotionally vulnerable with each other and practice sitting with difference (e.g., different feelings, thoughts, needs) while remaining connected. The therapist helps the patient and family members recognize how they influence each other and the importance of allowing others to connect and emotionally affect them. The therapist externalizes AN from the patient and family and reminds them that AN does not like us interacting in mutual ways. It will try to obstruct efforts to connect with ourselves (embracing our genuine thoughts, feelings, and needs) and others. Although it is important to point out and reinforce when patients and family members are responding in mutually empathic and empowering ways, opportunities to engage in a mutual way often emerge when attention is drawn to how they are

88   *Mary Tantillo, Jennifer Sanftner McGraw, and Daniel Le Grange*

experiencing disconnections due to AN's attempts to divide them. Following is a vignette of the therapist engaging a family in the review of points of tension and disconnections they described during Session 1. The therapist takes an opportunity to promote mutuality in the relationship between the patient and his father when they comment on differing perceptions regarding one of the items they both noted during Session 1. Present in the office are mom, dad, Sam (19-year-old patient with AN) and Jane (Sam's 23-year-old sister).

Therapist: *So last week you all did a great job naming points of tension and disconnections that you felt AN helped create for everyone in the family. I want to review what they are so we can compare notes with each other. We might have similar or different views on them, so it is good to get feedback from everyone. We can start practicing being "different in connection" like we discussed last week. AN hates when we can do that because it likes to split us up and isolate us from each other. That is how it maintains its connection with the person in recovery.*

Mom: *Yes, I was curious about how many of the disconnections would be the same for all of us. Or if we would see things really differently.*

Therapist: *Mom, that feeling of curiosity is so important in life and in recovery. Curiosity keeps us open to each other and eliminates judgment and all-or-nothing thinking that AN likes us to have. As it turns out, there are actually many disconnections that both Sam and you and your husband and Jane all agreed on. (The therapist posts the list of points of tension and disconnections on the board so everyone can see them.) Here is what I learned from everyone last week. The common points of tension and situations leading to disconnections include:*

- *Disagreement about Sam being in the kitchen when food is being prepared*
- *No one talks about feelings*
- *Needing to be perfect*
- *Comments about working out*
- *Feeling you cannot say no to family member requests*
- *Sam not wanting to be with his friends*
- *Decisions about when Sam can return to the cross-country team*

Did I forget anything?

Mom: *You captured everything I think we talked about. Dad and Jane both nod in response.*

Therapist: *Sam, is there anything I forgot from what we discussed?*

Sam: *Nope. (He says this while slightly rolling his eyes toward the ceiling.)*

Therapist: *Now that we are together, does anyone feel like they want to add any others to the list? And since we are just meeting together now to compare notes, does anyone feel that an item should be deleted from the list? Sounds like I made a complete list, but it is also important to get everyone's views about*

Session 2: Engaging and Evaluating Young Adults 89

the overall list. We could have different views about the situations that lead to disconnection, and that would be good for us to say out loud. This is part of practicing being different in connection.
There is silence for a moment. Then, Sam speaks.

Sam: *Well, I agree with most of what is there, but I don't agree with how the item about my friends is worded. It's not that I don't want to be with my friends.*

Dad: *But Sam, you spend so much time in your room and in the house on your computer. You refuse to go to team social events and school events. Kyle (Sam's best friend) called you about going over his house with a couple friends last weekend and you declined that too. It does not seem like you want to be with them.*

Therapist: *Sam, I am wondering whether you experience things in the way dad describes or if you experience them differently.*

Sam: *Silent and looking down at the floor.*

Jane: *Dad, he doesn't feel well. He doesn't want to go out sometimes.*

Dad: *It is not sometimes. It is all the time. It is not healthy.*

Therapist: *Dad and Jane, you both sound very worried about Sam. Sam, I want to be sure dad accurately understands what you are experiencing about your friends or he will continue to perceive things in the same way. Is what you are experiencing the same or different from what Dad is saying?*

Mom: *Sam, go ahead. It is OK to say something different.*

Sam: *Looks up at the therapist. It is different, and he still does not get it. I don't want to get in a fight about it. That is where this ends up going every time.*

Therapist: *Well then it is very important for us to figure out how you can share your different experience while staying connected with dad. I am guessing the eating disorder likes to swoop in and take advantage of you at these times. Can you share with us how you see the situation?*

Sam: *Yes, it does. I start thinking that I should just isolate even more and feel like eating less. I feel like no one understands. I WANT to be with my friends, but I don't want to be around food. I don't want to watch my friends binge eat pizza and soda and everything else they might eat. It is overwhelming to be with them at social events involving a ton of food. And some of the guys keep telling me I should eat. It is very awkward. No matter what they say, I feel I am not lean enough. They don't get it either.*

Therapist: *So, it is important to let your family know exactly how you might be feeling when you think about being with your friends. You said you feel awkward. Are there other feelings too? If you need me to give you the feelings sheet to help you come up with the names of feelings, I can do that too.*

Sam: *I am super anxious. I feel out of control when I think about all the food and the comments they might make. I also feel like a failure because I am not able to run right now. I let everyone down.*

Therapist: *Sam, those are really painful feelings to have. I can see why you end up isolating and not seeing your friends. Can you also let your family know what it*

	feels like when you feel like they don't understand what you are experiencing with your friends?
Sam:	*More anxiety and…Sam shakes his head and looks down.*
Therapist:	*Can you tell what you are feeling right now?*
Sam:	*I don't know. He is still looking down, each hand clenched on a thigh.*
Therapist:	*Sam, sometimes it is hard to name feelings. Can you tell where you are experiencing the feeling? Do you feel anything in your head, your chest, your stomach, or your limbs?*
Sam:	*It is like a pressure in my chest and head.*
Therapist:	*And did you notice your hands are kind of clenched on your legs right now? That can give us a clue too. Do you remember other times when you have felt like this?*
Sam:	*Yes. Every time people don't understand what is really going on. It's so frustrating. I already feel like a failure and then I feel frustrated on top of it.*
Therapist:	*Dad, I am wondering if you knew that Sam felt this way about his friends and about what happens when he feels misunderstood?*
Dad:	*Sam, I just want to do what will help you. I don't mean to make things worse. It's hard to watch you stay to yourself day after day. It can't help your mood or your outlook on things. I don't know what to do.*
Therapist:	*Dad, can you share what you are feeling now?*
Dad:	*I am feeling frustrated, too, because I am supposed to be able to fix things for my kids, and I can't fix this for Sam. I feel helpless. Like I am a failure as a dad.*
Therapist:	*It is very painful to be a dad and not be able to fix things for your kids. And what is really interesting is that you and Sam are feeling some of the same feelings. You both want to do what is helpful but also feel stuck. Sam, did you know dad felt this way?*
Sam:	*Not exactly. You aren't a failure, dad. But you can't reach in and fix what is happening for me. What really helps me is when people listen to me.*
Mom:	*Well, this is much better than where we usually end up with this conversation. We love Sam, and we want to help. I guess we just need help knowing exactly the best way to help.*
Jane:	*Sam, I am glad you finally said what you felt out loud to dad. It only makes it worse when you keep it in.*
Therapist:	*So, Jane, it seems you are feeling relieved with Sam being more open with his feelings?*
Jane:	*Yes, because the alternative is fighting and then less eating at the next meal. That is what is frustrating for me.*
Mom:	*I guess what we are experiencing today also relates to how hard it is for us to say our feelings out loud. We don't want to hurt each other but end up doing it anyway when we stay quiet.*
Therapist:	*Well you all did a great job not being quiet today. When we start talking about goal setting in a little bit, let's remember what we just discussed and consider creating a goal that will keep everyone working together on talking out loud about*

Session 2: Engaging and Evaluating Young Adults 91

feelings and checking things out with each other. There is less room for the eating disorder to operate when everyone is more connected to what is happening inside them and connecting with each other about those experiences. If we can stay connected even in the face of intense emotions and different perspectives, it allows us to be creative with how to approach the challenges we experience in recovery.

In this vignette the therapist introduces the patient and family to how the R4R therapist will help them name and work through disconnections created by AN. Throughout the scenario the therapist uses normalizing statements (e.g., *Sometimes it is hard to name feelings. We could have different views about the situations.*) and validation (*I can see why you end up isolating and not seeing your friends. It is very painful to be a dad and not be able to fix things for your kids.*) in an effort to reduce anxiety and shame and increase openness and self-disclosure. She also emphasizes how patient, family, and therapist are "in this together," and strengthens a sense of "we" by often using the word "we" or "us" or emphasizing the importance of hearing everyone's voice (e.g., *Is there anything I forgot from what we discussed? It is important to get everyone's views about the overall list. If we can stay connected even in the face of intense emotions... it allows us to be creative with how to approach the challenges we experience in recovery*). These interventions promote a collaborative stance in recovery work and increase patient and family willingness to voice different perspectives, feelings, values, or needs. Through normalizing statements, validation, and strengthening the "we," the therapist creates the path leading family members toward practicing being "different in connection." The therapist deliberately asks Sam if his experiences are "similar or different" (e.g., *Is what you are experiencing the same or different from what Dad is saying?*). This intervention foreshadows what is to come in group, where the therapist will strategically often ask this question in an effort to normalize that group members may think similarly or differently about issues.

In the preceding vignette the therapist teaches members how to practice being different in connection by first helping them connect with what they are experiencing inside (emotions and biological states) and outside (behavioral cues), and then encouraging them to connect with one another and share these experiences. The therapist also takes the opportunity during this vignette to point out how the eating disorder may take advantage of disconnections (e.g., *I am guessing the eating disorder likes to swoop in and take advantage of you at these times.*) by tempting the patient to turn toward symptoms to regulate intense emotion. Throughout the interaction with patient and family, the R4R therapist maintains a "can do attitude" and conveys her confidence in group members' abilities to identify and work through disconnections. She emphasizes how difference can be a good thing and that it can strengthen relationships. In the preceding scenario the therapist ends by positively reinforcing the hard

92 *Mary Tantillo, Jennifer Sanftner McGraw, and Daniel Le Grange*

work accomplished by the patient and family. She explicitly notes how their ability to respond differently helps eliminate AN and foster ongoing recovery.

Although not mentioned in the vignette, the therapist also has the option to use a "hip-pocket patient or family member" if the patient or family members are reticent to speak. For example, the therapist can recount what other patients or family members have said under the same circumstances. This is normalizing and encourages patients and family members to then self-disclose (e.g., "I have heard from other patients/family members that they have felt "X" in this situation. I am wondering if you are feeling similarly or differently?"). Alternatively, the therapist can turn to others in the family and ask if they have a sense of what the other person may be feeling. This is more helpful to do when the therapist has a sense that another person in the room can empathize with the person who is struggling to express themselves.

Additionally, since the therapist is promoting perceived mutuality, she can model this in relationship with the patient and/or family members. For example, if the patient or family members cannot or will not express what they are experiencing inside, the therapist can share what she is feeling in response to what has transpired in an interaction (Tantillo, 2004). For example, if Sam was unable to share what he felt with his dad, she could share how she felt witnessing their interaction. For example, she could say, "Both of you seem to be having very painful feelings related to Sam not spending time with friends. I am feeling sad and frustrated about this for both of you. The eating disorder seems to be working very hard to keep Sam all to itself regardless of whether he actually wants to be with his friends. This has to be very hard for you Sam and for your dad. I am not sure if you are feeling something similar or different from what I am experiencing about this, Sam."

Finally, the therapist can bring some levity to situations with the use of humor if appropriate. For example, if Sam hinted that dad or mom is overly involved with trying to ensure he spends time with friends and the parents can handle some humor, the therapist could use a combination of self-disclosure and humor by saying, "Sam, it is hard being loved so much by your parents. My son says that to me a lot. He calls me a helicopter or kangaroo parent sometimes. Parents are not perfect. I know I am not. Is this what it is like for you at times?" A combination of warmth and caring can ease the anxiety and tension experienced by young adults with AN and their family members.

Establishing Patient and Family Group Goals

After completing the review of points of tension and disconnections created by AN, the therapist assists the patient and family members to establish two to three goals for R4R MFTG. These goals should be informed by the points of tension and disconnections discussed earlier. Goals should promote internal

Session 2: Engaging and Evaluating Young Adults   93

and interpersonal connections and ideally be specific, measurable, action-oriented, and achievable by the end of R4R. For example, based on the points of tension and disconnections reviewed by Sam and his family, three goals could include:

- Family members will practice naming and assertively expressing their perspectives, feelings, and needs, even if they are different from those of other family members.
- Family members will practice being "imperfect" and "good enough" as evidenced by more compassionate self-talk, self-care, and realistic goal-setting.
- Work with Sam to identify and implement constructive strategies to help him increase time spent with friends and decrease his related anxiety.

The family will not be able to resolve all challenges related to recovery during the 16 sessions. However, the therapist can help them prioritize what they want to focus on. Additionally, some goals can target a number of points of tension and disconnections. For example, the patient and family may agree that working on the first goal would actually help address several points of tension and disconnections (e.g., Sam being in the kitchen during meals, no one talking about feelings, comments about working out, and decisions about Sam's return to cross-country). Goals should be recorded on a goal sheet and signed by the patient, family members, and therapist. The therapist keeps a copy and also gives copies to the patient and family members. See Box 6.1 for an example of the goal sheet.

Box 6.1   R4R MFTG Patient and Family Goal Sheet

The _____ **Family**
    Here are the goals we will work on during the Multifamily Therapy Group. (Identify at least two that are specific, measurable, action-oriented, and achievable.)
1.
2.
3.
Patient Signature: _____ **Date:** _____
Family Member Signature: _____ **Date:** _____
Family Member Signature: _____ **Date:** _____
Family Member Signature: _____ **Date:** _____
Family Member Signature: _____ **Date:** _____
Therapist Signature: _____ **Date:** _____

Complete Orientation to R4R MFTG

The therapist finishes Session 2 by reviewing the nature and goals of R4R MFTG, as well as R4R norms/expectations and syllabus. The therapist reminds the patient and family about how MFTG works by saying something like:

> *As I mentioned during the last session, Multifamily Therapy Group is a kind of therapy that involves several families and patients working together to identify challenges experienced in recovery and practice skills and strategies in order to overcome these challenges and move forward together in recovery. Patients and families find MFTG very helpful because everyone shares a common experience, like recovering from AN, while also being able to share many different viewpoints and feelings about the challenges that are part of recovery and ways to tackle them.*

The therapist can again distribute the handout *Description of R4R Multifamily Therapy Group,* used in Session 1, and briefly call attention to what was discussed during the last session (see Chapter 5) regarding R4R MFTG. The therapist then reviews the R4R MFTG goals. The goals are provided on a handout and include:

- Increase understanding regarding how AN promotes disconnection in relationships with others and obstructs recovery.
- Increase understanding regarding the impact of disconnections on AN symptoms and recovery.
- Increase perceived mutuality among patients and families.
- Practice new emotional and relational skills that promote recovery.
- Increase understanding regarding the illness and stages and processes of change so families can interact in ways that promote motivation for ongoing treatment and recovery.
- Promote a sense of hopefulness and positive, healing energy that enables patients and families to remain connected and engaged in their recovery work.
- Decrease isolation and expand families' and patients' social networks.

The therapist then reviews the R4R MFTG norms and expectations handout and the syllabus. Group members may also add to the norms and expectations once group begins. Norms and expectations include:

- I will attend every group. If I am sick, I will call (insert therapist name and phone number).
- I will be on time for each group session.
- I understand we can drink (non-diet) fluids during group but will refrain from eating food.
- I will actively participate because my thoughts, feelings, and perspectives are important for my work, as well as for the work of other patients and families. Everyone has wisdom to share in the room.

Session 2: Engaging and Evaluating Young Adults   95

- I promise to support one person speaking at a time. We want to hear everyone's voice.
- I understand that it is therapeutic to be able to offer thoughts, feelings, or perspectives that might be different from those of others. I promise to share them respectfully. Being able to be different *and* connected with ourselves and others is a big goal of group.
- Over time, patients or family members in group may desire to connect and support one another outside of group. I understand that if I spend time with a group member outside of group, that this is considered part of the material that can be discussed in group.

The R4R MFTG syllabus is then reviewed. It can be distributed as a handout in a format shown in Table 6.1.

Table 6.1 Reconnecting for Recovery Syllabus (R4R)

Session Topic	Date
Session 1: Single Family Session: Assessment, joining, and orientation	
Session 2: Single Family Session: Assessment, joining, and orientation (continued)	
R4R Multifamily Therapy Group Sessions Begin	
Session 3: Anorexia nervosa (AN): A disease of disconnection— Introduction, recovery process, and the spiral of change	
Session 4: Recovery process, the spiral of change and supporting patients to stay motivated for change in recovery	
Session 5: Biopsychosocial risk factors for AN and common accompanying behavioral health conditions	
Session 6: Biopsychosocial risk factors (continued), disconnections, and functional analysis skills (understanding the ABC's of how AN affects everyone in the family)	
Session 7: Strategies to promote mutual connections	
Session 8: AN and the family context: Rules and relationships	
Session 9: Identifying points of tension and disconnections related to AN, recovery, and relationships	
Session 10: Nourishing and empowering the "We" in relationships	
Session 11: How to name and work through conflict in connection*	
Session 12: Moving from disconnection to connection: Building strong connections to work through tension and disconnections related to young adulthood and recovery*	
Session 13: Relapse prevention and maintaining good connections*	
Session 14: Relapse prevention (continued) and preparing for group termination*	
Session 15: Relapse prevention (continued), termination, and next steps for continued connections in recovery**	
Session 16: Relapse prevention (continued), termination, and next steps for continued connections in recovery**	

Note: * = every other week; ** = monthly.

At the end of Session 2 the patient and family members are offered another opportunity to raise any other questions. They are reminded that next week will be our first R4R group session including all patients and families. At the end of Session 2 patients and family members leave with a folder containing orientation paperwork including the handouts and a list of recommended readings below. (Session 2 handouts are available upon request from the first author, MT. The content of these handouts is reviewed in Chapters 3 through 8.)

- Description of R4R Multifamily Therapy Group
- R4R MFTG Goals
- R4R MFTG Norms and Expectations
- R4R Syllabus
- Eating Disorders Are Diseases of Disconnection
- Spiral, Stages and Processes of Change
- Motivational Interviewing Principles
- Helping Relationships and the Stages of Change
- The Five Good Things
- Perceived Mutuality Is Essential for Psychological Growth
- Mutuality Venn Diagram and Circles of Disconnection
- Eating Disorder Websites
- Recommended Readings:

  - How Do Connections Lead to Growth? (pp. 24–41) and The Source of Psychological Problems (pp. 65–83). In Miller, J. B., & Stiver, I. P. (1997). *The healing connection.* Boston, MA: Beacon Press.
  - How You Change (pp. 21–35). In Prochaska, J. O., Norcross, J. C., & DiClemente, C. C. (1994). *In Changing for good: A revolutionary six-stage program for overcoming bad habits and moving your life positively forward.* New York: William Morrow and Company, Inc.
  - Helping to Eliminate the Eating Disorder (pp. 93–111). In Treasure, J., & Alexander, J. (2013). *Anorexia Nervosa: A recovery guide for sufferers, families and friends* (2nd edition). New York, NY: Routledge.
  - Caring Styles of Close Others (pp. 42–55) and Caregiving Relationships (pp. 118–131). In Treasure, J., Smith, G., & Crane, A. (2017). *Skills-based learning for caring for a loved one with an eating disorder* (2nd edition). New York, NY: Routledge.

We encourage each family to purchase or borrow from the library *Changing for Good* (Prochaska, Norcross, & DiClemente, 1994), *The Healing Connection* (Miller & Stiver, 1997), *Anorexia Nervosa: A Recovery Guide for Sufferers, Family and Friends* (Treasure & Alexander, 2013), and *Skills-Based Caring for a Loved One with an Eating Disorder: The New Maudsley Method* (Treasure, Smith, & Crane, 2017). We have copies of these books available for borrowing as well. The goals, materials, and handouts for Session 2 are outlined in Box 6.2.

> **Box 6.2 Session 2: Engaging and Evaluating Young Adults with AN and Their Families: Assessment, Joining, and Orientation (Continued)**
>
> ## Goals
>
> - Review Session 1 points of tension and disconnections related to AN
> - Strengthen a sense of "we" and promote perceived mutuality for recovery
> - Develop patient and family MFTG goals
> - Complete orientation to R4R MFTG
> - Briefly review description of R4R MFTG
> - Review R4R MFTG goals, norms/expectations, and syllabus
> - Distribute R4R orientation folder
>
> ## Materials
>
> - Easel paper to display points of tension and disconnections
>
> ## Handouts
>
> - R4R MFTG patient and family goal sheets
> - R4R description of R4R MFTG
> - R4R MFTG norms/expectations
> - R4R MFTG syllabus
> - R4R MFTG orientation folder

References

No DOI

*Miller, J. B., & Stiver, I. P. (1997). *The healing connection: How women form relationships in therapy and in life*. Beacon Press.

*Prochaska, J. O., Norcross, J. C., DiClemente, C. C. (1994). *Changing for good: A revolutionary six-stage program for overcoming bad habits and moving your life positively forward*. William Morrow.

Tantillo, M. D. (2004). The therapist's use of self-disclosure in a Relational Therapy approach for eating disorders. *Eating Disorders: Journal of Treatment and Prevention, 12*, 51–73. https://dx.doi.org/10.1080/10640260490267760.

*Treasure, J., & Alexander, J. (2013). *Anorexia Nervosa: A recovery guide for sufferers, families and friends* (2nd ed.). Routledge.

Treasure, J., Smith, G., & Crane, A. (2017). *Skills-based learning for caring for a loved one with an eating disorder* (2nd ed.). Routledge. https://dx.doi.org/10.4324/9781315735610.

7 Session 3: Anorexia Nervosa—A Disease of Disconnection—Introduction, Recovery Process, Motivational Interviewing Principles, and the Spiral of Change

Mary Tantillo, Jennifer Sanftner McGraw, and Daniel Le Grange

Session 3 is the first R4R MFTG group session to include all patients and families. Both R4R therapists are present for this and all future sessions. Their main aims in Session 3 are to:

- Promote group cohesiveness, universality, and a sense of mutual trust, empathy, and empowerment
- Begin education regarding the spiral, stages, and processes of change (Prochaska, Norcross, & DiClemente, 1994) and Motivational Interviewing principles (Miller & Rollnick, 2013)
- Encourage the use of strategies for connection to strengthen relationships and collaborative caring in recovery (an ongoing homework assignment over the course of the group)

Session 3 begins with the therapists welcoming members and facilitating introductions that include first names, the person(s) with whom the group member is "connected," (strategically use this word as part of initiating members into the language of R4R), and a goal the patient or family member hopes to accomplish by the end of MFTG. The R4R therapists can encourage members to share some of the excellent goals they set as individual families during the last session. Therapists can promote a sense of universality and connection among members by confirming that families established many similar goals.

After the introductions the therapists discuss an icebreaker they would like to conduct with the group to help members get to know each other a little more. We have used an icebreaker that involves having members work together to identify three to five of their favorite animals or movies and the reasons for their choices. Begin by having the members count off by threes and then ask them to divide into groups comprised of all the ones, twos and threes. Tell them that each group has up to ten minutes to complete the icebreaker and that a scribe needs to report their findings to the larger group. An alternative is to have each member write down an animal that represents them on a sticker. Ask them to wear their stickers and walk around the room for ten minutes looking at each other's stickers and asking one another about their choice of animal. There are many different icebreakers that can be used. See Asen and Scholz (2010) for additional MFTG icebreaker examples. At the end of the icebreaker, spend about five more minutes discussing member responses to the icebreaker.

Next, the R4R therapists quickly remind members about the overall goals of R4R MFTG, norms/expectations, and the importance of separating patients from the eating disorder. The therapists continue to externalize AN and remind members that despite AN's efforts to get in "our way," "we" will work "together" to build a "community" that supports recovery. The therapists strategically strengthen the "we" in group by using words that foster member connectedness and universality. They validate the burden of the illness for the patient and the family and reinforce that neither the family nor the patient caused the illness, and that they cannot control or cure it alone.

The therapists then provide psychoeducation in the form of handouts or PowerPoint slides regarding the spiral, stages, and processes of change (Prochaska, Norcross, & DiClemente, 1994). (The PowerPoint slides include information described in this chapter. The reader may construct their own slides using this information or request slides used in R4R from the first author, MT.) Members are also referred to their orientation folders for copies of the spiral, stages, and processes of change handouts (also see Chapter 5 and 6). During the psychoeducation regarding how individuals change and how family members can help maintain patient motivation for change, the therapists emphasize that all humans heal and grow in connection. They discuss how the eating disorder, as a *disease of disconnection*, will try to obstruct healing, change, and growth through creating and maintaining disconnections inside the patient and between the patient and others. We always begin this presentation with a slide that emphasizes how AN is a disease of disconnection and the four levels of disconnection it creates (see Box 7.1).

Box 7.1   The Eating Disorder Is a Disease of Disconnection

- Disconnects the patient from self/body and others
- Disconnects the immediate family or family of origin from extended family and friends
- Disconnects the patient and family from professional treatment team members
- Disconnects professional treatment team members from one another

100 *Mary Tantillo, Jennifer Sanftner McGraw, and Daniel Le Grange*

This PowerPoint slide or handout also facilitates an understanding that disconnections can extend in a parallel way from the patient and family toward the treatment team or from the treatment team toward the patient and family.

With regard to the first level of disconnections from self, body, and others (see the first item in Box 7.1), the R4R therapists quickly note that patients experience a number of interacting biopsychosocial risk factors that go on to create and maintain AN and that these risk factors can involve processes of disconnection. They say that they will defer a more comprehensive discussion of these disconnections until Session 5, but a couple of examples include the disconnections that go on neurochemically or with regard to how brain areas process information. These processes of disconnection may exist before the onset of illness and/or be the consequence of the illness. Either way, the patient is left feeling disconnected from their genuine feelings, thoughts, and needs, as well as feeling disconnected from others in relationships. For example, once AN takes hold, the patient's brain experiences the effects of malnutrition, starvation, dehydration, compulsive exercise, and electrolyte disturbance if they are vomiting or abusing laxatives. Patients feel increasingly irritable, distracted, and exhausted and experience more social withdrawal and cognitive rigidity (e.g., black and white thinking and not being able to flexibly adjust their thinking when rules in a situation change). These experiences further distance the patient from being able to make accurate sense of what they are experiencing internally and interpersonally. Because patients are unable to accurately process what is happening with regard to AN and its impact on them, they are less able to share their experiences with others. Additionally, anosognosia (i.e., not recognizing one is ill) (Nunn, Frampton, Fuglset, Törzsök-Sonnevend, & Lask, 2011; Vandereycken, 2006) can be part of AN, and the illness initially presents itself as a friend—meeting patient needs (e.g., regulation of emotions or a need to feel unique, accomplished, or in control). These factors contribute to the length of time it takes for family members to know something is wrong with their loved one. When family members do notice something is awry, their concerns can be met with avoidance, denial, or anger. AN will make the patient dismiss or minimize others' concerns. If family members continue to voice concerns or try to intervene to increase intake or interrupt symptoms, patients can become increasingly anxious, fearful, and avoidant. The anxiety and fear can also manifest as increased anger. The preceding discussion helps family members and patients consider each other's experiences and understand why change can be so challenging for everyone. One story we use to represent what this is like to the patient is as follows:

Pretend you are in the woods and you are holding your compass and it is telling you that you are going north, but your family members keep running in from different places in the forest telling you that you are actually going south. This experience can be irritating over time and eventually can be very anxiety provoking and unsettling. It is difficult to

Session 3: Anorexia Nervosa   101

believe others when one's compass is saying something different. And it is frightening to think that one's external or internal compass is broken. Denial is a common response in this situation. In AN, one's information processing compass is broken, which is why the patient is disconnected from what is really happening inside emotionally and physically. The only way through this dilemma is to find family and professionals you trust deeply in order to find your way to true north—reconnecting with yourself and others on the road to recovery.

This story increases empathy for the patient, helps separate the patient from AN, and reinforces how scary change can be for the patient. In response to the interpersonal disconnections that family members experience with their loved one, they may reach out to other family members and friends for support but become frustrated, ashamed, or deflated when their close others do not understand AN or its impact on the patient and family. Or the family may isolate more, not seek out support, and avoid socially awkward situations that could occur due to their loved one's AN. These experiences lead to the second level of disconnections involving family of origin, extended family and friends (see #2 in Box 7.1), the outcome of which is less positive, healing energy coming into the family system to deal with AN. Now AN is isolating the whole family from the support of others.

The third level of disconnections (see #3, Box 7.1) happens when AN creates disconnections between the patient and family and professional treatment staff. (Treatment staff include all professionals seeing the patient and family, not just the R4R therapists.) These disconnections can occur when AN is making patient, family, and/or treatment staff think in all-or-nothing ways and respond in less flexible ways that ignore context. These disconnections often occur in the face of intense emotion and include, for example, conflict experienced regarding a patient's target weight or contingencies that should follow when a patient is not eating according to the prescribed meal plan. AN tries to prevent patient, family, and clinicians from listening to one another's concerns. For example, treatment staff may be unwittingly sending a message that is experienced as shaming by the family or patient (e.g., "We don't understand what went wrong over the weekend. We reviewed the meal plan before you left the session last week.") Alternatively, the patient or family may begin discussing terminating treatment unless the target weight or mealtime requirements are lowered. The latter often happens when family members start negotiating with the eating disorder about necessary nutrition and self-care.

The fourth level of disconnections involving the professional treatment team (see #4, Box 7.1) can occur any time during treatment, often when there is cognitive rigidity and intense emotion on the scene. Various professional team members can point fingers at each other out of frustration or helplessness because of AN. Splitting (i.e., an unconscious defense mechanism involving dichotomous thinking that fails to bring together positive and negative characteristics of the self and others into a cohesive, reality-based whole) may occur and manifest itself in how team members respond to each other. For example, without realizing it, the team social worker may start believing that the team RN is being punitive, when she is actually just following through with contingencies related to meal completion. This scenario is similar to splitting and disconnections that may be occurring at home when the patient's mother sees the father as punitive for delivering contingencies in response to their son's refusal to complete prescribed meals. The social worker and the mom may feel tempted to be extra flexible in their response to the patient and, perhaps, make allowances or not deliver contingencies in a way that the whole treatment team agreed upon. In both scenarios it is stressful to remain firm and deliver consistent contingencies while being warm and supportive to the patient. It is difficult to walk the line between acting in a way that is perceived as frustrating but supportive versus punitive to the patient. Caring for an individual with AN can feel intense and overwhelming at times. AN capitalizes on this situation by disconnecting caregivers from one another in order to remain connected with the patient.

After reviewing the different levels of disconnection that AN creates to obstruct change, the therapists can continue with the other handouts/PowerPoint slides more specifically addressing the stages, spiral, and processes of change (Prochaska, Norcross, & DiClemente, 1994) and Motivational Interviewing principles (Miller & Rollnick, 2013). We begin this set of slides with quotes from past patients to help family members understand the severe anxiety and fear associated with making changes and letting go of an ED. We call attention to the intense emotions and experiences in these quotes. Examples follow:

"Having an ED is like being in a frying pan surrounded by *horrendous* flames. On the other side of those flames is recovery. My therapist and others are on the recovery side telling me to step out of the pan into the flames and to walk through the fire to reach recovery. I think to myself, 'Are they nuts?! Don't they know how *frightened* I am to step into the fire? It will *destroy* me. I will *die*.' This frying pan (eating disorder) is safe and protective because I know how to live in it. I know how to 'be' in the pan."

(Tantillo, Bitter, & Adams, 2001, pp. 206–207)

"When I thought of giving up my eating ED before, I would feel *petrified*. I would feel the *fear* right here, like in my chest. I don't feel that so much anymore. I feel readier to give it up … less *frightened*. Like I won't *lose all of me* if I do. I used to be *afraid* that if I gave up the eating disorder, I would *lose a sense* of me. Like I would *vaporize, become invisible … cease to exist*. Like without the eating disorder there would be *nothingness*."

(Member of Outpatient Contemplation Group, personal communication, 2010)

While reviewing these slides, the therapist can provide additional metaphors for what it is like to have AN and the challenges involved in making changes to let go of it. For example, the therapist may give the example of the patient being a rose and AN being a weed that overcomes the rose. Over time it is difficult for the rose to separate itself from the weed. They seem like one. The patient may feel this way about AN and may fear for her/his ability to survive without the ED. These metaphors remind family members of the important purposes AN serves in the lives of patients (e.g., emotional regulation, coping, control, mastery, uniqueness, and a sense of identity) and how it is frightening to eliminate AN without knowing how to meet various needs in alternative ways. Patients are often unsure of *who they will be and how they will exist* without AN.

Next, the therapist can proceed with instruction regarding motivational principles (Miller & Rollnick, 2013) and the stages, spiral, and processes of change (Prochaska, Norcross, & DiClemente, 1994). The therapist begins with a slide that highlights motivational principles that strengthen relationships for the work of change and recovery. (See Box 7.2 for the summary slide of the motivational principles.) These principles include:

- **Express empathy:** Emphasize the importance of maintaining an empathic stance and using validation with patients. Ask family members to remember that AN serves many purposes for the patient and has associated meanings/values. Encourage them to radically accept the importance of these things for the patient while not agreeing with or enabling AN. When AN tries to disconnect the patient from him/herself or others through symptom use, have family members respond by first conveying an understanding of why the patient responded in this way. Then they can help the patient explore antecedents to symptom use and the possibility of working together to help the patient meet needs in more adaptive ways in the future. Starting with validation strengthens mutual trust, understanding, and respect needed for collaborative caring. Here is an example:

  > *"I can understand why you want to restrict more after talking with your co-worker today. It sounds like that conversation was very stressful. I am wondering if you compared yourself to her and found yourself lacking in some way. Based on what you have told me in the past, it sounds like the ED may have helped you numb out the anxiety and embarrassment you felt. I am not sure what you discussed, but I want you to know I am happy to talk more with you about it. Maybe we can figure out another way for you to cope with what was discussed."*

- **Develop discrepancy:** Encourage family members to help patients examine if AN is helping them or hindering them in (a) living according to their *life values* and (b) living out their *life goals*. This examination will lead to a feeling of discrepancy between what they value/seek to do in their lives and what AN allows. The discrepancy can fuel change because it can clarify that AN is not growth-fostering and that it increases disconnection from self and others. Discrepancy is more powerful than lectures because it occurs inside the patient and is not imposed. It is important to remind family members and patients that the goal of AN is to make patients forget their cherished values, goals, dreams, and aspirations. It is essential that family members remind patients to explore and remember what is truly important to them and examine whether AN is honoring these things. The therapist can give the following example to group members:

> *"If a person's life goals include going to college 500 miles away to increase their autonomy, eventually becoming a social worker, getting married, and having a child, is AN (e.g., daily food restriction with inability to complete a prescribed meal plan and twice daily purging) helping or hindering them in accomplishing these goals?"*

> *"If a person's life values are honesty, integrity, and transparency, is AN allowing them to live according to these values?"*

One story we share when discussing the importance of developing discrepancy involves a music student who had a full scholarship to attend a prestigious music school. This particular patient had loved playing the piano since the age of 5 and sought from an early age to someday be a concert pianist. When she fell ill with AN in the transition from high school to college, she lost interest in playing piano and ended up needing to take a medical leave from school. Her parents and older siblings would gently remind her of what she used to say to them about loving music and being a concert pianist one day. They did not lecture her but would ask her if AN was helping her live out her dreams. Eventually the patient recognized that AN was eliminating her true love, music, and she went on to recover and attend music school.

- **Avoid argumentation:** Remind family members that when we fight with an ED, the ED usually wins. Encourage them to use empathy and validation and increase discrepancy as noted earlier. These actions preserve patient self-worth and can promote self-confidence and trusting connections with loved ones in recovery. The therapist can also refer to the animal metaphors representative of caregiving styles (Treasure, Smith, & Crane, 2017) and encourage family members to respond like dolphins (swimming alongside their loved one) or St. Bernards (being centered, compassionate, and steady), instead of ostriches (avoidant), jellyfish (emotionally dysregulated), terriers (nagging and critical), rhinoceroses (aggressive), or kangaroos (overprotective/enabling).

- **Roll with resistance:** Encourage family members to come alongside the patient when there are challenges in recovery instead of going straight at a problem full speed or immediately pushing back. Encourage them to use validation and empathy and acknowledge how difficult things may be for the patient, while expressing concern, developing discrepancy, and holding out the possibility of working through challenges without use of the ED. Describe the process of *going with* the resistance versus *against it* by asking family members to consider what they should do if they are swimming in the ocean or large lake and experience an undercurrent in the water. If they do not know the answer, tell them they should swim parallel to the shore, not straight at it because the undercurrent will not permit this and could carry them away. Similarly, they can interact with their loved one in a way that acknowledges the current challenge in recovery while also offering the opportunity to tackle the challenge differently, perhaps after an initial cooling down time. Another metaphor to help them understand how to interact at times that are emotionally charged is that of a sailboat. A sailboat does not sail straight into the shore. Instead, it tacks back and forth. In conversation with a loved one, it is important to interact in a dialectical way, tacking back and forth in the conversation between the patient's experience informed by AN and an alternative way to think about the situation. This approach involves talking in a caring "both/and" motivational way (Miller & Rollnick, 2013). Here is an example:

  > *"I love you and hear how important it is for you to go to college out of town and how great this would feel in terms of your being independent and building your self-confidence. And at the same time, I am concerned about your difficulty with the meal plan and inability to adequately meet your daily energy needs as an active full-time student athlete. I want to help you accomplish your goals."*

- **Support self-efficacy:** Encourage family members to foster in patients a sense of competence and confidence related to their choices and self-care efforts. Direct family members to positively reinforce patient assertiveness and efforts to try new things (e.g., new foods, new social experiences, etc.). Reinforce that young adults developmentally want to feel they can handle things on their own. Encourage family members to promote autonomy while also providing support. Have them offer the young adult patient choices whenever possible, even if this means parents have identified several choices because AN prevents the young adult from identifying healthy choices. The young adult patient still appreciates having some kind of choice in this scenario versus having no choice. Encourage parents and partners to move out of a "control" or "power over" position into a position of caring. The ED will make the patient

106　*Mary Tantillo, Jennifer Sanftner McGraw, and Daniel Le Grange*

push back if it feels controlled. Instead, family needs to interact with the patient in a way that helps them feel more in control of their choices and lives. Also, tell family to remember the importance of reinforcing the patient's efforts at taking control in healthy ways (e.g., coping by expressing feelings and needs versus remaining silent and avoiding them or deciding not to go to a potentially triggering event versus being passive and accompanying friends to that event). Patients quickly identify what they experience as flaws or failures, but they are slow to notice accomplishments and positive efforts. Catch them doing something well (especially actions unrelated to food, exercise, and body image) and let them know. The more mastery they experience with life skills and coping, the less they need to turn to eating disorder symptoms to meet their needs.

Box 7.2　Motivational Principles

Express empathy (Validate and consider the pros/purposes/ meanings related to AN.)

Develop discrepancy (Help the patient consider whether AN is helping or hindering attainment of their life goals and living out their life values.)

Avoid argumentation (If you fight with the ED, it usually wins. Instead of arguing, use empathy, develop discrepancy, and promote patient self-worth and confidence. Be a dolphin or St. Bernard, not a rhinoceros, ostrich, jellyfish, or terrier.)

Roll with resistance (Instead of going straight at a problem full speed or immediately pushing back, come alongside the patient. Validate and use empathy [e.g., noting how challenging things must be for the patient] while also expressing concern and creating discrepancy. Go with the resistance versus against it.)

Support self-efficacy (Help patients to experience a sense of competence and confidence in caring for themselves. Positively reinforce assertiveness and their taking risks by trying new things. Young adults especially crave the feeling that they can handle things on their own. Promote autonomy while also providing support. Move out of a "control" or "power over" position into a position of caring. You don't want to control the patient. You want the patient to feel more in control of their choices and lives. Reinforce their use of healthy controls.)

Note: Motivational Principles. Adapted from *Motivational interviewing: Helping people change* (3rd edition), by W. R. Miller and S. Rollnick, 2013, New York, NY: The Guilford Press. Copyright 2013 by Guilford Press. Adapted with permission of The Guilford Press.

During this discussion about self-efficacy the first author often shares the following example of how she as a nurse on the inpatient unit practiced moving out of a position in which a young adult felt controlled into one that left her feeling cared for. This example shows how the ED will try to bait the caregiver into a "power over" (controlling top-down) versus "power with" (caring alongside) position. The example shows how the caregiver can avoid or work through disconnection by using empathy and validation, separate the patient from AN, and use a "hip-pocket patient" (stories from other real or fictional patients) to maintain connection with the patient.

Nurse: *I can help you with your shower now.*

Patient: *Yes and I will be fine. I feel like I can do that without any problems right now.*

Nurse: *I believe you and I know how hard you are working. At the same time, it is important to have someone with you in case the ED gives you a hard time.*

Patient: *You mean you actually have to be near me when I take the shower? You don't trust me.*

Nurse: *I do trust you and at the same time, I don't trust the ED. I know right now you intend to not let it bully you. Additionally, though, many patients have told me that when they are alone, the ED comes and gives them trouble. Then they feel vulnerable and overwhelmed, and it is easier to experience a symptom. It is not something they planned. In time you can definitely shower on your own. Right now you are early in recovery, and I want to be present to offer you support.*

Patient: *Well, I still think I will be OK, but it sounds like you are worried about me. Maybe if you can see me be OK, it will show you I can do this.*

Nurse: *Excellent way of thinking about this.*

After reviewing the preceding motivational principles, the therapists ask for any feedback or questions from the group members. One of the therapists then draws on the board or uses a handout or PowerPoint slide to present the spiral, stages, and processes of change (Prochaska, Norcross, & DiClemente, 1994). The stages of change include:

- **Precontemplation:** Involves denial and little or no awareness of having a problem. No intention to change in foreseeable future.
- **Contemplation:** Involves ambivalence and having awareness of having a problem. There is a desire to change in the next six months.
- **Preparation:** Getting ready for change by setting small goals and telling others of your intent to make a change. There is a desire to change in the next month.
- **Action:** Making active behavioral and environmental changes.
- **Maintenance:** Consolidating gains and being free of symptoms for at least six months.
- **Termination:** The problem behavior is no longer experienced as a temptation and there is high confidence in coping without relapse.

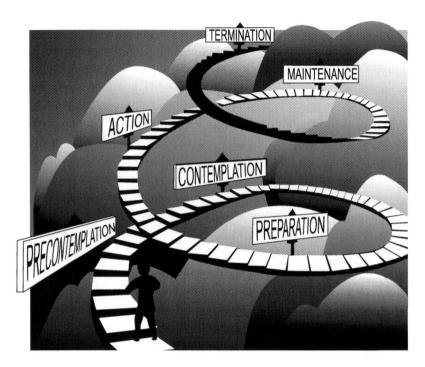

Figure 7.1 The Spiral of Change (pg. 49) from CHANGING FOR GOOD by JAMES O. PROCHASKA, JOHN C. NORCROSS, and CARLO C. DICLEMENT. Copyright © 1994 by James O. Prochaska, John C. Norcross, and Carlo C. DiClemente. Reprinted by permission of HarperCollins Publishers.

The therapists emphasize that a patient can be in a different stage of change with different eating disorder behaviors. For example, a patient may feel they are in action with purging, preparation for action with binge eating, and contemplation with food restriction. The therapists describe how the process of change is a spiral, rather than a straight line, and that the young adult may move up and down the spiral of change four to five times on average (Prochaska, Norcross, & DiClemente, 1994) (see Figure 7.1).

The therapists note that change occurs in a back and forth way; five steps forward and three steps back, four steps forward and two steps back. They emphasize that when lapses or relapses occur in recovery (and they will), patients and family members need to view these as learning opportunities and not failures. They help reframe these instances as experiences in which the patient's body is speaking for them because the patient is not yet aware of what is triggering the AN symptom. The therapists encourage group members to use the symptoms to their advantage versus disadvantage and to be curious about them and about what has triggered symptom use. Patients and families are asked to be like "Sherlock Holmes" and discover what is creating stress for the patients, leaving them feeling vulnerable to AN symptoms. The therapists reinforce that at these higher risk times patients need to engage in relapse prevention activities like meal planning, journaling (or other modes of self-expression like drawing), reaching out to others for support, and structuring their time.

The therapists emphasize how being an adult means being honest with oneself and others about our limitations and imperfections and asking for help. They emphasize interdependence with others as opposed to a distorted notion that young adults must be ultra-autonomous and accomplish recovery on their own. The latter message is one that AN amplifies, and it is easy for a young adult to buy into this message because they are at a stage of development that involves increasing independence. Young adults are either hungry for independence or feel they should be hungry for it. If they are fearful of independence, they may feel they cannot admit this. This admission may be associated with a sense of shame or failure, especially when engaging in self-comparisons to peers. AN symptoms can disconnect the young adult from the push-pull of wanting versus fearing increased autonomy, especially when they are feeling anxiety in their attempts to achieve developmental milestones.

The therapists then discuss the processes of change and examples of how group members can engage in these processes in daily life (Prochaska, Norcross, & DiClemente, 1994). The processes of change include:

- **Consciousness-raising:** Raising consciousness about (a) AN, (b) the recovery process, (c) how AN will obstruct the patient's efforts to recover, and (d) how we get in our own way during recovery.
- **Helping relationships:** Establishing and using supportive relationships that facilitate recovery work.
- **Social liberation:** Engaging in efforts that support recovery work and contribute to creating an environment that prevents eating disorders and promotes health and wellness. For example, engaging in social activism to eliminate media images that promote the thin ideal and damage body-esteem.
- **Emotional arousal:** Experiencing increased emotional responsiveness to the impact of AN on one's life.
- **Self-reevaluation:** Self-reappraisal to examine if AN is helping or hindering one in achieving life goals and living out one's life values.
- **Commitment:** Strengthening beliefs that you can make behavioral change. Includes activities like telling others about your desire to change and small realistic goals.
- **Countering:** Engaging in healthy thoughts and behaviors that counter use of symptoms. Trying out new skills and adaptive behaviors.
- **Environmental control:** Changing the environment to support recovery including controlling stimuli that would trigger symptoms.
- **Reward:** Rewarding positive, healthy behaviors and decreasing rewards that follow unhealthy behaviors.

110 *Mary Tantillo, Jennifer Sanftner McGraw, and Daniel Le Grange*

Table 7.1 Processes of Change Interventions to Promote Eating Disorder Recovery

Consciousness-raising: Help increase knowledge regarding self, the eating disorder, and the recovery process. Practice functional analysis of behavior (i.e., identify antecedents and consequences to behaviors).

Helping relationships: Encourage/assist with development of open and trusting relationships in therapy and the community to promote recovery.

Social liberation: Explore and practice new alternatives in the community that promote change efforts, e.g., social activism. For example, be part of a media watch group.

Emotional arousal: Assist the patient to experience/express feelings related to negative consequences created by the eating disorder.

Self-reevaluation: Assist with the assessment of how the patient thinks and feels about her/himself in regards to the eating disorder. Create discrepancy by examining goals/values in relation to the eating disorder and practice decisional balance (i.e., identify pros/cons related to behaviors).

Commitment: Strengthen beliefs that the patient can change. Create a realistic plan of action.

Countering: Assist the patient to identify and practice alternative coping/self-care strategies.

Environmental control: Help to assess and restructure the environment to promote recovery.

Reward: Assist with identifying rewards from self and others to celebrate changes.

Note

Processes of Change and Interventions to Promote Eating Disorder Recovery. Reprinted from "Mutuality and Motivation" (p. 320), by M. Tantillo and J. Sanftner in M. Maine, B. Hartman McGilley, and D. Bunnell (Eds.), *Treatment of Eating Disorders*, 2010, London, UK: Elsevier. Copyright 2010 by Elsevier Inc. Reprinted with permission. The "Processes of Change" from *Changing for Good*, James O. Prochaska, John C. Norcross, & Carlo C. Diclemente. Copyright 1994 by James O. Prochaska, John C. Norcross, and Carlo C. DiClemente, 1994. Reprinted by permission of HarperCollins Publishers.

The therapists also distribute a handout that summarizes the processes of change and associated interventions that promote recovery (see Table 7.1).

After reviewing the spiral, stages, and processes of change, the therapists ask for any questions or feedback. They then ask group members to get into their smaller family units for ten minutes to discuss each person's idea of where the patient may be on the spiral of change with regard to AN behaviors. They emphasize that the patient and family members may have different ideas about the stage. They encourage them to be curious and not defensive or judgmental about these differences, especially because our goal is to practice being "different-in-connection" in recovery and in life. Everyone should share and compare their observations and consider this a brainstorming session. We are learning together about where patients believe they are on the spiral of change and how to best support them as they move along from one stage of change to the next.

Next, the large MFTG is reconvened and members are asked to share their experience of the exercise and observations. If there is not enough time to reconvene the larger group today, it may be left for the beginning of next session. The therapists will end this session assigning homework to patients to

Session 3: Anorexia Nervosa   111

Figure 7.2   How Do You Feel Today? Reprinted from The Children's Involvement Team, http://www.sheffkids.co.uk/adultssite/documents/worksheets/Feelings.pdf?LMCL=MGxDHF, retrieved May, 2018, Sheffield City Council, Sheffield, UK. Reprinted with permission from The Children's Involvement Team, Sheffield, UK.

connect with another person (family or friends) in some way before the next meeting. They will say that this is an ongoing assignment because it will help patients practice connecting with others to bring in positive energy for recovery. If time permits, facilitate a very short discussion about how family members currently connect. Remind them that AN tries to keep patients isolated and stuck in negative thoughts and emotions.

Throughout this first group session it is important to help group members identify and express emotions as they come up during group. If they need help with identifying emotions, the therapists can help them identify the biological and behavioral cues to emotions. This intervention promotes connection to self and one's bodily states. They can ask, "Are you experiencing anything in your body right now? Like butterflies in your stomach or tension in your arms or heaviness in your chest?" They can reflect behaviors by saying, "I noticed you started shaking your leg more when you were talking just now. I am wondering if that gives us a clue about which feeling you might be having?" They can also distribute the feelings handout that includes faces depicting emotions—*How Do You Feel Today?* (The Children's Involvement Team, Sheffield City Council, Sheffield, UK, 2018; see Figure 7.2)—to help members identify feelings and can enlist the aid of other group members.

The therapists can ask other members how they might be feeling given what another member has just shared. This intervention is done in a non-shaming and inviting way, conveying a sense of curiosity, exploration, and discovery. The therapists emphasize that AN capitalizes on unnamed feelings and the unspoken points of tension and disconnections that can emerge from them. The main goals, materials, and handouts for Session 3 are outlined in Box 7.3.

Box 7.3 Session 3: Anorexia Nervosa: A Disease of Disconnection—Introduction, Recovery Process, Motivational Interviewing Principles, and the Spiral of Change

Goals

Help patients and family members to:

- Orient to the nature of MFTG group and group goals and norms and increase connection with one another. (AN is a Disease of Disconnection, and goal = reconnection with self and others.)
- Describe Motivational Interviewing principles and spiral, stages, and processes of change to foster continued patient motivation. Identify where patient is on spiral of change.
- Begin discussion of current ways the families connect (ongoing homework).

- Begin to identify and express emotions as they come up in discussion. (Use *How do you feel today?* emotions sheet and identify biological and behavioral cues to feelings as needed.)

Materials

- Large poster size circles and Venn diagram showing disconnections and mutual connection
- Icebreaker exercise—paper and pens for each family
- Show Motivational Interviewing slides/spiral, stages, and processes of change.

Handouts

- Refer patients and families to review Motivational Interviewing and stages of change handouts in orientation folders.
- Faces depicting emotions sheet—*How do you feel today?* (The Children's Involvement Team, Sheffield City Council, Sheffield, UK)

References

No DOI

Asen, E., & Scholz, M. (2010). *Multi-family therapy: Concepts and techniques.* Routledge. https://dx.doi.org/10.1080/01609513.2011.620785.

*Miller, W. R., & Rollnick, S. (2013). *Motivational interviewing: Helping people change* (3rd ed.). The Guilford Press.

Nunn, K. P., Frampton, I., Fuglset, T. S., Törzsök-Sonnevend, M., & Lask, B. (2011). Anorexia nervosa and the insula. *Medical Hypotheses, 76*(3), 353–357. https://dx.doi.org/10.1016/j.mehy.2010.10.038.

*Prochaska, J. O., Norcross, J. C., DiClemente, C. C. (1994). *Changing for good: A revolutionary six-stage program for overcoming bad habits and moving your life positively forward.* William Morrow.

*Tantillo, M., Bitter, C. N., & Adams, B. (2001). Enhancing readiness for eating disorder treatment: A relational/motivational group model for change. *Eating Disorders: The Journal of Treatment and Prevention, 9*, 203–216.

The Children's Involvement Team, Sheffield City Council, Sheffield, United Kingdom. (2018).

Treasure, J., Smith, G., & Crane, A. (2017). *Skills-based learning for caring for a loved one with an eating disorder* (2nd ed.). Routledge. https://dx.doi.org/10.4324/9781315735610.

Vandereycken, W. (2006). Denial of illness in anorexia nervosa—a conceptual review: Part 2 different forms and meanings. *European Eating Disorders Review, 14*(5), 352–368. https://dx.doi.org/10.1002/erv.722.

8 Session 4: Anorexia Nervosa—A Disease of Disconnection—Introduction, Recovery Process, Motivational Interviewing Principles, and the Spiral of Change (Continued)

Mary Tantillo, Jennifer Sanftner McGraw, and Daniel Le Grange

Session 4 continues to focus on:

- The spiral, stages, and processes of change (Prochaska, Norcross, & DiClemente, 1994)
- Motivational Interviewing principles (Miller & Rollnick, 2013)
- Practice with being "different-in-connection"

Session 4 allows for more group discussion regarding these topics and ends with education regarding the continuum of care, team member roles, and local resources. The session begins with asking patients to take turns reporting back on how they connected with another person(s) between the previous and current groups. Any connection that promotes mutual trust, understanding, and empathy is considered. Some examples include calling or texting a friend, playing a board game with family members, watching a movie with a sibling, meeting a friend at a coffee shop, or attending a social event with a number of friends or family. Again, the therapists reinforce that this homework assignment helps patients practice strengthening current relationships or building new ones, both of which can bring in positive energy for recovery. Being in relationships where we feel increasingly able to be more connected with ourselves (i.e., our genuine thoughts, feelings, and needs) and others makes the relationship with AN less inviting and necessary.

If there was no time to complete the small and/or large group exercises from Session 3, Session 4 continues with their completion. Remind patients and families that during the ten minutes of small group work with one's own family unit, they need to discuss each person's idea of where the patient may be on the spiral of change with regard to AN behaviors. Also remind them that each person may have a different perspective about the patient's stage of

Session 4: Anorexia Nervosa   115

change, and that curiosity and a nonjudgmental attitude are important. The goal is to brainstorm responses, rather than critique one another, and to understand what each person thinks and the context for each other's beliefs. Being able to be "different-in-connection" is an ongoing group goal. We can better support the patient when we understand their perspective, even if it differs from that of other family members. Additionally, by hearing each other's responses, patients and family members are able to reflect on their beliefs and experiences and potentially modify these with feedback from others. The therapists remind members that none of us can "step outside of ourselves" and know clearly 100% of the time what is going on inside of us or between us and others. Having feedback from others can be helpful.

After the small group work, the large group reconvenes, and the therapists have each family share their experience of the exercise. Questions to raise include: "How did everyone experience this exercise? Was it challenging or easy? What was it like for folks?"

It is important to promote universality and connection in response to member feedback, normalizing how patients and families often experience similar things. In response to one family's responses, the therapists can ask, "I am wondering if others experienced something *similar or different?*" This response encourages members to join with others when there are similar experiences, while also giving them an opportunity to discuss different experiences. Again, this promotes the ability to be "different-in-connection" with one's family and the group.

Next, the therapists will ask patients and families to share what they discovered while discussing which stage of change the patient is in with regards to AN behaviors. Therapists should remind families that there may have been agreement or a difference of opinion. If there is hesitation in starting this discussion, the therapists can ask one of the patients to begin. Again, in response to what patients and families share, the therapists will normalize their responses and promote universality and connection and thank them for sharing. Each patient and family unit should respond during this exercise. Following is an example of how the therapist responded to a family where the patient's assessment of his stage of change was different from that of his parents. The therapist facilitates a discussion of their different ideas about the stage of change (fostering difference-in-connection) and also helps with identification of emotions that, if left unspoken, could impede their ability to collaborate in recovery.

Dan (20-year-old patient):	*Well, we had a difference of opinion about my stage of change. I think I am in Preparation for Change, and they think I am still in Contemplation.*
Therapist:	*Say more about that Dan. And then we can hear from your folks. I am glad you guys could be honest with one another about your difference of opinion. It would be tempting to stay quiet about the difference.*

Dan:	*Well, I have told other people, like my parents and a couple close friends, about my ED now. I am not keeping it a total secret like I used to. And I agreed to come to MFTG and agreed to see an individual therapist. I am making goals to try and stop the ED and am trying to eat more and not exercise. But they are saying that I am still not eating enough and that I am exercising too much. They feel that I am still not convinced about giving up the ED. (He is shaking his head while he talks.)*
Therapist:	*And, Dan, do you know what you are feeling as you share this with the group?*
Dan:	*I feel they don't believe me and my intentions.*
Therapist:	*Those are important thoughts. Can you also tell how you are feeling—in your heart? If you are not sure, I can pass the emotions list to you.*
Dan:	*I don't know (pausing and looking down for a few seconds), probably like annoyed.*
Therapist:	*The tone of your voice seems like you might be more than annoyed. But I could be wrong. Feelings occur on a continuum and anger runs from things like irritation and annoyance and aggravation to frustration, and onto anger, fury, and rage. Can you tell where you are on that continuum?*
Dan:	*Well maybe closer to frustrated.*
Therapist:	*Were you able to share that with your family?*
Dan:	*Well, not exactly that feeling, but I did tell them that I don't think they are understanding me and what is really going on sometimes.*
Therapist:	*Turning to Dan's parents. Did you folks know that Dan felt frustrated about the difference of opinion on his stage of change?*
Mom:	*I could guess at the frustration when hearing his tone of voice, but we did not talk specifically about that. I did not want to upset him. I am hearing what he says about his stage of change but also have observed behaviors that leave me thinking it is still very hard for him to let go of the eating disorder. Like maybe he still feels ambivalent.*
Dad:	*I tend to equate preparing for change with following through on goals. For example, Dan does try to eat more at meals but still has trouble getting in the nutrition he needs. I see him delay eating or miss meals or snacks some days. And he still goes on a run a couple times per week. He may still feel unsure about giving up the ED. I get that he is frustrated, but I am frustrated too because I want to help and am unsure what to do.*
Therapist:	*And mom are you feeling frustrated too? Or a different feeling?*

Mom:	*I am feeling a little frustrated at times but more anxious than frustrated. I want to do what is most helpful and am not sure of the best way to support Dan all the time.*
Therapist:	*So it is interesting how all of you are feeling some similar things. And of course, the ED likes this because it leaves everyone disconnected and not on the same page. Dan, we heard how the ED gets your folks feeling frustrated or anxious. Do you have a sense of what makes you feel most frustrated?*
Dan:	*I guess the biggest thing is that they don't seem to believe me and my intentions. They doubt me and my efforts. And they see only what they think I am not doing.*
Therapist:	*Yes, Dan, it can feel very frustrating and possibly deflating if we feel that others don't believe us and our efforts. I wonder if your folks believe in you, and at the same time, worry about the influence of the ED on your decisions.*
Mom:	*Yes, Dan, we believe and trust in you, but we don't trust the ED. It is difficult to know who we are talking with and who is in charge at times, you or the ED.*
Therapist:	*Dad would you agree with that?*
Dad:	*Yes, and I guess I tend to see where things are stuck versus what Dan is achieving. I want him to keep moving ahead and I am not sure how to make this happen at times. That is probably more about me than him.*
Therapist:	*It is hard to be a dad when you can't fix things for your child, no matter how old they are. And it is hard to be a mom when you can't protect your son from things that can hurt him.*
	Dan, is there anything you would like your folks to do differently to help you continue moving along the spiral of change? It does sound like you are making efforts to move toward action and you need continued support, especially when the ED starts tempting you to eat less or exercise more. We can be in preparation for action, experience a tough time, and dip into contemplation. And we can also get back on track and return to preparing for action and ultimately get to action.
Dan:	*It would help that if they feel stuck, they take a breath and not immediately assume I can't take care of myself. Maybe they can remember I am trying as best I can to take care of myself and ask me what they can do to help me meet the goals I set for myself, like getting back to college. This reminds me of what is most important and helps me refocus.*
Therapist:	*Mom and Dad, what do you think about this?*
Mom:	*I will try to calm my own anxiety when I feel the ED is in control and instead refocus Dan on what is important to him and try to work together to get back on track.*

Dad:	*I will try to do the same. It is challenging because I wish I could just make this go away. I am still trying to understand why all this is happening to him.*
Therapist:	*And Dan is probably feeling similarly at times, dad." I bet that Dan and his folks were not the only ones in the group who felt the way they did while doing the small group work. Let's keep going and see what others found when they discussed their loved one's stage of change.*

The vignette shows how a discussion about stage of change can reveal not only different ideas about patient progress in recovery but also unspoken feelings, meanings, and disconnections that can threaten development of the mutual trust, understanding, and empathy in relationships that are required to move ahead together in recovery. The therapist modeled the importance of obtaining information about everyone's emotions and thoughts regarding a point of tension or disconnection (i.e., the differing ideas about Dan's stage of change and the associated assumptions/feelings) and separated the illness from Dan. She validated the patient's and parents' feelings while inviting them to make a change (i.e., encouraging Dan to express his needs and encouraging his parents to consider supporting him in a different way). While a main goal in Session 4 is educating members about the stages of change, an overarching goal that continues throughout duration of MFTG is helping families to identify and repair disconnections obstructing continued recovery. The latter goal includes helping them name, modulate, and express emotions and practice relational skills that foster patient self-empathy, autonomy, and agency, as well as mutual connections with family members. We can become more genuinely and fully who we are when we are in mutual connections with others, and we can forge stronger mutual connections when we represent ourselves more authentically and fully in relationships. Box 8.1 outlines interventions the therapist can employ to process and repair disconnections in order to help patients and family members practice being "different-in connection" in R4R MFTG.

Box 8.1   Interventions to Process and Repair Disconnections and Practice Being "Different-In-Connection"

- Begin by obtaining the context of the disconnection from the patient and family members including the story line (content), meanings attached to the content (how the person is making sense of the content), and the associated feelings.

Session 4: Anorexia Nervosa 119

- Promote validation, universality, and self-disclosure by reinforcing that it is likely that a particular member or family unit is not the only one in the group who has experienced their particular disconnection.
- Be sure that group members are separating AN from the patient. (If the young adult is averse to this approach, be sure there is an understanding that AN can influence our perceptions and the feelings and meanings we attach to our experiences.)
- Reinforce how members' experiences may be the same or different in comparison to those of others. Explicitly ask, "Was your experience similar or different?" to normalize that there may be differences and encourage expression of differences in the face of anxiety or other strong emotions.
- If a member has trouble identifying what they feel, promote connection with self by helping them note the biological and behavioral cues of feeling states. For example, ask them where they feel it in their body and if they can connect it with behaviors they may be evidencing (e.g., a clenched jaw or shaking their leg). Another option is to distribute the emotions sheet with faces that represent a menu of feelings. Or the therapist can ask other members if they have a sense of what the member might be feeling. This intervention helps patients and families practice mutual empathy (with one another) and self-empathy (being able to identify, acknowledge, and accept one's own emotions). This work increases the experience of perceived mutuality in relationships.
- Once a member can recognize what emotion they are experiencing, help them identify where they are located on the continuum for that emotion, e.g., anger ranges from annoyance to rage.
- Reinforce that we can have two or more emotions or experiences at the same time, e.g., feeling love and anger or trusting one's young adult child but not AN.
- Promote mutual empathy by asking if the patient and family members knew how each of them was feeling about the disconnection. Help them share how they feel now, knowing what their loved one has been feeling. This work promotes a sense of perceived mutuality in relationships.
- Help members view events from their own and others' perspectives. If a patient or family member has difficulty with this work, again promote validation and universality by reinforcing that it is likely that a particular member or family unit is not the only one who has experienced their particular disconnection. Consider engaging other patients or family members and ask how they have felt in the identified situation. Because other patients and families can deliver or receive information with less defensiveness, they can often assist with expanding or deepening the understanding of an event.

- When asking others if they have experienced the disconnection discussed by another family unit, obtain their thoughts, feelings, and meanings associated with the disconnection. The therapist can ask other patients first for their perspective if a patient initiated the discussion of the disconnection or can ask other parents first if a parent initiated the discussion. It is important to foster an exchange of patient and family perspectives on disconnections. This intervention promotes being "different-in-connection" and helps members leverage differences to strengthen relationships and problem solve new ways to respond to one another. This work fosters new positive images of oneself in relationships with others (e.g., "I guess I am good enough in my relationship with my partner") and new positive relational patterns ("When I am angry, it is important to reach out to others and check out my assumptions.")
- If a family or the group is struggling to discuss a particular disconnection, the therapist can ask "Who likes it when patients and families are experiencing disconnection?" Of course, the answer is AN, and someone in the room usually knows the answer to this question. This question can rally group members to work together because the therapist externalizes the disconnection and blames AN for it. This approach helps members reconnect in the face of a "common enemy"—AN, and helps them self-disclose despite feeling tension, high anxiety, shame, or blame. The therapist reminds the group that "AN is trying to create disconnection right now in our group. It is trying to have its way with us, even here. We can work together to put a stop to this."
- Once the context (content, meanings, and feelings about a disconnection) are addressed, explore strategies to respond differently to one another in order to repair (and avoid reenacting) the identified disconnection. For example, this work can include practice in naming, modulating, and assertively expressing emotions. Often, new ways of responding to one another include empowering the patient (e.g., promoting autonomy through providing choices), using distraction, changing the environment, or taking a time out when emotions feel too intense and reframing situations (e.g., "My daughter is feeling overwhelmed and frightened right now (versus resistant) and this is why she is struggling with her meal." It is helpful to remind family members to reframe what might be experienced as "controlling" to what should be experienced as "caring." For example, when patients are highly anxious and tempted to use AN behaviors, gently remind them of the life goals and values they have shared and ask if AN is helping them live these out. Another strategy that parents and partners may find helpful is to practice quieting their own intense emotion first before interacting with their young adult. This work can involve reaching out to others for support and practicing mindfulness,

i.e., staying in the moment and observing and describing what one experiences but not negatively judging it.

- If patients have difficulty letting family members know more helpful alternative responses in the face of a particular disconnection, remind them that MFTG provides a unique opportunity to educate their family members. Reinforce that family members want to be supportive, and without feedback, they will unknowingly repeat what they consider to be supportive behaviors. Or ask the patients what they think will happen if "we" don't come up with alternative responses during a disconnection. There is usually at least one patient who will say that the same thing will keep happening. Tell the young adults this is an opportunity for them to consider and share responses that could be more useful. Additionally, normalize how AN may try to stop patients and families from problem-solving alternatives because it wants to stay connected to the patient.

- Throughout the processing of a disconnection, simultaneously validate patient and family member experiences, while asking them to consider making changes in how they relationally respond to one another. Patients and families can also be encouraged to continue processing disconnections explored in group in their own individual family work. R4R provides members with practice processing disconnections and being different-in-connection, so they can continue this work outside R4R.

- It is essential to explore feelings and meanings attached to situations before moving quickly into problem-solving alternative responses. As members grapple with the tension, anxiety, and other intense emotions involved with naming and discussing disconnections, it can be tempting to gloss over a full discussion of the context surrounding them. Members may want to jump immediately to problem solving what to do differently in order to prevent or repair a disconnection. Unspoken/unprocessed emotions and their associated negative relational images (e.g., "Whatever I say or do is not good enough for my father"); meanings ("This is because I am defective and dumb"); and feelings (unworthiness, inadequacy, and shame) can foster continued disconnection from self and others and obstruct relational repair. Instead, the therapist is working to make explicit what is implicit, promote patient and family member ability to stay connected in the face of difference (thoughts, feelings, and needs), and foster reconnection to self and others. In order to do this work, the R4R therapists must be mindful, remaining connected with their own thoughts and feelings and practice being at home with the anxiety and tension that occur during group and AN's attempts to derail and sabotage the group.

After exploring with each patient and family their observations related to patient stage of change, the therapists can ask if there are any other questions related to Motivational Interviewing principles or stages of change information shared during the previous and current sessions. The remaining time can be spent on describing the continuum and levels of care associated with treatment of AN. Patients and families have shared with us that they appreciate this information because it helps them think about treatment along a trajectory, as opposed to disconnected episodes of care. This continuous view of treatment and recovery reinforces the importance of sustaining connections with others during recovery and reminds everyone that recovery is a marathon, not a sprint. We also review the symptoms that are commonly associated with each level of care, as well as local resources within the continuum of care. We end Session 4 with a review of the roles of treatment team professionals (e.g., primary therapist, dietitian, primary care provider, psychiatrist, care manager, peer mentor, parent peer mentor; see Box 8.2) and the importance of working as a team to ensure continued recovery. The main goals, materials, and handouts for Session 4 are outlined in Box 8.3.

Box 8.2 Professional Treatment Team Member Roles

The treatment team is comprised of the patient, family, and professional treatment team members. Descriptions of professional treatment team roles follow.

Primary care provider: Primary care providers are commonly licensed physicians (e.g., MD or DO family practitioners, internists, pediatricians, adolescent medicine specialists, and obstetricians/gynecologists) or nurse practitioners who practice general medicine and oversee the medical treatment of the patient.

Psychiatrist: Psychiatrists are licensed physicians (MD or DO) who specialize in the evaluation, diagnosis, and treatment of mental disorders. Their medical and psychiatric training prepares them to treat adults individually, as part of a family unit, and/or in a group setting. Additional training in development and psychiatric conditions in youth prepares them to treat children and adolescents. Psychiatrists can prescribe medication or other biological treatments like ECT, if needed.

Psychologist: Psychologists are licensed mental health professional (PhD or PsyD) who specialize in the evaluation, diagnosis, and treatment of mental health conditions. Their training prepares them to treat adults and children either individually, as part of a family unit, and/or in a group setting. Psychologists are also trained to conduct and interpret tests evaluating mental abilities and interests, neuropsychological functioning, and personality.

Social worker, or licensed clinical social worker (LCSW): Social workers have bachelor's master's, or doctoral education. They are trained to consider the ecological/systems issues influencing patient and family functioning and often work with patients and families to develop and achieve long- and short-term treatment goals. Social workers identify resources and services, and provide direct services such as counseling, psychotherapy, and case management. Those with graduate education engage in evaluation, diagnosis, and treatment of mental disorders and conduct individual, group, and/or family therapy.

Marriage and family therapist: Marriage and family therapists provide evaluation, diagnosis, and treatment of mental disorders with a specialized focus on the family system. They may have received master's or doctoral education and may be the patient's (and family's) primary therapist or work closely with the patient's primary therapist to ensure comprehensive, continuous, and coordinated care. Marriage and family therapists focus not only on the individual patient but on the context and relationships in which the person participates, including the couple, family, school, work, social, community, and other relational systems.

Advanced practice psychiatric nurse: Psychiatric-Mental Health Advanced Practice Registered Nurses (APRN) are master's or doctoral-level prepared psychiatric nurses, specializing in mental health nursing. In the United States, these nurses may be clinical specialists (CNS) or nurse practitioners (NP). They specialize in the evaluation, diagnosis, and treatment of mental health disorders. Depending on their training, they may treat adults and/or children and adolescents individually, as a family, or in group settings. Nurse practitioners are able to prescribe and manage medications.

Registered dietitian: Registered dietitians (RD) have bachelor's, master's, or doctoral education that allows them to use principles from nutrition, biochemistry, physiology, food management, and behavioral and social sciences to foster health and wellness. RDs assess nutritional needs and food patterns, collaborate with medical providers to develop meal plans that meet nutritional needs, conduct individual or group nutritional counseling, and direct food preparation to meet nutritional needs.

Care manager: Care managers have bachelor's or master's degree education and demonstrate advanced knowledge of community resources. Care managers conduct outreach and advocacy and assist with service referral. They identify patients and families at risk in terms of their ability to engage and remain engaged in treatment and work with the treatment team to alleviate barriers. Care managers assist with smooth transition among levels of care, work with patients to identify rehabilitation goals, foster the development of community living skills, and promote a recovery-based treatment plan of support.

Life coach: Life coaches have associate's, bachelor's, or master's level education and life coaching certification and demonstrate advanced knowledge of life coaching for individuals with eating disorders. They assist individuals to identify needs, life goals (related to living, learning, working, and socializing), and values that influence achievement of full recovery and the ability to create a life in the community without illness. Life coaches help patients to meet needs and learn life skills through provision of group-based and individual services. They collaborate with the treatment team to facilitate patient transitions among levels of care and re-entry into community living.

Peer mentor: Peer mentors demonstrate advanced knowledge of educational and community resources in assisting individuals with eating disorders. They use their lived experience to help individuals with eating disorders identify and meet needs and goals for recovery and life and work with the treatment team to refer them to other community resources as needed. Peer Mentors may also assist siblings to identify needs and goals related to supporting their loved one with an eating disorder and work with the treatment team to refer them to other community resources. Peer Mentors also engage in advocacy and service referral in collaboration with the treatment team and assist with patient and family transitions among levels of care and re-entry to community living.

Parent Peer Mentor: Parent Peer Mentors demonstrate advanced knowledge of educational and community resources in assisting parents and other family members supporting individuals with eating disorders. They use their lived experience to help parents and other family members identify needs and goals related to supporting their loved one with an eating disorder. Parent peer mentors promote skill building related to mealtime coaching and other caregiving behaviors supportive of recovery. They also engage in advocacy and service referral in collaboration with the treatment team. They assist with patient and family transitions among levels of care and re-entry to community living.

Box 8.3 Session 4: Anorexia Nervosa—A Disease of Disconnection—Introduction, Recovery Process, Motivational Interviewing Principles, and the Spiral of Change (Continued)

Goals

Help patients and family members to:

* Participate in large group discussion of where patients are on the spiral of change.

Session 4: Anorexia Nervosa   125

- Continue discussion about spiral of change, Motivational Interviewing principles, and recovery process.
- Continue to help members practice being different-in-connection.
- Describe continuum and levels of care for AN, symptoms that indicate need for particular levels, available local help in the continuum of care, roles of treatment team professionals, importance of team work, and idea that recovery is a marathon, not a sprint.

Materials

None

Handouts

- Continuum of Care for Eating Disorders
- The Eating Disorder Multidisciplinary Treatment Team and Roles of Treatment Team Professionals
- Local Treatment Resources and Community Supports

References

*No DOI

*Miller, W. R., & Rollnick, S. (2013). *Motivational interviewing: Helping people change* (3rd ed.). The Guilford Press.
*Prochaska, J. O., Norcross, J. C., & DiClemente, C. C. (1994). *Changing for good: A revolutionary six-stage program for overcoming bad habits and moving your life positively forward.* William Morrow.

9 Session 5: Biopsychosocial Factors for Anorexia Nervosa and Co-morbidity

Mary Tantillo, Jennifer Sanftner McGraw, and Daniel Le Grange

The aims of Session 5 include:

- Identify biopsychosocial factors related to development and maintenance of eating disorders (ED)
- Relationally reframe these factors into *intrapersonal* (e.g., not accurately perceiving internal states) and *interpersonal* (e.g., avoiding intense emotion and conflict, self-silencing) *processes of disconnection* related to AN and how they can contribute to *interpersonal disconnections with loved ones (see Chapters 1 and 3 and 5–6)*
- Begin to discuss how interpersonal disconnections can decrease perceived mutuality needed for recovery and how the eating disorder capitalizes on disconnections by creating, amplifying and perpetuating them
- Discuss the connection between AN and other co-morbid conditions and behaviors such as anxiety, depression, addictions, and self-harm (e.g., cutting).

Session 5 begins with the weekly review of strategies for connection patients used since the last group. The therapists then provide psychoeducation about biopsychosocial factors and relationally reframe these factors. The R4R therapists can begin by reviewing how the individual with AN experiences interplaying *internal processes of disconnection* that contribute to *interpersonal disconnections with loved ones*. The two main kinds of internal processes of disconnection include *intrapersonal and interpersonal processes of disconnection*. *Intrapersonal processes* of disconnection involve a series of activities (biological and psychological) that create disconnection from the self or body. They disrupt growth and development of a clear and integrated sense of self and obstruct the patient from accurately sensing and effectively processing thoughts, feelings and information from internal organs. They can make it more challenging for the patient to embrace, tolerate, and regulate what they experience internally and externally in the environment (Gratz & Roemer, 2004; Miller & Stiver, 1997; Schore, 1994). Thus, intrapersonal processes of disconnection can adversely influence the ability to be connected with one's authentic self and body (Siegel, 2012; Tantillo, Sanftner, & Hauenstein, 2013; Winnicott, 1965). (See Table 9.1 for examples of intrapersonal processes of disconnection. The R4R therapist may also distribute this table to patients and families in the group.)

Session 5: Biopsychosocial Factors 127

The patient also experiences *interpersonal processes of disconnection* comprised of a series of activities (affective [involving feelings and emotions] and behavioral) occurring between individuals in relationship that obstruct development of a strong and intimate bond with others and a sense of perceived mutuality (i.e., mutual empathy, trust and understanding) (Genero, Miller, Surrey, & Baldwin, 1992; Jordan, 2018; Miller & Stiver, 1997). These processes can also affect development of identity, self-worth and self-efficacy because they can prevent patients from engaging with others who could provide positive reflected appraisals, validation, and positive reinforcement (Sullivan, 1953; Tantillo, Sanftner, & Hauenstein, 2013). (See Table 9.2 for interpersonal processes of disconnection.)

R4R therapists can remind group members that *intra- and interpersonal processes of disconnection* interplay with one another because our embodied self grows within the context of connections with others (Bowlby, 1969; Chodorow, 1978; Miller & Stiver, 1997). Their interplay can contribute to *interpersonal disconnections* (e.g., relational misalignments or mismatches and

Table 9.1 Phenomena Involving Intrapersonal Processes of Disconnection

Alexithymia (difficulties identifying and describing feelings)
Poor interoceptive awareness (difficulties accurately sensing internal bodily states)
Dysfunction or "disconnection" of neural networks converging upon the insula (disrupting synthesis of external sensory information with visceral, affective and cognitive information)
Weak central coherence (ability to focus on details but difficulty seeing the big picture)
Cognitive rigidity (difficulty thinking about things in a different way)
Difficulties reading others' facial expressions
Anxiety, Harm Avoidance, Inhibition (Difficulty with uncertainty, ambiguity and unpredictability and discomfort with new or surprising experiences)
Numbing effects of starvation

Note
See Chapters 1, 3, 5 6 and Tantillo, Sanftner, & Hauenstein (2013) for more information on definition and description of intra- and interpersonal processes of disconnection and resulting interpersonal disconnections.

Table 9.2 Phenomena Involving Interpersonal Processes of Disconnection

Conflict avoidance
Avoidance of intense emotions
Self-silencing
Isolation in the face of intense emotion or conflict
Minimizing or denying one's feelings and needs
Self-comparison with perception that one is "less than" others
Not seeking clarification regarding interactions or intentions of others
Assuming others expect perfection

Note
See Chapters 1, 3, 5 6 and Tantillo, Sanftner, & Hauenstein (2013) for more information on definition and description of intra- and interpersonal processes of disconnection and resulting interpersonal disconnections.

128   *Mary Tantillo, Jennifer Sanftner McGraw, and Daniel Le Grange*

Table 9.3 Interpersonal Disconnections with Close Others

Focus on detail at the expense of seeing the whole situation
Overprotectiveness and not allowing for increased autonomy
Pseudomutuality with conflict avoidance (everything "looks OK" but it really is not
  ("walking on eggshells")
Criticism
Invalidation
Inability to compromise
Hostile interactions/Blaming
Shaming/Invoking Guilt

Note
See Chapters 1, 3, 5–6 and Tantillo, Sanftner, & Hauenstein (2013) for more information on definition and description of intra- and interpersonal processes of disconnection and resulting interpersonal disconnections.

misunderstandings) especially when close others experience distress and a high caregiving burden. (See Table 9.3 for examples of interpersonal disconnections with close others). Patients may respond to interpersonal disconnections with family and friends by engaging in AN symptoms to cope with these disconnections and the associated intense emotions. In R4R, AN is seen as a *"disease of disconnection"* because it is characterized by the above internal and interpersonal disconnections that can unwittingly perpetuate illness. The goal in R4R is to foster connection with self, the body and others to foster recovery and reclaim wellness and one's life (Tantillo, McGraw, Hauenstein, & Groth, 2015; Tantillo, Sanftner, & Hauenstein, 2013).

The R4R therapists can present the following typical example of *internal* (intrapersonal and interpersonal processes of) disconnections associated with AN and how they culminate in an *interpersonal disconnection* between a young adult and her partner:

Jane:	*(She is calling to her husband from upstairs.) I am almost ready to meet Nancy and Tom (close friends) for dinner.*
Doug (Jane's partner):	*Oh, I forgot to tell you, Nancy called while you were in the shower. They said that the Pine Inn (restaurant) is closing early today for renovations and suggested we go to the other restaurant across the street, Elm Place.*
Jane:	*silence*
Doug:	*Jane, did you hear me?*
Jane:	*Uhm, yeah.*
Doug:	*Is anything wrong with that? We have been trying to meet with them for months now.*
Jane:	*Uhm. (pause) No, it's fine.*
Doug:	*OK, how much longer will you be?*
Jane:	*Ten more minutes.*
Doug:	*(Thirty minutes later). Jane, you said you would be ready in 10 minutes and it's been 30 minutes now. We need to get in the car or we are going to be super late.*

Session 5: Biopsychosocial Factors   129

Jane:	*I am coming now. She walks past him and into the garage to get in the car.*
Doug:	*(A little later while driving). You are being really quiet. We have been driving for 20 minutes and you have not said a thing.*
Jane:	*I am just thinking.*
Doug:	*About what?*
Jane:	*Nothing big.*
Doug:	*OK, then. (With a tone that does not sound convinced, but he does not want to pry.)*
Jane:	*Maybe we should have cancelled for tonight, since the restaurant we wanted to go to is closed.*
Doug:	*What do you mean? We have been looking forward to seeing Nancy and Tom for months now. It's more about seeing them than the restaurant anyway.*
Jane:	*Yeah, but I am not even sure what they serve at the other restaurant. They may not have a good selection (her voice is sounding more stressed).*
Doug:	*I don't understand why you are getting so worked up about going to the other restaurant. You are being so rigid about this.*
Jane:	*I am being rigid? How can you say that? I am in the car and we are going, even though I am not sure it is the best idea (sounding irritated now).*
Doug:	*Silent*
Jane:	*Now you are not talking with me, and you are mad at me. I don't want to go on this date if you aren't going to talk with me.*
Doug:	*You know what, maybe we should just turn around and go home. This is not going in the right direction.*
Jane:	*Fine! Go home! You don't understand what I am going through and it seems like you don't care.*
Doug:	*You can call Nancy and tell her we are not going. I am turning around and going home. This is not working. I am so tired of these arguments. You don't talk with me about what is going on inside, and when you do, it's about me not understanding you and not caring. I'm done.*
Jane:	*Tearful, hurt, angry and sitting silently as they drive back home.*
Doug:	*(Entering the house and walking through the kitchen.) Do you want me to get a frozen dinner out of the freezer? I am making one for myself.*
Jane:	*Silent and walks by him and up the stairs to her room.*
Doug:	*You are not eating anything?*
Jane:	*No (and slams the door of their bedroom).*

In this vignette, Jane is likely highly anxious about going to a different restaurant. Her lack of knowledge about the menu at the other restaurant is probably a significant stressor and so is the general sense of uncertainty, unpredictability and lack of control she experiences with this change. However, she was having difficulty clearly identifying what she was feeling and expressing this to Doug (*intrapersonal process of disconnection*). Doug did try to clarify if there was anything wrong, but she could not respond in the moment. She also used avoidance (taking more time to get ready), self-silencing, and minimizing her experience (*all interpersonal processes of disconnection*) in the house and/or in the car when asked if anything was wrong. The interplay of these processes of disconnection likely continued to heighten Jane's anxiety. Eventually, Doug, feeling thwarted in his initial efforts to get her to talk, says she is being rigid and is feeling more exasperated because he does not understand why she can't be more flexible. The couple is now experiencing an *interpersonal disconnection* and the eating disorder capitalizes on this, fueling Jane's anger and hurt, inviting her to focus on Doug's lack of understanding and caring for her. She is not necessarily aware that the eating disorder is also helping her avoid going to a new restaurant and her feelings about this. Doug, feeling increasingly upset about the conflict, chooses to avoid any further potential tension and returns home. He tries to calm down and invites her to eat something, but the eating disorder has the upper hand because Jane feels overwhelmed by the intense emotions bubbling inside and tries to mute them by isolating herself and not eating dinner.

Relationally Reframe Biopsychosocial Factors that Promote and/or Perpetuate AN

After providing the example of how the eating disorder perpetuates itself by maintaining internal and interpersonal disconnections, the therapists can proceed with Powerpoint slides regarding the biopsychosocial factors that contribute to development and maintenance of AN. (The reader may construct their own slides based on information presented in this chapter. For a review of Session 5 PowerPoint slides used in R4R, please contact the first author MT.) They relationally reframe the factors by asking members to consider how these factors promote disconnection from self, the body, and others. The R4R therapists can also show members the posters of the Circles of Disconnection (See Chapters 5) to visually remind group members about the types of disconnection that can occur in recovery and how AN tries to create and/or maintain these disconnections to obstruct perceived mutuality in relationships. The poster showing the Venn Diagram of mutual connections can be shown (See Chapter 5) to illustrate how healthy relationships in recovery honor each unique person (with their different perspectives, feelings and needs), as well as the "we" in relationships, thus, allowing for continued growth in connection.

It will be impossible to comprehensively review all biopsychosocial factors that potentially contribute to development and maintenance of AN, but the following can be highlighted as examples:

Session 5: Biopsychosocial Factors 131

- Genetic vulnerability
- Neurochemical alterations: alterations with serotonin and dopamine
- Neurobiological alteration: insular dysfunction
- Temperament (anxiety, obsessionality, perfectionism, inhibition, avoidance, compulsiveness and impulsiveness)
- Poor interoceptive awareness and alexithymia
- Cognitive rigidity (all or nothing thinking and difficulties shifting set)
- Detail focus at the expense of the big picture
- Biological impact of starvation on the brain (findings from the Keys Study, 1950)
- Interpersonal disconnections created by AN and adverse impact on perceived mutuality
- Socio-cultural influences that socialize us to value ourselves from the outside in (versus inside out) and equate thinness with success, beauty and control

Since those conducting R4R should have already received eating disorder specialty-training and had experience treating patients with AN, they should be familiar with the biopsychosocial factors contributing to etiology and perpetuation of AN. R4R therapists may desire to review articles and book chapters that comprehensively review biopsychosocial factors (e.g., Culbert, Racine, & Klump, 2015; Kaye, Fudge & Paulus, 2009; Maine, Bunnell, & McGilley, 2010; Munro, Randall, & Lawrie, 2017; Rose & Frampton, 2011; Strober & Johnson, 2012) before conducting Session 5.

While reviewing information on the biopsychosocial factors, the therapists reinforce that no one factor guarantees an ED. Even having genetic vulnerability in itself does not guarantee someone will have AN. Instead, it is important to convey that AN is multidetermined and multidimensional. The therapists note that many biopsychosocial factors interact together to create AN. It is like several rivers that run from different directions and eventually join together to create a large lake. AN occurs from the interaction of vulnerable genes and environmental stressors. The stressors turn on vulnerable genes. This is the traditional way to think about gene and environment interaction (Klump, Suisman, Burt, McGue, & Iacono, 2009; Thornton, Mazzeo, & Bulik, 2011; Trace, Baker, Peñas-Lledó, & Bulik, 2013).

The therapists can also provide brief information on how the environment can *epigenetically* influence genes (Strober, Peris, & Steiger, 2014). In this scenario the gene itself does not change (DNA sequence remains the same), but its *expression* is affected by the epigenome. The epigenome is comprised of many chemicals and proteins that tell our genes what to do. If the epigenome provides our genes different instructions, then they will express themselves differently. For example, lifestyle and environmental factors such as stress could affect the epigenome. Changes in the epigenome can, for example, affect the methyl groups (groupings of carbon and hydrogen atoms) on a gene. Methyl groups turn genes on or off by affecting interactions between DNA and other proteins, potentially leading to certain health problems and symptoms. Epigenetic changes may also be passed on to subsequent generations. (See https://www.genome.gov/about-genomics/fact-sheets/Epigenomics-Fact-Sheet and Strober, Peris, & Steiger, 2014 for more information). This means that even if someone did not have genetic vulnerability to AN, there is a chance AN could develop in the face of an environmental stressor like trauma. The trauma can change the expression of an individual's genes, contributing to development of AN (Hill, 2017; Strober, Peris, & Steiger, 2014; Toyokawa, Uddin, Koenen, & Galea, 2012).

The therapists can also share that since a person may epigenetically develop an eating disorder due to adverse environmental conditions, the opposite could also be true. For example, social support and perceived mutuality, which are positive environmental conditions, can also exert influence on genes. Interpersonal relationships are a main source of experience that shape gene expression within the brain, as well as ongoing brain function during our lifetime (Siegel, 2012; Tantillo, Sanftner, & Hauenstein, 2013). They heavily influence the brain because the circuits responsible for social perception are the same as or are tightly linked to circuits that integrate the important functions controlling the creation of meaning, regulation of bodily and emotional states, organization of memory, and capacity for interpersonal communication (Schore, 1994; Siegel, 2012). Therefore, helping young adults and family members identify and repair disconnections and strengthen mutual connections can potentially exert a positive influence on gene expression that may ultimately improve ability to process and respond to internal and external information. Further research is needed in this area (Sherman, Cheng, Fingeman, & Schnyer, 2016; Strober & Johnson, 2012; Tantillo, Sanftner, & Hauenstein, 2013).

Review Comorbid Conditions Accompanying AN

Session 5 ends with a brief discussion about the association between AN and other comorbid conditions and behaviors including anxiety, depression, substance use disorders, personality disorders, and self-harm (e.g., cutting) (APA, 2013; Woodside & Staab, 2006). While a comprehensive discussion of each of these comorbid illnesses is unnecessary for Session 5, it is helpful for family members to know that patients often experience them. R4R therapists can reinforce that anxious temperament commonly exists before the onset of AN and that approximately half of patients may experience anxiety disorders including generalized anxiety, social phobia, and/or panic attacks (Ulfvebrand, Birgegard, Norring, Högdahl, & van Hausswolff-Juhlin, 2015). They may also experience obsessive-compulsive disorder, as well as obsessive-compulsive personality disorder. Cluster C personality disorders are more common with AN restricting type and impulsive personality features are more commonly associated with bulimic symptoms (Diaz- Marssá, Carrasco, & Sáiz, 2000444). For example, borderline personality is the most common personality disorder in binge-eating/purging type anorexia nervosa (Sansone, Levitt, & Sansone, 2005). Additionally, some individuals with AN may suffer from post-traumatic stress disorder (PTSD) (APA, 2013; Reyes-Rodriguez et al., 2011; Woodside & Staab, 2006).

Session 5: Biopsychosocial Factors   133

R4R therapists can discuss how depression may have existed before AN but can also occur after onset of AN. Thirty-three to 50% of individuals with AN have a comorbid mood disorder such as depression (Ulfvebrand, Birgegard, Norring, Högdahl, & van Hausswolff-Juhlin, 2015). The starvation and isolation that accompany AN can contribute to low self-esteem, depressed mood and suicidal ideation. Twenty percent of individuals with AN die due to suicide (Arcelus, Mitchell, Wales, & Nielsen, 2011; Bulik et al., 2008; Franko, Keshaviah, Eddy, Krishna, Davis, Keep, & Herzog, 2013). Depression can complicate recovery from AN and AN can obstruct treatment for depression.

R4R therapists can also note that substance use disorders and eating disorders share some of the same biopsychosocial factors that contribute to etiology and illness maintenance (Harrop & Marlatt, 2010). Similar to eating disorders, substance use disorders can create and maintain many internal and interpersonal disconnections for an individual. Both illnesses can serve similar purposes, e.g., emotion regulation, coping, and providing a sense of connection (Covington & Surrey, 2000). Individuals with a lifetime diagnosis of both AN and Bulimia Nervosa and those who experience bulimic behaviors demonstrate more alcohol abuse/dependence and drug abuse/dependence than individuals who engage only in restricting behaviors (Root, Pisetsky, Thornton, Lichtenstein, Pedersen, & Bulik, 2010). Those struggling with substance use disorders and AN are at increased risk for physical and mental health conditions, as well as a higher risk of suicide (Bulik et al., 2004).

R4R therapists can also note that patients with AN may experience self-harm (Favaro & Santonastaso, 2000; Koutek, Kocourkova, & Dudova, 2016). Self-harm, similar to eating disorder behaviors, may be compulsive or impulsive in nature (Favaro & Santonastaso, 2000) and may serve purposes such as emotion regulation, distress tolerance, and self-punishment (Linehan, 2015). Self-harm can maintain disconnections from the authentic self, the body and/or others and may be used to cope with PTSD (Banks, 2006; Dixon-Gordon, Tull, & Gratz, 2014; Kress, Haiyasoso, Zoldan, & Headley, 2018). The main goals, materials and handouts for Session 5 are outlined in Box 9.1.

Box 9.1   Session 5: Biopsychosocial factors for Anorexia Nervosa & Co-morbidity

Goals:

Help patients and family members to:

- Identify biopsychosocial factors related to development and maintenance of eating disorders.
- Discuss the *intra- and interpersonal* processes of disconnection related to AN (e.g., not accurately perceiving internal states, inaccurate

134 *Mary Tantillo, Jennifer Sanftner McGraw, and Daniel Le Grange*

information processing, avoiding intense emotion and conflict, self-silencing, etc.) and how they can complicate interpersonal communication and contribute to *interpersonal disconnections.*

- Begin to discuss how interpersonal disconnections can decrease perceived mutuality and how the eating disorder capitalizes on disconnections (creating, amplifying and perpetuating them).
- Discuss the connection between AN and other comorbid conditions and behaviors such as anxiety, depression, substance use disorders, and self-harm (e.g., cutting).

Materials

- Large poster size circles and Venn Diagram showing Disconnections and Mutual Connection.
- Powerpoint slides on biopsychosocial factors contributing to development and maintenance of AN.

Handouts

- FEAST Handout about Puzzling Symptoms: Eating Disorders and the Brain: Refer patients and family members to: https://simplebooklet.com/neuroguide#page=0
- Examples of Intra- and Interpersonal Processes of Disconnection and Resulting Interpersonal Disconnections with Close Others

References

*No DOI

Arcelus, J., Mitchell, A. J., Wales, J., & Nielsen, S. (2011). Mortality rates in patients with anorexia nervosa and other eating disorders: A meta-analysis of 36 studies. *Archives of General Psychiatry, 68*(7), 724–731. http://dx.doi.org./10.1001/archgenpsychiatry.2011.74.

American Psychiatric Association (2013). *Diagnostic and statistical manual of mental disorders* (3rd ed.). Author.

Bowlby, J. (1969). *Attachment and loss: Vol. 1: Attachment.* Basic Books.

Banks, A. (2006). Relational therapy for trauma. *Journal of Trauma Practice, 5,* 25–47. https://dx.doi.org/10.1300/J189v05n01_03.

Bulik, C. M., Klump, K. L., Thornton, L., Kaplan, A. S., Devlin, B., Fichter, M. M., Halmi, K. A., Strober, M., Woodside, B., Crow, S., Mitchell, J. E., Rotondo, A., Mauri, M., Cassano, G. B., Keel, P. K., Berrettini, W., Kaye, W. H. (2004). Alcohol use disorder comorbidity in eating disorders: A multicenter study. *Journal of Clinical Psychiatry, 65*(7), 1000–1006. https://dx.doi.org/10.4088/JCP.v65n0718.

Session 5: Biopsychosocial Factors   135

Bulik, C. M., Thornton, L., Pinhiero, A. P., Plotnicov, K., Klump, K. L., Brandt, H., Crawford, S., Fichter, M. M., Halmi, K. A., Johnson, C., Kaplan, A., Mitchell, J. E., Nutzinger, D., Strober, M., Treasure, J., Woodside, B., Berrettini, W. H., & Kaye, W. H. (2008). Suicide attempts in anorexia nervosa. *Psychosomatic Medicine, 70*(3), 378–383. https://dx.doi.org/10.1097/PSY.0b013e3181646765.

Chodorow, N. (1978). *The reproduction of mothering*. University of California Press.

Covington, S., & Surrey, J. (2000). The relational model of women's psychological development: Implications for substance use. *Work in Progress (#91)*. Wellesley Centers for Women.

Culbert, K. M., Racine, S. E., & Klump, K. L. (2015). Research review: What we have learned about the causes of eating disorders – a synthesis of sociocultural, psychological, and biological research. *Journal of Child Psychology and Psychiatry, 56*(11), 1141–1164. https://dx.doi.org/10.1111/jcpp.12441.

Diaz-Marssá, M., Carrasco, J. L., & Sáiz, J. (2000). A study of temperament and personality in anorexia and bulimia nervosa. *Journal of Personality Disorders, 14*(4), 352–359. https://dx.doi.org/10.1521/pedi.2000.14.4.352.

Dixon-Gordon, K. L., Tull, M. T., & Gratz, K. M. (2014). Self-injurious behaviors in posttraumatic stress disorder: An examination of potential moderators. *Journal of Affective Disorders, 166*, 359–367. https://dx.doi.org/10.1016/j.jad.2014.05.033.

Favaro, A., & Santonastaso, P. (2000). Self-injurious behavior in anorexia nervosa. *Nervous and Mental Disease, 188*(8), 537–542. https://dx.doi.org/10.1097/00005053-200008000-00010.

Franko, D. L., Keshaviah, A., Eddy, K. T., Krishna, M., Davis, M. C., Keel, P. K., & Herzog, D. B. (2013). A longitudinal investigation of mortality in anorexia nervosa and bulimia nervosa. *American Journal of Psychiatry, 170*(8), 917–925. https://dx.doi.org/10.1176/appi.ajp.2013.12070868.

Genero, N. P., Miller, J. B., Surrey, J., & Baldwin, L. M. (1992). Measuring perceived mutuality in close relationships: Validation of the Mutual Psychological Development Questionnaire. *Journal of Family Psychology, 6*, 36–48. https://dx.doi.org/10.1037/0893-3200.6.1.36.

Gratz, K. L., & Roemer, L. (2004). Multidimensional assessment of emotion regulation and dysregulation: Development, factor structure, and initial validation of the Difficulties in Emotion Regulation Scale. *Journal of Psychopathology & Behavioral Assessment, 26*(1), 41–54. https://dx.doi.org/10.1023/B:JOBA.0000007455.08539.94.

Harrop, E. N., & Marlatt, G. A. (2010). The comorbidity of substance use disorders and eating disorders in women: Prevalence, etiology, and treatment. *Addictive Behaviors, 35*(5), 392–398. https://dx.doi.org/10.1016/j.addbeh.2009.12.016.

Hill, L. (2017). A brain-based approach to eating disorder treatment: A temperament-based therapy with supports (TBT-S). *The Center for Balanced Living*. https://www.brainbasedeatingdisorders.org/etext.

Jordan, J. (2018). *Relational-cultural therapy* (2nd ed). American Psychological Association. https://dx.doi.org/10.1037/0000063-001.

Kaye, W. H., Fudge, J. L., & Paulus, M. (2009). New insights into symptoms and neurocircuit function of anorexia nervosa. *Nature Reviews Neuroscience, 10*(8), 573–584. https://dx.doi.org/10.1038/nrn2682.

Keys, A., Brozek, J., Henschel, A., Mickelsen, O., & Taylor, H. L. (1950). *The biology of human starvation*. University of Minnesota Press.

Klump, K., Suisman, J. L., Burt, A., McGue, M., & Iacono, W. G. (2009). Genetic and environmental influences on disordered eating: An adoption study. *Journal of Abnormal Psychology*, *118*(4), 797–805. https://dx.doi.org/10.1037/a0017204.

Koutek, J., Kocourkova, J., & Dudova, I. (2016). Suicidal behavior and self-harm in girls with eating disorders. *Neuropsychiatric Disease and Treatment*, *11*(2), 787–793. https://dx.doi.org/10.2147/NDT.S103015.

Kress, V. E., Haiyasoso, M., Zoldan, C. A., Headley, J. A., & Trepal, H. (2018). The use of relational-cultural theory in counseling clients who have traumatic stress disorders. *Journal of Counseling & Development*, *96*(1), 106–114. https://dx.doi.org/10.1002/jcad.12182.

*Linehan, M. M. (2015). *DBT skills training manual* (2nd ed.). The Guilford Press.

*Maine, M., Bunnel, D., & McGilley, B. (2010). *Treatment of eating disorders: Bridging the gap between research and practice*. Elsevier.

*Miller, J. B., & Stiver, I. P. (1997). *The healing connection: How women form relationships in therapy and in life*. Beacon Press.

Munro, C., Randell, L., & Lawrie, S. M. (2017). An integrative bio-psycho-social theory of anorexia nervosa. *Clinical Psychology and Psychotherapy*, *24*(1), 1–21. https://dx.doi.org/10.1002/cpp.2047.

Reyes-Rodriguez, M. L., Von Holle, A., Ulman, T. F., Thornton, L. M., Klump, K. L., Brandt, H., Crawford, S., FIchter, M. M., Halmi, K. A., Huber, T., Johnson, C., Jones, I., Kaplan, A. S., Mitchell, J. E., Strober, M., Treasure, T., Woodside, D. B., Berrettini, W. H., Kaye, W. H., & Bulik, C. M. (2011). Posttraumatic stress disorder in anorexia nervosa. *Psychosomatic Medicine*, *73*(6), 491–497. https://dx.doi.org/10.1097/PSY.0b013e31822232bb.

Root, T. L., Pisetsky, E. M., Thornton, L., Lichtenstein, P., Pedersen, J. L., & Bulik, C. M. (2010). Patterns of co-morbidity of eating disorders and substance use in Swedish families. *Psychological Medicine*, *40*(1), 105–115. https://dx.doi.org/10.1017/S0033291709005662.

Rose, M., & Frampton, I. (2011). Conceptual models. In B. Lask & I. Frampton (Eds.), *Eating disorders and the brain*. John Wiley & Sons, Ltd. https://dx.doi.org/10.1002/9781119998402.ch7.

Sansone, R. A., Levitt, J. L., & Sansone, L. A. (2005). The prevalence of personality disorders among those with eating disorders. *Eating Disorders: The Journal of Treatment and Prevention*, *13*(1), 7–12. https://dx.doi.org/10.1080/10640260590893593.

Schore, A. N. (1994). *Affect regulation and the origins of self: The neurobiology of emotional development*. Lawrence Erlbaum Associates, Inc. https://dx.doi.org/10.4324/9781315680019.

Sherman, S. M., Cheng, Y. P., Fingerman, K. L., & Schnyer, D. M. (2016). Social support, stress and the aging brain. *Social Cognitive and Affective Neuroscience*, *11*(7), 1050–1058. https://dx.doi.org/10.1093/scan/nsv071.

*Siegel, D. (2012). *The developing mind: How relationships and the brain interact to shape who we are*. The Guilford Press.

Strober, M., & Johnson, C. (2012). The need for complex ideas in anorexia nervosa: Why biology, environment, and psyche all matter, why therapists make mistakes, and why clinical benchmarks are needed for managing weight correction. *International Journal of Eating Disorders*, *45*(2), 155–178. https://dx.doi.org/10.1002/eat.22005.

Strober, M., Peris, T., & Steiger, H. (2014). The plasticity of development: How knowledge of epigenetics may advance understanding of eating disorders. *International Journal of Eating Disorders*, *47*(7), 696–704. https://dx.doi.org/10.1002/eat.22322.

*Sullivan, H. S. (1953). *The interpersonal theory of psychiatry.* New York: Norton.

Tantillo, M., Sanftner, J. L., & Hauenstien, E. (2013). Restoring connection in the face of disconnection: An integrative approach to understanding and treating anorexia nervosa. *Advances in Eating Disorders: Theory, Research, and Practice, 1,* 21–38. https://dx.doi.org/10.1080/21662630.2013.742980.

Thornton, L. M., Mazzeo, S. E., & Bulik, C. M. (2011). The heritability of eating disorders: methods and current findings. *Current Topics in Behavioral Neuroscience, 6,* 141–156. https://dx.doi.org/10.1007/7854_2010_91.

Toyokawa, S., Uddin, M., Koenen, K. C., & Galea, S. (2012). How does the social environment 'get into the mind?' Epigenetics at the intersection of social and psychiatric epidemiology. *Social Science and Medicine, 74*(1), 67–74. https://dx.doi.org/10.1016/j.socscimed.2011.09.036.

Trace, S. E., Baker, J. H., Peñas-Lledó, E., & Bulik, C. M. (2013). The genetics of eating disorders. *Annual Review of Clinical Psychology, 9,* 589–620. https://dx.doi.org/10.1146/annurev-clinpsy-050212-185546.

Ulfvebrand, S., Birgegard, A., Norring, C., Högdahl, L., & von Hausswolff-Juhlin, Y. (2015). Psychiatric comorbidity in women and men with eating disorders: Results from a large clinical database. *Psychiatric Research, 230*(2), 294–299. https://dx.doi.org/10.1016/j.psychres.2015.09.008.

*Winnicott, D. W. (1965). *The maturational processes and the facilitating environment: Studies in the theory of emotional development.* Hogarth Press.

Woodside, B. D., & Staab, R. (2006). Management of psychiatric comorbidity in anorexia nervosa and bulimia nervosa. *CNS Drugs, 20*(8), 655–663. https://dx.doi.org/10.2165/00023210-200620080-00004.

10 Session 6: Biopsychosocial Factors (Continued), Disconnection and Functional Analysis Skills

Mary Tantillo, Jennifer Sanftner McGraw, and Daniel Le Grange

During Session 6 the R4R therapists continue to discuss the relational factors that contribute to development and maintenance of and recovery from AN. Specifically, the aims of Session 6 are:

- Discuss how the interplay between internal disconnections, negative relational images and meanings, and caregiver stress can contribute to interpersonal disconnections and unwittingly perpetuate AN.
- Describe how relational images and meanings become the unconscious interpersonal blueprint for future relational patterns, thus enabling or fortifying the patient from AN.
- Discuss the importance of examining and altering relational images and meanings; improving emotional and relational processing skills; and understanding the meanings, purposes, and functions of AN as strategies to increase perceived mutuality and strengthen connections with self and others.
- Emphasize that PM promotes our ability to be different-in-connection, decreases AN's attempts to use our differences to increase disconnection from ourselves and others, and maximizes repair of disconnections.
- Introduce functional analysis to improve understanding of triggers, relational patterns, and functions of AN.

Session 6 begins with the weekly review of strategies for connection that patients have used since the previous group. Next, picking up from the last group, the R4R therapists emphasize again how the interplay of internal disconnections (refer to examples from Tables 9.1 and 9.2) contribute to interpersonal disconnections (see Table 9.3). They reinforce how interpersonal disconnections can also emerge from and contribute to negative relational images (i.e., [often unconscious] mental representations of the self in relationship with others) and meanings (i.e., how we make sense of the image). An example of a negative relational image and meanings and the resulting disconnections, which can be used as a handout and reviewed with group members, is described in Box 10.1.

Session 6: Biopsychosocial Factors   139

Box 10.1   Negative Relational Image and Meaning

Negative relational image: "When I talk to my mom, she doesn't hear me."

Negative relational meanings: "This is because I must be unlovable, unimportant, or wrong."

Resulting disconnections: In the face of the emotional pain related to this negative relational image and meanings, the person with AN experiences more AN thoughts and behaviors (i.e., engages in restriction and/or purging or exercise to mute or numb emotions). Additional disconnections that can follow this relational image and associated meanings can include self-silencing, minimizing one's needs, isolation, and other phenomena involving interpersonal processes of disconnection outlined in Chapter 9, Table 9.2. The interplay of the negative relational image and meanings and internal disconnections can contribute to interpersonal disconnections with loved ones (see Table 9.3 for examples), because they are not aware of the patient's negative relational image and meanings and resulting emotions and do not understand how AN helps the patient deal with them. Loved ones may unwittingly reinforce negative relational images and meanings and their associated intense emotions and resulting disconnections including AN.

The R4R therapists share with group members that as we mature, we develop positive and negative relational images based on what happens in relationships with others. Since AN is associated with negative, dichotomous thoughts that widen the gap between realistic and unrealistic self-expectations (Fairburn, 2008; Murphy & Straebler, 2010), it can lead to the formation of new distorted, negative relational images and meanings and/or amplify those the patient experienced before the onset of AN. The goal is to identify these negative relational images and meanings and associated emotions and understand how they can reinforce internal and interpersonal disconnections with family members and maintain AN (see Figure 10.1). Then the patient can re-examine and alter these negative, distorted images and meanings with feedback from others. This work is important because relational images and meanings are our interpersonal blueprint for future interactions with loved ones. We cannot change how we view ourselves in relationships and change the nature of our interactions with others unless we are more cognizant of these images and meanings and how they influence our interactions and the responses of others.

For example, the parent in Box 10.1 does not know her daughter experiences the stated negative relational image and meanings. Once the patient is aware of these images and meanings and shares them with her mother, her mother can share what she is really thinking and feeling in relation to the

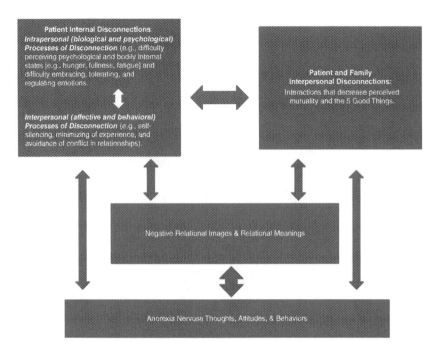

Figure 10.1 The Interactions Among Patient Internal Disconnections; Interpersonal Disconnections with Loved Ones; Negative Relational Images and Meanings; and Anorexia Nervosa Thoughts, Attitudes, and Behaviors.

patient. This activity supports the bidirectional nature of mutual relationships and promotes perceived mutuality between mother and daughter. For example, the mother may say she does not view her daughter as unimportant, but instead, can reinforce that the patient is very important to her and that she loves her very much. It may be that AN (with its rigid, dichotomous cognitions and demands) is what makes listening to her daughter challenging or anxiety-provoking at times. She can let her daughter know that she considers her daughter separate from the illness. The perceived mutuality experienced by the patient in response to her mother's disclosure can strengthen their connection. It assists in altering the patient's negative relational images and meanings, promotes the patient's connection with her authentic self, and leads to alternative emotion regulation and coping strategies. For example, as a result of the dialogue with mother, the patient could alter her distorted negative relational image and meanings to a more realistic and positive image and meanings (e.g., **Relational image:** "When I talk with my mother and AN is more in control, it is difficult for my mother to understand what I really need." **Relational meanings:** "This is because AN makes it hard for me to be clear about what I want, and my mom feels highly anxious, uncertain, or confused at these times.").

Session 6: Biopsychosocial Factors   141

Additionally, there are times when the negative relational image is accurate, but the negative relational meanings are distorted. In this case, the patient can be helped to change the relational meanings. For example, if the patient above had a mother who really was unable to listen because she had her own untreated major depression, the relational image in Box 10.1 would be correct. However, the patient who is blaming herself for the negative outcome of their interactions (see negative relational meanings in Box 10.1) can, with help from the group members and therapist, construct a different relational meaning to explain why her mother is not able to listen to her, e.g., "This is so because my mother is sick with untreated major depression and is unable to listen."

In addition to reviewing the example in Box 10.1 with group members in a didactic way, the R4R therapists can engage in this kind of emotional and relational work when situations present themselves in the "here and now" of the group. The following vignette illustrates how the R4R therapist could help a young adult and her mother identify and alter a negative relational image and meaning, thus, allowing them to repair their disconnection that previously led to reinforcement of the patient's felt invalidation and aloneness and the unwitting perpetuation of AN behaviors. This intervention can occur during Session 6 or a subsequent session and can be used as a learning opportunity for members directly involved in the scenario, as well as other group members who can assist with identification of negative relational images and meanings and resulting emotions and disconnections.

Therapist:	*Emily, I noticed that when we were talking about the importance of sharing what we really feel or think with our family members, you shook your head and looked down. Can you share a little with us about what that was about? It is important to know everyone's view on that. Your view may be different and you could have a good reason for why it's different.*
Emily:	*It's nothing. I'm fine.*
Therapist:	*You know that when I hear the word "fine" I worry that things may not be fine. What you are thinking is important. Plus, someone else in group might be having the same thought as you and you could help them voice a different idea too.*
Emily:	*It's OK. I am really fine (shooting a quick look over to her mother).*
Emily's mother:	*It sounds like you have something to say. Just say it. It is OK.*
Therapist:	*I am wondering if you are protecting mom from whatever you are not saying?*
Emily:	*Yes, in a way, I guess. It's just that when I talk with my mom, I feel she does not listen to me at times.*
Therapist:	*Well, that is a very important thing to share, and I appreciate your taking the risk to say that out loud. It would be very tempting to keep that to yourself. So, when you think of yourself in your relationship with your mom, you feel she is not hearing you (**negative relational image**).*

Emily:	Yes.
Therapist:	And how do you make sense of that? Why do you think this happens?
Emily:	I feel like it is because she does not think what I have to say is worthwhile or credible. Like she sees me as being sick and always thinks it is my eating disorder talking, so she does not listen to what I am saying **(negative relational meanings)**.
Therapist:	And then, how do you end up feeling when you make sense of things in this way?
Emily:	(Silent first) I – (having difficulty putting emotions into words).
Therapist:	Do you need help with finding the words to describe your feelings? Do you want the emotions sheet?
Emily:	Yes.
Therapist:	(Therapist passes her the emotions sheet.) While you are looking at the emotions sheet, I am also wondering if your friends here can help you with what feelings you might be having? Can other patients share some examples of feelings you might have in the scenario Emily described. I don't think she is the only patient who has experienced something like this. And sometimes our family members don't know we are feeling this way because we protect them from how we are feeling.
Jan:	I would feel inadequate.
Beth:	I would feel invalidated and frustrated.
Ellen:	I have had this experience with my parents at times. And when it happens, I also feel like they don't value what I have to say. I feel alone and sad at those times.
Therapist:	Emily, after looking at the sheet and hearing from Jan, Beth, and Ellen, do any of the feelings you read or heard seem to fit your experience?
Emily:	I think the feelings are invalidated and alone. I feel misunderstood and like no one understands what is really going on inside at times **(feelings associated with negative relational image and meanings)**. They don't get it.
Therapist:	These are tough feelings to carry around. Do you know what has made it difficult to share this information with mom?
Emily:	I know she is already stressed out trying to help me, and I don't want to upset her more. It's not worth it.
Therapist:	So, the beauty of Multifamily Therapy Group is that mom is right beside you and you can check this out with her. Can you do that?
Emily:	Mom, this would make you more upset if I told you this, right?
Emily's mother:	Emily, you don't need to protect me from what you really think and feel. I will be OK. It is more upsetting thinking that you are protecting me from hearing something. I do listen to you, but I will also admit that sometimes I have trouble knowing how to make sense of what you are saying or asking because I am not sure if I am talking with the illness or you. Like when you want to try something on your own, and I want to support your being independent, but I am not sure if you are ready yet for whatever you are asking for. But I don't want you feeling alone, that I don't care, or

Session 6: Biopsychosocial Factors   143

	that what you say doesn't matter. I admit I don't always know how to respond to you, especially when I am feeling anxious about what to do. But what you say is important to me and I do love you very much. I am still learning. And if you don't tell me what is really going on inside, then I am afraid of what could happen next.
Therapist:	*What might that be mom?*
Emily's mother:	*I am afraid she will eat less and have more symptoms.*
Therapist:	*Emily, what do you think about what mom is saying?*
Emily:	*Makes sense.*
Therapist:	*What happens when you feel invalidated and alone in response to what you and mom discuss?*
Emily:	*I don't want to stick to my meal plan. I want to restrict or delay eating and isolate more. I don't like feeling the tension that goes with feeling misunderstood, alone, and invalidated. I just want to numb out (**resulting internal and interpersonal disconnections**).*
Therapist:	*So, it sounds like the eating disorder takes advantage of your feelings and your being alone and encourages you to use it as a solution to how you feel in relationship to mom. You bravely started out this conversation saying that you did not think mom hears what you say to her and that is because what you say is not seen as credible or worthwhile. What did you hear mom say about her experience of what happens between the two of you at these times (**clarifying and reinforcing new information that can lead to a more positive and less distorted relational image and meanings**)?*
Emily:	*She said she does listen and that what I say does matter. But she feels unsure of how to make sense of what I am saying because she feels nervous and is not sure she is talking with the healthy part of me or the eating disorder (**new positive, more accurate relational image and meanings**).*
Therapist:	*Yes, and I am pretty sure that you two are not alone in this challenging situation and the resulting disconnections. AN can take full advantage of this situation. It is difficult to discern, especially initially, if a recovering person's request or explanation is reflective of healthy self-care and where they are in development or if it is the eating disorder. I am wondering who else in group may have experienced this challenge and what signs may help us know if we are talking with the eating disorder or the healthy part of the person in recovery? It is very helpful to get patient and family feedback on this issue.*

In this clinical vignette, the R4R therapist assists the patient to share her negative relational image and meaning, as well as the feelings associated with them. She also involves other patients in this work to support the patient. The therapist promotes mutuality by helping mother respond to her daughter. Through sharing how she actually sees and experiences her daughter (*how she is influenced by her*), mother provides information needed to alter the patient's initial negative relational image and meaning. The patient hears information that counters her desire to protect her mother from her genuine thoughts and feelings and her initial negative relational image and meanings. The therapist reinforces how the negative relational image and meanings can lead to painful emotions and disconnections to manage these emotions, including use of AN behaviors. She normalizes how the scenario is likely experienced by other members, too, and invites further discussion to promote universality, raise awareness, and foster problem solving related to discernment of when a loved one is talking with AN versus the healthy self of the patient.

It is important to note that there are some instances when a patient's relational image and/or meanings may be negative but not distorted. For example, a patient's parent or partner may have historically had difficulty hearing the patient because of their own challenges (sometimes even before the onset of AN), e.g., severe anxiety and/or depression or personality difficulties. If this is the case, the R4R therapist can help the patient and family member name the relational image and meaning and again clarify what is happening for each person in the relationship, with a focus on promoting mutual empathy and understanding. Again, group members can be useful in sharing their perspectives and emotions in response to what a family is sharing with the group. Other parents and patients can support and educate the family member who is having difficulties understanding the needs of their young adult. Also, a family can be encouraged to continue their work related to negative relational images and meanings and disconnections in their own single-family therapy meetings and/or with the patient's individual therapist.

After reviewing information about negative relational images and meanings, the R4R therapists reinforce how positive relational images and meanings promote perceived mutuality and encourage the patient to connect with themselves and others. They remind members about the importance of the "Five Good Things" that characterize mutual relationships and graphically show them via a poster or handout (see Chapter 5, Figure 5.4). They can also graphically display what a mutual relationship looks like through sharing a handout or using a poster of the Venn diagram reviewed in Session 1 (see Chapter 5, Figure 5.3). For homework, group members can be encouraged to review the chapter by Jean Baker Miller and Irene Stiver, How Connections Lead to Growth (pp. 24–41) from *The Healing Connection*. Boston, MA: Beacon Press (1997). This chapter provides further reading about how mutual connections foster connection with self and others.

The R4R therapists emphasize that perceived mutuality in relationships develops when we are emotionally vulnerable and open to allowing others to influence us *and* when we have an accurate understanding of how we influence others. They remind group members that perceived mutuality involves honoring and building on *difference within relationships*. It involves balancing attention to the needs of each individual in the relationship (the "I and You"), while also attending to the integrity of the connection with the other person (the "We"). They reinforce that when connection *and* acknowledgment of difference are present in relationships, AN is less able to create or amplify internal

Session 6: Biopsychosocial Factors 145

and interpersonal disconnections or negative relational images and meanings that can unwittingly perpetuate AN and maintain disconnection among patients and caregivers. Showing the Session 1 Venn diagram depicting mutual relationships can be helpful while discussing this material (see Chapter 5, Figure 5.3).

Session 6 ends with an introduction to the concept of functional analysis. The R4R therapists explain that functional analysis can be used to examine a particular behavioral cycle when AN is controlling what is happening in an interaction. The cycle includes what happens before the behavior (A—antecedent stimuli or triggers), during the behavior (B—behavior), and after the behavior (C—consequences including reinforcers that maintain the behavior) (Goddard, Raenker, & Treasure, 2012; Treasure, 2010). The therapists explain that conducting functional analysis allows patient and family members to recognize internal and external triggers to patient anxiety and use of AN behaviors and how family responses can unwittingly lead to disconnection, maintain the behavioral cycle, and reinforce AN behaviors. Once the behavioral cycle is understood, family members can learn how to respond in different ways that support the patient and promote recovery (Goddard, Raenker, & Treasure, 2012; Treasure, 2010). Since a functional analysis can facilitate an understanding of the advantages, meanings, and functions of AN, family members can use this understanding to inform their responses and help the patient replace AN behaviors with other self-care and coping strategies. Box 10.2 provides an example of how the therapists can describe functional analysis to group members.

Box 10.2 Functional Analysis: Understanding Eating Disorder Behavior Traps

Functional analysis can help loved ones figure out if they are unknowingly responding in ways that trigger or are not helpful with regard to eating disorder behaviors. Without realizing it, they may end up in a disconnection with the patient when they really want to establish connection and offer support.

A functional analysis has three parts, including:

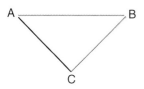

- Antecedent (A)
- Behavior (B)
- Consequence (C)

146 *Mary Tantillo, Jennifer Sanftner McGraw, and Daniel Le Grange*

This ABC approach to understanding our behaviors and their influence on others helps promote mutuality because we can develop more insight into how we influence others and learn to change our responses. This work strengthens our relationships and facilitates movement toward recovery.

Antecedents can be identified by asking questions about what is happening inside the patient and in the patient's environment. **Behaviors** are the eating disorder behaviors. **Consequences** are others' verbal and behavioral responses to the eating disorder behavior. These responses can either encourage movement toward healthy behaviors or unknowingly reinforce eating disorder behaviors. The eating disorder does all it can to create conditions for the latter so it can continue to exist.

Antecedents	*Behavior*	*Consequences*
EXTERNAL	Specific behavior, intensity, duration of time	Positive
When, Where, What, Who, How	What purpose is the behavior serving?	
INTERNAL		Negative
Thoughts, Feelings, Sensations, Memories		

Note. Functional Analysis Example—Rhinoceros and Dolphin Caregiver Responses. Adapted from Involving Carers: A Skills-Based Learning Approach (pp. 149–162), by E. Goddard, S. Raenker, and J. Treasure, in *A collaborative approach to eating disorders*, by J. Alexander and J. Treasure (Eds.), 2012, London: Routledge. Copyright by J. Alexander and J. Treasure. Adapted with permission. Changing Behaviors in the Family, by J. Treasure, in *The clinician's guide to collaborative caring for eating disorders* (pp. 104–121), by J. Treasure, U. Schmidt, and P. MacDonald (Eds.), 2010, London: Routledge. Copyright by J. Treasure, U. Schmidt, and P. Macdonald. Adapted with permission.

The therapists will demonstrate how to complete a functional analysis by reviewing the example in Table 10.1. This example also includes a rhinoceros and dolphin caregiver response as a consequence to food restriction, so that group members can consider what might occur next in the behavioral chain when using one response versus the other. The R4R therapists can ask group members, "Which of the responses would be more apt to lead to negative feelings and disconnection and unwittingly maintain AN behaviors? Which would be more apt to lead to positive feelings, increased mutuality, and continued recovery?"

Table 10.1 Functional Analysis Example—Rhinoceros and Dolphin Caregiver Responses

Antecedents (A)	Behavior (B)	Consequences (C)
EXTERNAL*	**Note specific behavior and its intensity and duration of time**	**Note Positive and Negative**
When? Where? What? Who? How?	**What purpose is the behavior serving?**	**Positive**
Failed an exam at college and was told that if he does not get a 90% on next exam he cannot continue in the program.	*Restricting at the meal and not following healthy meal plan. Picking at food throughout meal time for over 40 minutes. Restriction to feel control or success over something.*	• *Short-lived avoidance of intense negative feelings.* • *Feeling a sense of control or success related to restriction.*
INTERNAL* Thoughts, Feelings, Sensations, Memories		**Negative**
Believes he is a failure and feels inadequate and worthless. Feels full of negative emotion and sick to his stomach. Internal tension. Memories of previous perceived failures. Fear of extra cheese on sandwich.		• *Avoidance of facing and problem solving real challenges and fears.* • *No opportunity to check out with others the validity of thoughts and assumptions.* • *No practice with identifying and regulating emotions in healthier way.* • *Alone with negative emotions and feelings of failure.* • *Reinforcement of eating disorder symptoms that lead to a short-lived sense of control or success.*

(Continued)

Table 10.1 (Continued)

Antecedents (A)	Behavior (B)	Consequences (C)
		Caregiver Rhinoceros response during meal: *"Your not eating is destructive to your body. It has to stop now. You are a smart person and should know that this is bad for you. I'll be watching you like a hawk because you can't be trusted to take care of yourself."* **Caregiver Dolphin response after the meal:** *"I recognize you are doing the best you can to take care of yourself when the ED starts talking to you. I am wondering what happened today that might be affecting your self-care. I want to work with you on what we can do at higher risk times to ensure that you can continue caring nutritionally for yourself. When is a good time today to talk more and make a plan to help you going forward?"*

*Functional analysis can be used to understand a patient's *internal* (e.g., uncomfortable thoughts or feelings) or *external* (e.g., isolation from others, conflict, anxiety-provoking environmental conditions) triggers for eating disorder behaviors. Understanding and discussing one's internal and external triggers can decrease internal and interpersonal disconnections. Patients and family members can work together to help the patient experience decreased anxiety and increased self-worth and confidence for recovery.

Note

Functional Analysis Example—Rhinoceros and Dolphin Caregiver Responses. Adapted from Involving Carers: A Skills-Based Learning Approach (pp. 149–162), by E. Goddard, S. Raenker, and J. Treasure, in *A collaborative approach to eating disorders*, by J. Alexander and J. Treasure (Eds.), 2012, London: Routledge. Copyright by J. Alexander and J. Treasure. Adapted with permission. Changing Behaviors in the Family, by J. Treasure, in *The clinician's guide to collaborative caring for eating disorders* (pp. 104–121), by J. Treasure, U. Schmidt, and P. MacDonald (Eds.), 2010, London: Routledge. Copyright by J. Treasure, U. Schmidt, and P. Macdonald. Adapted with permission.

Session 6: Biopsychosocial Factors   149

Table 10.2 Functional Analysis Worksheet

Antecedents	Behavior	Consequences
EXTERNAL	Specific behavior, intensity, duration of time	**Positive**
When, Where, What, Who, How	What purpose is the behavior serving?	
INTERNAL		**Negative**
Thoughts, Feelings, Sensations, Memories		

Group members will then be asked to break out into smaller groups of patients and family members. All the patients may remain together in one group and family members can be divided into smaller groups, e.g., four or five people. The subgroups are asked to practice doing a functional analysis by identifying a scenario that triggers AN symptoms and use the ABC model to examine patient internal and external triggers, patient behavioral responses to these triggers, and possible family member responses to the patient's behaviors (see Table 10.2). The R4R therapists should circulate around the room to touch base with the small groups in case they need any additional help completing the small group exercise.

During their small group work, members should discuss the impact of family member behaviors on maintenance or interruption of AN behaviors and identify at least one dolphin caregiver response. This work furthers development of perceived mutuality as patients and family members recognize how they influence one another and how they can change responses to one another to foster continued recovery. The R4R therapists tell group members that they will report on their work at the start of the next session. Session 10 goals, materials, and handouts are outlined in Box 10.3.

Box 10.3   Session 6 Biopsychosocial Factors (continued), Disconnection and Functional Analysis Skills

Goals

Help patients and family members to:

- Continue to discuss how *internal disconnections* can contribute to disconnection from self (one's genuine thoughts, feelings, bodily needs/sensations) and from others, leading to *interpersonal disconnections* and perpetuation of AN symptoms
- Describe how interpersonal disconnections can lead to and emerge from negative/distorted relational (mental) images of oneself in relationship (e.g., "When I talk, my mom doesn't hear me.") and meanings (e.g., "This is because I must be unlovable, unimportant, or wrong.")

150 *Mary Tantillo, Jennifer Sanftner McGraw, and Daniel Le Grange*

- Describe how negative and distorted relational images and meanings become the unconscious interpersonal blueprint for future interpersonal disconnections and relational patterns and how AN tries to take advantage of this, thus perpetuating itself
- Describe (a) the importance of perceived mutuality, (b) the Five Good Things related to mutual relationships, and (c) the importance of being different-in-connection to reduce and repair disconnections
- Discuss the concept of functional or behavioral chain analysis and practice completing an analysis to identify triggers and purposes that AN serves for the patient

Materials

- Posters of Venn diagram and disconnection circles
- Poster of "Five Good Things of Mutual Relationships"

Handouts

- Relational Image slide handout to revisit interpersonal disconnections
- Handout of "Five Good Things of Mutual Relationships"
- Functional analysis worksheets: "Functional Analysis: Understanding Eating Disorder Behavior Traps" and uncompleted "Functional Analysis Worksheet"
- Baker, J.M., & Stiver, I.P. (1997). How connections lead to growth (pp. 24–41). In *The Healing Connection*. Boston, MA: Beacon Press.

Exercise

- Small group work (*this time with patients in a small group and family members in small groups*) where they apply the ABC model and identify a scenario that triggers AN symptoms. Identify patient and family member responses, as well as any additional impact on AN symptoms and recovery.

References

*No DOI

*Fairburn, C. G. (2008). *Cognitive behavior therapy and eating disorders*. The Guilford Press.
Goddard, E., Raenker, S., & Treasure, J. (2012). Involving carers: A skills-based learning approach. In J. Treasure & J. Alexander (Eds.), *A collaborative approach to eating disorders* (pp. 151–162). Routledge.
*Miller, J. B., & Stiver, I. P. (1997). *The healing connection: How women form relationships in therapy and in life*. Beacon Press.

Murphy, R., Strabler, S., Cooper, Z., & Fairburn, C. G. (2010). Cognitive behavioral therapy for eating disorders. *Psychiatric Clinics of North America, 33*(3), 611–627. https://dx.doi.org/10.1016/j.psc.2010.04.004

Treasure, J. (2010). Changing behaviors in the family. In J. Treasure, U. Schmidt, & P. MacDonald (Eds.), *The clinician's guide to collaborative caring for eating disorders* (pp. 104–112). Routledge. https://dx.doi.org/10.4324/9780203864685

11 Session 7: Strategies to Promote Mutual Connection

Mary Tantillo, Jennifer Sanftner McGraw, and Daniel Le Grange

Session 7 begins with patients noting at least one way they connected with others since the last session. In today's session the patients and families will have time to discuss additional strategies for connection, the destructive sociocultural messages that erode connection, and how they can resist these messages. Before doing that work, the R4R therapists will help patients and family members review what they discovered during the last session when they completed the functional analysis worksheet. Specifically, during session 7 the R4R therapists:

- Facilitate large group discussion about the last session's subgroup work related to functional analysis
- Help patients identify the purposes AN serves and alternative healthier ways to meet their needs
- Increase awareness of toxic sociocultural values that foster disconnection with the self and others
- Promote patient and family member openness to difference while remaining connected with one another
- Help members identify additional strategies for connection that do not include AN

After opening the group, patients and families are asked to share the examples they used while completing the functional analysis from the last session. Each subgroup reports back on a scenario that triggers AN symptoms and how they used the ABC functional analysis model to examine patient internal and external triggers, patient behavioral responses to these triggers, and possible family member responses to patient behaviors (see Table 10.2 for functional analysis worksheet). Therapists should foster discussion about whether family member responses would maintain or interrupt AN behaviors and encourage each subgroup to identify at least one dolphin or St. Bernard caregiver response. This work fosters perceived mutuality because group members increase their awareness of how they influence one another (often unknowingly) and how they can alter their responses to help the patients connect with their genuine selves (authentic feelings, thoughts, and needs) and with family members during recovery.

Part of this discussion should also include each patient identifying at least one purpose that AN serves for them. The R4R therapists reinforce that the goal of AN is to keep patients disconnected from what is really going on inside themselves and in relationships with others in order to maintain itself as the only solution to patient needs and distress. AN does not want them practicing alternative healthier self-care and coping strategies. This practice threatens AN because it creates less need for AN behaviors and fosters ongoing recovery. Identifying these purposes helps family members reflect on ways they can better respond during times of disconnection when the eating disorder is loud. They will then be able to problem solve more effectively with patients regarding how to meet certain needs without AN. This information can also inform strategies for connection they will identify at the end of group today.

After the large group discussion about the functional analysis worksheet, the R4R therapists continue to reinforce the importance of functional analysis. They emphasize its ability to increase patient and family member awareness of how AN adversely impacts everyone. They note how patients and families often enter group feeling depleted, as the illness has inserted itself into every aspect of their personal and family lives. Therapists explicitly state that AN tries to stop self and family development. Additionally, they point out how AN's efforts to foster disconnections are also supported by toxic Western (especially American) dominant sociocultural values that place a premium on control, rugged individualism, ultra-independence, and ultra-autonomy (Jordan, 2018). These values make us believe that as we mature we are supposed to be accomplishing things on our own and "picking ourselves up by the bootstraps" when the going gets tough. We do not feel comfortable asking for help because we assume that this will lead to others perceiving us as incapable and immature. We do not learn to value interdependence with others. These sociocultural messages are destructive for both recovery and life. The therapists can show the group members the Venn diagram poster of mutual relationships and the two examples of disconnection (See Chapter 5) to visually depict how the toxic sociocultural values emphasize the separate "I" and "You" in the diagram, but not the "We."

The R4R therapists note that these values are also especially damaging for young adults with eating disorders because developmentally they are already seeking or thinking they are supposed to be seeking increased autonomy and independence from their family (Dimitropoulos, Lock, Le Grange, & Anderson, 2015). AN will amplify the pressure or desire to emotionally and/or physically separate from family. The ego-syntonic nature of AN, the possible experience of anosognosia (Vandereycken, 2006), and the ambivalence and avoidance that characterize AN obstruct the development of true autonomy and healthy self-development (Dimitropoulos, Lock, Le Grange, & Anderson, 2015; Strauss & Ryan, 1987). Instead of promoting perceived mutuality and continued growth-in-connection with family, these factors promote internal and interpersonal disconnections. Parents are also ambivalent about denying their young adults an opportunity to achieve developmental milestones and may overestimate patient abilities and readiness for what seem like normal developmental challenges. They may support their young adult child's desire to separate and individuate because they do not realize that AN may be at work in motivating this request and the disconnections that follow.

The R4R therapists end group by emphasizing the importance of mutual connections for recovery. They note that mutual connections promote perceived mutuality, a main factor that promotes healing and psychological growth in recovery (Jordan, 2018; Miller and Stiver, 1997; Tantillo, Sanftner, & Hauenstein, 2013). They encourage group members to increase their practice of strategies for connection with one another in order to bring in positive energy for recovery and continue building mutual connections with one another. As part of this effort, they ask members to end the group session by breaking into their small family units for ten minutes and brainstorming additional strategies of connection. The therapists distribute pens and paper to facilitate recording these strategies. Each family unit chooses a scribe to record their strategies and someone from each family will report on them to the large group at the very end of the session.

The therapists tell group members that there are only two main rules attached to the exercise. The first rule is that they can only brainstorm and cannot "critique" one another. All strategies for connection are good contributions, even if there is disagreement about them. For example, the patient may want to connect by going to a particular coffee house and playing a board game, while one of the parents is not too excited by this idea. Or a parent or partner may suggest going to a particular favorite location and looking up at the constellations together, but the patient may not feel excited about this. They are reminded that "difference" is good and being different-in-connection is an important group goal. This exercise is an opportunity to practice listening and responding to each person's unique requests and desires, while being attentive to the "We" and remaining in connection. Everyone's contributions are important because they will be shared with the large group at the very end of the session. Additionally, strategies can include ones they have tried in the past and ones they would like to try in the future. They can be practical or zany suggestions. The strategies for connection can involve all members in the family unit or different relational combinations (e.g., patient and mother, patient and father, patient and partner, patient and friends). The majority of strategies should involve individuals within the group but can also involve others outside of group (e.g., sponsor, mentor, close friend) who support the patient's recovery.

The second rule is that the strategies for connection cannot include AN. That means that if the strategy might be triggering in any way and potentially lead to AN thoughts and behaviors, it cannot be included. For example, if a patient states that shopping together would be a good way to connect, it would be important to think through whether clothes shopping is really a good strategy for connection at this point in recovery. If it could be triggering in some way, it is probably safer to shop for shoes or housewares. Other examples of strategies for connection that may actually be triggering and lead

Session 7: Strategies 155

to AN symptoms include eating out together and visiting extended family members or friends. The patient generally needs to be farther along in recovery before tackling meals outside the home, and visits with extended family or friends are connecting when the environment is safe, welcoming, and supportive of one's meal plan and overall recovery goals.

After the ten minutes of brainstorming in small family subgroups, the members are asked to return to the large group and report on their strategies. Members are in control of what they share, and family unit scribes take turns reporting on their strategies. One of the R4R therapists records the strategies on easel paper (or whiteboard) so everyone can see them. The R4R therapists reassure members that it is OK if their strategies are duplicates of other family strategies. The therapist can put an asterisk next to each item that is repeated to show its strong endorsement. See Box 11.1 for an example of the list of strategies for connection that families have identified in previous R4R MFTG groups.

Box 11.1   Strategies for Connection

- Going to the coffee house and talking or playing a board game***
- Walking the dog/playing with pets***
- Going to a concert***
- Volunteering at a community nonprofit**
- Doing a house improvement project**
- Going on a drive**
- Going on vacation to a favorite place**
- Going to the movies**
- Going to festivals**
- Playing cards**
- Having a game night at home**
- Going to craft shows*
- Going to the theater
- Going to the museum or planetarium
- Decorating for the holidays
- Going to Barnes and Noble and reading
- Going shopping for shoes
- Going to a sports game
- Looking at the constellations
- Going to the beach
- Going to the park
- Making a bonfire
- Doing crafts/making things
- Skyping/Facetime to touch base
- Going mini-golfing

156 *Mary Tantillo, Jennifer Sanftner McGraw, and Daniel Le Grange*

The R4R therapists will inform families that they will create a list of the strategies for connection and distribute a copy to each member during the next session. The leader asks each family to engage in at least one of their recorded strategies for connection before the next session. Session 7 tends to ease family burden and decreases the demoralization and stigma patients and families often experience when they start MFTG. Session 7 goals, materials, and handouts are outlined in Box 11.2.

Box 11.2   Session 7: Strategies to Promote Mutual Connections

Goals

Help patients and family members to:

- Increase understanding and application of functional analysis so as not to unwittingly perpetuate AN.
- Understand the purposes AN serves.
- Identify ways to help patients fulfill the above purposes in healthier ways.
- Increase awareness of destructive dominant cultural messages that promote disconnection with oneself and others (emphasis on I/You versus We; external appearance versus what is inside of us).
- Practice being open to difference (internally and interpersonally); practice being different *and* connected with each other—including identifying additional ways they can connect without AN.

Materials

- Venn diagram and circles of disconnection posters.
- Paper and pens.
- Easel and easel paper with marker.

Exercise

- Review as a large group the *small group examples using the functional analysis worksheet from the last session*. Discuss internal and external triggers, patient behavioral responses to the triggers, and family responses to patient behaviors. Identify at least one dolphin caregiver response.
- During the preceding discussion, each patient should share at least one *purpose the eating disorder serves for them*. Therapists will have assessed these purposes during Session 1 and can help the patients discuss examples.

- Meet in family subgroups to brainstorm additional ways they can *connect with one another* that do not include AN (to externalize the illness, bring in energy, and strengthen family ties). Then review strategies as a large group.

Handouts

- Functional analysis worksheet from last week

References

*No DOI

*Dimitropoulos, G., Lock, J., Le Grange, D., & Anderson, K. (2015). Family therapy for transition youth. In K. Loeb, D. Le Grange, & J. Lock (Eds.), *Family therapy for adolescent eating and weight disorders: New applications* (pp. 230–255). Routledge/Taylor & Francis Group.

Jordan, J. (2018). *Relational-cultural therapy* (2nd ed.). American Psychological Association. https://dx.doi.org/10.1037/0000063-001.

*Miller, J. B., & Stiver, I. P. (1997). *The healing connection: How women form relationships in therapy and in life.* Beacon Press.

Strauss, J., & Ryan, R. (1987). Autonomy disturbances in subtypes of anorexia nervosa. *Journal of Abnormal Psychology, 96*(3), 254–258. https://dx.doi.org/10.1037//0021-843X.96.3.254.

Tantillo, M., Sanftner, J. L., & Hauenstein, E. (2013). Restoring connection in the face of disconnection: An integrative approach to understanding and treating anorexia nervosa. *Advances in Eating Disorders: Theory, Research, and Practice, 1*, 21–38.

Vandereycken, W. (2006). Denial of illness in anorexia nervosa—a conceptual review: Part 2 different forms and meanings. *European Eating Disorders Review, 14*(5), 352–368. https://dx.doi.org/10.1002/erv.722.

12 Session 8: Anorexia Nervosa and the Family Context

Rules and Relationships

Mary Tantillo, Jennifer Sanftner McGraw, and Daniel Le Grange

Session 8 begins with completion of last week's group work related to strategies for connection, including (a) distribute the list of strategies of connection identified during Session 7; (b) review strategies of connection that patients used since last session (members were encouraged to use at least one strategy from the list they jointly generated during Session 7); and (c) take turns reading aloud items from the "Strategies to Promote Mutual Connections and Recovery" handout to increase knowledge of various ways to promote mutual connections during recovery. The R4R therapists can follow this review with a very brief large group discussion (five to eight minutes) about responses (thoughts/feelings) about the items. They can ask if any of the items stood out for members. Additionally, they can ask for any other strategies that members would like to add to the list that was reviewed (see Table 12.1).

The remainder of Session 8 is devoted to understanding the importance of implicit and explicit rules related to the eating disorder, recovery, and relationships. Specifically, during Session 8 the R4R therapists will:

- Provide education about the origin of explicit and implicit rules and their impact on recovery
- Discuss how AN's rules obstruct individual and family system growth and development
- Help members identify their own implicit and explicit rules related to AN, recovery, and relationships
- Assist members to rate one of their stated rules based on its ability to promote or obstruct member ability to be "different-in-connection."

The R4R therapists begin the group work on implicit and explicit rules by first defining these terms. They can ask the group what "explicit" means and usually at least one of the members knows that explicit means something that is clearly stated. Therefore, explicit rules are those that are directly spoken out loud and are known. Then the therapists ask what "implicit" means. Again, at least one member usually knows that implicit means something that is implied but not clearly stated. Implicit rules are those that are implied, unspoken, and possibly unrecognized at first. The R4R therapists can provide an example of

Rules and Relationships 159

Table 12.1 Strategies to Promote Mutual Connections and Recovery

Create Safety: Embrace the differences among one another. Work through conflict in connection. Strong relationships are based on a willingness of all concerned to tolerate difference (e.g., different thoughts, feelings, and needs).

Observe, Listen, and Share: Carefully observe and listen to your child, partner, or friend. Take risks to state your genuine feelings, thoughts, and needs.

Increase Connection: Find alternative places for connection in your relationships. Bring energy into relationships and create time to do things together.

Offer Validation: Validate your own experience and the experience of others. Validation does not equal agreement. A little validation can go a long way. Admit when you have missed the mark with someone. Your admission of failures and mistakes can help restore connection with others, even if this seems contrary to what you believe. Also, you can validate someone's experience while still voicing your own concerns and inviting the other person to make healthy choices.

Check Things Out: Check out your perceptions and assumptions with others to construct new relational images and meanings. Do not do this work in a vacuum, because what you construct could be wrong. How you see yourself or others in relationships (relational images) may or may not be the same as the way they see you or themselves in relationships. Also, each person may make sense of how they see themselves in relationships with others (relational meanings) in different ways. Checking out perceptions and assumptions about relational images and meanings creates more accuracy in how we see and experience ourselves in connections with others.

Be Accessible: Be physically and emotionally accessible to your loved ones and decrease secrets among you. It is as important to understand others as it is to feel understood, even if the understanding does not completely fix things or involves some pain. None of us is perfect. We each have our limitations. It is important for others to see this.

Be Realistic: Be realistic about what you expect from yourself and others. Check out your expectations with others who can help you reality test.

Engage in Grief Work: Begin to do the grief work related to the realization that we all have failings. We all have flaws, and people who say they love us cannot always be who we would like them to be or respond in ways that we would like them to respond. Sometimes this fact is due to others' inabilities, not their willingness, to make changes in their behavior.

It Takes Two (or More): Remember, it takes two to have a relationship. You cannot do all the work yourself. A healthy relationship is just that—a relationship. Healthy relationships are based on risk-taking that can feel very frightening to one or all persons in a relationship. However, if you do not check out your thoughts and feelings with those in relationship with you, you will not be representing yourself genuinely with them. As we hold more of ourselves out of connection with others, others know less and less about us. This can be safe, but, ultimately, it leads us down the road to more disconnection from ourselves and others and toward more isolation.

(Continued)

160 *Mary Tantillo, Jennifer Sanftner McGraw, and Daniel Le Grange*

Table 12.1 (Continued)

No One Is to Blame: Know that neither you nor any other person or singular event can directly cause someone else's or your own psychological difficulties. Psychological difficulties such as eating disorders are more complicated than that. Moving away from blame and toward understanding is what promotes mutual relationships. However, we also need to take responsibility for what we can control.

Increase Connections: Create an increasing number of growth-fostering connections in your life. These include connections with yourself and mutual connections with others, as well as connections with pets, nature, or a higher power. All kinds of growth-fostering connections bring in energy needed to continue building existing and new relationships.

Improve Self-Care: Strengthen your connection with yourself and increase your self-care. Learn to listen to what you and your body really need and enjoy. Routinely create time, even if it is initially brief, for such things as meditation, yoga, prayer, relaxation, and quiet. Practice mindfulness—learn how to observe and describe and be in the moment without negative evaluation of yourself and others. Routinely do one good thing for yourself, even if it is only once a week to start. This self-care activity could be a physical one such as a facial or massage, or it could be an emotional one such as driving to a favorite spot and taking in the sunset.

Find and Connect with Trusted Others: Find people in your life whom you trust and who validate your experience. Spend time with them and try not to run or isolate when they fail you (and they will) or when you feel increasingly close to them. Instead, slow yourself down and think about why you want to respond in these ways. Share your experience. Acknowledge when you are anxious or scared and why. Sometimes, when we finally get what we wish for, we don't know how to handle it. We may feel the urge to disconnect in the face of a potentially growth-fostering connection because we have assumed that only more hurt can come from relationships. The eating disorder wants us to believe this, so we remain isolated and connected to it.

Be a Resister and Social Activist: Encourage and participate in political resistance and social justice. Participate in activities that help eliminate damaging societal values and norms. Challenge yourself and others to not subscribe to the myth that beauty, happiness, and success are contingent on being thin. Join efforts to stamp out the stigma of obesity and boycott the weight-loss industry. Do not join diet programs and do not spend every free moment in the gym. Try not to focus only on achievement, performance, self-sufficiency, independence, and competitiveness. Instead, balance these values with a focus on mutual relationships, interdependence, and a sense of community.

Remember that Mutual Relationships Take Continual Work: Remember that despite all the idealized and romanticized relationships we see in the media, there are no perfect relationships. The best connections are those that involve continual hard work and relational repair on the part of both or all persons in a relationship. As we learn to move toward mutual relationships with others, instead of a relationship with the eating disorder, we also feel more connected to ourselves.

each kind of rule. For example, some explicit rules that govern relationships and interactions at home include things like, "Call if you will be late," "Don't take someone else's things without permission," and "Apologize if you did something to hurt someone." The R4R therapists can provide an example of implicit rules by sharing a story from their own lives or from the lives of other "hip-pocket" (readily available hypothetical or real cases) patients/family members. In previous MFTGs, the first author (MT) has often used humor and engaged in therapist self-disclosure to provide a real-life example of implicit rules at work:

> *"Implicit" rules are funny things. We may not even know they exist until we get into a disagreement or experience conflict in our relationships. AN loves to take advantage of implicit rules because it thrives on what is unspoken, i.e., unspoken needs, feelings, perspectives, etc. It can amplify the tension related to unspoken implicit rule(s) because it pushes on us to engage in all or nothing thinking regarding these rules. Negative emotion results from this all or nothing thinking and the interpersonal demands often associated with it. Once the negative emotions and tension occur, then AN doubles back and offers itself as a solution to avoid or mute the tension and negative emotion. This scenario then leads to more disconnection due to a lack of communication and isolation. This situation can happen regardless of whether we are in recovery or not. It is part of the human condition and AN capitalizes on this situation when a person is in recovery. Let me share with you how implicit rules affected my husband and I when we were first married. We did not realize it at first, but we started our relationship with very different rules about how to respond to one another when we got home after work. These were implicit rules because we initially had not spoken them to each other and did not even know they existed. So, from what you have learned about me, do you think when I get home that I like to debrief and talk about my day or do you think I dislike talking about my day? (There are always at least a few patients and family members who will guess that I would want to talk about my day.) Yes, I am the one in the relationship who wants to talk about my day. So, my implicit rule was, "When we get home from work, we should connect and debrief with each other about the day." However, I soon discovered that my husband is the one in the relationship that does NOT want to talk about his day the moment he gets home. I learned that he wants to disengage and chill out and watch TV for about 30 minutes. These actions helped him unwind because he does not want to continue thinking about work. His implicit rule was, "When we get home from work we should chill and not initially discuss work." You can imagine what followed these very different, unspoken, implicit rules. I felt shut out when I asked him how his day went, and he didn't answer me. I also felt he didn't care enough about me to ask how my day went and discuss this with me. He felt annoyed and controlled because he did not want to discuss the day at first and could not understand why I kept trying to talk about work.*
>
> *Eventually, after enough disagreements and frustration, we made explicit what was implicit. We ended up recognizing and sharing with one another our implicit rules. We realized that the issue was less about being "right" or "wrong" and more about being open to different rules and the underlying needs, meanings, and feelings that*

accompany them. I learned to give him some breathing time when he got home and after that, he would ask me about my day. We agreed I could ask him how his day was because I felt that was a caring thing to do, but I would not personalize it if he did not want to discuss his day. The funny thing is that over time, he needed less and less time to make the transition from work to home and more frequently than not, discussed highlights from his day. And I learned to do other things (e.g., take the dogs for a walk, ride my bike, start dinner) during the brief transition time when he was coming down from the day. We both learned that we could be "different while remaining connected." We learned not to interpret these differences as negative but learned to use them to respect each other's needs and strengthen our relationship.

After providing the definition and examples of explicit and implicit rules, the R4R therapists note that rules develop within the context of one's parenting, previous generations, developmental stage, personalities, sociocultural variables, and other factors. As individuals and family systems grow and develop, the rules guiding each person and the family system should change to permit healthy maturation (Maine, 2004; Miller & Stiver, 1997; Siegel, Brisman, & Weinshel, 2009). Unfortunately, AN can impede the growth and development of individuals and the family system. For example, as children mature, they seek opportunities to be increasingly autonomous and self-efficacious. They experience implicit and explicit rules that tell them that they should be able to do more on their own, and they come to expect this. The family system that is also growing and maturing allows for increased autonomy of children by altering rules and expectations over time. For example, parents' explicit and/or implicit rules increasingly allow their older adolescent and young adult children more freedom and choice. However, this natural progression of changes in rules is disrupted or stalled in the face of AN. The young adult's emotional and psychosocial development is delayed, and the family system cannot effectively progress to a place that supports young adult developmental milestones. This situation can cause stress for the young adult, individual family members, and the family as a whole. For example, parents may maintain rules that keep them very involved in the care of their ill young adult, similar to when their child was younger. Siblings may develop rules that they cannot complain or ask for support from their parents because their sibling with AN is sick and needs a great deal of their time and attention. A number of different implicit and explicit rules can coexist in this scenario. For example, the young adult with AN may have a **relationship rule** that says, "He should be able to have meals with friends and stay out till midnight," but his **AN (rule)** says, "He should not eat anything after 3 p.m. and not tell his parents." Additionally, the **recovery rules** he is supposed to live by state, "He needs to complete all meals according to his meal plan" and "He should be honest with his parents about his intake." His parents may have a **recovery rule** that "they have to be with him at every meal and provide him supervision one hour after meals for now." A **relationship rule** they may have is that "they will do all they can

Rules and Relationships   163

to protect their son and will believe him but not the illness." (See Table 12.2 for examples of eating disorder, recovery, and relationship implicit and explicit rules.)

After providing education about the impact of AN on patient and family member development and rules, as well as the different and competing implicit and explicit rules that can exist during recovery, the R4R therapists emphasize that the goal of group today is to help members identify their implicit and explicit rules related to AN, recovery, and relationships. They will work together to raise awareness of these rules, make the implicit ones explicit and eventually will choose one of these rules and examine whether it helps them embrace or avoid being different-in-connection (being open to different thoughts, feelings, needs, perspectives and leveraging these for the good of the relationship). The therapists ask the group participants to begin this work by discussing within their own family subgroups for the next ten minutes the implicit and explicit rules related to AN, recovery, and re-lationships. They are again asked not to critique one another but to "brain-storm" and accept everyone's contributions. They are reminded that each family member may have a different perspective on the rules that exist in each family. For example, one family member may cite a rule and another may say that they don't experience that rule. It is important to normalize that this can happen in families, and that if there are seven family members, there could be seven different experiences of a situation and the related rules. They are re-minded that if they experience disagreement, that this is a good thing and an opportunity to practice being curious, open, and "different-in-connection." They are encouraged to discuss this experience when they return to the large group and process the exercise.

During this break-out period, the R4R therapists circulate through the room to touch base with each family subgroup while they are brain-storming. They can get a sense of what issues need to be addressed, nor-malize concerns and challenges, facilitate naming of explicit and implicit rules when this work involves anxiety and tension, and model ways to be curious and open toward difference in order to move from disconnection to better connection. If during the break-out time members are still struggling to identify implicit rules, the R4R therapists can help them by giving them additional examples. One example can involve the different implicit rules at work in a couple or friendship in the face of an argument. One person may have a relationship rule that makes them want to talk immediately to repair what has transpired, and the other person has a relationship rule that they need to take a time-out first to collect themselves and regain control before further discussing the incident. Acknowledge that implicit rules are more difficult to identify because we often are not aware of them until we experience a disconnection. Then, in hindsight, we may be more aware of them and can use them to strengthen mutual under-standing and trust versus allowing AN to use our differences to cause more disconnection.

164 Mary Tantillo, Jennifer Sanftner McGraw, and Daniel Le Grange

Table 12.2 Implicit and Explicit Rules Regarding the Eating Disorder, Recovery, and Relationships

Eating Disorder
Implicit Rules

- The thinner I am, the more successful I am.*
- I have to be the best at restriction, exercise, and everything else.*
- I need to delay eating.*
- I need to read the labels on all food items.*
- I have to watch my parents prepare my food.*

Explicit Rules

- Do not order any trigger foods.*
- I can't vary the foods I eat.*
- Do not eat certain foods in front of me.*
- Don't force me to eat things.*
- Don't make me eat anything after dinner.*

Recovery
Implicit Rules

- Don't demand to know how my eating disorder is. Give me time to share.
- Don't make comments on how I look. This is triggering.
- Don't talk about food, dieting, or exercise or physical appearance.
- Don't call out my behaviors.*
- Kindly call out the eating disorder when it acts up.
- Help me try new things and be more spontaneous again.
- Avoid conflict at mealtimes.
- Don't let me go to the bathroom or be alone after meals.
- Find balance.

Explicit Rules

- Don't take food to the bedroom.
- Eat in the kitchen and dining room.
- Eat together and offer each other support.
- Touch base regarding where we are through the day.
- Don't hide symptoms.
- Ask for help.
- Don't hibernate in my room.
- Be honest about what I ate.
- Don't hide food.
- Follow the meal plan and complete my meals.

Relationships
Implicit Rules

- Respect each other's privacy, need for space, differences, and idiosyncrasies.
- It's not OK to be mad (at least not for very long).*
- Be sensitive to each other's weaknesses and don't use them against each other.
- Do not expect things to be perfect.

(Continued)

Table 12.2 (Continued)

- Share thoughts with one another. We can't mind read.
- Don't talk about negative emotions at home. Avoid conflict so no one gets hurt.*
- Try to make things look OK, even if they aren't.*
- What happens in the family always stays in the family.*
- Our family feels like it has to be perfect.*
- Everything is about competition.*

Explicit Rules

- Be responsible and respect yourself and others at home.
- Be honest and open.
- Be kind and courteous to others.
- Clean up after yourself.
- If you are going to be late, call.
- Don't take anything without asking first.
- Don't solve a problem by lecturing.
- Actively listen to others before responding.
- Be assertive versus passive or passive aggressive.
- Don't go to bed angry—try to have resolution.

Note

*Denotes those rules that can maintain ED symptoms because they promote disconnection from self and/or others.

After approximately ten minutes of subgroup discussion have members return to the large group and share their experiences of the exercise for an additional ten minutes. The R4R therapists can ask for member feelings and thoughts about the exercise. Was it challenging? Straightforward? Acknowledge that each family may have different experiences and some families may have found that they had many rules, while others felt that they had few or no rules. It is not an issue of wrong or right but more about just observing and being curious about what they discovered. Following is an example of a dialogue between a newly married husband and wife (patient) (ages 28 and 27, respectively) during the large group discussion and the therapist's work to help them identify rules that can strengthen their relationship and recovery, instead of allowing AN to use their rules to hurt their relationship and maintain itself.

Therapist:	*So, how was that exercise for folks? Some find it challenging to identify rules and some find it fairly easy. There can be differences of opinion about the rules in each family, and each family member may even experience the same rule differently. It is good to be curious about and learn from all of these things.*
Matthew:	*Well, it was kind of challenging and created some tension for us. (His wife, Andrea, is looking down at the floor.)*
Therapist:	*Can you guys share more about that with us? I am sure you are not the only group members who may have experienced some tension or anxiety while coming up with the rules. It can be*

166 *Mary Tantillo, Jennifer Sanftner McGraw, and Daniel Le Grange*

	challenging to make explicit what previously may have been implicit.
Matthew:	*Well, Andrea said that she thought we had a rule that involved my being supportive to her recovery but that she did not always feel that at dinnertimes. I told her that I do have that rule, but I also can't control everything that goes on at work. Sometimes I am late getting home and can't be there right at dinnertime. She has to eat by 6 p.m. or she gets really nervous and upset. She says when I am late, she does not feel like I care about her and that I value my job over her. She says another rule takes over about my needing to show my colleagues that I am a hard worker because I am the newest at the (architectural) agency. It is true that I feel stressed out trying to figure out what to do when I am running late on a deadline, but it does not mean I love or value her less. (His voice tone is getting slightly more pressured as he speaks.)*
Therapist:	*Matthew, that is a tough dilemma that you and Andrea are experiencing. Can you tell what you are feeling right now as you describe it to us?*
Matthew:	*I feel like she doesn't understand what is actually happening at those moments for me.*
Therapist:	*Those are very important thoughts, and they are more about Andrea than you. What are YOU feeling in your heart? Can you tell?*
Matthew:	*It doesn't feel good. It doesn't feel fair because I love her and want what is best for her. It's...It's frustrating. I feel pressured to be back right at 6 p.m. every night for her and sometimes feel the pressure of needing to complete a project due to a particular last-minute deadline. Sometimes everyone in the office is late getting home.*
Therapist:	*So, you love Andrea, and at the same time, you feel frustrated because you feel caught in a bind of caring for her or completing work in the face of a surprise time demand.*
Matthew:	*Yes.*
Therapist:	*Andrea, I was wondering if you saw things similarly or differently from Matthew. You may see and experience things differently.*
Andrea:	*I know that Matthew loves me, but he does not understand how stressed out I get when I have to eat dinner alone. By the end of the day I am a stress case at meals, and I have told him how important it is to eat with him.*
Therapist:	*So, it sounds like eating dinner can feel really overwhelming.*
Andrea:	*Yes, exactly.*
Therapist:	*And is it true that you feel he values work over you? Is that a rule that you feel exists?*
Andrea:	*Right now, I would say, no, that is not true, but when he is not at dinner, it feels that way. I am all alone and feeling out of*

Rules and Relationships   167

	control. I can't eat what is in front of me and complete my meal plan. Then he gets mad at me because I restricted. He says that it should be OK for me to occasionally eat alone and just leave his dinner for him to eat when he gets home, if I can't wait to eat. I know he has to perform well at work, and I know how important that is. I love him too, but I feel so overwhelmed.
Therapist:	So, this is tough because the eating disorder is working hard to leave both of you feeling alone and with very intense emotions. You both feel misunderstood, and Matthew loves you but also feels frustrated. You love him but also feel overwhelmed. The eating disorder is probably very happy about this because it is stopping you from working together to develop a new rule and a compromise position that could help both of you. I wonder what others are thinking or feeling as you are listening to the dilemma that Matthew and Andrea are facing?
Doug:	My girlfriend also wants me to sit with her at meals. It is still hard for me to understand exactly how frightening this is for her, but I believe her when she says this. I can see how tough it is for both of you. It's like you are stuck between taking care of your wife and doing what your boss is asking you to do.
Sally (Doug's girlfriend):	Yes, Doug and I went through something similar. He finally figured out a way to consistently be with me four out of seven days per week at dinnertime. It took some jockeying of his schedule, and I really appreciate it. In order to deal with the times he could not be with me, I had to try something new. I reached out to my best friend and my sister to ask if they would be with me. I felt very anxious doing that. I was not sure how they would respond. But until I let myself do that, it kept all the pressure on him. I had an implicit rule, I guess, that said he was the only one I could trust to have dinner with me. I did not realize this until he told me how pressured he felt.
Doug:	Yes, I would either feel like a failed boyfriend or get really angry at her, well the eating disorder, I mean. I felt trapped and like the only one who could help.
Matthew:	That is how I feel, I guess. I don't like saying that out loud because I don't want her to think I don't care. It is not her fault that she has an eating disorder and it is not my fault that I get last minute work demands.
Therapist:	Sally, it is interesting how when you uncovered your implicit rule about Doug being the only one to help, that that helped you create a new rule to support your recovery and your relationship. Andrea, did you notice if there were any other rules that were getting in your way of figuring out a compromise that would help both of you?

168 *Mary Tantillo, Jennifer Sanftner McGraw, and Daniel Le Grange*

Andrea:	*I am not sure. I guess I need to think more about that.*
Susan (another patient):	*Andrea, what about your rule about eating at 6 p.m.? Could that be changed? I know that could feel stressful. Or could you let someone else support you like Sally did? Like change the rule that only Matthew can be at dinner with you sometimes?*
Andrea:	*I get really stressed the later we eat. I know that is probably the eating disorder. I just can't change that right now. I am already trying new foods, and I need one thing to remain the same for right now. Maybe I can ask someone else for help. It is just so embarrassing. I am 27 and need someone to eat meals with me. It seems ridiculous.*
Doug:	*It is not ridiculous, Andrea. Sally felt the same way when she asked her sister and best friend for help. They were very happy to help, but she did not know that till she asked.*
Therapist:	*Sounds like the eating disorder works very hard to keep us from asking loved ones for help and makes us worry about how others will view us. It keeps us isolated from others and feeling badly about ourselves. Makes it hard to ask for help then. Andrea, is there anyone else you trust that you could ask for help at dinners?*
Andrea:	*I guess I could ask my mom. I just didn't want her to worry about me, and I wanted her to feel like I am taking care of myself.*
Sally:	*But you ARE taking care of yourself by asking her to be with you when Matthew is late. That is self-care and it does not mean you will always need it. You need it for now.*
Matthew:	*Andrea, do you feel OK doing that? I do think your mom would not mind. She loves you so much. I know you don't want to feel like a teenager needing her help again, but you are not a teenager. You are an adult experiencing a relapse, and you need and deserve extra support from all of us till you get your sea legs. I can talk with my boss again about him trying not to give me surprise last-minute projects right now, but I can't totally control everything that goes on at the office. I will do my best.*
Andrea:	*OK, I can talk to mom. She has been asking how to help. I just have not given her options. I guess it would take the pressure off both of us right now.*
Therapist:	*Excellent self-care move Andrea, and your decision also helps Matthew and strengthens your relationship. Thanks to both of you for starting us off. Who else would like to share a little about how the exercise was for them?*

In this vignette the R4R therapist helps the couple identify the rules that might be obstructing recovery, as well as their relationship, and how AN is capitalizing on this situation (leading to isolation and intense negative

Rules and Relationships   169

emotions for Andrea and Matthew, as well as Andrea's food restriction at meals when Matthew is absent). The therapist helps them compare their perspectives on the stated rules, as well as the feelings they experience because of them. Other group members are invited to offer their thoughts and feelings about Andrea's and Matthew's dilemma and associated rules. The group members provide validation and promote a different way to problem-solve a solution to the dilemma. They facilitate Andrea's ability to re-examine her rigid rule about eating by 6 p.m. and its impact on her and her partner. With their help and the therapist's encouragement, she is able to identify her mother as a possible mealtime support and explore what has made it difficult to previously pursue this option. Her ability to create a new rule, i.e., my mother can also help me at dinnertimes, promotes her self-care and continued recovery and also supports her husband and their relationship.

Next, the therapists ask members to take turns sharing some of their explicit and implicit rules related to AN, recovery, and relationships. They record the rules on easel paper and can separate the rules into explicit and implicit rules or just write them as they are presented by each member, noting verbally if they were explicit or implicit. Of course, technically, they are now all explicit because they have been shared out loud. The therapists let group members know they did a great job because AN thrives on what is implicit and unspoken. It is like jet fuel for AN. Today they helped disempower AN because they made explicit a number of rules that were implicit. The R4R therapists tell the members that they will make a copy of the rules recorded today and distribute them next session.

The therapists end group by asking members to quickly meet together (about five minutes) in their family subgroups to choose one of their rules and evaluate together if that rule helps them embrace or avoid difference (different feelings, thoughts, needs, perspectives). Next, the R4R therapists return the members to the large group for a brief discussion of what they discovered. They ask each family to identify the rule they chose and what they found with regard to its allowing them to be different-in-connection. The therapists end group by asking if there are any other thoughts or feelings about the work on rules today. They also distribute the handout "Rules and Relationships: The Family Context of Eating Disorders" (see Table 12.3), which summarizes highlights about family rules and relationships and provides additional criteria group members can use to evaluate whether a rule is helpful or harmful for family relationships and recovery (Siegel, Brisman, & Weinshel, 2009).

Session 8 helps the patient and family members become more aware of the rules that drive their interactions. They practice being open and curious about these rules versus allowing AN to leverage them to hurt their relationships with one another. This work can be challenging for some families and may lead to tension. It is important to normalize that this can happen when we finally make what is implicit explicit. Group members are

170   *Mary Tantillo, Jennifer Sanftner McGraw, and Daniel Le Grange*

Table 12.3 Rules and Relationships: The Family Context of Eating Disorders

Families with an eating disordered young adult vary tremendously. However, there is one common thread within these families. The existing relationships, rules, and practices that bind the family together are not accommodating the shifting needs of individual family members. Family rules and practices affect the kind of connections family members can have with one another. While connections in the family are important, what often needs to change is the nature of these connections. For example, the nature of parent-child connections normally shifts as the child moves from toddler to teenager to young adult. Connection is still important, but there should be some alteration in the kind of connection that exists between parents and children. There needs to be space for each person in the relationship and a two-way movement of feelings, thoughts, and actions between people in the relationship (the "We"). When movement and growth in relationship are somehow constrained, there may be increased strain or stress experienced by individual family members and by the family as a whole. This strain or stress can be even more overwhelming in the context of an eating disorder. Sometimes family relationships are strained and stressed before the onset of a family member's eating disorder and other times they are strained and stressed after the onset of the disorder.

In recovery it is important to reexamine family rules, e.g., regarding how to live together, show intimacy, deal with conflict, and express needs. Here are some questions to consider:

- Are the rules inconsistent or unpredictable? Or are they rigid? Do they apply to some family members and not others?
- Do the rules inhibit or promote emotional expression?
- Do the rules facilitate or inhibit conflict negotiation?
- Do the rules help family members embrace or avoid differences?
- Do the rules encourage family members to check things out with one another or to assume and fill in the blanks with whatever each "thinks is happening" to others?
- Do the rules promote or discourage family secrets?
- Do the rules inhibit freedom or sacrifice boundaries and privacy?
- Do the rules foster or inhibit growth and movement in relationships?
- Do the rules focus mainly on physical appearance and performance?
- What are the pros and cons for changing the rules?

Note
Rules and Relationships: The Family Context of Eating Disorders. Agent-approved abridgement of Chapter 3: pp. 56–79 from Surviving an Eating Disorder, 3rd Ed. by Michele Siegel, PhD, Judith Brisman, PhD, and Margot Weinshel, MSW. Copyright © 1988, 1997, 2009 by Judith Brisman, Margot Weinshel, and the estate of Michele Siegel. Reprinted by permission of HarperCollins Publishers.

supported to practice sitting with strong emotions and differences, which is an important skill for recovery and life. During Session 8, members realize that family rules and practices affect the kind of connections they can have with one another, as well as the recovery process. The R4R therapists emphasize that connections with family members continue to be very important for young adults. However, what often needs to change are the rules and the nature of these connections as recovery progresses and the young adult moves along their developmental trajectory. Session 8 goals, materials, and handouts are outlined in Box 12.1.

Rules and Relationships 171

Box 12.1 Session 8: Anorexia Nervosa and the Family Context: Rules and Relationships

Goals

Help patients and family members to:

- Understand how individual and family "rules" are formed and that they ideally change over time during development in order to promote growth.
- Understand how individual and family growth and development are hampered by AN and its rules, contributing to internal and interpersonal disconnections.
- Identify implicit and explicit rules related to AN, recovery, and relationships.
- Identify which rules help members embrace difference in connection versus avoid it and perpetuate AN.

Materials

- Paper and pens.
- Easel paper and easel.
- Poster that lists criteria used to evaluate rules. (You can show all of them but will be using the criterion about whether a rule helps *embrace or avoid difference* later during the group today.)

Exercise

- In small family groups, brainstorm a list of implicit and explicit rules related to AN, recovery, and relationships. Then return for large group discussion.
- In small family groups, choose one rule from their list and rate it according to the criteria of whether or not the rule helps family members embrace and tolerate difference (e.g., helps everyone be open to different perspectives; name, tolerate, regulate, and express different emotions; negotiate conflict; and repair relationships after interpersonal disconnections). Then return to large group discussion.

Handouts

- Distribute list of strategies for connection created last week.
- Strategies to Promote Mutual Connections and Recovery (members read out loud at start of group).
- Rules and Relationships: The Family Context of Eating Disorders.

References

*No DOI

Maine, M. (2004). *Father hunger: Fathers, daughters, and the pursuit of thinness* (2nd ed.). Gurze Books.

*Miller, J. B., & Stiver, I. P. (1997). *The healing connection: How women form relationships in therapy and in life.* Beacon Press.

Siegel, M., Brisman, J., & Weinshel, M. (2009). *Surviving an eating disorders: Strategies for family and friends* (3rd ed.). Harper Collins.

13 Session 9: Identifying Points of Tension and Disconnections Related to Anorexia Nervosa, Recovery, and Relationships

Mary Tantillo, Jennifer Sanftner McGraw, and Daniel Le Grange

Session 9 begins like other sessions with the review of strategies of connection. This session flows naturally from Session 8 because group discussion of implicit and explicit rules usually leads to identification of points of tension and disconnections experienced by patients and family members. The R4R therapists can begin the group with this statement and reinforce the notion that unhelpful rules promote tension and disconnection. The therapists should remind the group that these rules need to be revised or discarded in order to strengthen mutual connections and move ahead together in recovery. They should note that today members will work on identifying the specific points of tension and disconnections created, amplified, and/or maintained by AN. During Session 9 the R4R therapist aims include:

- Help group members identify points of tension and disconnections related to AN, recovery, and relationships (including mealtime and non-mealtime examples)
- Assist members to identify strategies that move them from disconnection to better connection with self and others

Before moving into the work related to points of tension and disconnections, the R4R therapists distribute the copies of implicit and explicit rules related to AN, recovery, and relationships developed during the last session. They encourage members to refer to the copies when doing small group work related to points of tension and disconnections. A number of the rules may give them a "jump start" if needed. The therapists state that they will do some large group discussion about points of tension and disconnections first. Then members will be asked to break out into their individual family units to do some small group work on identifying points of tension and disconnections related to AN. Next, the large group will be re-convened for discussion of their findings and development of a list of points of tension and disconnections that will be used for large group discussion in future sessions. Finally, the large group will review a handout regarding strategies to facilitate movement from disconnection to better connection.

Next, the R4R therapists ask members if they can remember the two main kinds of disconnection that AN creates and/or maintains. The therapists will have the posters of the circles of disconnection (Chapter 5) available so they can display the circles and ask what might be happening in relationships in each disconnection example (i.e., one set of completely separated I and You circles and one set of I and You circles superimposed on one another). The therapists remind group members that as discussed in previous sessions, AN can create and maintain disconnections internally (e.g., due to difficulty identifying and regulating emotions, challenges discerning physical from emotional fullness or hunger, conflict avoidance, etc.) and interpersonally (e.g., due to rigid, all or nothing thinking, focus on detail at the expense of the big picture, the stress and fatigue related to the illness state and caregiving efforts, etc.). These disconnections can be signaled early on by a feeling of tension in the relationship. Being aware of the points of tension (related to AN, recovery, and relationships) and the disconnections created and maintained by AN is essential to sustained and full recovery. The faster members can anticipate or name points of tension and disconnections, the faster they can change course or engage in relational repair. It is then more difficult for AN to maintain itself because family members are working together to empower the patient and disempower the illness (Banks & Hirschman, 2016; Miller & Stiver, 1997; Siegel & Hartzell, 2003; Tantillo, 2006; Tantillo, McGraw, Hauenstein, & Groth, 2015; Tantillo, Sanftner, & Hauenstein, 2013).

The therapists then ask members to divide into their family subunits for ten minutes to generate a list of possible points of tension and disconnections related to AN, recovery, and relationships. They note that the large group will reconvene after small group work to list examples from all families and that the list will inform future group work. They are asked again to remember that the small group work involves brainstorming and not critique. Family members may have different perspectives on what constitutes a point of tension or disconnection and they may each feel differently about a particular point of tension or disconnection. Everyone's contribution is important and needs to be recorded. Again, therapists emphasize that when differences exist in how family members experience points of tension and disconnections, this is a great opportunity for curiosity and understanding different perspectives. This situation gives members more opportunity to practice being "different-in-connection" and increases mutual understanding, empathy, and trust. Examples of points of tension and disconnections include statements regarding the patient's weight, appearance, and progress in treatment; certain "rigid" family rules; and challenges balancing siblings' needs and the patient's needs. See Table 13.1 for a list of points of tension and disconnections identified by patients and family members in previous R4R MFTGs.

During the break-out part of this session the R4R therapists circulate throughout the room, touching base with each family. They can get a sense of issues that need to be raised during the large group discussion. They can also

Session 9: Identifying Points of Tension 175

Table 13.1 Points of Tension and Disconnections Related to Anorexia Nervosa, Recovery, and Relationships

- Grocery shopping
- Food preparation
- Being policed at meals
- Comments on what I am eating
- Big family dinners with large quantities of food
- Having trigger food around
- Eating at restaurants
- Commenting on physical appearance
- Separating the eating disorder voice from the person's voice
- Jumping to conclusions about eating disorder behavior
- Jumping to extremes in general
- Feeling like a burden
- Privacy versus secrecy
- Not sharing emotions
- Telling people how they feel versus asking them
- Dishonesty
- Feeling mistrusted
- Having intense emotions
- The silent treatment
- When I am expected to mind read
- When my mother is a helicopter mother
- Comparing myself with others
- Feeling like I have to be the best at everything
- If I can't do something perfectly, don't bother trying
- Wanting to please everyone
- I have to do it all on my own; asking for help means I am a failure
- Lack of flexibility; trouble changing plans
- When he isolates in his room
- Siblings feeling left out
- Discussion about whether to return to college
- Dealing with others who are not educated about eating disorders

normalize concerns and challenges and encourage members to bring them forward to the group. Additionally, if patients and families experience tension just from discussing points of tension and disconnection, therapists can model and discuss various ways to move from interpersonal disconnection into better or new connection. The therapists can normalize this situation as something families may experience, and they should ask families to add this situation to their list of points of tension and disconnections. Sometimes using externalization and humor about this can lighten up the situation, e.g., "So, it looks like AN might be trying to take advantage of the situation right now by creating tension and disconnection while we are just trying to name points of tension and disconnections. It tries to get in our way whenever it thinks it has a chance." Alternatively, the therapist can engage in some brief family work, helping the patient or family member name the point of tension or disconnection (and associated feelings) that is occurring in the immediacy of

176 *Mary Tantillo, Jennifer Sanftner McGraw, and Daniel Le Grange*

the small group work. If the patient becomes defensive or shuts down during the small group work, despite therapist and family efforts to process issues and continue with the small group work, offer encouragement and normalize that this work is very challenging. Promote universality and remind them that they are not alone in the challenge. Encourage them to consider discussing what transpired when the large group reconvenes. Their scenario, if appropriate, could be discussed in the larger group as an example of how to move out of disconnection into better connection. Support and feedback from other patients and family members can often decrease tension, promote validation, and increase flexible thinking and problem solving.

After the small group, the therapists ask members to reconvene as a large group to share what it was like to do the exercise (e.g., 10–15 minutes) and some of their points of tension and interpersonal disconnections (e.g., 10–15 minutes). The R4R therapists record these points of tension and disconnections on an easel sheet of paper and tell members they will distribute copies of the list during the next session. They note that the points of tension and disconnections will also inform the discussion in future groups. Following is a clinical vignette showing how the R4R therapist helped a patient and her parents and siblings identify and move through a disconnection that came up during large group discussion. Their ability to practice new emotional and relational skills and move into better connection provided a great example for other families.

Therapist: So, I am wondering how the small group exercise went for folks. What was it like to work together to name points of tension and disconnections?

Mom: Well, it was a little challenging for us because we ended up having a point of tension while trying to do the assignment. We kind of got stuck part way through.

Therapist: It is excellent that you noticed that you were experiencing a point of tension during the group work and that you can share this with us. That is exactly what is required in recovery, even if it might feel uncomfortable or unfamiliar. Can you say more about that mom?

Mom: We started out OK and were able to list off some disconnections that happen, but we got stuck on what happens during mealtimes. (She looks over at her daughter, Lindsey [age 21], who shoots her a quick look. Lindsey then looks at her father and readjusts her body to sit looking away from him.) Lindsey eventually stopped talking, and I think she and her dad don't see eye to eye on what should happen at meals. My husband wants to help but it is how he goes about it that can be challenging.

Therapist: Lindsey, would you agree with mom's interpretation of what goes on at meals? Or do you think differently about what she is saying?

Lindsey: I don't think that talking about this is going to get us anywhere.

Therapist: You are worried it will lead to more tension or disconnection?

Lindsey: Yes.

Therapist: Do you know how you are feeling right now, in your heart?

Session 9: Identifying Points of Tension   177

Lindsey:	*Shakes her head to indicate she does not know.*
Therapist:	*Do you want the feelings sheet to try and help you figure it out? We can send it over to you.*
Lindsey:	*OK.*
Therapist:	*Here you go (and passes the sheet to her).*
Lindsey:	*(Looking over the sheet.)*
Therapist:	*If you are having a hard time figuring out the feeling, try to also focus on where you feel it in your body. Are you feeling anything physically right now like in your stomach or head or chest or limbs?*
Lindsey:	*I feel tension in my head and a heaviness in my chest.*
Therapist:	*When you have felt these things before, do you remember what you were feeling in your heart? Do any of the feeling words you see on the sheet fit with the physical experiences you are having?*
Lindsey:	*I guess sad and frustrated. And... probably hurt.*
Therapist:	*Excellent work. Can you say more about where those feelings are coming from? How are they related to what goes on at meals?*
Lindsey:	*I know my dad wants to help me, but the way he does this is NOT working. It seems like no matter what I say to him, he does not get that his approach is not helping.*
Therapist:	*So, you are feeling sad, frustrated, and hurt because you do not feel heard by dad?*
Lindsey:	*Yes.*
Therapist:	*And those are the feelings at the table too? Yes, but also just overwhelmed. My dad keeps pushing. I just want him to let me take a breath sometimes.*
Therapist:	*Dad, your wife and daughter see your desire to help Lindsey at meals. At the same time, it sounds like you may feel somewhat challenged by the eating disorder with how to best support Lindsey. Do you see it that way or is your experience different from what they are saying?*
Dad:	*Yes, they have told me that my approach is not helpful, but I am tired of watching my daughter not get the proper nutrition. I feel like my wife does not take the bull by the horns at times. I end up feeling like I have to do that, so the eating disorder does not win.*
Therapist:	*So, you feel pressured to step in and try to fix things as her dad. Dads do feel a pressure to fix things. That makes sense. Do you know exactly what you are feeling as you describe this to us?*
Dad:	*I feel like I am the bad guy all the time. I have to have the heavy hand. It does not feel good, but I will do whatever it takes to help my daughter get her life back.*
Therapist:	*Dad, those are excellent thoughts. Can you tell specifically what you FEEL in your heart about what goes on at meals? If you need the feelings sheet, we can pass that down to you too. We are all practicing today. (She smiles at dad.)*
Dad:	*I can tell you what I feel at meals. I feel afraid that my daughter is getting taken advantage of by this illness that won't let go. I feel like I am in a battle at the table to help my daughter get free.*
Therapist:	*That sounds like a lot of pressure for you at meals. And it sounds like your daughter is also feeling a lot of pressure. You both are having pretty intense*

178   *Mary Tantillo, Jennifer Sanftner McGraw, and Daniel Le Grange*

emotions while trying to do some very challenging work at meals. Did you know that Lindsey was feeling sad, frustrated, hurt, and overwhelmed at meals? I don't think you intend for her to feel those feelings. It sounds like you intend to help.

Dad: *I did not know she felt all those things. I figured she was mad at me for pushing her, but I do it because I love her. Lindsey, I don't mean for you to feel that way, but I don't know what to do when you are not completing your meal plan. In other places in my life, when I am faced with the enemy, I learn to keep going regardless of the pain involved. I am concentrating on the final outcome.*

Mom: *My husband has been enlisted in the armed forces for over 20 years now. He is not used to backing off in the face of the enemy. I keep telling him this is more complicated though because his daughter is also at the table. We have to find a way to support her while not supporting the illness.*

Therapist: *So, dad, now I can understand even more how painful mealtimes must be for you and Lindsey. Tell me, what do you do in the military after you try using a rifle and that does not do the job?*

Dad: *I could throw a grenade.*

Therapist: *And what if that doesn't work?*

Dad: *(He smiles.) I can use an artillery cannon.*

Therapist: *I think you know where I am going with this. As your wife said, you have learned to keep going and do more in the face of the enemy. (She then looks at Lindsey.) Lindsey, whatever we ask your dad to do to help you, the good soldier in him needs to feel like he is truly helping you and battling the eating disorder. Earlier you said you would like for him to let you take a breath sometimes. He may feel like allowing for this is not helping your recovery. Can you let him know why this is important for you?*

Lindsey: *Dad, I need to a break sometimes at the table. I have to calm down when I feel a bad wave of anxiety. I feel totally out of control, and I know you want me to push through it. But sometimes I need to take a breath and slow down for a minute.*

Therapist: *So, you would like dad to let you pace yourself a little differently at those times because the anxiety feels like a tidal wave. It feels immobilizing.*

Lindsey: *Yes, exactly. And he thinks I am just trying to avoid eating. Yes, it is true I want to avoid it, but I also know I need to keep going. I just need to recenter for a minute.*

Therapist: *So, it is excellent that you suggest to dad that you breathe at those times. You are reminding him that it is important for him to breathe too. I am wondering if you can tell him this at those times? Can you say, dad, I need to breathe for a minute?*

Lindsey: *Yes, I can try, but sometimes, I am just so overwhelmed, I am not even thinking clearly enough to say that.*

Therapist: *Dad, here is where you can help. Can you ask her if taking a breath would be helpful? Can you actually take a long deep breath with her at those times and acknowledge her need to pace herself a little slower? You are not backing off from the meal completion goal, but you are pacing her differently to achieve it.*

Session 9: Identifying Points of Tension   179

	You allowing her to breathe and breathing with her helps her slow down the intense emotions inside and allows her to feel more freed up to do what is required to care for herself. Sometimes we have to slow down or back up to be able to move ahead. I think the best soldiers would agree that sometimes you have to pull back a bit during a particular battle in order to move ahead and win the war.
Dad:	*I never thought of it that way. It makes sense.*
Therapist:	*This approach helps you stay connected with your daughter while you work against the eating disorder. If she feels connected to you during meals despite her intense emotions, she won't feel inclined to restrict to deal with them. And if you remain open to one another and connected at the table, you can come up with additional strategies to get through the meal together. Lindsey is there any other strategy that might help at these times when you need to breathe and slow down a bit?*
Lindsey:	*Seeing all the food on my tray starts to feel overwhelming. Maybe set aside some of the food in front of me so I can concentrate on one thing at a time.*
Therapist:	*That sounds like a great idea. The eating disorder wants you both to feel fear and out of control so that it can continue to take advantage of Lindsey and stay connected with her. Taking a breath and focusing on one food item at a time can help her feel a sense of control so the eating disorder doesn't take advantage of her. (The therapist turns to Lindsey's siblings, Sarah [age 18] and Tom [age 24]. Sarah and Tom, I am curious about your thoughts about the mealtime point of tension we discussed and the solution we came up with.*
Sarah:	*I am the one who is usually at meals, and it is hard because dad does want to help but things backfire when he gets intense at the table and insists that Lindsey continue to eat at a pace that he sets.*
Therapist:	*How do you feel while all that is going on?*
Sarah:	*It makes me very tense and, honestly, I don't want to be at the table. It makes eating together very stressful. I want to support my sister, but it is frustrating when meals turn into a battle of the wills. The more my dad pushes at times, the more the eating disorder pushes back. My dad and my sister are very similar. Both very strong willed. I do think that both of them taking a breath at times during the meal would help. They could probably come up with additional ways to deal with the meal if they could stop the action for a minute and reset.*
Therapist:	*Thank you Sarah for your honesty about how stressful and frustrating things can feel at mealtimes. Siblings often have these experiences. You are not alone. Tom, how about you?*
Tom:	*I am not home for meals like I was in the past because I live with my buddies. When I am here for a meal on the weekend, Sarah is right. It is stressful at the table at times. I want to tell my dad to back off, but I am afraid it will only piss him off more. So, I stay quiet. My mom tries to tell him, but he worries that if he backs off even a little, my sister won't get well. It makes me not want to come home for meals sometimes because I know what will happen when we get to the table. I want to support my sister, but I am not sure how to do that.*

180 *Mary Tantillo, Jennifer Sanftner McGraw, and Daniel Le Grange*

Therapist: Well, I believe you two are already supporting her just by showing up here at group and being willing to discuss these points of tension and disconnections created by the eating disorder. Your honesty and desire to help are so essential. Lindsey, what else can your siblings do to support you?

Lindsey: Showing up for family meals on weekends helps me because I am not alone at the table with mom and dad. We can talk about other things you guys are doing. It helps. Plus, I guess if I could do something with you guys after meals that would help. It feels awful not being able to do anything after meals on my own or with my friends away from mom and dad. I am 21, and I have to stay near them in a common area for an hour after meals right now. Having you guys around makes it more normal and enjoyable. It is lonely without you around. I know I make it hard for you to want to be around me.

Sarah: It is not your fault Lindsey. It is the eating disorder. We care about you. I can try to remember to stick around after meals at least on Mondays, Wednesdays, Fridays, and Sundays. Tuesdays and Thursdays are harder because I have soccer practice. And I may go out Saturday nights sometimes.

Tom: I can try to come over on Saturdays at least once a month, and I can try to be there Tuesdays and Thursdays after dinner, if not during dinner. I will try to be there for Sunday dinners together.

Therapist: Sarah and Tom, thank you for supporting your sister in this way. Your connections with her are so important to her healing and recovery. As Lindsey progresses in recovery, she will not always need the structure and supervision she is receiving from your parents right now. Having you available at the times you note sounds like it is a great comfort to her.

Lindsey: Thanks, you guys.

Therapist: I am sure that Lindsey and her family are not the only family that has experienced points of tension or disconnections like the ones they have shared. I am wondering how others are feeling in response to what they have shared with us? For example, are your experiences similar to or different from theirs at mealtimes? (After hearing the responses from other patients and families, the therapist asks if there were any other feelings or thoughts members wanted to share about the exercise before beginning to jointly create a list of group member points of tension and disconnections.)

In this vignette the R4R therapist helps Lindsey's family work through a point of tension experienced at mealtimes in order to model for group members how to engage in the emotional and relational work required to move from disconnection to better connection. The therapist intentionally begins with *validation* for Lindsey's *and* her father's experiences of the point of tension related to meals (i.e., Lindsey's need to slow down at times in the face of intense emotion and dad's need to keep her eating). This intervention fosters safety, trust, openness to being emotionally vulnerable, and further exploration and dialogue. The therapist also intentionally asks them if they feel *similarly or differently* about the point of tension as described by others

Session 9: Identifying Points of Tension 181

(promoting the possibility of difference-in-connection). The therapist helps Lindsey and her father move toward one another in relationship by first helping them connect with what they each are feeling about the point of tension at meals. The therapist deliberately offers the feelings sheet to Lindsey and her father to help them connect with their own genuine feelings. They can then practice sharing these with one another while also listening to one another's feelings. Specifically, this work involves engaging in self-empathy (figuring out and embracing what one feels inside) and then sharing emotions with the other, which promotes mutual empathy (being attentive to one's own and the other's emotional experiences). The therapist also facilitates Lindsey connecting with herself (her genuine experience) by encouraging her to attend to her internal bodily states. The therapist does this to help her link emotions with particular bodily states. She also could have helped Lindsey connect feelings with behavioral states like clenching her jaw or nervously shaking her leg if these were occurring. These emotional and relational skills facilitate connection with self and self-disclosure that can foster mutuality (bidirectional movement of thoughts, feelings, and activity in relationships) with loved ones.

In addition to helping Lindsey and her dad identify their feelings associated with the point of tension at meals, the R4R therapist helps them examine the meanings related to the point of tension and associated feelings. For example, Lindsey says she feels overwhelmed with emotions and this is what leads to her need to take a breath and slow down. Her dad has intense fear at meals when her eating slows down and feels like he is not helping her battle the eating disorder and move ahead in recovery if he allows her to slow her pace of eating. The therapist notes that dad intends to be helpful and asks if he realized that Lindsey experiences the intense negative feelings she describes at mealtimes when he is pushing the pace he feels comfortable with. She does this, again, to promote mutual understanding of the intense emotions both experience during mealtime.

The therapist also makes use of analogies or metaphors that aptly express what Lindsey and her father experience. For example, she frames Lindsey's anxiety as a "tidal wave" and she describes her father as a "good soldier." She intentionally uses military terms to help dad understand that his desire to push his daughter through the meal may not bring the desired outcomes. He cannot treat the mealtime scenario exactly as he would a battle with an enemy because he may end up sacrificing his relationship with his daughter. She needs this relationship to move ahead during the meal and recovery, while at the same time, they both need to push back on the eating disorder. The therapist relationally reframes the point of tension for Lindsey's dad so he can understand it and the needed solutions in a different way. She encourages the patient to assert her need to breathe at meals and focus on one food item at a time, while also asking her father to help her accomplish this if she is too emotionally vulnerable and overwhelmed to advocate for herself. This intervention promotes mutual empowerment, because Lindsey and her dad are encouraged to act as their own advocates (Lindsey for her need to breathe and pace herself and dad for his need to battle the eating disorder and support his daughter) while advocating for each other and their relationship (the I, You, and We).

In addition to clarifying what needs to change relationally for Lindsey and her dad, the therapist also invites Lindsey's siblings into the conversation. She understands that they can further buttress Lindsey in her recovery attempts and support her continued development as a young adult. She also recognizes they need to name their feelings in relation to the stated point of tension at meals. This activity can free them up to be more emotionally available to their sister. She was able to solicit their feelings of tension and frustration and the temptation to engage in avoidance of family meals and the patient. Through naming the point of tension and their related feelings, Lindsey's siblings were freed up to offer her more connection and support after meals.

Whenever processing points of tension and disconnections, it is important for the R4R therapist to defer problem solving of solutions until later in the discussion. Anxiety and the desire to avoid conflict may push group members to problem solve solutions to points of tension and disconnections prematurely, before examining the associated emotions and meanings. For example, the therapist did not return to the discussion of Lindsey wanting to "take a breath" at meals until she and her father had processed the feelings and meanings related to the point of tension at meals and what taking a breath meant to the patient and her dad. Patients and family members will be more open to effective problem solving once feelings and meanings are fully explored. These feelings and meanings can then accurately inform strategies that will move group members out of disconnection to better connection. When exploring strategies for moving from disconnection to better connection, the therapists can call upon the patients as "experts" who can educate their loved ones regarding possible solutions. Alternatively, the therapists can begin problem-solving solutions to move from disconnection to better connection by validating that the whole room is full of experts (patients and families) with much lived experience. The therapists reinforce that they have confidence in how the group can brainstorm together ways out of disconnection to better or new connection.

The R4R therapists end group today having members take turns reading aloud items from the handout "Moving Through Disconnection to Better Connection" (see Table 13.2). Each item is a strategy that puts connection at the heart of the relationship and assists in the movement from disconnection to mutual connection.

The R4R therapist will ask members their thoughts and feelings about the strategies, if any stood out to them, and if they have tried other strategies not present on the worksheets. The therapists will note that "I statements" (e.g., "I feel frustrated. I need more help.") and paying attention to one's own internal experience are very important in developing

Session 9: Identifying Points of Tension 183

Table 13.2 Moving Through Disconnection to Better Connection: Learning a New Relational Language and Process

It is important to learn and practice the language of "connection and disconnection" and place the connection, instead of the self or other, at the heart of experience.

- Recognize that "connection comes first."
  When trouble arises in the relationship, focus on the connection versus the issue or individual. If people are in connection, anything can be discussed well; if people are in disconnection, nothing can be discussed well. Moving from a language of *self* to a language of *connections* helps heal things in paradoxical ways. For example, instead of saying "*You're* such a jerk," or "*I* feel neglected," say, "*We're* in a disconnect." The latter is a connecting thing to say. While it is important to own your feelings in an interaction, it is easy to get stuck focusing only on your feelings. Talk about the relationship, not just you or me.

- Identify difficult transitions that threaten the "we."
  Relationships have three phases of transition: moving into connection (getting engaged), holding the connection, and disengaging (but not necessarily disconnecting). All families face times that threaten connection. For some it is the transition from the end of the workday to the beginning of time together at home. For some it is Sunday nights, as they prepare for the Monday workday. Holidays, anniversaries, visits to extended families in distant places – all of these can make the relationships with one another more vulnerable. We have to take extra care of relationships at these times, since family members can be more easily hurt and there is increased risk for disconnection. The goal is to identify your family's high-risk vulnerable times – times that threaten connection between some or all of the members.

- Hold the "we" through the disconnection.
  Move from being alone in your differences to being with each other in your differences. Differences add to, instead of detract from, growth in the relationship and can lead to increased mutuality. Family members can hold the "We" without abandoning the "I" or "You." Forces of culture, gender, and personality pull us to abandon the "We" for the "I" or "You." Everyone makes mistakes and experiences disconnections in relationships. What matters is the relational repair that follows. Feeling the feelings together without having to fix them, analyze them, or act on them through binging, purging, restricting exercising, or medicating them with drugs or alcohol invites shared understanding and validation. Validation is key. Shared understanding leads to shared experience and mutual empathy. Family members can learn to identify with one another, not compare. They can learn together.

- Check-In
  Checking in maintains the continuity of connection. It takes the pulse of the relationship. Anyone can call for a check-in. The first person says, briefly, where he or she is in thought or feeling about the other person and the relationship. The other says only "I hear you," and responds in kind. The first person says "I hear you," and that's it.

(Continued)

184 *Mary Tantillo, Jennifer Sanftner McGraw, and Daniel Le Grange*

Table 13.2 (Continued)

- Check-Out
  Checking out prevents destructive disconnection. If things get too heated too fast, feel out of control and overwhelming or nonproductive, either person can call for a check-out. Check-out means I am stopping the conversation and leaving right now. However, if you check out, you are responsible for bringing the issue back up again in a reasonable period of time, e.g., five minutes to the next morning, but no more than 24 hours. Don't let the impasse last. This approach capitalizes on early intervention and letting go and coming back.

- The 20-Minute Rule
  Every day set aside 20 minutes to discuss a particular issue, no more, no less. You can split up the time into ten minutes for each person, so one listens while the other speaks. At high-risk times, interactive dialogue may be too dangerous, but attentive listening can help. Twenty minutes gives the person who worries the discussion won't stop, a sense of comfort and control, and it allows the person who fears her experience is minimized or dismissed to feel heard.

- Reframe Common Dilemmas in Terms of "We"
  When feelings or issues arise, try to see them in terms of the "We" versus seeing them residing within the individual. For example, do not locate the eating disorder entirely within your loved one. Instead, shift the focus onto the priority of the relationship. Also, the loved one's recovery becomes less the focus, and the building of better or new connection with the family becomes more the focus.

- Bring Your Outside Creativity Inside the Relationship
  Relationship is a creative process. Growth-fostering connections have much in common with creative processes: curiosity, flexibility, spontaneity, freedom of movement, patience, persistence, humility, playfulness, humor, intuition, risk-taking, holding opposites simultaneously, knowing when to hold on and when to let go, and openness to change and revision. Bring individual creative skills into the service of the relationship. Find "our" way out of problems or along the change process.

- Use Humor
  Laughing together promotes connection when used appropriately. (Humor can be disconnecting or distracting as well.) Humor can sometimes move family members out of a stuck place in relationships. Humor can be found in the worst impasses. Develop catch phrases that trigger a way out through humor and that add a perspective on how ridiculous the whole thing is. For example, one couple found humor by prescribing how many times they needed to apologize based on the severity of the offense. Here is what they said: Dan: "I'm sorry. I'm sorry. I'm sorry." Chelsea: Silence. Dan: "How many more times do I have to say I'm sorry?" Chelsea: "Two more times." Dan: "I'm sorry. I'm sorry." Chelsea: "OK."

(Continued)

Session 9: Identifying Points of Tension   185

Table 13.2 (Continued)

- Be Mindful and Stay in the Present Moment, Not the Past
Practice observing and describing what is happening currently in the relationship without using negative evaluation. For example, say "We both are pretty upset right now and are having a tough time listening to each other" versus "You're being ridiculous and unfair, and you never listen to me because you don't care." Avoid reducing the present to the past because this can lead to disconnection and obstructs growth in the relationship in the now. A focus on the past may also be used as an escape from the work of connecting, since connecting always occurs in the present. Even old grudges cannot be negotiated if there is no good communication in the present. When we are more connected in the present, we can go to the past in a more meaningful way.

Note

Moving Through Disconnection to Better Connection: Learning a New Relational Language and Process. Adapted from *We have to talk: Healing dialogues between men and women* (pp. 92–164), by S. Shem & J. Surrey, 1998, New York, NY: Basic Books. Copyright 1998 by S. Bergman and J. Surrey. Adapted with permission.

mutual relationships and identifying and repairing interpersonal disconnections. However, this work should be done with a simultaneous focus on respecting and strengthening the "We" in the relationship (e.g., using "We" statements like "We are in a disconnect right now. We don't seem to be a good place right now. We both seem to feel alone and misunderstood. We both might need a little space right now."). The therapists can remind members again how in the dominant American culture, the "We" gets less attention because there is a hypertrophied emphasis on the autonomous "I." This is also true in terms of the traditional hallmark of healthy psychological maturation, i.e., the individuated and separate "I" has been more valued in our culture than the interdependent "We" (Jordan, 1986; 2018; Miller and Stiver, 1997). True mutually empathic, authentic, and empowering relationships that contribute to sustained full recovery respect each person in the relationship, as well as the connection binding those in relationship (Jordan, 2018; Tantillo, Sanftner & Hauenstein, 2013). Before concluding the session, the R4R therapists distribute the following handouts (see Tables 13.3 and 13.4 and Figure 13.1) for review before Session 10:

- Mealtime Guidelines and Support Strategies for Recovery handout
- *Coaching* and Mealtime Assistance handout
- Recovery Plate Diagram handout

These handouts offer mealtime support strategies and information that can reduce the occurrence of points of tension and disconnections specifically related to mealtimes. Session 9 goals, materials, and handouts are outlined in Box 13.1 at the end of this chapter.

186 *Mary Tantillo, Jennifer Sanftner McGraw, and Daniel Le Grange*

Table 13.3 Mealtime Guidelines and Support Strategies for Recovery

- **Maintain a regular eating schedule.** The eating disorder will push you to delay or skip meals or fast for long periods of time. Starvation makes us think more about food though. To avoid this preoccupation, eat every three hours. If you need support with shopping, planning, or preparing meals, get a trusted support person to help. These activities can be very anxiety-provoking early in recovery. Initially you may want to purchase foods that don't need a lot of preparation so you can reduce anxiety.
- **Plan ahead for meals and snacks.** Writing a meal plan ahead of time will help you feel less anxious when it is time to eat. It might be helpful to develop a meal plan for a week's time. If you work with a dietitian, she/he can prescribe you the right amount and type of foods so that you will know you are not overeating or undereating. Each meal should consist of some carbohydrate, protein, and fat. Have a support person help you develop a meal plan if it is too anxiety-provoking to do alone. Try not to work on your weekly meal plan for more than an hour. Get help if you start obsessing about the food and the plan.
- **Eliminate diet products, low-fat, fat-free, or other "special" food items from your meal plan unless they are needed due to medical necessity.** You and those with whom you eat should have meals that don't perpetuate the eating disorder. As long as you use diet, low-fat, fat-free or other "special" food items, the eating disorder has a hold on you. Avoidance of fat or high-calorie foods fuels the eating disorder.
- **Grocery shop at times that are not high risk and/or get a support person to help.** Going to the grocery story can feel overwhelming. Make a grocery list ahead of time and be sure to include the foods you noted on your meal plan. Take a friend with you if needed and go shopping during times that are not high risk. For example, shopping late at night can be very risky. You might feel more anxious, have more eating disorder thoughts, be tempted to binge, buy extra food/trigger foods, etc. Do not buy in bulk if you can help it because if you binge eat, this can be triggering and lead to symptoms.
- **Set a time frame of 30–45 minutes for meals and 15–20 minutes for snacks.** The eating disorder will push you to restrict and avoid or delay meal or snack completion. Meals are normally completed within 30–45 minutes and snacks within 15–20 minutes.
- **Challenge your strict eating rules.** The eating disorder makes you stick to strict rules about food and eating. Each time you follow a rule, it fuels the eating disorder. It is important to replace eating disorder rules with healthier eating rules. For example, if you have a rule forbidding *all* desserts, change it into a less rigid guideline such as, "I won't eat dessert every day" or " I won't gain weight by enjoying an occasional dessert." Make a list of all your eating disorder rules and prioritize them from the least scary to the scariest. Start with the least scary rule and break it first for one week. You can rate your anxiety on a scale from 0–100 before and after you break it. When your anxiety goes down to 20–30 points after

(Continued)

Session 9: Identifying Points of Tension 187

Table 13.3 (Continued)

you break a rule, work on the next scariest rule. Involve a support person who can help you and practice something distracting or relaxing after you break a rule.

- **Don't diet.** Healthy eating (through the day)—not dieting—is the key to being in a healthy weight range. Instead of focusing on what you shouldn't eat, focus on nutritious foods that will give you energy and make your body strong. Think of food as fuel (energy) for your body. Your body knows when the tank is low, so listen to it. Eat when you're hungry, then stop when you're full. **If the eating disorder has eliminated your hunger and fullness cues**, then first re-establish a pattern of mechanical eating (eating at set times even if you are not hungry) e.g., 8 a.m., noon, and 6 p.m. or break up meals into six smaller meals that you have routinely through the day. It is common to have three meals and a couple small snacks each day. The pattern of eating helps your brain and stomach talk to each other and helps restore your hunger and fullness cues. It is important to stop binge eating and purging too because these behaviors also interrupt the re-establishment of these cues. It could take several months for your hunger and fullness cues to re-establish themselves.
- **Incorporate fear foods into your menu.** The eating disorder will make you especially fearful of certain foods, commonly those high in carbohydrates and/or fat. It will tell you that these foods will make you fat. These foods may also be triggers for binge eating. Each time you avoid these foods, it strengthens the eating disorder and the avoidance of these foods. In order to decrease anxiety, fear, and feelings of loss of control related to these foods, you need to incorporate them in a planned and gradual way. Make a list of all your fear foods/binge foods and prioritize them from the least scary/triggering to the scariest/most triggering. Start with the least scary/least triggering one and try it first. You can rate your anxiety on a scale from 0–100 before and after you try it. When your anxiety goes down to 20–30 points after you eat it, work on the next scariest/next triggering food. Involve a trusted support person who can support you when you try the food item. Stay with that person for an hour after you complete the fear/binge food item. Also practice something distracting or relaxing after you eat it in order to decrease anxiety and prevent vomiting or any other way of compensating for eating the food item. Remember to choose a safe place and less high-risk time of the day when you do this work. Only one serving of the food item should be available. Remember that you will be more successful incorporating fear/binge foods if you have eaten normally earlier that day. Binge eating of trigger foods is more apt to happen if you don't eat earlier in the day. Binge eating is caused by starvation and stress.
- **Create a pleasant atmosphere during meals.** Eat in safe places. Add things that help you feel calm, for example, music. Eat with supportive others and engage in social conversation (movies, TV shows, weather, vacation plans, etc.) that has nothing to do with dieting, body image, exercise or any other triggering issues. Create a code word you will use if the conversation becomes triggering. The code word will signal people to stop talking about these issues without getting

(Continued)

188 *Mary Tantillo, Jennifer Sanftner McGraw, and Daniel Le Grange*

Table 13.3 (Continued)

into a big discussion about this at the meal. Alternatively, you can play a game during the meal with your support person. Try to avoid watching TV while eating when you are re-establishing hunger and fullness cues. You need to remain aware of signals from your body letting you know when you are hungry and full. If eating at home alone creates anxiety, and you can't schedule a meal with a support person, consider eating out in a smaller safe, enjoyable place like a favorite coffee house or bookstore.

- **Get support from others and engage in distracting activities for an hour after meals and 30 minutes after snacks.** You may feel very anxious and out of control after eating. The eating disorder may push you to compensate in some way for eating. Purging could occur through vomiting, exercise, and other behaviors. Staying in a common area versus going up to your bedroom is much safer and helps you avoid the isolation the eating disorder takes advantage of. Do not remain at the table after meals if this is triggering. Change your environment and leave the house if you feel this will help decrease post-meal anxiety. Also, use the bathroom (toileting or showering) before meals or snacks because the eating disorder may use post-mealtime as an opportunity to encourage you to purge after meals. Plan out post-meal distracting activities in advance so you don't have to make a decision about these activities after the meal when you already feel anxious and unsettled.

- **Caregiver support during meals.** Separate the illness from your loved one. An individual with an eating disorder can become highly anxious, panicked, irritable, and/or angry during mealtimes. They can feel very frightened and out of control. Early in refeeding your loved one can experience much gastric discomfort (early sense of fullness, bloating, indigestion, constipation, and/or gas). The physical sense of fullness at meals can combine with the emotional fullness (due to high levels of anxiety, fear, and other negative emotions) experienced at meals. This can feel very overwhelming. Avoid criticism and do not get embroiled in power struggles. Instead focus on being a St. Bernard or Dolphin – come alongside the person and be caring, compassionate, calm, confident, and consistent. If you need a time out, then offer meal support with someone else so you can take turns if needed. Intense emotions and criticism at the table perpetuate the eating disorder and are hurtful to the part of the patient that wants to recover but is scared and overwhelmed due to the bullying of the eating disorder. Be warm, down to earth, and remind your loved one that food is medicine for them. Find ways to encourage additional "bites" to complete their meal.

- **Caregiver support after meals.** After meals help your loved engage in a distracting or relaxing activity. If your loved one is feeling anxious, out of control, or having other intense emotions, help them name them. If this feels too overwhelming at that moment, then help them get distracted by playing cards, a game, going outside to a favorite place, etc. They need help to regulate their intense emotions and eliminate eating disorder thoughts. Validate their experience while acknowledging you don't know exactly what they are feeling.

(Continued)

Session 9: Identifying Points of Tension 189

Table 13.3 (Continued)

Emphasize your love for the person and your desire to help. Remain positive, offer reassurance, and emphasize that treatment is important because it will help him or her to attain their goals and live life more fully. Remember that the person with the eating disorder experiences two voices: one that is saying "You are fat, bad, and ugly, and should not eat" and another that is saying "You are sick and should eat." You cannot reason with the eating disorder voice. It is better to speak to the healthy part of your loved one.

Table 13.4 Coaching and Mealtime Assistance

Mealtime stance. The mealtime stance is one of coaching and involves support, structure, and promotion of the social aspects of eating. The coach is someone who can confidently and comfortably model healthy eating and self-care.

Characteristics of the mealtime coach:

- Externalizes the illness from the recovering individual.
- Is collaborative, emotionally calm, and secure.
- Maintains a positive relationship with the recovering individual.
- Avoids expressing intense negative emotions at the meal and helps the recovering individual regulate emotion.
- Treats mealtime as an opportunity for learning versus a time for success/failure.
- Helps the recovering individual avoid feelings of shame and guilt.
- Uses humor in helpful ways.
- Demonstrates active listening, clarifies questions, and does not make assumptions.
- Uses validation and reflection.
- Involves recovering individual in finding solutions to challenges at the table.
- Offers options within healthy parameters.
- Reinforces the importance of mealtime support (decreases the adverse physical and psychological impact of eating disorders on health and life goals/values. Helps the person see the forest through the trees.)
- Communicates that food is medicine and fuel.
- Consumes no diet foods at the meal.
- Avoids extremes/communicates a flexible attitude about food (e.g., no "good" and "bad" foods).
- Offers distractions, support, and ways to tolerate distress after meals.
- Communicates positive messages about body image.
- Fosters a relationship with the recovering individual outside mealtimes.
- Models self-care.

What does not work at meals: force, guilt trips, lectures, bribes, bargaining, quick return to eating in public (it takes time and should be well-planned)

Box 13.1 Session 9: Identifying Points of Tension and Disconnections Related to Anorexia Nervosa, Recovery, and Relationships

Goals

Help patients and family members to:

- Identify disconnections and points of tension related to AN, recovery, and relationships (including mealtime concerns)
- Practice strategies that move them from disconnection to new and better mutual connections (including strategies supporting patients at mealtimes)
- Identify and express authentic internal experiences while also honoring and nurturing the "We" (what is important to maintain healthy connection) in the relationship
- Identify and express what is similar *and* different across their experiences to help them practice being different in connection

Materials

- Paper and pens
- Easel paper and easel
- Posters or handouts of circles of disconnections (Chapter 5)

Exercise

- Brainstorm a list of disconnections and points of tension related to AN, recovery, and relationships in small family groups. Then return to large group discussion.

Handouts

- Distribute the list of *implicit and explicit rules* developed during the last session. (Discuss how these can help identify disconnections and points of tension today.)
- **At end of group have members take turns** reviewing items on the worksheet *Moving Through Disconnection to Better Connection: Learning a New Relational Language and Process*. This handout emphasizes putting connection at the heart of the relationship and reviews strategies for moving from disconnection to mutual connection.

Session 9: Identifying Points of Tension 191

- Distribute for review by the next meeting:
  - *Mealtime Guidelines and Support Strategies for Recovery handout*
  - *Coaching and Mealtime Assistance handout*
  - *Recovery Plate Diagram handout*

What to Do if Members Have Difficulty Identifying and Discussing Points of Tension and Disconnections

If any particular group member(s) have difficulty naming and exploring points of tension and disconnections, the R4R therapist can employ several strategies. First, the therapists' biggest resource is other patients and families. For example, in the preceding clinical vignette the therapist could have called on other members at several points if Lindsey and/or her father were having challenges processing their point of tension regarding meals. If Lindsey had trouble identifying her feelings despite looking at the feelings sheet or if she declined to see the sheet or shut down, the therapist could have promoted universality and normalized the difficulty in naming intense emotions. She could then ask other patients how they might feel in a similar situation. The validation and clarifications offered by other patients is empowering for the patient who is more disconnected from their internal experiences or too fearful, anxious, hurt, angry, or overwhelmed to state them.

Similarly, the R4R therapist could call on other parents (especially the dads) to state what they might be feeling if Lindsey's dad was struggling with naming his feelings. The therapist might also ask other dads (or moms if there are no dads) how a dad feels when he cannot "fix things" in order to validate how frustrating this situation is. In the vignette, the therapist did not call on other group members until the end of the work with Lindsey's family because she and her family members were able to engage in the processing and practicing of emotional and relational skills to move out of disconnection into better connection.

Additionally, if a member questions whether an activity or situation is representative of a point of tension or disconnection, the therapist can ask for help from the group in evaluating this further. For example, in the vignette, if Lindsey's father maintained that pushing her to eat according to his pace did not create a point of tension or disconnection, the therapist could engage group members in a decisional balance (Prochaska, Norcross & DiClemente, 1994) activity regarding that strategy. The therapist would ask the group to first note the pros of using the strategy, and then the cons. The therapist could then repeat the examination of pros and cons for not using this strategy. Usually, others in the group can identify more cons than pros for points of tension and disconnections, helping the member who is stuck to see things from a different viewpoint. The therapists can also ask members to evaluate whether the action or situation (a) helps you feel more or less connected with yourself (your genuine thoughts, feelings and needs) and (b) helps you feel more or less connected

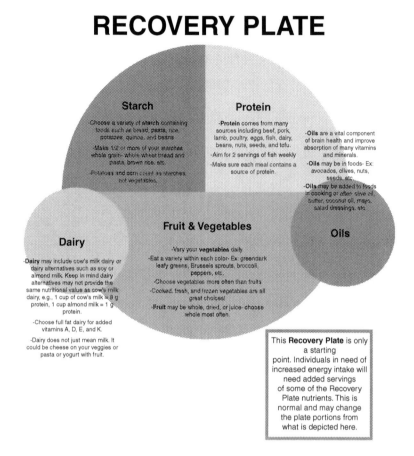

Figure 13.1 Recovery plate. Reprinted from artwork, by Marie Bieber RD, 2019, Copyright 2019 by Marie Bieber RD. Reprinted with permission.

with others. If the particular action or situation leads to more disconnection from yourself and others, it generally involves a point of tension and disconnection. It generally is an action that would obstruct the "Five Good Things" (Chapter 5) in relationship, decrease a sense of perceived mutuality, push the patient to engage in symptoms, and enable AN to maintain itself.

If particular family members get stuck in working through a point of tension or disconnection with one another, it is also important to encourage them not to *"do the relationship for both people"* (i.e., assume how the person will respond and behave accordingly). As noted earlier, the therapists can ask the group to examine the pros and cons of engaging or not engaging in this behavior (decisional balance). Group members can usually quickly identify how *doing the relationship for both people* can be a safe, more controlled, and predictable way of interacting with others, while it also can be painful and lead to more

Session 9: Identifying Points of Tension 193

interpersonal disconnection because each individual's genuine experience does not accurately or fully make it into the relationship.

Finally, if the whole group is having difficulty discussing points of tension and disconnections in the larger group, the R4R therapist can wonder out loud "if AN is taking advantage of all of us in group tonight and trying to disconnect us from one another." The therapists can normalize that this can happen at times because naming points of tension and disconnections requires courage, energy, and perseverance. Members could be feeling very fatigued, anxious, and overburdened due to AN. They may fear that explicitly identifying points of tension and disconnections related to AN may eliminate the last shred of connection they have with one another. It is important for the therapist to note this possibility and to say that AN wants us to think this way. The therapists can explore with the group if this situation is occurring and encourage members to push back on AN by identifying points of tension and disconnections in order to maintain and deepen the mutual connections needed for recovery.

References

No DOI

*Banks, A., & Hirschman, L. A. (2016). *Wired to connect: The surprising link between brain science and strong, healthy relationships.* Jeremy P. Tarcher/Penguin.

Jordan, J. (2018). *Relational-cultural therapy* (2nd ed.). American Psychological Association. https://dx.doi.org/10.1037/0000063-001.

*Miller, J. B., & Stiver, I. P. (1997). *The healing connection: How women form relationships in therapy and in life.* Beacon Press.

*Prochaska, J. O., Norcross, J. C., DiClemente, C. C. (1994). *Changing for good: A revolutionary six-stage program for overcoming bad habits and moving your life positively forward.* William Morrow.

*Siegel, D., & Hartzell, M. (2003). *Parenting from the inside out: How a deeper self-understanding can help you raise children who thrive.* Jeremy P. Tarcher/Putnam.

Tantillo, M. (2006). A relational approach to eating disorders multifamily therapy group: Moving from difference and disconnection to mutual connection. *Families, Systems, & Health, 23*(1), 82–102. https://dx.doi.org/10.1037/1091-7527.24.1.82.

Tantillo, M., McGraw, J. S., Hauenstein, E., & Groth, S. W. (2015). Partnering with patients and families to develop an innovative multifamily therapy group treatment for adults with anorexia nervosa. *Advances in Eating Disorders: Theory, Research, and Practice, 3*(3), 269–287. https://dx.doi.org/10.1080/21662630.2015.1048478.

Tantillo, M., Sanftner, J. L., & Hauenstein, E. (2013). Restoring connection in the face of disconnection: An integrative approach to understanding and treating anorexia nervosa. *Advances in Eating Disorders: Theory, Research, and Practice, 1*, 21–38. https://dx.doi.org/10.1080/21662630.2013.742980.

14 Session 10: Nourishing and Empowering the "We" in Relationships

Mary Tantillo, Jennifer Sanftner McGraw, and Daniel Le Grange

After reviewing the strategies for connection at the start of Session 10, the R4R therapists begin by reminding group members that Session 10 is the last weekly group. They note that Sessions 11–14 will meet every other week, and Sessions 15 and 16 will meet monthly to give members an opportunity to practice skills learned in MFTG and report back. They continue by reinforcing that today the group will continue to discuss points of tension and disconnections, factors that contribute to their development and maintenance, and strategies to empower the "We" in relationships. They tell members that they will choose one point of tension/disconnection from the list they generated last week and jointly discuss the item, as well as problem-solve strategies to move out of disconnection into better and/or new mutual connections. Therefore, the therapist aims during Session 10 are to:

- Assist members to continue identifying and working through points of tension and disconnections
- Discuss interacting forces that push us to focus on the "I" and "You" at the expense of the "We"
- Discuss strategies to empower the "We" and increase mutual connections for continued recovery

The R4R therapists begin the review of previously identified points of tension and disconnections related to AN, recovery, and relationships by distributing copies of the points of tension and disconnections that were identified in the large group discussion during the last session. They give members an opportunity to review these items and point out that both mealtime and non-mealtime points of tension and disconnections can be discussed in the group. They remind members of the handouts regarding mealtime support strategies that were distributed during the last session. The therapists state that they provided the handouts as a resource for members with the hope that their review will facilitate discussion of any additional related mealtime points of tension or disconnections. The R4R therapists can inquire whether there are any other points of tension and disconnections that members would like to add to the list. These items should be added onto the list, which will be redistributed at the next session. The therapists tell members they will return to the list a little later in group.

Next, the R4R therapists should review the numerous forces that pull us to abandon the "We" and move us to focus on the "I" and the "You." They can distribute the handout, *Forces that Perpetuate Interpersonal Disconnections and AN* to aid in this discussion (Figure 14.1).

The therapists remind members that numerous cultural, gender socialization, developmental, neurobiological, and personality factors will pull at us to abandon the "We" and move toward the "I" or the "You," thus increasing the chances of interpersonal disconnections (see Chapters 1, 3, and 9). AN capitalizes on these forces because it adversely affects information processing (e.g., difficulties discerning our internal affective and bodily states), is characterized by all-or-nothing thinking, and makes it challenging to move back and forth between details and the big picture. These experiences increase the chances of disconnections among patients and their loved ones and the perpetuation of AN. While reviewing the handout, the therapists can provide the following examples of the identified forces:

> Neurobiological: Insula dysfunction that may have been present before or after AN obstructs accurate visceral, cognitive, and affective information processing (Nunn, Frampton, & Lask, 2008).
> Personality: Some individuals have an anxious temperament, are avoidant of new stimuli, are introverted and tend to respond with negative emotions, whereas others are impulsive, willing to approach new stimuli, extraverted,

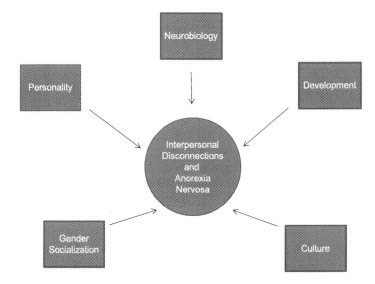

Figure 14.1 Forces that Perpetuate Interpersonal Disconnections and Anorexia Nervosa.

196 *Mary Tantillo, Jennifer Sanftner McGraw, and Daniel Le Grange*

and tend to respond with positive emotions (Cassin & von Ranson, 2005; Kaye, Fudge & Paulus, 2009).

Gender Socialization: The dominant culture socializes women in a way that leaves them struggling with how to be nice and kind while also being assertive and achieving. It socializes men in a way that leaves them thinking they should not verbalize vulnerability or feelings and should not ask for help (Gilligan, 1993; Steiner-Adair, 1991; Tantillo & Kreipe, 2006).

Dominant Culture: The dominant culture promotes ultra-independence, individuation, and separation and touts these experiences as the signs of "mature development" instead of promoting interdependence (Jordan, 2018).

Development: When we are young adults, we practice being more autonomous and demonstrate our competence by doing things on our own, including going to college, getting a job and financially supporting ourselves, establishing a separate residence, and developing close relationships with others outside our family of origin (Tanner & Arnett, 2013).

All these forces can interplay in the face of AN and end up detracting from a young adult's ability to ask for help. AN capitalizes on the vulnerabilities of young adults. It amplifies the isolation from others, while offering itself as a solution to developmental challenges and disconnections experienced by young adults with AN and their caregivers.

Next, the R4R therapists emphasize that given the increased possibility of disconnections in the face of the preceding interacting forces, we need to focus on and strengthen the "We" in relationships. They note that when everyone is in good connection, almost anything can be discussed and resolved, but if people remain in disconnection, little can be shared and meaningfully worked through. The therapists then have the group members take turns reading aloud items from the handout *Nourishing and Empowering the We* (see Box 14.1). The items are strategies that strengthen the "We" and increase the possibility that patients and families will move toward each other in relationship in the face of a threatening disconnection, or enable them to ask for help from the treatment team and others in the community to accomplish this task. Following review of the handout, the R4R therapists briefly discuss member responses (thoughts/feelings). They ask members whether any items stood out for them and why, and whether they have any other items they would add to the list of strategies.

Box 14.1   Nourishing and Empowering the We

Create Time for the "We": We all have different emotional time scales. It is important to set aside time each week to discuss how relationships are going. Start with the 20-minute rule and increase time if necessary, e.g., an hour. Some families use family therapy to do this work initially. Try to set aside time to be in connection with the whole family, individuals in the family, and individuals outside the family.

Create a Place for the "We": Think together about the best place for the entire family and particular members in the family to connect. Is there a particular room inside the home? Is there a favorite spot outside the home? Is there a favorite vacation spot? Is there a favorite entertainment place (e.g., baseball stadium, theater, museum, etc.)?

Develop the "We" in Action Projects: Physical activity and shared projects can increase movement in the relationship. It takes more than talking to create good connection with others. It is important to spend time being, doing, and creating together. How does the family as a whole and its members play together? How does the family as a whole and its members learn together? Does the family or any of its members do creative projects together? Do they do any volunteer work together? Do they do home improvement projects together? Could they create a garden together? Do they walk the dog or play with the pets together?

Engaging in service and volunteering in the world also helps us be in touch with a "We" that is larger than our immediate family "We." Nourishing others helps nourish us. Healing involves receiving and giving and, of course, it is important to balance these things.

Engage in Stress Reduction and Relaxation Strategies: Hold weekly meetings that examine where the stressors are in the "we" and in each individual person. Use daily check-ins and goal setting slowly and realistically over time. Move from self-care to mutual care (of self, others, and the relationship). Progressive muscle relaxation, yoga, stretching, mindfulness, relaxation tapes, mental imagery, and breathing exercises can be helpful.

Finding "Our" Spirit: Relationship is greater than the sum of its part. The relationship is a power greater than the self. There is a spiritual momentum at the root of psychological change and growth. Spirituality is not the same as organized religion. It is a sense of connection with something bigger than ourselves. Engage in activities that access and develop this spirit. Clarify spiritual beliefs (individual and shared) and examine your spiritual history (individual and shared).

Connect Through Silence, Meditation, and Prayer: Consider setting aside time together to be silent, pray, or meditate. Connection does not only happen in dialogue. It can be powerfully present in our quiet moments too.

Note: Nourishing and Empowering the We. Adapted from *We have to talk: Healing dialogues between men and women* (pp. 118–164), by S. Shem & J. Surrey, 1998, New York, NY: Basic Books. Copyright 1998 by Stephen Bergman and Janet Surrey. Adapted with permission.

The R4R therapists then return to the list of points of tension and disconnections created during the last session, including any newly added items from the current group. They ask the members to initially identify a few points of tension and disconnection that they would like to discuss in a more in-depth way as a larger group. The therapists state that this discussion will include how the points of tension or disconnections are experienced by patients and family members and the associated feelings and meanings. The therapists emphasize universality again by stating that if one family is experiencing a point of tension or disconnection, chances are that at least one other family is also experiencing it. And while there are likely many similarities across experiences, the therapists state that there may also be differences in experiences for patients and family members or across families. It is important to be curious about similarities and differences, especially since "being-different-in-connection" is a group goal. The therapists emphasize that people can grow through interpersonal disconnection into new and better connection if everyone remains committed ("at the table") to working on the relationship. This willingness involves emotional vulnerability, hard work, and, for patients, food – the fuel to do the work. The group is then asked to choose one of the points of tension and disconnections to address tonight. They can vote by a show of hands on which point of tension or disconnection they will begin discussing.

Similar to the approach described in Chapter 13, the R4R therapists help the group members describe the nature of the points of tension or disconnection they select. Their main job is to help members learn and practice emotional and relational skills required to name points of tension and disconnections and repair any relational ruptures with the help of group members. As noted above, members are asked to discuss the feelings and meanings attached to the point of tension or disconnection before identifying strategies that could move members out of disconnection into better connection. Naming and processing points of tension and disconnections can also reduce their recurrence in the future.

As reviewed in Chapter 13, the therapists can assist patients and family members with identification of feelings through helping members connect internal bodily and affective states with behavioral cues. The therapists may offer members the faces/feelings sheet (*How Do You Feel Today* handout; see Chapter 7) to help them identify feelings, as well as ask other patients or family members to help name feelings. Additionally, if members get stuck examining whether a particular strategy could move individuals from disconnection to better connection with self and others, the therapists can engage members in a decisional balance activity. This work involves examination of pros and cons associated with the strategy. One example of this is the pros and cons related to sleeping in and eating breakfast later in the morning versus eating according to a set breakfast time regardless of the day (a strategy). The R4R therapists can end this decisional balance work by asking members to discuss whether a strategy fosters or hinders connection with self and others.

Session 10: Nourishing and Empowering   199

Decisional balance work can also be used when the group members are stuck in the here and now of the group. For example, if the group seems reticent about discussing a particular topic, the therapists can ask them to examine the pros and cons of discussing versus not discussing the topic. At the end of the decisional balance work, they can then ask the group if not discussing the topic leads to more or less connection with the self and others. The goal is to identify strategies and behaviors that lead to more connection with self and others in order to promote continued recovery.

During this session group members may continue to discuss points of tension and disconnections they have experienced outside the group room. However, by Session 10 patients and family members may be more open to discussing a disconnection occurring in the here and now (in the immediacy of the group). An example of this situation is when a frustrated young adult may not answer a parent's question, responds in a curt way, or minimizes his/her experiences/needs. Patients may respond better to cross-parenting (receiving parental responses and support from another set of parents) than to feedback from their own parents. Similarly, parents may respond less defensively to an adult child from another family than to their own young adult child. During these times it can be helpful to emphasize that AN wants to divide patients and families from each other, so it can have the patient all to it itself. It wants the patient to only have a strong relationship with it, and not others.

The following vignette shows how the R4R therapist, with the help of group members, assisted a young adult and her parents negotiate her return to college. This work involved discussing disconnections and problem-solving strategies that moved the patient and family into better connection and positioned the patient for a successful return to college. The group members include Ann (20-year-old patient), Bob (Ann's father), Fran (Ann's mother), Lesley and Shannon (other young adults [ages 21 and 25 respectively] in group), Sharon (Lesley's mother), and Doug (Shannon's father).

R4R Therapist:	*So, it sounds like today the group would like to talk about returning to college as a source of disconnection. Who would like to start us off on what happens when this topic comes up at home?*
Group members:	*(Silence. They look at each other to see who wants to start.)*
R4R therapist:	*I know this can be a challenging disconnection to talk about. Maybe those of us who voted on discussing this particular disconnection can help us out and go first.*
Fran:	*Well, we voted on it because we are worried about Ann's return to college in the fall. We are four months away from that, and we want to be sure we are doing whatever we can to help her be successful.*
R4R therapist:	*Dad (Bob), mom is saying you are worried. Is that the feeling word you would use to describe what you feel or something else?*
Bob:	*Well, I have confidence in Ann. I just don't want the eating disorder to take over.*

R4R therapist:	OK, and how does this situation leave you feeling in your heart about her return to college? Worried like your wife or something different?
Bob:	Um. All I can think of is I don't want her to get in trouble because of this illness.
R4R therapist:	That is an excellent thought, dad, and makes total sense. I am wondering if the group could help us out and say what they might be feeling in this situation.
Sharon:	I know what you two are experiencing because we are also worried about Lesley's return to college in the fall. I guess I also have moments of fear, if I am being honest. She is so hard on herself. We want her to return in the best possible position. We agree about the importance of her being healthier before she goes back, but we disagree about what specifically needs to be accomplished before she returns.
Doug:	We were where you are now, four years ago. In hindsight, which is 20/20, I wished we had stuck to our guns more about the return to college. Shannon did OK on her return, but I believe if we had held firmer with some of our expectations, she would have had her sea legs when she got back on campus and would not have struggled as much as she initially did. I remember feeling worried and frustrated about her going back, and I feel the same things listening to you now, Bob. You believe in your daughter and you want her to move along in life like her friends. But this illness inserts itself and changes everything. Good outcomes can happen, but they need to be accomplished in a different way and at a different pace sometimes.
R4R therapist:	So, dad, Sharon and Doug shared how they felt related to Lesley and Shannon returning to college. Would you say your feelings are similar to or different from the feelings they expressed?
Bob:	Similar. I guess I am worried and sometimes feel frustrated. Like Doug says, I wish Ann did not have to deal with this illness and could just experience college without this extra challenge. I believe in her, but I am worried about the eating disorder going with her to college.
R4R therapist:	So, Ann, we heard your parents' concerns and feelings. What are you thinking and feeling about the return to college in the fall?
Ann:	I keep telling my parents that I will be fine. I am doing what everyone is telling me to do. I am not perfect though. No one is. I should not have to be perfectly recovered to return to school. That is where we disagree.
R4R therapist:	So, as you discuss this with us, Ann, how are you feeling in your heart?
Ann:	I just want them to stop focusing on how the eating disorder can cause me trouble when I get back. I am getting better at taking care of myself now.
R4R therapist:	Those are very important thoughts that you are sharing with us. In addition, what do you feel about the situation? Can you tell or maybe the group can give you some help? Maybe Lesley and Shannon can help here? (The therapist smiles and looks over at Shannon and Lesley.)
Lesley:	Ann, I know exactly what you are talking about. My parents talk about the return to college like every other week. It creates stress for me. I get

Session 10: Nourishing and Empowering 201

	irritated because we are four months away, and I am trying to do what is needed to get back to college. For example, I came to group because they felt strongly about attending.
Shannon:	*I remember when I was in the middle of this, that regardless of what my parents said, I felt I knew myself better than anyone. I was determined to show them I could go back and get through. I wanted to be with my friends, and I was angry with my parents because I felt they did not trust me and my judgment. I see now that they did not trust the eating disorder. And if I am being honest, the eating disorder did come with me to college. Its voice got louder when I got to campus and it grew stronger with each week away from home. I ended up getting a counselor off-campus, but things were really rough for several months. I thought I would have to come back home again. It didn't go that way, but it was close. And I think that if I had done more to get stabilized then, I would not be sitting here now. Things just went underground for a while after graduation, and when I got this new job, they kind of exploded again.*
R4R therapist:	*So, Ann, having heard what Lesley and Shannon felt, do you connect with any of the feelings they are sharing, or do you have different feelings? Theirs included irritation and anger.*
Ann:	*I know my parents care about me, but I guess I am annoyed when they keep bringing up the college return and how I need to meet certain expectations to go back. I feel like a child when they talk like this. And I feel like I have to do things perfectly to be able to go back.*
R4R therapist:	*So, mom and dad, did you know Ann felt this way?*
Fran:	*I can see how she might feel like that, but we don't intend her to feel that way. We love her and want her to be successful.*
R4R therapist:	*Mom, can you turn toward Ann and let her know how you feel about what she is experiencing.*
Fran:	*Ann, we love you and don't expect you to be perfect. Just further along in your recovery before you go back to school.*
Ann:	*But that's the whole problem because we define further along differently.*
Bob:	*Further along means eating according to your meal plan and not using the illness to cope with stress.*
Ann:	*But I don't think I should have to be 100% at this every single day until August 20th when I am supposed to go back. No one is perfect in recovery.*
R4R therapist:	*So, Ann, it sounds like where the disconnection is happening is related to how you think people define "further along" and to your feeling like you have to do what is required at 100% between now and then. Is that correct?*
Ann:	*Yes.*
R4R therapist:	*It sounds like some of us in addition to Ann and her family may be familiar with the kind of disconnection they are experiencing. I am wondering what the group is thinking and feeling in response to what they have shared.*

Shannon:	Ann, maybe your mom and dad want to see that you can take care of yourself more days than not versus being perfect. I can understand the pressure you are feeling because I felt it in the past too. I am someone who probably should have waited a little longer before I returned to school. I convinced my parents that I was ready. They saw me eat dinner every night but did not know that I restricted at breakfast and lunch at times. They also did not know that I was still occasionally purging at night before I went back. I told them I was ready, and they believed me. Are your parents actually saying that you have to be perfect?
Ann:	They say that I have to complete all meals per my meal plan, and I can't compensate for stress or eating with restriction or exercise.
Bob:	Ann, you don't need to be perfect, but we have to know that you can take care of yourself when you are away and feeling more stressed.
Sharon:	So maybe you and your parents can talk more specifically about what is "good enough," so that you don't feel so pressured Ann? We are struggling to try and figure that out with Lesley as well. We don't expect perfection, but we want to be sure she can advocate for herself and her health when she feels vulnerable. Have you actually asked your parents, specifically, what they expect with regard to what is "good enough" for return to school?
Ann:	I have tried but every time we start talking, I get upset because I don't think they understand the pressure I feel. I feel like they don't have confidence in me either.
Bob:	We do have confidence in you Ann, but we don't trust the eating disorder. We need to know that you can send it away when it tries to take advantage of you.
Doug:	I watched Shannon go through this and as a dad, you wish you could somehow fix this for your daughter. Like guarantee everything will be alright, but you can't. You feel somewhat helpless. This is challenging for you and your parents. I did hear your parents say they love you a lot Ann and your dad said he has confidence in you, but he does not trust the illness. Sounds like he just wants to be sure you can take care of yourself if the illness tries to get the upper hand when you are away at school. Maybe it would help to discuss what you need to show them to convince them that you can take care of yourself, even if you feel vulnerable and are tempted to use or begin to use eating disorder behaviors in the face of stress. Like what would show them that you know how to stay or quickly get back on track when you are away from them.
Lesley:	That would be way better than feeling like we have to be 100% all the time. That just leads to more stress and possibly more restriction.
R4R therapist:	So maybe it would be good to take some time and think about how we would define "good enough." That is a great concept. Let's compare notes on how we would define that. Ann, Shannon, and Lesley, what do you think defines "good enough"?

Session 10: Nourishing and Empowering 203

Ann:	*I need to think about this more but maybe eating according to my meal plan at least 90% of the time. And coming up with ways to compensate for what I miss sooner versus later if I have a tough time. Plus, I need an opportunity to prepare my own meals for whole days at a time so that they know I can do this.*
Shannon:	*I think what is also important is agreeing on what you will do if you are having a tough time and cannot eat according to the meal plan. Like agreeing you will let someone know and use them as a support person. And using other strategies like journaling or drawing to figure out what is going on that is stressing you out.*
Lesley:	*My parents asked me to identify a support person on campus, if I am having a hard time and could not talk with them for any reason. (The patients share several other ideas, and the R4R therapist turns to the parents and other group members.)*
R4R therapist:	*This is an excellent start. I am wondering what our parents and other group members think about the proposed strategies so far? You may have some additional ideas too.*
Bob:	*I think the strategies sound good. I also would feel way more comfortable if I knew Ann had a designated support person on campus, continued to see her off-campus therapist weekly, and agreed to reach out to us if she was having difficulties with completing her meal plan or with self-care in general.*
Fran:	*And, Ann, I like your idea about making up for missed nutrition. Having an agreement about how you would nutritionally compensate for non-completion of a snack or meal would make me feel better. I know the goal is to stick with the meal plan 100% but in reality, this may not happen at times. I would like to see her being able to practice this before she leaves home as well.*
Sharon:	*And it would be great if we could make a plan on how nutritional self-care will happen on days when classes are close together so that lunchtimes are a challenge. Like is the plan to take lunch and eat in class? Or does she eat later that day and adjust dinnertime? (The parents and other group members make a few more suggestions.)*
R4R therapist:	*This was great work today. I would encourage folks to continue this discussion in their individual and family therapy sessions too. It might be helpful to sit together and draft some ideas about the college return soon after tonight's session so thoughts will be fresh in everyone's minds. And, of course, we can continue to discuss how to approach the return to college in future sessions so that everyone's voice is heard, and we support our college students and not enable the eating disorder.*

In this vignette, the R4R therapist moves through a number of steps to promote exploration and repair of the disconnection experienced by Ann and her parents. The therapist strategically involves group members at various points to assist with the emotional and relational work required to help the family navigate the move from disconnection to better connection. This movement allows Ann, her parents and other group members to make what is implicit (e.g., worries, feelings, meanings, expectations, and strategies) explicit. This work is very important because AN thrives on what is hidden and unspoken. Outlined next are the steps the therapist took to foster mutuality, motivation, and continued recovery.

- Help the patient and parents connect with themselves and identify their feelings about the return to college. Nonverbally and verbally create openness to and an expectation that members may see and experience things differently. Normalizing that their feelings may be similar or different can decrease anxiety about expressing differences and promotes "difference-in-connection."
- Recognize important "thoughts" that members share about the disconnection while encouraging them to get at their feelings.
- Call on other group members to help patients and families identify their feelings. This intervention increases a sense of universality and validation and reduces anxiety, shame, guilt, and blame.
- Help members explore the meanings related to the disconnection, i.e., return to college, and help them, again, be open to differences in these meanings and the experiences of the disconnection across family members.
- Clarify the disconnection. For example, the therapist states that the disconnection seems related to Ann feeling pressured to be "perfect" in her recovery" and assuming her parents are not confident about her self-care efforts. Her parents are focused mainly on ensuring a successful re-entry to college because they want her to feel good about herself and confident about her self-care and recovery.
- Ask for the group's feedback (thoughts and feelings) about the disconnection. Promote cross-parenting and/or feedback from peers to promote validation, universality, and connection. These experiences can free up members who are feeling stuck in the rigid thoughts and distress associated with disconnections and help make explicit was is implicit, e.g., What is "good enough"? Members are then able to move bidirectionally between the details and the big picture involved with the disconnection (e.g., realistic expectations and strategies along with overall success with self-care and recovery on re-entry).
- Empower the young adult patients by asking them first (ahead of other members) to define what "good enough" is. Help them problem-solve and identify recovery-oriented strategies first, so they can feel self-efficacious, autonomous, and successful (important young adult developmental experiences).
- Invite parents and the rest of the group to comment on ideas offered by the young adult patients and offer any additional ideas.

Session 10: Nourishing and Empowering 205

- Positively reinforce group member efforts throughout the discussion. Encourage them to continue strengthening the "we" by meeting together as a family to draft a document reflective of their joint ideas. This helps them continue to make explicit the strategies that will increase the chances of a successful college return. The plan should incorporate patient and parent ideas and could be jointly constructed or be initially drafted by the young adult (practicing more autonomy) and reviewed with parents, R4R group members, and other treatment team members.
- Emphasize that moving through disconnection to better connection with ourselves and others simultaneously disables the illness and enables the young adult patient and their continued recovery.

At the end of today's session, the therapists remind members that the next group will meet in two weeks. They note again that Session 10 is the last weekly group and that Sessions 11–14 will meet every other week and Sessions 15 and 16 will meet monthly. Session 10 goals, materials, and handouts are outlined in Box 14.2.

Box 14.2 Session: 10: Nourishing and Empowering the "We" in Relationships

Goals

Help patients and family members to:

- Nourish and empower the "We" in relationships.
- Identify forces (e.g., culture, gender socialization, development, neurobiology, and personality factors) that interact and pull at us to abandon the "we" and move to the "I" or the "you," thus perpetuating interpersonal disconnections and AN.
- Continue identifying interpersonal disconnections and points of tension.
- Continue practicing emotional and relational skills to repair relationships and restore/build mutual connections.

Materials

- None

Exercise

- Continue identifying disconnections and points of tension from list distributed today and choose/address one item. Have members address feelings and meanings (and do decisional

---

206 *Mary Tantillo, Jennifer Sanftner McGraw, and Daniel Le Grange*

balance [pros/cons] if indicated) regarding the item before problem-solving better ways to connect and elbow out AN.

Handouts

- At start of group review the handout *Forces that Perpetuate Interpersonal Disconnections and AN.*
- Next have members take turns reading items from *Nourishing and Empowering the We* handout *Forces Perpetuate Interpersonal Disconnections AN.*
- Distribute Review the list of *Points of Tension and Disconnections Related to the Eating Disorder, Recovery and Relationships* developed last session. Choose one item and jointly discuss.

*Remind members that Session 10 is the last weekly group. Sessions 11–14 will meet every other week and Sessions 15 and 16 will meet monthly to give members an opportunity to practice skills learned in group and report back.

References

*No DOI

Cassin, S. E., von Ranson, K. M. (2005). Personality and eating disorders: A decade in review. *Clinical Psychology Review, 25*(7), 895–916. https://dx.doi.org/10: 1016/j.cpr.2005.04.012.

*Gilligan, C. (1993). *In a different voice: Psychological theory and women's development.* Harvard University.

Jordan, J. (2018). *Relational-cultural therapy* (2nd ed.). American Psychological Association. https://dx.doi.org/10.1037/0000063-001.

Kaye, W. H., Fudge, J. L., & Paulus, M. (2009). New insights into symptoms and neurocircuit function of anorexia nervosa. *Nature Reviews Neuroscience, 10*(8), 573–584. https://dx.doi.org/10.1038/nrn2682.

Nunn, K., Frampton, I., Gordon, I., & Lask, I. (2008). Anorexia nervosa – A noradrenergic dysregulation hypothesis. *Medical Hypothesis, 78*(5), 580–584. https://dx.doi.org/10.1016/j.mehy.2012.01.033.

Steiner-Adair, C. (1991). New maps of development, new models of therapy: The psychology of women and the treatment of eating disorders. In C. Johnson (Ed.), *Psychodynamic treatment of anorexia nervosa and bulimia* (pp. 225–241). The Guilford Press.

Tanner, J. L., & Arnett, J. J. (2013). Approaching young adult health and medicine from a developmental perspective. *Adolescent Medicine, 24,* 485–506.

*Tantillo, M., & Kreipe, R. E. (2006). The impact of gender socialization on group treatment of eating disorders. *Group: The Journal of the Eastern Group Psychotherapy Society, 30*(4), 281–306.

15 Session 11: Waging Good Conflict in Connection

Mary Tantillo, Jennifer Sanftner McGraw, and Daniel Le Grange

R4R therapists begin Session 11 by welcoming members back after a two-week period of time. They remind members that Sessions 12–14 will occur every two weeks and that Sessions 15–16 will occur monthly. Next, instead of asking group members to review their strategies for connection since the last group, the therapists ask to review **peaks and valleys** group members have experienced over the previous two weeks. Peaks are defined as high points comprised of connections with self and others, and, in general, accomplishments and successes in relation to recovery, relationships, and life. Valleys are defined as low points comprised of challenges, struggles, lapses (experiences of increased symptoms), and disconnections. The R4R therapists emphasize that low points are part of recovery and life and present opportunities for continued learning and connection. Members are encouraged to use the group for additional support and feedback related to low points. They are told that low points can be incorporated into group discussion related to points of tension and disconnections and that it is likely that a number of patients and families may have experienced similar low points. The group can assist with further exploration and problem solving and offer additional validation and support.

During Session 11 the R4R therapists continue to help members:

- Identify and process points of tension and disconnections
- Practice emotional and relational skills required to repair disconnections
- Effectively move through conflict in connection (*wage good [constructive] conflict*) and use differences to strengthen versus weaken relationships

After completing a review of patient peaks and valleys, the R4R therapists then have the members take turns reading items from the *Transforming Disconnections into Stronger Connections—Waging Good Conflict* handout (see Box 15.1).

Box 15.1 Transforming Disconnections into Stronger Connections: Waging Good Conflict

- Acknowledge the importance of the connection with the other person(s).
  Example: *You are my best friend in the world. You have always been there for me, and I have appreciated that so much.*
- Honor the history and potential future of the relationship(s).
  Example: *We have been through a lot together, and I look forward to other adventures we will have together.*
- Name the disconnection.
  Example: *And that is why I want to talk with you about what happened last night. When we were talking, you said that by now you thought I would have been over the eating disorder. I felt hurt by that because you know this is a marathon and not a sprint for me. I am trying so hard. It felt like you did not see this.*
- Embrace the differences each person experiences (e.g., thoughts, feelings, needs, values, etc.). *Yes, I can understand why you would feel frustrated and think that after six months I should be able to try new foods without feeling totally panicked. Eating with friends is a social thing I used to be able to do. At the same time, there are still some foods that scare me a lot, especially if I eat them really late at night. I can try them a little at a time. But I can't eat a whole ice cream cone yet. Just because I could not eat an ice cream cone last night does not mean I have not progressed. I am not perfect, but I am working hard in recovery.*
- Apologize if you have hurt the other person(s).
  I also want to apologize for swearing at you last night before you left. I was feeling hurt and probably a little pissed off. I should not have done that. Hurting you does not fix the hurt that I felt. I am sorry for adding to our disconnection.
- Take a "time out" if needed.
  If we get into a situation where I feel hurt in the future and feel the push to swear or get sarcastic, I need to just leave for a few minutes to calm down. That would probably help me slow down to figure out what I am feeling. Then I could tell you how I feel. If you need a time out to slow down because you feel frustrated with me, that is totally fine with me.
- Ask a third person to help you and the other person(s) resolve conflict and use differences to strengthen instead of weaken the relationship. *I am wondering if you would come to my next therapist appointment with me so we can talk about what happened the other night. We ended up in a disconnection because we have different ideas and feelings about where I should be in recovery. And we could not figure a way through the disconnection. I think it could help both of us. I would really appreciate it.*

Session 11: Waging Good Conflict in Connection   209

Note: Transforming Disconnections into Stronger Connections. Adapted from *Relational practice in action: A group manual* (p. 40, by J.V. Jordan & C. Dooley, 2000, Wellesley, MA: Stone Center, Wellesley College. Copyright 2000 by J. Jordan and C. Dooley, Wellesley College. Adapted with permission.

After reviewing these items, the therapists can briefly solicit member feedback about them. For example, they can ask for group member thoughts and feelings about the items, whether any stood out for them, and whether they would add any items to the list. The therapists end this discussion by saying that the handout is a reminder of how to engage in dialogue with others while naming points of tension and disconnections. They note that the handout can help group members navigate disconnections that are discussed in the current and future sessions. The therapists then ask the group members to choose one point of tension/disconnection from the group list generated during the previous sessions. This point of tension/disconnection can be one of the ones previously voted upon or could be a new one. For example, at the start of group, a patient and family may have shared a disconnection that occurred during a valley (low point) over the past two weeks. Other members may have identified with their experience of this low point, and the group may desire to help that particular family further explore the point of tension/ disconnection. Through the work of group curative factors like interpersonal learning (Yalom & Leszcs, 2005), the discussion and repair of a disconnection within one family will also help other families.

During Session 11 the R4R therapists engage in work that is similar to that of Sessions 9 and 10. They assist members in practicing emotional (e.g., identifying and regulating emotions) and relational (e.g., see handouts from today and Session 9 [*Moving Through Disconnection to Better Connection*]) skills required to identify points of tension and disconnection and engage in relational repair. They can concretely refer back to items listed in Session 9 and 11 handouts as needed during the group discussion. The therapists should continue helping members explore feelings and meanings attached to disconnections before allowing the group to move into identification of concrete strategies for transforming disconnections into better connections. They should continue to solicit what aspects are similar and different among members with regard to their experiences when exploring meanings, feelings, and values, which helps members practice being "different-in-connection." The therapists can continue to use the faces/feelings sheet (How Do You Feel Today?; see Session 3) to help patients identify feelings and connect biological and behavioral cues with feelings as indicated. Similar to Sessions 9 and 10, they can ask other patients or loved ones to assist with naming emotions and help them employ decisional balance (review pros and cons of choices/behaviors). They can also continue to ask if the identified strategies to solve relational dilemmas and work through disconnection will lead to more or less connection with self

210   *Mary Tantillo, Jennifer Sanftner McGraw, and Daniel Le Grange*

or others. The clinical vignette that follows illustrates how the R4R therapist can help patients and families "wage good conflict" and transform disconnections into stronger connections with one another. Sarah is a 20-year-old who is presently attending a local college and began experiencing AN at the age of 18. Her parents (Kelly and Sam) have been engaging in family-based treatment for AN with her over the past few months.

R4R Therapist:	*So, I wonder if we should circle back to what was discussed during our review of peaks and valleys a short time ago. I heard Sarah say that she felt a low point for her was feeling like her parents did not believe that she could begin having meals alone. I wonder if we can use that as our point of tension/disconnection today. I am sure that other patients and family members can identify with what Sarah shared.*
Sarah:	*(Smiles nervously) It is probably not going to change their minds. I have kind of given up on them understanding I am ready for this. It seems that unless they hear something from a therapist, I can never take the next step. It is like what I think does not matter. They always worry that the eating disorder, not me, is talking to them.*
Kelly:	*Sarah, we are just trying to do what is best for you and following directions from Dr. Andrews (family therapist). We do listen to what you say, and at the same time, we also have experienced times when we thought you, not the eating disorder, was talking to us and you ended up hiding food.*
R4R Therapist:	*So, let's slow this down a bit and talk first about how folks are feeling about this particular disconnection. It is important for us to understand both sides of the disconnection.* Sarah, how are you feeling as you describe this situation to us today?
Sarah:	*The same way I felt about it when it came up again over the weekend. They don't understand I am more ready to take care of myself. They don't believe in me.*
R4R Therapist:	*These are important thoughts and they are mainly focused on your parents. Can you tell what feelings you are having, in your heart, that go along with those thoughts? What you are experiencing sounds like it is painful.*
Sarah:	*Probably…annoyed and probably some other things too. I am not sure.*
R4R Therapist:	*I can pass the feelings sheet down to you if that might help (sends the sheet over to Sarah). And while you are looking at that, I wonder if your fellow group members can help you out too. I am wondering as other patients hear what Sarah is sharing, what feelings you might be feeling in this situation?*
Ann (another patient):	*I would probably feel angry over time and let down and disappointed or hurt. It is hard to feel like your parents don't*

Session 11: Waging Good Conflict in Connection   211

	believe you, especially if you really think you are ready to try something new.
Terry (another patient):	I would feel the same things and probably deflated and worthless. Like it would not matter how hard I am working if my parents can't hear what I am trying to say to them. It is probably hard being a parent in this situation because you probably don't know what to believe. At the same time, it is hard being the person in recovery because you want others to know you are trying hard and are ready to take better care of yourself.
R4R Therapist:	Anyone else have similar or different feelings?
Melissa (another patient):	I would feel many of the same things but also feel like a little kid. Like incapable and helpless because regardless of what I am trying to do, it is not seen. Like what I am doing is invisible and who I am becoming is invisible.
R4R Therapist:	I appreciate everyone helping out Sarah. Sarah are any of those feelings similar to yours?
Sarah:	Yes. Definitely like a little kid and deflated. I do feel like what I do is unseen and I feel like a failure. I think about where my friends are and what they are doing with their lives, and I can't even get an opportunity to eat a snack alone or even with a friend.
R4R Therapist:	Those are tough feelings to have, especially as a young adult. I hear how tempting it is to compare yourself to your friends, which is not fair to you. But it is very easy to do. You would like to be able to move ahead with your life and you want your parents' support in this. It is important when there is a disconnection, for us to understand both sides of it. Mom and dad, did you know Sarah felt like this? I am wondering, too, what you are feeling as you hear her describe her experience of things?
Kelly:	Sarah, we don't intend to make you feel badly about yourself. We are just worried about you and want you to be successful with your recovery. We don't want the eating disorder to take advantage of you. It has done it before.
R4R Therapist:	So, mom it sounds like you are worried about Sarah. Are there any other feelings you are having in addition to the worry?
Kelly:	Well, yes, I... (She takes a deep breath and seems to be fighting back tears.) I fluctuate between being angry with myself for not intervening more actively when she was younger and started showing symptoms that I did not recognize and feeling frustrated that this illness has taken away so much from her. She wanted to go away to school and we had to say no. She wanted to be involved with sports, and we had to say no again. We never anticipated saying no

	to so many things we knew she looked forward to. (Kelly becomes tearful.)
R4R Therapist:	Mom, it sounds like you love Sarah very much and that you feel very protective of her and her recovery. It sounds like it has been painful having to say no so often when you want to see your daughter move ahead in life. It also seems like you can be hard on yourself and blame yourself for not seeing the eating disorder as quickly as you would have liked. I am sure you are not alone with this experience. It is a very secretive and deceptive illness. You do not want it to have the upper hand again. I am sure other parents and partners can identify with what you are sharing. I am wondering what others are thinking and feeling about this?
Martha (another mother):	Kelly I did not see Karen's (Martha's daughter) eating disorder right away either. It took a long time and she protected us from it. At first, she did not think anything was wrong and then, when she finally recognized that things were not going well, she was afraid to tell us. I felt upset and powerless. I was angry that this happened to my daughter and angry with myself because I somehow should have magically seen it coming sooner.
Frank (father of another patient, Joseph):	Kelly, Joseph was sick for several years before we even knew he was struggling with his eating disorder. When he was away at college, he started losing more weight, but we had no idea it was AN. He was always slender because he was a cross country runner. But we never thought he was sick. He saw a number of doctors and no one diagnosed this. When we look back now, we all can see he was struggling in his senior year in high school. It feels bad to have missed the early signs, like we let him down. Hindsight is always 20/20 though. You are doing the best you can. And what matters is that you are here with your daughter today.
R4R Therapist:	Do any other parents, partners or patients have anything else they would like to add? I am sure many of us can identify with what Sarah and her parents are experiencing.
Joseph:	I just wanted to say that being a parent in a situation like this must be hard. I can totally understand why Sarah feels the way she does because I have felt similarly. At the same time, I can understand why you (looking at Sarah's parents) would feel worried and angry. You cannot blame yourself for Sarah's eating disorder. I have told my parents this repeatedly because they also felt they missed the signs. I just appreciate my parents supporting me today. We try to listen to each other when I feel able to try something new. Sometimes it works out and sometimes it doesn't. Some of this is trial and error. There is no game book for exactly how recovery should go for each of us.

Session 11: Waging Good Conflict in Connection 213

R4R Therapist (Looks at Sam, Sarah's father,):	Dad, I was wondering what you were feeling about Sarah and the discussion we have had so far.
Sam:	I have told Sarah that I want her to do the things she has been looking forward to, but some of those things can't happen till she is better recovered.
R4R Therapist:	That is a very important thought dad. Can you tell what feelings in your heart go along with that thought?
Sam:	Probably...frustration. Frustration because we love our daughter and want a full life for her, and this thing has slowed her down. But we want to do whatever we can to get it out of her way.
Sarah:	Dad, I am going to tell you again what I said last weekend. You can't get it out of my way. Only I can do that. That is why I need to start practicing eating on my own and taking care of myself more. I need to feel I can do that, or I am not going to feel confident in my recovery.
R4R Therapist:	Sarah can you tell what you are feeling now?
Sarah:	I am frustrated too. No matter when I try to do more on my own, it will worry them. And I worry about disappointing them if I end up listening to the eating disorder. But we have to start somewhere.
R4R Therapist:	So, Sarah, you and your parents are having some similar feelings that come from similar and different places. You want to practice feeling more capable and confident in your recovery and they worry about giving you more to do in your recovery because the eating disorder might take advantage of you when you are alone. But it is clear you all love each other and that you all are in agreement that your recovery and living a full life is important. So, I am wondering what one small realistic step toward self-care might look like. You would have to of course further discuss this together and with your therapist. I am just wondering what it might look like. Sarah, do you have an idea about this?
Sarah:	Well, I wanted to eat dinner with friends one night on the weekend, but I know my parents are too anxious to let me do that yet. I would like to at least try to eat a snack out with my best friend. She knows I am in recovery, and she would encourage me during the snack. She would eat with me.
Terry:	That seems like a good idea. I assume your parents know your best friend and if they trust her, that would be a safe way to start self-care.
Kelly:	Yes, Sarah and her friend Jenny grew up together. Jenny loves her and supports her. I guess we could start there. She looks at her husband.

Sam:	*I can get on board with that, but don't you think we should have a back-up plan, Sarah, if you get there and start feeling more anxious than you anticipated?*
Sarah:	*Dad, I promise if I get anxious, I will text or call you from wherever Jenny and I are.*
Melissa:	*And maybe you can go to a place that you feel safe in to start. Like maybe a less crowded coffeehouse that you feel comfortable in. Then your anxiety will be lower to start. You would be with your best friend in a comfortable environment.*
Sarah:	*I know exactly where that would be. That is a good idea.*
R4R Therapist:	*Great idea. Are there any other plans we could put in place to help Sarah feel confident about her self-care step? So the eating disorder is less apt to have its way with her.*
Joseph:	*You could put a limit around the time you spend there if your anxiety might increase over time. Like you could tell Jenny that you want to go to the café for 30 minutes. Then you will feel in control of the time spent there.*

The group continues to help Sarah and her parents make a concrete plan for the following weekend that they can discuss with their family therapist the next day. They also discuss how Sarah would know if the eating disorder is getting stronger and attempting to hold her back from achieving her self-care goal. This work helped her parents see that she is better equipped in knowing when her healthy versus eating disorder voice is getting louder and that she can create a plan for how to obtain support if it threatens her recovery work.

In this vignette, the R4R therapist assists Sarah and her parents to transform their disconnection (related to their different feelings regarding her wanting to have a snack with a friend) to strengthened connection. The therapist employs some of the interventions listed on the handout in Box 15.1 (*Transforming Disconnections into Stronger Connections: Waging Good Conflict*). For example, the R4R therapist acknowledges the importance of the connection between Sarah and her parents, their love for one another, and their joint desire to have her reclaim her health and life. By noting these, the therapist honors the history and potential future of their relationship. She also helps Sarah and her parents name their disconnection and embrace the similar and different feelings they each experience regarding the disconnection. The therapist slows down the interaction to help them first identify the feelings and meanings associated with the disconnection. For example, Sarah wants to feel more competent and confident in performing her own self-care. She sees her parents' support in allowing her to eat a snack with a friend as a beginning step toward this goal. Her parents want her to be successful and move ahead, but they also are fearful of the eating disorder taking advantage of her without their support during meals. They worry about her readiness, and this issue is even more

Session 11: Waging Good Conflict in Connection   215

sensitive for Kelly because she still blames herself for not picking up on her daughter's symptoms earlier.

The therapist purposefully starts the work of identifying feelings and meanings associated with the disconnection with Sarah because she is a young adult who wants to experience more autonomy. As the therapist empowers Sarah to share her experience, she also models for her parents how to do the same. The therapist then affirms the importance of the young adult hearing her parents' perspective and follows up with questions about their feelings and meanings associated with the disconnection. This intervention reinforces the importance of mutual understanding, empathy, and respect in resolving conflict and moving through disconnections. The therapist seeks the feedback of the group throughout the discussion so that Sarah and her parents see the usefulness of "asking a third person for help to resolve conflict and use differences to strengthen relationships" (see Box 15.1). During this vignette, the therapist assists the patients and family members to connect with themselves (e.g., asks about their genuine feelings and needs) and with one another (e.g., encourages them to be authentic and assertive about their experiences with one another). After processing the disconnection (examining feelings, needs, and meanings) with Sarah, her parents and the group, the R4R therapist moves on to helping them problem solve possible strategies that would increase the possibility of success for Sarah if she were to meet a friend for a snack. Again, the therapist starts this work with Sarah because she desires to feel more competent and confident about setting and achieving self-care goals. She is modeling for Sarah's parents and the group that the plan should begin with querying the young adult for their ideas. If the young adult's ideas are unrealistic and not supportive of recovery, then discussion about this issue would follow. The therapist would ask for group feedback about this as well. There are usually several parents and/or patients in group who can offer validation while reality-testing about possible options with a patient and family members who are in a disconnection. Sarah knew her parents were not supportive of her having a full meal with her friend yet, and she set a smaller, more attainable initial goal. This was probably more possible in this scenario because she felt heard by the therapist, her parents, and the group.

Throughout Session 11 the R4R therapists positively reinforce member use of emotional and relational skills that foster connection with self and others. They emphasize how growth in recovery and life can come from moving through disconnection and building on *difference within strong connection* because AN has a hard time flourishing in this situation. They reinforce how the ability to *wage good conflict* (staying connected with ourselves and others in the face of conflict, tension, and disconnection) reduces the patient's need to resolve conflict and tension through the use of AN symptoms. Session 11 goals, materials, and handouts are outlined in Box 15.2.

216 *Mary Tantillo, Jennifer Sanftner McGraw, and Daniel Le Grange*

Box 15.2   Session 11: Waging Good Conflict

Goals

Help patients and family members to:

- Continue identifying interpersonal disconnections and points of tension.
- Continue practicing emotional and relational skills to repair relationships and restore/build mutual connections.
- Practice sitting with and building on difference (thoughts/meanings, feelings, needs, values) within strong connection.

Materials

- Easel paper and marker

Exercise

- Review **peaks and valleys** (instead of strategies for connection) in order to conduct a fuller check in after the two-week time between group sessions.
- Add Points of Tension and Disconnections to group list (if indicated).

Handouts

- Members will take turns reading items from *Transforming Disconnections into Strong Connections.*
- Add other points of tension and disconnections to the group list generated in the previous session (if indicated).
- Choose one item from Points of Tension and Disconnections list and discuss.

Reference

*No DOI

Yalom, I., & Leszcz, M. (2005). *The theory and practice of group psychotherapy* (5th ed.). New York, NY: Basic Books.

16 Session 12: Moving from Disconnection to Connection

Building Strong Connections to Work through Tension and Disconnections Related to Adulthood and Recovery

Mary Tantillo, Jennifer Sanftner McGraw, and Daniel Le Grange

Session 12 extends the work patients and families have been doing in previous sessions on points of tension and disconnections, while helping them shift their focus more specifically on points of tension and disconnections related to a young adult's transition from adolescence to young adulthood. The R4R therapists' aims in Session 12 include helping group members:

- Identify interpersonal disconnections and points of tension specifically related to the transition into young adulthood and its related developmental milestones
- Identify the earliest signs that AN is offering itself as a solution to the tension/anxiety associated with adult developmental challenges
- Discuss alternative coping strategies and support needed from others to navigate this transition
- Practice emotional and relational skills to repair relationships and restore/build mutual connections

Conducting the First Half of Session 12

Similar to Session 11, the R4R therapists begin Session 12 with a review of peaks and valleys group members have experienced over the previous two weeks. For the first half of the session they continue to help patients and families identify and process interpersonal disconnections and points of tension, including those from the list they previously developed and newly identified ones that emerge from the current session. For example, after the review of peaks and valleys, there is often a valley that has been experienced by a number of patients that can be used in a general discussion about that point of tension/disconnection. The R4R therapists can decide whether to promote a general discussion about the point of tension/disconnection or if they think it would be more beneficial to process it with a particular family in mind and obtain group support while doing so, similar to the work done with Sarah and her family in Session 11. If the

218 *Mary Tantillo, Jennifer Sanftner McGraw, and Daniel Le Grange*

therapists choose to conduct a general discussion, they would encourage disclosure of everyone's feelings and meanings associated with a particular point of tension/disconnection, followed by joint problem solving regarding more effective responses to one another. Examples of statements the R4R therapist uses to foster a general discussion are in Box 16.1.

Box 16.1 R4R Therapist Statements that Foster General Discussion of Points of Tension/Disconnections

Example of the Point of Tension/Disconnection: Trouble finding time to eat at work or school

- So, it sounds like, based on our check-in today, that there are several patients who experienced a similar kind of valley or low point over the past couple weeks. I am thinking it might be very helpful to further discuss that point of tension/disconnection as a larger group. Then we could capitalize on all the ideas, wisdom, and creativity we have in the room.
- So, Ann, Theresa, and Emily (patients), can we start with you first, since you noted the same valley over the past two weeks? Sounds like the valley related to having trouble consistently finding time to eat at work or school. It seems like it has created tension and disconnection. Can you share more about what this challenge is like and the feelings that go along with it?
- I am wondering what other patients and family members are thinking and feeling as they hear Ann, Theresa, and Emily describing this point of tension and disconnection. (Again, the therapist ensures that members share their thoughts and feelings about the challenges related to not consistently finding a time to eat at work or school.)
- So, now that we have discussed our thoughts and feelings about the challenges that Ann, Theresa, and Emily have experienced, I am wondering what might be helpful to them in terms of finding a solution to their challenge. Ann, Theresa, and Emily, do you have any ideas you think might be helpful going forward? And we can of course also ask everyone else for some help. Asking for help is a super important skill to practice here, because the eating disorder was telling you that you needed to fix things on your own. It loves to do that, especially with young adults. It knows that young adults want to feel independent. It capitalizes on that to increase isolation from others, and of course, eventually offers itself up as the solution to a problem. (Go to the young adults first to ask if they have any ideas about how to promote their self-care despite AN's attempts to disconnect them from their self-care needs and from others when they need to eat at school and work. This intervention fosters their autonomy and practice with

Session 12: Moving from Disconnection to Connection 219

> problem solving. Then ask for feedback from others. As strategies are
> offered, check in with the young adults to assess if they seem helpful or
> not. If not, ask them to share why.)

Regardless of whether the R4R therapist chooses to conduct a general discussion about points of tension/disconnections or addresses a point of tension/disconnection with a particular patient and family in mind, the therapist continues to assist group members in practicing emotional and relational skills that repair current disconnections and strengthen connections with oneself and others. Their promotion of joint problem solving leads to collaborative caring (Treasure, Schmidt, & Macdonald, 2010) among young adult patients and their family members, thus reducing the frequency of future disconnections.

Possible Challenges with Working Through Points of Tension/Disconnections

Some potential challenges that may occur during the discussion of points of tension/disconnections include group members talking more about thoughts than feelings, patients being reticent to share about points of tension/disconnections, and/or the entire group becoming quiet and hesitant to speak about a point of tension/disconnection.

Talking about Thoughts versus Feelings

If patients or family members discuss only their thoughts during either a general discussion of points of tension/disconnections or when working on them with a particular family, remind them that their thoughts are important and *at the same time*, you want them to also share their feelings ["from their heart"]. If they continue to have trouble identifying feelings, they can use the *How Do You Feel Today* sheet (see Chapter 7). The therapist can help the group members note biological and behavioral cues that would facilitate their identifying a feeling state. Or the therapist can ask other members to comment on how they would feel in a situation similar to that of the patient or family member. The therapist would then check back with the patient or family member to ask if any of the disclosed feelings were similar or different from what they felt. Alternatively, instead of asking how members would feel in a similar situation, the therapist can also ask members how they feel listening to another member describe how they are experiencing an event. The first approach (i.e., soliciting others' feelings in a similar situation) promotes validation, universality, and self-empathy because it helps the patient to feel less alone, normalizes patient concerns, and helps them compare their internal states with those described by others. The second approach (i.e., asking members how they feel as the patient describes her experience in the "here and now" of the group), promotes mutual empathy because members, in the moment, let the patient know how they have been influenced by the patient's self-disclosure. And, in turn, the patient can take in these feelings and reflect on whether s/he feels similarly or differently (self-empathy) because of the disclosure to the group. These interventions help members connect with themselves while connecting with others during the discussion about a point of tension/disconnection, thus enlarging relational possibilities and reducing the temptation of using AN for self-expression, emotion regulation, connection, and coping.

Patient Reticence to Share about Points of Tension/ Disconnections

If the young adults seem reticent to disclose about certain points of tension/ disconnections or why certain suggested solutions won't help them overcome the challenges they experience in relation to these points of tension/ disconnections, remind them that this group offers them an opportunity to jointly educate their family members about points of tension/disconnections and the effectiveness of solutions. If patients do not educate family members, then family members will likely respond in ways they have responded in the past, which may or may not be experienced as helpful by the patients. If the patients are still reticent to disclose, conduct a decisional balance activity on the pros and cons of sharing vs not sharing information (also see Chapter 13, p. 18). Include in this decisional balance activity a question about whether patients will feel more or less connected with themselves and others if they share information with others versus not share information.

The Whole Group Becomes Quiet

If for any reason the entire group is having difficulty engaging regarding a particular point of tension/disconnection, the therapist can employ a "group as a whole" intervention (Yalom & Leszcz, 2005) and state that the "eating disorder seems to be trying to create disconnection for all of us tonight. It is important for us to figure out what is making it challenging for us to talk right now." This intervention puts a focus on the "we" by reminding members that AN may have the upper hand right now, empowering them to regroup and not allow this, and it reinforces that members are not alone with whatever they are experiencing. They can call upon others for support. The preceding intervention is an invitation to reflect contemporaneously on what is transpiring in a safe way, something that patients and families need to practice outside group as well. After making the "group as a whole" in-tervention, the therapist then asks members what they think and feel about the preceding statement and/or can do a check in with each member if they are not spontaneously offering feedback. During this discussion, the point of tension/disconnection that is at work in the group usually emerges for further discussion. The therapist needs to model how to name tension and

Session 12: Moving from Disconnection to Connection 221

disconnection when it is at work in group. She/he does so in a curious, warm, and engaging way. Well-timed humor can also help in this situation because it can decrease anxiety and reconnect members. For example, the first author has made the following statements in a "group as a whole" intervention while wearing a curious and inviting smile: "Well, the eating disorder is trying to work it's magic with all of us right now," or "Well, the eating disorder is trying to have its way with us right now," or "You know who is having a good time with all of our silence right now?" The skill of naming points of tension and disconnections amidst high anxiety and other intense emotions is important for patients and family members to practice because it promotes reconnection with self and others and does not allow AN to maintain disconnection among patients and family members. Watching the therapist model this skill can help group members know this is possible.

The R4R therapists end the first half of Session 12 by having members take turns reviewing items from a handout, "Strategies for Promoting Mutuality and Motivation during Recovery" (see Box 16.2). These items represent additional strategies that foster perceived mutuality and motivation during recovery, thus helping members move from interpersonal disconnection to new and better connection.

Box 16.2 Strategies for Promoting Mutuality and Motivation during Recovery

- Build and empower the "We"; put connection at the heart ❤ of the relationship.
- Remember the eating disorder will do whatever it can to disconnect the patient from her/his genuine feelings, thoughts, and needs and from loved ones to maintain its existence. Eating disorders are *Diseases of Disconnection.*
- Separate the illness from the patient.
- Remember you are more than the eating disorder. Identify and remember your strengths. Connect with others who will remind you of these things too.
- Acknowledge the burden and strain created by the eating disorder for patient and family. Engage in self-care and ask for support from trusted others.
- Use validation and avoid shame and blame with one another.
- Be empathic and warm while being deliberate and consistent with support.
- Be real, genuine, and emotionally present and responsive.
- Remember that lapses and mistakes are opportunities for learning, not failures.

The anxiety involved in transitions and trying something new can leave us more vulnerable to lapses. Increase self-care and seek more support at these times.

- Model, encourage, and reinforce flexibility, openness to change and difference, and the ability to tolerate uncertainty, unpredictability, and ambiguity.
- Try to understand and empathize with the meanings the patient attaches to the eating disorder and the purposes it serves. Help the patient find alternative healthy ways to meet the needs and purposes served by the eating disorder.
- Encourage opportunities for connection that don't include the eating disorder.
- Learn the language of the eating disorder and adjust how you communicate. For example, telling a patient that she/he looks healthy can be interpreted as "I am fat."
- Be on the lookout for rigid thinking patterns, black and white thinking, and a focus on details at the expense of the big picture. Try to identify when this is happening in relationships and practice more flexible thinking and seeing the big picture.
- Encourage the patient to remember his/her life values and goals when the eating disorder tries to make her/him forget these things.
- Name points of tension and disconnection and your responses to these events.
- Be aware of your own strategies for disconnection, e.g., isolation, avoidance, etc.
- Acknowledge and apologize for errors.
- Convey humility, use well-timed humor, and foster the "we" (a team feeling).
- Share with one another how you influence each other by using "I statements" to clarify your experience and "we statements" to strengthen your connection. This helps you practice being "different in connection" with each other.
- Be respectful of everyone's different thoughts, feelings, and needs and use these to strengthen versus weaken relationships.
- Name relational dilemmas and allow loved ones to see how you are thinking and feeling in response to their verbal and nonverbal communication. For example, "I want to respect your desire to be autonomous, while also wanting to be honest about my concerns regarding your skipping dinner tonight."
- Do not assume what others think/feel. Check it out.
- Remember that all relationships naturally move from connection to disconnection and back and that there are no perfect relationships. The best ones come from continual hard work and repair.
- Find and use personal and professional support people with whom you experience mutuality. Remember you are part of a team.

Note: Strategies for Promoting Mutuality and Motivation During Recovery. Reprinted from "Mutuality and Motivation" (p. 325), by M. Tantillo and J. Sanftner, in M. Maine, B. Hartman McGilley, and D. Bunnell (Eds.), *Treatment of eating disorders*, 2010, London, UK: Elsevier. Copyright 2010 by Elsevier Inc. Reprinted with permission.

Conducting the Last Half of Session 12

During the last half of group, the R4R therapists help members focus on the points of tension and disconnections related specifically to the transition into young adulthood. They begin this work by reviewing the highlights from a handout (Transitioning from Adolescence to Young Adulthood) describing emerging adulthood and young adulthood (see Box 16.3). The highlights include what to expect during this developmental transition (e.g., new expectations, responsibilities, role changes in relation to school, work, relationships, etc.). They discuss how any transition, especially the move into young adulthood can involve ambiguity, uncertainty, and unpredictability, all things that patients may experience as uncomfortable. Anxiety and fear can increase at these times, as well as less flexible thinking, e.g., black and white thoughts, "shoulds," and an increased focus on detail at the expense of the big picture. The therapists note how AN finds ways to offer itself as a solution to the tension and anxiety involved with this transition.

Box 16.3 Transitioning from Adolescence to Young Adulthood

Eating Disorders often begin during adolescence and their effects can spill over into "Emerging Adulthood" (ages 18–25) and Young Adulthood (ages 26–40). Eating disorders can also begin during Emerging Adulthood. Therefore, it is important to consider what is going on during these developmental periods and the impact on health and recovery.

Process of growth and development from adolescence through emerging adulthood and into young adulthood.

Stage 1 Adolescence (10–17)

Goals

- Achieve autonomy while maintaining connections with parents and others.
- Practice being responsible for meeting one's own needs and eventually those of others who will be dependent on you in the future.

Stage 2 Emerging Adulthood (18–25)

Goals

- Achieve responsibility and develop the ability to meet one's needs without obstructing others' ability to meet their needs.
- Consolidate and strengthen identity through decisions and experiences related to education, employment and social networking that influence one's ability to achieve and maintain financial independence throughout adulthood.

Stage 3 Young adulthood (26–40)

Goals

- Invest oneself in adult social roles, relationships, and responsibilities in ways that connect the person to new systems (work, family and community).
- The responsibilities and associated demands influence adult development.

Emerging Adulthood

Emerging Adulthood (18–25)

- Accept responsibility for the consequences of one's actions.
- Decide on personal beliefs and values independently from parents and other influences.
- Spend time preparing for adulthood.
- Make decisions about when and with whom one lives.
- Make decisions about entering and leaving school and work.
- Make decisions about committed relationships with intimate partners.
- Subjective sense of being "in between" (feeling like an adult or not).
- Identity development occurs in the context of real-life experiences instead of in your head (like when you were an adolescent).

Five Characteristics of Emerging Adulthood

Instability along one's life plan	Emerging adults experience challenges and complications with regard to their initial "life plan" necessitating changes in their college majors, employment, intimate partners, and residences.

(continued on next page)

Session 12: Moving from Disconnection to Connection 225

Five Characteristics of Emerging Adulthood

Self-discovery and identity exploration	Emerging adults try out new things in their quest to figure out who they are and who they want to become, especially related to romantic partners and careers. This aids in the process of looking for a satisfactory life partner and a fulfilling career.
Focus on personal needs	Emerging adults tend to focus on themselves and their personal needs, thus delaying major adult responsibilities (e.g., getting married and having children) to enjoy a sense of freedom.
Feeling "in between" adolescence and adulthood	Emerging adults subjectively feel like they are and they aren't adults. They do feel more independent and mature than when they were adolescents.
Future possibilities	Emerging adults often feel positively about the future, believing they can accomplish their dreams and overcome past hardships to become the person they want to be.

Implications of Health in Emerging Adulthood on Future Health

It is important to optimize health during Emerging Adulthood because the health accumulated during this time influences pathways of health, disease, and disability across adulthood. Helping emerging adults maximize their level of functioning contributes to continued high functioning and health later on.

The effects of early health risks such as eating disorders spill over into adulthood. These health risks can persist or become amplified in Emerging Adulthood. Sometimes eating disorders can also begin in Emerging Adulthood. A person's health risks contribute to their overall health vulnerability.

In Emerging Adulthood health vulnerability is influenced by:

- Health and previous health risk exposures before age 18 (e.g., genetic vulnerabilities, illness, trauma, environmental hazards)
- Instability and transitions experienced during Emerging Adulthood (18–25)
- Combined effect of health promotion and risk factors affecting the Emerging Adult in their lives (e.g., neighborhood and physical environment, social support, education, food, economic stability, access to health care)

Emerging Adulthood is a good window for health promotion because individuals are still developing their identity, life preferences, values, and beliefs. And even though the eating disorder will try to capitalize on the Emerging Adult's freedom to make (potentially unhealthy) decisions, developmentally, the Emerging Adult is seeking out new information and experiences. New information and experiences can be presented within a context of mutual understanding, trust, and empathy, which is respectful of the person's autonomy and fosters self-worth, self-efficacy, and the ability to authentically be who they are in relationships with others.

Note: For more information on Emerging Adulthood see Arnett, 2000, 2004, 2006; Tanner & Arnett, 2013.

After reviewing the highlights, the therapists divide members into small groups—one comprised of all the patients and several others comprised of family members from different families. Patients are intentionally allowed to comprise their own subgroup during this session because they may initially feel freer to identify the points of tension and disconnections that accompany young adulthood without family members present. Family members are asked to count off, for example, by threes and divide up into three groups comprised of different family members. The therapists ask patient and family member subgroups to identify and discuss challenges, interpersonal disconnections, points of tension, and triggers for the ED related specifically to the transition from adolescence to adulthood and the challenges associated with achieving adult developmental milestones. Members are also asked to identify the earliest signs of AN indicative of stress related to the preceding experiences. Group members are given 15 minutes to complete this task and should record their responses on the handout, "Challenges, Points of Tension, Interpersonal Disconnections, and Triggers for Eating Disorder Behaviors in Young Adults" (see Box 16.4).

Session 12: Moving from Disconnection to Connection   227

Box 16.4   Challenges, Points of Tension, Interpersonal Disconnections, and Triggers for Eating Disorder Behaviors in Young Adults

- What are the challenges, points of tension, interpersonal disconnections, and triggers for eating disorder behaviors experienced by young adults?
- What are the **earliest signs** the young adult in recovery experiences in the face of these challenges, points of tension, interpersonal disconnections, and triggers just noted? These signs can include:

  -*Internal* (e.g., biological and emotional) signs like certain feelings (e.g., panic, anxiety, irritability); racing thoughts; inflexible ways of thinking like black and white thinking and shoulds; an increased focus on detail versus the big picture; changes in heart rate and breathing; butterflies in the stomach; tightening of one's chest, etc., and

  -*External* (e.g., behavioral) signs like the clenching of one's jaw, nervously jiggling one's leg up and down, not being able to make eye contact with others, leaving the room emotionally, yelling, avoiding, isolating, etc

---

After 15 minutes of small group work, the R4R therapists reconvene the large group and facilitate discussion about member findings. The therapists can begin with a quick discussion (no more than five to ten minutes) of what it was like to do the exercise. The therapists can use easel paper to create a list of challenges, points of tension, interpersonal disconnections, and triggers for eating disorder behaviors experienced by the young adult patients. Some of the responses may duplicate points of tension and interpersonal disconnections mentioned previously, whereas others may be new responses. Group members often cite challenges, points of tensions, interpersonal disconnections, and triggers related to the stress involved with going to or returning to college; starting one's first paid employment position; moving out of the family home into an independent living situation; beginning a serious relationship with a new romantic partner; and shopping for, planning, and eating meals more independently. These experiences reflect the new expectations, responsibilities, and roles that accompany young adulthood.

After documenting the first list on easel paper, the therapists then use easel paper to outline the earliest internal and external signs indicating that patients may be experiencing challenges, points of tension, interpersonal disconnections, and triggers for eating disorder behaviors. Internal signs can include, for example, negative and rigid all or nothing thoughts such as rationalizing food restriction

228 *Mary Tantillo, Jennifer Sanftner McGraw, and Daniel Le Grange*

and telling oneself that she/he should be doing things totally independently; biological cues such as increased heart rate, headache, and heaviness in the chest; and emotions such as anxiety and irritation. External signs can include, for example, behaviors such as clenching of teeth, pacing, avoidance, withdrawal, isolation, negative self-talk, and silence. After constructing the list of earliest signs, the group can then begin problem solving together how to respond to these signs. The therapists (with the help of group members) assist patients to identify alternate coping, emotion-regulation, and self-care strategies and explore how loved ones can offer support during the transition to young adulthood. The following clinical vignette shows how the R4R therapist assisted Karen, a 20-year-old athlete, to discuss a point of tension/disconnection (i.e., her compulsion to exercise more after cross-country practice) and the earliest signs indicative of this point of tension/disconnection. The therapist also facilitates group discussion to help Karen problem-solve alternative coping and self-care strategies to prevent AN from succeeding in offering itself as a solution to her feelings of inadequacy, anxiety, and out of control feelings.

Therapist:	*So, now that we have listed everyone's thoughts about possible points of tension/disconnections related to moving into young adulthood, as well as some earliest signs of these points of tension/disconnections, I wonder if anyone would feel brave enough to help us practice applying what we learned as it relates to their particular point of tension/disconnection?*
Group:	*Members look at each other waiting for someone to offer a suggestion.*
Therapist:	*There were so many excellent points of tension and disconnections. Who would like to share more about one of theirs? This is a great opportunity to learn how to support one another.*
Ann:	*(a young adult in group is looking at Karen and is smiling and nodding)*
Therapist:	*Ann, you look like you have an idea about an example. It looks like you think Karen has something good to offer.*
Ann:	*Well, I don't want to put her on the spot, but I think her example is something that would help all of us. It is realistic and could happen to any of us.*
Therapist:	*Karen, Ann has confidence that you have a great example. Do you feel up to sharing it with us? What do you think?*
Karen:	*Thanks a lot Ann (facetious tone)! Ok. I will share it, but I hated even admitting it because I don't want my parents to think I am having trouble all the time with track.*
Susan (Karen's mother):	*I would rather hear, than not hear about what it is. Your speaking about it actually makes me less nervous about whatever it is because you are identifying it as a point of tension and not hiding it from yourself or us.*

Session 12: Moving from Disconnection to Connection 229

Dave (Karen's father):	*I agree with your mother. We would rather know than not know. And we are glad you are speaking up in group.*
Karen:	*Well, I was the one who came up with the point of tension related to feeling pushed to practice more after I already attended track practice. I have been cleared to return to track, but I have only been back at it for a month. It can be triggering at times, especially when I am feeling less positive about my body or feeling more competitive with other team members. Like I used to be the fastest on the team. But I have an exercise plan now, and I promised my coach and my parents that I would stick with it.*
Therapist:	*Karen, thanks so much for being honest about this point of tension. I am sure others in group can identify with what you are saying, even if they are not athletes. The eating disorder tries to take advantage of us when we feel vulnerable, and it is important to know the earliest signs of this when it is coming on. Can you tell what the earliest internal and external signs might be?*
Karen:	*Well, I guess just before I feel pushed to run more, I start thinking that I should be farther ahead in my performance on the team. Like I have to make up for lost time. This is worse on days where I feel my time was not good, but I see others performing well. Plus, then I can start thinking that I am behind my friends with so many things. For example, treatment for an eating disorder cost me an entire year of school. I won't be able to graduate this year with my friends.*
Therapist:	*So, you are comparing yourself to others and finding your performance does not stack up somehow? And this thinking, if left unchecked, can affect how you feel about your life in general.*
Karen:	*Yes.*
Therapist:	*Any other thoughts that you might be having?*
Karen:	*Well, that I may not be good enough to be back on the team, and maybe I should quit.*
Therapist:	*And these thoughts leave you feeling how?*
Karen:	*Like not good enough. And anxious and more out of control.*
Therapist:	*So, the earliest signs that you may be headed toward compulsive exercise include your comparing yourself to others, negative all or nothing thoughts and feelings of inadequacy, anxiety, and feeling out of control?*
Karen:	*Yes, I feel all those.*
Therapist:	*And are there any other internal signs like biological cues such as headache, muscle tension, an increased heart rate or external signs that would tip you off? Like a change in your behavior?*

Karen: Well, I get like a knot in my stomach and probably withdraw more and avoid the team. Like we try to do something social after practice, and if I am feeling the things I shared, I don't hang out with them. I end up going to my dorm room, which only probably makes things worse because I am alone with my thoughts.

Ann: And the eating disorder.

Karen: Yes, and the eating disorder.

Therapist: So that can be dangerous because the eating disorder likes to take advantage of us, especially when we are alone.

Karen: Yes, because while I am sitting there, the thoughts about going out to run more get louder in my ahead. And my feelings of inadequacy and anxiety only get worse.

Therapist: Sounds like you are concerned that the compulsion to run could get worse.

Karen: Yes, and I have been able to avoid this up till now. I don't want it to get worse.

Therapist: Karen, it is so good that you had courage to share this with us. The eating disorder lives off of what is unspoken. Your disclosing this information helps disempower the eating disorder and return the power to you.

Therapist: So, Karen, based on our discussion so far, is there anything you think you could try to do, once you start experiencing the earliest signs that you might be tempted to exercise more.

Karen: Well, I am not sure. I feel like I should be able to figure this out on my own. But so far, that hasn't worked.

Therapist: That is because you are being hard on yourself, expecting yourself to figure things out totally on your own. The eating disorder probably encourages this thinking because it can keep you away from others who could problem-solve with you. Young adults often want to figure things out on their own and that makes sense. At the same time, they can feel pressured to figure things out on their own, even when feedback from others might help. Part of being an adult means knowing when we need help and asking for it. We are all interdependent on each other. And we are lucky because here we are surrounded by people who care for you. Is it OK for us to ask them what they think about possible solutions?

Karen: (Nods yes in affirmation.)

Therapist: So, I am wondering what Karen can do when she is feeling vulnerable and the eating disorder is pushing her to exercise more?

Ann: Well, it sounds like being alone is not a good idea. Karen, can you make yourself hang out with the team, even if it is

Session 12: Moving from Disconnection to Connection 231

	tough. Or at least a couple of your teammates that you are closer to? Are there any you feel closer to? Like do any of them know you are in recovery?
Karen:	*Yes, at least two know. Jennie and Kayla. I guess I could talk with them about what is going on. It is just hard to admit it because I don't want everyone worrying about me.*
Therapist:	*If things were the reverse and Jenny or Kayla were having trouble, would you want to know or not know?*
Karen:	*Of course, I would want to know. I would want to help.*
Therapist:	*OK. And if they were here right now, what would they say if they knew you were being hard on yourself and feeling compelled to listen to the eating disorder?*
Karen:	*They would say they want to support me.*
Therapist:	*So, is Ann's suggestion to hang out with them realistic? Could you do it?*
Karen:	*Yes, I just have to be honest with Jenny and Kayla about it. I guess I could let them know ahead of time that I need to hang with them if I am feeling extra vulnerable and having negative thoughts.*
Therapist:	*Ok. Good work. Any other suggestions for Karen?*
Linda (another patient's mom):	*Karen, can you change your negative self-talk and tell yourself different messages in order to outsmart the eating disorder? For example, when you start comparing yourself to others, can you tell yourself that the eating disorder wants you to do this and that you need to compare yourself to yourself, not to others. Can you tell yourself that you are improving your performance a little each day, and talk to yourself in the way you would talk with Jenny or Kayla? What would you tell them if they were in your position?*
Karen:	*I would tell them not to be so hard on themselves while also validating the pressure they feel to perform well. I would remind them to pay attention to their own running times and reinforce that they are getting better each day. I would tell them they have only been back on the team for a month.*
Therapist:	*So, do you think you can do that for yourself, as Linda suggests? Is it realistic?*
Karen:	*It probably would work better if I write down the new self-talk statements, so I have them when I feel out of control, anxious, and inadequate about my performance. I can keep them in my locker and look at them before and after practice. It would be helpful if I could remind myself that it is the eating disorder tempting me to compare myself with others.*
Ann:	*And maybe if you feel comfortable, you could let Jenny and Kayla know about these positive self-talk statements and they could use them with you too.*

Karen:	That is a good point. I will think more about that. I want them to say whatever they want to me without a script but maybe them knowing what I am working on would be helpful too.

The group continues to offer a few more suggestions and Karen's parents encourage her to let them know if she is having a tough time. They would be happy to remind her of the strategies we discussed today. The R4R therapist ends the discussion by asking Karen if she has any other ideas for self-care the group has not yet mentioned. The therapist encourages Karen to discuss the strategies discussed today with her individual and family therapists as well, so they can encourage her to employ the strategies and assess their impact. Karen was also invited to report back to group her implementation of the strategies, so they could get follow-up on her efforts to decrease her anxiety, out of control feelings, and inadequacy without using compulsive exercise or other AN symptoms.

During Session 12, the therapists emphasize the importance of asking for help and how true maturity is characterized by knowing our limitations, behaving in interdependent ways, and asking for assistance when needed. They reinforce that we all heal and grow in connection with others and that during young adulthood these "others" can include immediate and extended family and new relationships with adults outside the immediate family (at school, work, and in the broader community). The eating disorder often leaves young adults feeling guilty, ashamed, inadequate, and with a sense of failure when they want to reach out to others for support. These feelings can often be masked by irritation, defensiveness, and rejection of support, when in reality, support is needed and beneficial. Experiencing an eating disorder as a young adult is a perfect storm because the normal strivings for autonomy, competence, and confidence in living out one's life (Arnett, 2000, 2004, 2006; Dimitropoulos, Lock, Le Grange, & Anderson, 2015) converge with AN, which amplifies and twists these striving to serve its aims—disconnection from one's genuine needs and feelings and isolation from others (Tantillo, Sanftner, & Hauenstein, 2013). Western dominant culture only serves to further amplify the desire for ultra-independence, individuation, and separation from others (Jordan, 2018). It is in this crucible that the R4R therapist repeatedly reinforces through modeling, psychoeducation, discussion, and emotional and relational skills-building that growth in recovery and life come from being more connected to one's genuine self and others throughout development.

Due to the breadth and depth of discussion that can occur during Session 12 about young adult challenges, points of tension, disconnections, triggers, and the earliest signs of these experiences, the work from this session may extend naturally to Session 13. For example, due to time constraints, Session 12 could end with construction of the list of the preceding experiences, as well as the earliest signs of these experiences. More discussion about them could follow in Session 13 where members will discuss caregiving styles and begin focusing on relapse prevention. Session 12 goals, materials, and handouts are outlined in Box 16.5.

Box 16.5 Session 12: Moving from Disconnection to Connection: Building Strong Connections to Work through Tension and Disconnections Related to Adulthood and Recovery

Goals

Help patients and family members to:

- Identify interpersonal disconnections and points of tension specifically related to transition from adolescence to adulthood and achieving adult developmental milestones.
- Identify earliest signs that AN is trying to solve tension/anxiety regarding adult developmental challenges, as well as alternative coping strategies and support needed from others.
- Continue practicing emotional and relational skills to repair relationships and restore/build mutual connections.

Materials

- Easel and marker, paper and pens

Exercise

- Review peaks and valleys
- After reviewing handouts on **Emerging and Young Adulthood,** use last half of group to divide members into **patient and family member small groups**. Have them identify and discuss challenges, interpersonal disconnections, points of tension, and triggers for ED related specifically to the *transition from adolescence to adulthood and achieving young adult developmental milestones*. Also have them identify the earliest signs of these struggles, points of tension, interpersonal disconnections, and triggers.
- Return to the large group to create a list of the above to be distributed next week.
- Explore how AN offers itself as a solution to the tension and anxiety involved with the transition to young adulthood.
- Identify and discuss alternate coping and self-care strategies and how loved ones can offer support during the transition to young adulthood.

Handouts

- Have members take turns reviewing items from the handout *Strategies for Promoting Mutuality and Motivation During Recovery*.

- Review highlights from handouts on *Transitioning from Adolescence to Young Adulthood* later in group before small group exercise.
- Review the following article for additional information about the transition from adolescence to young adulthood: Tanner, J. L., & Arnett, J. J. (2013). Approaching young adult health and medicine from a developmental perspective, *Adolescent Medicine: State of the Art Reviews, 24*(3), 485–506.
- Use the following handout to record small group responses: *Challenges, Points of Tension, Interpersonal Disconnections, and Triggers for Eating Disorder Behaviors in Young Adults.*

References

*No DOI

Arnett, J. J. (2000). Emerging adulthood: A theory of development from the late teens through the twenties. *American Psychologist, 55*(5), 469–480. https://dx.doi.org/10.1037/0003-066x.55.5.469.

Arnett, J. J. (2004). Emerging adulthood: The winding road from the late teens through the twenties. Oxford University Press.

Arnett, J. J. (2006). *Emerging adults in America: Coming of age in the 21st. century.* American Psychological Association. https://dx.doi.org/10.1037/11381-000.

*Dimitropoulos, G., Lock, J., Le Grange, D., & Anderson, K. (2015). Family therapy for transition youth. In K. Loeb, D. Le Grange, & J. Lock (Eds.), *Family therapy for adolescent eating and weight disorders: New applications* (pp. 230–255). Routledge/Taylor & Francis Group.

Jordan, J. (2018). *Relational-cultural therapy* (2nd ed.). American Psychological Association. https://dx.doi.org/10.1037/0000063-001.

*Tanner, J. L., & Arnett, J. J. (2013). Approaching young adult health and medicine from a developmental perspective. *Adolescent Medicine, 24*(3), 485–506.

Tantillo, M., Sanftner, J. L., & Hauenstein, E. (2013). Restoring connection in the face of disconnection: An integrative approach to understanding and treating anorexia nervosa. *Advances in Eating Disorders: Theory, Research, and Practice, 1*, 21–38.

Treasure, J., Schmidt, U., & MacDonald, P. (2010). *The clinician's guide to collaborative caring in eating disorders: The new Maudsley Method.* Routledge. https://dx.doi.org/10.4324/9780203864685.

*Yalom, I., & Leszcz, M. (2005). *The theory and practice of group psychotherapy* (5th ed.). New York, NY: Basic Books.

17 Session 13: Relapse Prevention and Maintaining Good Connection

Mary Tantillo, Jennifer Sanftner McGraw, and Daniel Le Grange

The R4R therapists begin Session 13 by continuing discussion from Session 12 regarding young adult challenges, points of tension, disconnections, and triggers. Patients and family members may not have had sufficient time to fully discuss these experiences in the previous session. For example, the discussion between Karen, the therapist, and group members in the Session 12 clinical vignette might occur in the first part of Session 13 due to time constraints in Session 12. This discussion allows members to consider how developmental challenges, points of tension, disconnections and triggers may contribute to relapse. During Session 13, the R4R therapists help patients and families identify the earliest signs of a potential relapse. During Session 13 the R4R therapist's aims include:

- Use animal metaphors (Langley, Todd, & Treasure, 2019; Treasure, Smith, & Crane, 2017) to educate regarding caregiver styles and help members develop and practice dolphin and St. Bernard caregiving responses
- Help group members identify high risk situations (especially transitions), triggers, and the earliest internal and external cues signaling a patient relapse
- Facilitate identification and practice of relapse prevention strategies
- Assist members to begin developing discharge plans that include community-based supports and promote the continuity of connections and patient/family care

At the very beginning of Session 13 the R4R therapists have patients review both peaks and valleys from the past two weeks. One or more of the stated valleys (or peaks) can again be used to extend and deepen the discussion about triggers, points of tension, interpersonal disconnections, and the earliest signs of relapse, as identified during Session 12. This beginning work may last for approximately 30 minutes of the session. During this discussion, the therapists emphasize the importance of recognizing the earliest signs of relapse, as well as solicit what patients will do in the face of these signs, i.e., the relapse prevention strategies they will employ. These strategies include but are not limited to asking for help, returning to meal planning, journaling, drawing, structuring time, and increasing mindfulness practices. The therapists can help patients identify the behavioral chains (events that link together) that occur on the way to symptomatic behaviors. Feedback about behavioral chains and the earliest signs of relapse should be solicited initially from young adults. Family members can then be engaged to assist with this task because they are in a position to potentially see signs that the patient is unaware of. The therapists acknowledge that none of us can step outside of ourselves and know exactly what we are doing all the time. They can reiterate that part of being a good support is working with patients to identify the earliest warning signs of a relapse. The therapists encourage family members to remind patients (in a caring way) about the warning signs they identified in group, when patients are evidencing one or more of those signs. The therapists reinforce that AN will try to obstruct the patient from seeing these signs when she/he is experiencing them. Therefore, having loved ones make explicit what is implicit, is a way to stop AN from perpetuating itself.

After completing discussion about triggers, points of tension, interpersonal disconnections, the earliest signs of relapse, and effective relapse prevention strategies, the R4R therapists then begin a discussion about caregiving styles in recovery through the use of various animal metaphors (Langley, Todd, & Treasure, 2019; Treasure, Smith, & Crane, 2017). The discussion begins with distribution of stuffed animals, including a rhinoceros, ostrich, terrier, jellyfish, kangaroo, dolphin, and St. Bernard. The first author (MT) has often started by asking who would like to be the caretaker of one of the stuffed animals for today's session. There is usually a flurry of requests to be the recipient of one of the animals. Alternatively, illustrations of these animals (see Figure 5.5) can be distributed to group members. We have found the stuffed animals to be more pleasurable from a visual and tactile perspective.

The R4R therapists begin the discussion about caregiving styles by reinforcing the importance of supporting patients in a way that fosters mutual trust, empathy, understanding, and empowerment. They mention the animal metaphors used in family-based work as elaborated by Treasure and colleagues (Langley, Todd, & Treasure, 2019; Treasure, Smith, & Crane, 2017) and state that we will be doing some of that work today. An example of how to open the discussion follows:

Therapist: *We have spent a great deal of time in group discussing how the eating disorder loves to create and maintain internal and interpersonal disconnections and how mutuality in relationships fosters repair in the face of disconnections and can promote growth for everyone in the relationship. In recovery the patients work hard to allow themselves to ask for and receive help. Family members work hard at responding to patient needs and requests in a way that promotes mutual trust, understanding, empathy and empowerment. This is especially difficult to do when the eating disorder is doing all it can to burden patients and families, for example, promoting psychological distress, distraction, and fatigue. One way for caregivers to learn and practice the skills required to respond effectively to their loved ones in recovery, is to think about our caregiving responses in terms of animal metaphors. Janet Treasure and colleagues in London came up with a way of teaching families about helpful caregiving responses by using these animal metaphors. So, we will be doing that*

Session 13: Relapse Prevention and Maintaining Good Connection   237

work today in group. We will think about each of the animals I distributed to you and reflect on what kind of caregiving style might be associated with that particular animal based on what we know about that animal. There are five animals that represent caregiving styles that are less helpful in comparison to the caregiving associated with two of our inspirational animals. After we finish our discussion about each animal and their associated caregiving style, we will divide into our smaller family groups and discuss patient and family member impressions about what caregiver styles their loved ones use. Then we will return to our larger family group to discuss what each family discovered during their discussion.

After orienting group members to the work they will do related to caregiving styles, the therapists introduce one animal at a time, and, for each animal, they lead a discussion based on the questions contained in Box 17.1. The questions are designed to help members understand the caregiving style associated with an animal, as well as promote mutual understanding and empathy about why that caregiving style might be employed and what it feels like to receive that caregiving style over time.

Box 17.1   Questions to Foster Discussion about Caregiving Animal Metaphors

- When we see a (insert name of animal you are discussing), what do we think of? What do we know about (insert animal name)? What are they like?
- When we think about a (insert name of animal) caregiving style, what might be happening that could lead a loved one to respond with that caregiving style? What might they be feeling and thinking about before employing that caregiving style?
- Now that we know what a caregiver might be feeling/thinking when using this caregiving style, it is also important to know how the person in recovery feels when repeatedly receiving that caregiving style. We need to understand both sides. What might the person in recovery feel, think or do when receiving (insert name of animal) caregiving?
- How might the eating disorder capitalize on these experiences?
- How might these experiences affect recovery?
- When needed as a reminder: Who enjoys it when patients and families are at odds because caregiving styles might not be matching patient needs? (The answer that group members usually say in unison is *the eating disorder.*)

By the end of the discussion regarding the animals and caregiving styles, family members can reflect without guilt, shame, or defensiveness about the

238   Mary Tantillo, Jennifer Sanftner McGraw, and Daniel Le Grange

caregiving style(s) they use. This self-reflection facilitates the small and large group discussions that follows. Discussion about the animal metaphors allows for the use of humor and a light-hearted approach to examining caregiving styles. Patients and family members can more clearly see the interplay between the caregiver's style, the patient's response and AN's efforts to capitalize on this situation when the caregiver response is not experienced as helpful. The patient may end up engaging in AN symptoms to cope with the tension and disconnection experienced in the interaction with loved ones. During this discussion, the therapist can normalize why loved ones might use particular styles given various situations and why patients feel the way they do on the receiving end of the caregiving. Again, this approach promotes perceived mutuality in relationships. An example of how the R4R therapist promotes discussion about the caregiving styles associated with the animals is shown next. In this clinical vignette the therapist is discussing the kangaroo caregiving style.

Therapist:	*So, let's start with the kangaroo. When we look at that kangaroo with joey in her pouch, what do you think about? What do we think of when we think about kangaroos?*
Michelle (mother of a patient):	*Kangaroos are protective. They want to shelter their young.*
Therapist:	*Good, so they are very caring of their young and want to keep them close. Anything else?*
Taylor (patient):	*They might keep them too close sometimes. Like the joey might want to be out but the mother kangaroo might be worried about that.*
Therapist:	*Very good. So, because mama kangaroo loves her joey and is very concerned about her baby, she may sometimes err on the side of keeping joey close to her when joey might want to go exploring.*
Taylor:	*Yes. If the mother kangaroo is worried about the environment, she will keep her baby close.*
Therapist:	*Good. Any other thoughts about what kangaroo caregiving might look like?*
Thomas (patient):	*The kangaroo caregiving reminds me of like a helicopter parent. (He whirls his finger around in the air like a propeller and the group members laugh.) Like they are right by your side because they are always worrying about you.*
Therapist:	*Yes, there is a potential for that to happen when we love our young and adult children a lot and have lots of worries about their well-being. Great job. Anything else about kangaroo caregiving?*
Group:	*(Members are quiet and seem done with providing responses.)*
Therapist:	*OK, now that we have described kangaroo caregiving a bit, what would make a parent or partner use kangaroo caring? We already alluded to this in some of our discussion just now, but it is worth looking at again.*

Session 13: Relapse Prevention and Maintaining Good Connection 239

	What would make a loved one respond like a kangaroo when caring for someone with an eating disorder?
Pete (father of a patient):	Well, like before we said that the parent could be really concerned about their child getting hurt somehow. That could lead to kangaroo caring.
Therapist:	Yes, that makes total sense. What else could be happening?
Ann (patient):	Well, maybe the parent or partner is afraid if they let their loved one try something new, they might not be ready for it and could fail and feel even worse. So, they don't want them to try new things yet.
Therapist:	Excellent thought. That definitely could be happening. Any other thoughts and feelings that might trigger kangaroo caring in a family member?
Sheila (mom of a patient):	Probably the parent or partner could be feeling highly anxious. It is hard to let someone you love try something new or go far away, if you are worried that they are not well enough to do that. You are afraid the eating disorder will take advantage of them.
Therapist:	Very good. Yes, that could happen. So, it is scary for a kangaroo to let a loved one be far apart from them or let them try something that seems too risky. It seems like the kangaroo's actions are protective and well-intentioned. OK. Now let's look at this from the other side. What might it feel like if someone continually receives kangaroo caregiving?
Thomas:	Like it could feel too much. The person receiving the caregiving might want to have more freedom and get frustrated that this is not allowed. You could not try anything new.
Therapist:	Yes, the person could be sheltered so much, that they don't get to try their hand at developing new skills. They will not learn to feel competent or confident trying new things.
Taylor:	Yes, and maybe they are too scared to try new things anyway. And having a kangaroo mom or dad would protect you and help you keep avoiding something you should be trying. That seems good in one way because it keeps your anxiety down, but it does not help you gain confidence in yourself over time.
Therapist:	Yes, and the funny thing about caregiving is that we often don't realize that we are employing a particular caregiving style until we slow down and examine more closely how we are responding. Plus, family members may not be sure if they are talking with the healthy part of their loved one or the eating disorder when their loved one makes a request. When we love our kids or partner, we can reflexively respond in the way we have been parented or in the way we believe is best based on our current knowledge, values, wiring, and

	personalities. That way may or may not match what our loved one really needs. For example, my son always makes the helicopter sound and the propeller motion that Thomas made for us a few minutes ago, when he thinks I am being too protective. (Group members laugh.) I have learned to laugh about it now too, but I tell him I can't help it sometimes. I do it because I love him so much. It is hard being a young adult and it is hard being the parent of a young adult, let alone needing to work together in recovery. (Group members nod in affirmation.) And of course, the eating disorder does all it can to burden patients and family members and create distress and disconnections.
Michelle:	*Yes, it is hard to let go sometimes. You want your kid to succeed and you never know if the new thing they want to try will be good for them. I admit that I become more of a kangaroo when I am anxious or sense that Kelly (her daughter) is anxious about doing something.*
Therapist:	*Kelly, do you agree with what mom says or do you see it differently?*
Kelly:	*She is right.*
Therapist:	*And what happens if every time you have an opportunity to do something new, you and/or your mom get(s) nervous?*
Kelly:	*I would avoid everything.*
Therapist:	*And when you end up avoiding things, how does that affect you and your recovery?*
Kelly:	*I can't move forward. I am too scared to try new things.*
Therapist:	*And how might the eating disorder take advantage of this situation?*
Kelly:	*I never thought about it this way. I guess… well, it probably helps me not think about the thing I am scared about.*
Therapist:	*Say more about what you mean. Sounds like you are on to something important.*
Kelly:	*I guess it distracts me in a way and numbs the anxiety associated with the thing I am afraid of. I probably end up focusing on the eating disorder or my weight or how much less I can eat at my next meal, instead of on the thing I am afraid of.*
Michelle:	*And then I can end up being a kangaroo without realizing it because I tell her she does not have to do something if it is going to totally stress her out. I get anxious watching her get anxious about the situation and then want to shelter her from the stress.*
Therapist:	*So, thank you Michelle and Kelly for sharing this example. It demonstrates how tempting it is to be a kangaroo caregiver when we love someone and don't want them to be upset. Their concern will only increase in the face of the eating*

Session 13: Relapse Prevention and Maintaining Good Connection   241

> *disorder. At the same time, kangaroo caregiving can help us avoid doing new things that could help us grow and positively impact our recovery. One way to decrease kangaroo caregiving is to alleviate our own anxiety. In the homework that caregivers will receive tonight, you will be asked to identify your supports. Caregivers also need to feel connected to trusted others from whom they can receive support. When caregivers have that support, the distress the eating disorder creates is lessened. Then we are better able to employ dolphin or St. Bernard caregiving responses when helping patients manage their anxiety and other intense emotions. AN wants all of us to feel overwhelmed with anxiety so it can immobilize and disconnect us and stay connected with the patient. OK, excellent work. Let's move on to the rhinoceros now....*

In this clinical vignette, the R4R therapist teaches members about kangaroo caregiving through, first, encouraging members to brainstorm the meanings associated with kangaroos. She then translates this feedback into a description of kangaroo caregiving. She does so through validating and normalizing what might trigger this caregiving style, while also giving voice to what it feels like to be a recipient of this kind of caregiving (thereby promoting perceived mutuality). The therapist also uses humor by disclosing how she has sometimes responded like a kangaroo caregiver with her own son. Her intervention creates a sense of "we" in which she is included as a loving *and* imperfect parent. Her disclosure is intended to decrease shame, guilt, or blame and to acknowledge that parenting is not a perfect science and that no child comes with an instruction kit. Parents do the best they can with parenting their children based on their own parenting and personalities, and they can learn to improve their parenting across development, as the needs of their children change. The therapist conveys that like many other things, parenting is a work in progress and that in order to do that work, parents need their own supports and need to practice regulating their own emotions, so they can help their children do the same. Much of what the R4R therapist says about parent caregiving styles can also be used to describe caregiving styles of partners/close friends. Examples of the language the therapist can use in discussing each animal metaphor are noted in Table 17.1. This information should also be shared as a handout with group members. For additional information about the animal metaphors, members are asked to review Chapter 5 (pp. 42–55) and Chapter 9 (pp. 118–131) in Treasure, Smith, & Crane, 2017.

After the large group teaching and discussion about the animal metaphors, the members are then divided into their smaller family units for approximately ten minutes to reflect on and discuss the caregiving styles of each parent, partner, or close friend(s) in each family unit. The group members are reminded that they are to brainstorm and not critique each other and that different family members may hold different perspectives on a loved one's

Table 17.1 Animal Metaphors for Caregiving Styles: Caregiver and Patient Responses and Impact on Recovery

Animal Metaphor	Caregiving Style	Triggers for This Caregiving Style	Loved One's Experience in Response to Repeatedly Receiving This Caregiving Style	Impact on Recovery
Kangaroo	Kangaroos protect and support their loved ones by keeping them close by. Though well-intentioned, this caregiving style can unwittingly prevent loved ones from exploring the environment and building new skills. Loved ones may not develop the competence and confidence in themselves and their skills that foster ongoing recovery and achievement of developmental milestones.	Caregivers may feel anxious, scared, and/or overwhelmed. They may doubt their loved one's ability to handle new experiences. They feel compelled to shield their loved one from something they consider too risky or threatening.	Loved ones who want more space and autonomy may feel overprotected and constricted. They may verbalize feeling controlled and "smothered" and may experience frustration and resentment over time. They can experience self-doubt about their abilities, inadequacy, and low self-esteem. Conversely, if they are afraid of trying new things, they may feel comforted and sheltered from anxiety-provoking situations.	Loved ones may lack the competence and confidence they need to try new skills and achieve developmental milestones. This experience can contribute to negative self-evaluation because loved ones may engage in social comparisons and find themselves behind their peers without a way of catching up. Those who are more comfortable avoiding new experiences will continue to be sheltered from gaining new coping skills and have difficulty moving ahead in their psychosocial development.
Ostrich	Ostriches tend to look the other way when something stressful occurs with their loved ones. They may feel highly anxious about their loved one's struggles and cope with this through avoidance. It may be difficult for them to embrace the	Caregivers may feel highly stressed, overwhelmed, inadequate, unprepared, or assume that their loved one's challenges are a normal part of growing up that will stabilize over time.	Loved ones can feel unloved, invisible, and invalidated. They may feel frustrated, angry, sad, and/or depressed. They assume the ostrich caregiver does not care about them or their recovery. They may experience tension, conflict and betrayal if	Loved ones may feel they are not worthy of support and this may decrease their motivation for recovery. Or they may get derailed from recovery work because of the intense emotion related to the ostrich's lack of involvement and/or seeming avoidance.

(*Continued*)

Session 13: Relapse Prevention and Maintaining Good Connection 243

Table 17.1 (Continued)

Animal Metaphor	Caregiving Style	Triggers for This Caregiving Style	Loved One's Experience in Response to Repeatedly Receiving This Caregiving Style	Impact on Recovery
	intense emotions associated with understanding AN and helping in recovery. Or they may think that their loved one's experience is a passing phase and assume things will eventually be OK in time. Additionally, they may lack information that would help them be more active and effectual in their caregiving response. They may also feel ill-prepared to help with recovery and assume that they will not be helpful (e.g., fathers assume mothers know what to do in response to their child's needs).		their efforts to repeatedly involve their ostrich caregiver are unsuccessful. Or loved ones may blame themselves. The lack of collaborative work in recovery may also hurt the overall relationship with the caregiver.	Loved ones may also be angry and rejecting of the ostrich caregiver, even when they finally seem ready to help.
Terrier	Terriers can be feisty and tireless in their efforts to remind us when they are concerned about something. The terrier caregiver is determined to help things go correctly and provides constant reminders when things are not going as expected or scheduled. While well-intentioned, over time a	Terrier caregiving can occur in the face of concerns that the loved one will not respond in a way that they "should." The terrier caregiving occurs with the hope that if the loved one is given a reminder, things will go as planned and the proper outcome	Loved ones may feel aggravated with the nipping and yipping characterizing terrier caregiving. They can become resentful and defensive or respond in a passive or passive-aggressive fashion. They may feel criticized, demoralized and/or feel like they are being treated like a child. The	Terrier reminders may decrease a loved one's motivation for recovery and obstruct their ability to take responsibility for their decisions and actions due to their dependence on reminders from the caregiver. A terrier's tireless reminders may lead to disconnection because the loved

(Continued)

244 *Mary Tantillo, Jennifer Sanftner McGraw, and Daniel Le Grange*

Table 17.1 (Continued)

Animal Metaphor	Caregiving Style	Triggers for This Caregiving Style	Loved One's Experience in Response to Repeatedly Receiving This Caregiving Style	Impact on Recovery
	terrier's "yipping at loved ones' heels" can be experienced as obnoxious and nagging.	will be achieved.	loved one may feel frustrated by the caregiver's assumption that they will not perform in expected ways. This may also decrease self-esteem and increase self-doubt.	one may distance themselves from the terrier or just learn to ignore the reminders. The overall relationship with the caregiver may be injured due to the annoyance experienced by the loved one.
Rhinoceros	The rhinoceros is aggressive and fast-moving in response to perceived threat. Rhinoceroses tend to use argumentation and confrontation when trying to persuade the loved one to act in a certain way. Their determined and intense caregiving response can be experienced as angry and bullying. In their efforts to respond swiftly and strongly, they can be perceived as charging and overwhelming to their loved one.	Rhinoceros caregiving can occur as caregiver emotions become intense and dysregulated. Concern about a loved one can lead to frustration and anger. Feelings of loss of control can contribute to rhinoceros caregiving. The caregiver may feel helpless and overwhelmed in the face of AN, and this experience may manifest itself in angry, threatening and/or aggressive responses to the loved one.	Loved ones may feel invalidated, bullied, threatened and/or abused. They experience themselves in a "power over" relationship with the caregiver and may experience increased vulnerability, shame, self-blame, fear, or panic and respond with passivity. Alternatively, they may become defensive and angry which can further escalate the rhinoceros caregiving response and increase tension and interpersonal disconnections. Loved ones may distance themselves from the caregiver or seemingly comply with rhinoceros demands but not genuinely adopt new behaviors	Loved ones may feel unsafe and learn to protect themselves from rhinoceros caregiving by isolating, silencing themselves, lying, or distorting information. These experiences can decrease motivation for recovery and obstruct loved ones from being genuine and honest with the caregiver. Rhinoceros caregiving can paradoxically obstruct recovery because loved ones may end up pushing back (aggressively, passive-aggressively, or passively) not only on the caregiver but also on the work of recovery that the caregiver is trying to ensure occurs.

(*Continued*)

Table 17.1 (Continued)

Animal Metaphor	Caregiving Style	Triggers for This Caregiving Style	Loved One's Experience in Response to Repeatedly Receiving This Caregiving Style	Impact on Recovery
Jellyfish	Jellyfish move freely in the water and can change direction quickly. When the tide changes, their direction changes. When experiencing threat and feeling overwhelmed by stimuli, they can sting other creatures. Jellyfish caregiving is characterized by intense and dysregulated emotion that can lead the caregiver to respond in ways that amplify the emotions that the loved one is experiencing. Those emotions can feel overwhelming for the caregiver and lead to emotionally unpredictable "stinging" responses such as harsh words. It is difficult for the jellyfish to steady their course in the face of a loved one's stress. The loved one's stress becomes their own and their attempts to empathize with the loved one lead the caregiver to lose their	Jellyfish caregiving may emerge from initial efforts to empathize with a loved one's emotions and challenges. It is more likely to occur as caregiver emotions intensify and overwhelm them and as they experience a loss of control. As the caregiver struggles to regulate their own emotions they may "sting" loved ones with their words and actions. Jellyfish caregiving can also happen when the caregiver experiences high levels of self-blame for their loved one's AN, high unrealistic and perfectionistic caregiving expectations, and/or has false assumptions about AN.	and attitudes the rhinoceros is advocating.

Loved ones may feel unsafe, hurt or betrayed by jellyfish caregiving. They may be mistrustful of the caregiver, never knowing exactly how the caregiver will respond. They may experience the caregiver as unpredictable and may increase isolation from them. They may have mixed feelings toward the caregiver who seems empathic one moment and then emotionally intense and dysregulated the next. Loved ones may also feel like a burden and feel that they are the cause of the caregiver's distress. | Collaborative work and forward movement in recovery may be obstructed by jellyfish caregiving. The loved one may increase distance from the caregiver due to caregiver unpredictable responses. They may not confide in the caregiver because they do not want to trigger intense dysregulated emotion and experience any associated "stinging." Alternatively, they may not confide in the caregiver because they don't want to burden the caregiver and create more distress. |

(Continued)

Table 17.1 (Continued)

Animal Metaphor	Caregiving Style	Triggers for This Caregiving Style	Loved One's Experience in Response to Repeatedly Receiving This Caregiving Style	Impact on Recovery
	emotional balance and feel overwhelmed with emotion. It is difficult for them to stay centered in their efforts to care for their loved one.			
Dolphin	Dolphins swim alongside one another, not going too far ahead and not dropping too far back. When another dolphin gets off course, the dolphin caregiver gently nudges them back on track. Dolphins are smart and attuned to what goes on with other dolphins. They are communicative and form strong bonds with one another. Dolphin caregiving is characterized by a devotion to remaining alongside the loved one in recovery. When assistance is needed, caregiving is provided in a gentle and kind way. Dolphin caregiving can also be playful in nature.	Dolphin caregiving occurs in response to the caregiver accurately sensing that the loved one needs emotional and/or technical support.	Loved ones experience perceived mutuality when receiving dolphin caregiving because they feel heard, seen and understood. They feel that they matter to their caregivers and that they can influence them. They experience their caregiver as attuned and responsive to their needs. They feel they can safely depend on them to offer the right amount of support. They feel empowered because they experience the relationship as one that is "power with" versus "power over."	Because loved ones feel validated and valued, they learn to validate and value themselves in recovery. Dolphin caregiving promotes motivation and psychological growth in recovery and promotes relational repair when disconnections occur. Loved ones feel their caregiver believes in them and their abilities to change and grow.
	St. Bernards are calm, relaxed, and grounded.	St. Bernard caregiving occurs when the	Because the St. Bernard caregiver is experienced as	St. Bernard caregiving promotes

(*Continued*)

Session 13: Relapse Prevention and Maintaining Good Connection   247

Table 17.1 (Continued)

Animal Metaphor	Caregiving Style	Triggers for This Caregiving Style	Loved One's Experience in Response to Repeatedly Receiving This Caregiving Style	Impact on Recovery
St. Bernard	They are also intelligent, friendly, and welcoming. St. Bernard caregiving is benevolent and patient. When a loved one needs support, it is offered in a centered, kind, and easy-going way. St. Bernard caregiving is also characterized by forbearance, compassion, and consistency.	caregiver accurately senses that the loved one needs emotional and/or technical support.	a stalwart supporter, the loved one can safely rely on this caregiver. This experience encourages the loved one to trust others as well. The loved one feels cared for, seen and heard and experiences perceived mutuality. The caregiver is experienced as dependable, attuned and responsive to the needs of the loved one. Similar to those receiving dolphin caregiving, loved ones receiving St. Bernard caregiving feel empowered because they experience the relationship with the caregiver as one that is "power with" versus "power over."	psychological growth and motivation for recovery because loved ones feel supported, valued and validated. Feeling understood and accepted increases connection with self and others in recovery. The loved one also feels safe to ask for help and depend on others in recovery. Loved ones feel hopeful about recovery and similar to those receiving dolphin caregiving, they feel their caregiver believes in them and their abilities to change and grow.

Note
Animal Metaphors for Caregiving Styles: Caregiver and Patient Responses and Impact on Recovery. Adapted from *Skills-based caring for a loved one with an eating disorder: The new Maudsley method* (2nd ed.) (pp. 42–55), by J. Treasure, G. Smith, & A. Crane, 2017, Abingdon, Oxon: Routledge. Copyright 2017 by J. Treasure, G. Smith, and A. Crane. Adapted with permission. In each of these caregiving scenarios, the caregiver may be unaware of their caregiving style until there is closer examination of it. AN can create caregiving burden and distress that contribute to kangaroo, ostrich, terrier, rhinoceros and jellyfish caregiving. AN can also capitalize on patient experiences of caregiving mismatches by fueling intense emotions, negative self-talk, avoidance, points of tension, and interpersonal disconnections. Patients may try to cope with caregiving mismatches and the associated tension and disconnection through eating disorder behaviors. This situation can perpetuate eating disorder symptoms. The goal in recovery is to practice dolphin and St. Bernard caregiving responses. AN will try to obstruct these efforts because it wants to maintain the patient's disconnections from self and others and remain connected with the patient.

248   *Mary Tantillo, Jennifer Sanftner McGraw, and Daniel Le Grange*

caregiving style. They are encouraged to be open and curious about different perspectives because these qualities help them practice being "different-in-connection" and to use their differences to strengthen their connections with one another. AN of course loves to use differences to weaken relationships and strengthen its relationship with the patient. The therapists circulate through the room to assess how each family unit is doing with this task and offer assistance if needed. For example, a parent may be surprised that she/he is experienced as one kind of animal when they thought they were another. The therapists encourage patients to give examples of behaviors that fit with a particular animal caregiving style. They remind everyone that there may be a difference of opinion about someone's caregiving style and this information can be shared in the large group discussion next. The family unit is reassured that they are probably not the only group wherein folks have a difference of opinion about caregiving styles (e.g., different siblings in each family may experience their parents' caregiving differently). If it seems like the discussion leads to a point of tension or disconnection, this should be named in the small group and can also be named during large group discussion. During this work, the therapists promote a sense of universality and validation, while helping clarify what the patient and family member experience (thoughts and feelings). The therapists should help patient and family members identify what a more "dolphin-like" or "St. Bernard-like" response might look like. Again, all group members can help with this activity during the large group discussion if a particular patient or family member is struggling to translate their experience into language.

After the small group work is completed, the large group discussion is conducted by having each family unit share their findings related to caregiving styles. As the R4R therapist goes around the room to have each family share, she/he should be sure to get patient and family member experiences. The therapist can acknowledge that sometimes parents, partners or friends have "hybrid" caregiving styles. This intervention can involve a play on words and some humor when the therapist, for example, discovers that a particular parent has a caregiving style that is a combination of a kangaroo and terrier and names this "terraroo." Additionally, some parents are able to use their own sense of humor about their caregiving style once they recognize what it is. For example, the first author (MT) had a father in the group who dubbed himself a "daddyroo." He said he felt proud of this fact because it came from a place of love for his daughter. At the same time, he agreed he would work on this caregiving style and aspire to be more like a dolphin or St. Bernard. The following session he presented himself to the group with a T-shirt that said "daddyroo." The group burst into laughter when he walked through the door. The following clinical vignette provides an example of the R4R therapist promoting dialogue between Kelly and Michelle (daughter and mother in the earlier vignette) about caregiving style.

Therapist:	*Well, Kelly, since you and your mom helped us discuss kangaroo caregiving qualities in the beginning of group, I was curious about whether you two agreed on that*

Session 13: Relapse Prevention and Maintaining Good Connection 249

	caregiving style during your smaller family unit discussion? What did you discover when you were brainstorming about her caregiving style? Is she a kangaroo or something else?
Kelly:	*Definitely a kangaroo and occasionally a terrier. She has been known to be a rhinoceros once or twice but that is not usual. I would say mainly a kangaroo and a little terrier.*
Therapist:	*So, she is a terraroo hybrid then. Very good. (The group laughs.) Mom would you agree or do you see that differently.*
Michelle:	*Yes, that makes sense. I think probably more kangaroo than terrier, but I can see her point. She says I bug her about things repeatedly sometimes and that it can feel like nagging.*
Therapist:	*Kelly were you able to share with mom specific examples of the kangaroo caregiving? Seems like you gave her some terrier examples.*
Kelly:	*The one example I shared is when I may want to go out with my friends, but they are going to go to a new place I am unfamiliar with. That creates a lot of stress. It is hard enough to make myself go with them, when I am already worried about what I will do if they are going to eat something. But then if they go to a new place, that makes it worse. I feel even more anxious. When I tell her this, she says I don't have to go if I am going to be super stressed.*
Therapist:	*And mom did you know this was happening for Kelly?*
Lisa (Kelly's mom):	*Yes, and I guess I did end up being a kangaroo because I could see the stress she was feeling and told her she did not have to go if it was going to totally stress her out. I probably kept her in my pouch. (The group chuckles.)*
Nancy (another mom):	*Kelly, you are not the only kangaroo in the room. I am one too.*
Linda (another mom):	*Yes, and you are not the only parent here that feels pulled to shield your child when you see them feeling vulnerable. It is hard to resist this sometimes.*
Therapist:	*Yes, absolutely, and the eating disorder of course knows this and will try to play off of this, increasing a parent's anxiety while it increases the patient's anxiety. Now it has everyone feeling super anxious and potentially wanting to avoid whatever challenge is on the horizon.* So, Kelly, what would be a more dolphin-like or St. Bernard-like response from your mom?
Kelly:	*Well, I hate even saying this out loud because it forces me to have to face more social stress. I guess she could*

250   *Mary Tantillo, Jennifer Sanftner McGraw, and Daniel Le Grange*

	ask me if there is anything that would help me be with my friends despite my stress. I am not sure what that would be yet but maybe say something like that.
Therapist:	I am wondering if any of the other patients can help Kelly identify some possible alternatives here.
Taylor (another patient):	Kelly, maybe you could think of things to help you feel more in control. Like do any of your friends know you are in recovery? Can you ask that person if everyone will be eating when they are out and if they are, you could either eat before you go and tell them you just ate with your family or just order something small and manageable from your meal plan.
Thomas (another patient):	Or just go be with them after they eat.
Therapist:	Great suggestions. Any other ideas from the group?
Nancy (another patient's mother):	Or if you are close to someone in your friend group, could you ask them to ask the other friends if they could change their plans and go to a place that you are more familiar with. Your friend could couch this as her request and not yours. They don't need to know that you and your friend spoke. Of course, if you feel comfortable and your friends are supportive of your recovery, you could make this request yourself and tell them this would help you.
Therapist:	Kelly, what do you think about these ideas? Do any of them sound realistic?
Kelly:	Well, I am closest to two of my friends. I never thought of asking them to see if they could change plans for where we will end up. And I did not think about the timing of when I could be with them. I get so overwhelmed that I want to avoid the whole thing. Those are good ideas. Part of me does not want to try them, but they make sense.
Michelle:	And I will try to remember to be less kangarooey next time and swim alongside you as a dolphin (she holds up the dolphin stuffed animal and group members chuckle) and encourage you to try something new, even if it creates some anxiety. And I will need to practice telling myself that your anxiety is something that the eating disorder will take advantage of, if we don't help you live through it.
Therapist:	Exactly, mom. Great work everyone. OK, who would like to go next with their findings from the small group work?

Although many patients and family members are able to openly share their challenges related to caregiving styles and even use humor when they share these challenges in Session 13, some may struggle with this task, especially if a family norm is that "you don't say things if others will feel hurt or upset." This norm

Session 13: Relapse Prevention and Maintaining Good Connection   251

and the associated tension and potential disconnection make naming a caregiving style a challenge, especially if the parent or partner does not agree with the patient's perception. If a point of tension or disconnection that occurred during the small group exercise reveals itself during the large group discussion, it should be named and processed in the way other points of tension and disconnections have previously been named and processed in group. As noted earlier, this work should include promotion of universality and mutuality while soliciting patient and family member experiences. Many families at this point in the group cycle are able to use a sense of humor while discussing caregiving styles. However, if a particular family is experiencing tension that is especially high and seems unable to process the disconnection with the help of the group, the therapist can acknowledge that they are likely not the only family that has experienced this disconnection and that they need and deserve more time than what the group can offer tonight in order to fully explore it. The therapist can recommend that the family bring the point of tension/disconnection to their single-family therapy work and further process it. In this situation, the R4R therapist would be sure to connect with the family after group, offer support, reinforce this recommendation and be in contact with the single-family therapist about what transpired in the group. (The consent to consult should have been obtained before the start of group.) If the family does not have a family therapist, then the R4R therapist can recommend that the patient and family discuss what transpired in group with the patient's individual therapist and follow up with that practitioner (encouraging the therapist to meet with the patient and family). The R4R therapist would also follow up with either the individual or single-family therapist after they had an opportunity to work with the family on the particular point of tension/disconnection. The therapist can then decide whether or not to encourage the family to share what they found during their single-family/individual therapy work in a future group session. This decision would be informed by considerations such as the outcome of the single-family therapy/individual therapy session and patient/family willingness and ability to share this information, for example, as a follow-up peak or valley in a future session without it dominating group discussion in an unhelpful way.

At the end of Session 13 the R4R therapists remind group members that there are three sessions left including one in two weeks and then two monthly sessions. They reinforce that it is important to start planning for continuous and coordinated treatment after discharge from the group. For example, if a young adult patient is going out of town to college, the patient and family members need to start identifying their treatment team providers (e.g., therapist(s) at home and college, primary care physician at home, college health medical providers, and dietitian at home or college). The R4R therapists reinforce that they will be discussing this planning in future group sessions. They end the group by encouraging members to complete the homework for the next session including development of the patient relapse prevention plan (see Box 17.2) and the family relapse prevention support plan (see Box 17.3), as well as review of the relapse prevention strategies handout (see Box 17.4) and animal metaphor caregiving styles handout (see Table 17.1). The therapists reinforce that the homework will continue to help members identify high risk situations/transitions that could lead to relapse, the earliest signs of relapse, effective relapse strategies, and dolphin-like and St. Bernard-like supports available to patients to enact these strategies. The homework helps patients and family members anticipate ways that AN will attempt to thwart their efforts at working collaboratively in recovery. Session 13 goals, materials, and handouts are outlined in Box 17.5.

Box 17.2   Patient Relapse Prevention Plan

1   High-risk situations/triggers (people, places, things):

2   Internal cues to a relapse: e.g., your bodily sensations, feelings, thoughts (e.g., negative self-talk), inflexible ways of thinking (e.g., black and white thinking and shoulds), increased focus on detail versus big picture, and eating disorder thoughts:

3   External cues to a relapse: e.g., your behavioral and interpersonal responses (including eating disorder behaviors like delaying breakfast), increased isolation:

4   Relapse prevention strategies: e.g., I will return to completing my daily meal plan. I will return to journaling each day:

5   Who are my supports and what kind of support do I need from loved ones (dolphin and St. Bernard strategies that promote a feeling of mutuality and motivation for recovery)?

Session 13: Relapse Prevention and Maintaining Good Connection   253

Box 17.3   Family Member Relapse Prevention Support Plan

1   Identify ways to offer your loved one support that are grounded in dolphin and St. Bernard caregiving approaches.

2   How will the eating disorder try to trip you up as you try to connect with and care for your loved one?

3   What can you do to remain compassionate, calm, consistent, clear, and confident in providing support in order to foster mutuality in your relationship and continued motivation for recovery?

4   What supports do *you* need in place to provide caregiving that promotes a sense of mutuality?

Box 17.4   Relapse Prevention Strategies

- Return to your meal plan (e.g., three meals per day and prescribed snacks). Plan meals ahead.
- Restart monitoring of your food and feelings (use self-monitoring log or journal).
- Identify connections between your relationships with food/AN and relationships with yourself and others. Do you need to make a change in a relationship?
- Remember when you start thinking more about your body shape and weight that you are feeling vulnerable, out of control, anxious, depressed, etc. Identify the source.

- Remember that everyone in recovery experiences lapses and can grow stronger from working through these times.
- Structure your time and plan your days ahead (e.g., avoid long periods of unstructured time and do not overbook and overextend yourself).
- Increase self-care: build in some rest and relaxation. Slow down.
- Engage in planned activities during high-risk times.
- Reach out for support from those you trust and with whom you have a mutual connection.
- Consider whether you need to make a change in your environment.
- Do not weigh yourself more than once per week.
- Use scientific problem solving to identify any problems.
- Be sure you are setting realistic goals for yourself.
- Remind yourself not to use black and white thinking, e.g., a lapse does not mean you have "blown your recovery." A lapse is an important opportunity for learning something about you and your experience that you haven't been able to put into words yet. Your body is trying to tell you something. You need to listen to yourself.
- Be mindful. Stay in the present and observe and describe what you experience without negatively judging yourself.

Box 17.5   Session 13: Relapse Prevention and Maintaining Good Connection

Goals

Help patients and family members to:

- Continue to identify internal and external triggers, cues, and relapse prevention strategies (especially during high risk times like transitions).
- Discuss how particular caregiving styles can help or hinder recovery and can unwittingly perpetuate the eating disorder.
- Identify ways loved ones can respond effectively (i.e., like dolphins and St. Bernards) in the face of possible relapse signs.
- Begin to discuss how patients can arrange for continuous/ coordinated treatment after MFTG to continue meeting their needs and recovery goals.

Materials

- Paper and pens
- Stuffed animals

Exercise

- Review peaks and valleys
- In the large group have patients and families identify internal and external triggers for relapse, helping them identify the **earliest signs** of these experiences. Also begin to discuss relapse prevention strategies and the best ways family members can respond in the face of triggers and signs of relapse.
- Conduct large group discussion about animal metaphors associated with caregiving styles.
- Divide into small family units to do small group work on identifying caregiving styles.
- Return to the large group to review the small group findings.
- Encourage members to begin planning for continuous and coordinated treatment.

Handouts

- Distribute *Animal Metaphors for Caregiving Styles*
- Encourage review of Chapter 5 (pp. 42–55) and Chapter 9 (pp. 118–131) in Treasure, Smith, and Crane (2017).
- Distribute *Relapse Prevention Plan, Family Member Relapse Prevention Support Plan*, and *Relapse Prevention Strategies*: Assign patient homework to develop relapse prevention plan and assign family to develop relapse support plan for review next group. Assign everyone to review relapse prevention strategies handout.

References

*No DOI

Langley, J., Todd, G., & Treasure, J. (2019). *Caring for a loved one with an eating disorder: The new Maudsley Skills-Based Training Manual.* Routledge. https://dx.doi.org/10.4324/9781351232593.

Treasure, J., Smith, G., & Crane, A. (2017). *Skills-based learning for caring for a loved one with an eating disorder* (2nd ed.). Routledge. https://dx.doi.org/10.4324/9781315735610.

18 Session 14: Relapse Prevention (Continued) and Preparing for Termination

Mary Tantillo, Jennifer Sanftner McGraw, and Daniel Le Grange

Session 14 begins with a review of peaks and valleys experienced by the patients over the last two weeks. The R4R therapists should look for opportunities to positively reinforce self-care, practice of R4R emotional and relational skills, and relapse prevention efforts. During Session 14 the R4R therapists aim to help patients and families:

- Discuss points of tension/disconnections and high risk situations that could lead to relapse, including how AN takes advantage of the patient by capitalizing on patient vulnerabilities (e.g., perfectionism) and twisting patient strengths (e.g., perseverance and attention to detail) to work against the patient
- Discuss effective relapse prevention strategies and potential dolphin and St. Bernard responses from family members that promote use of these strategies and ongoing recovery
- Continue to develop plans for social eating with family, peers, and others, including graduated exposures to eating outside the home
- Identify community supports for recovery and distinguish mutual from non-mutual supports
- Begin to address feelings and concerns related to termination.

After reviewing the peaks and valleys at the start of group, the therapists can use what has been shared to identify common points of tension/disconnections and high risk times that can potentially thwart continued recovery. If patients identify high risk times and urges to engage in symptoms or actual symptom use, the R4R therapists continue the relapse prevention work addressed in Session 13 by assisting patients and family members to identify the earliest signs of potential relapse. Additionally, they can, as needed, help the patients and family members construct a behavioral chain that clarifies events leading up to AN symptoms or the urge to engage in them. The behavioral chain should also include what followed the use of or urge to use AN symptoms. This information helps the R4R therapist know if patients sought help from family members or isolated from them. It also allows them to assess whether family members responded in a mutually empathic and empowering way or in a way that unwittingly created disconnection and perpetuated symptom use. The therapists encourage patients and families to identify relapse prevention strategies that have been or could have been employed during high risk situations shared during their check-in.

After briefly discussing peaks and valleys and using the information shared to engage in a brief discussion (about 15 minutes), patients and families will divide into their own smaller family units (for 15 minutes) to review the homework they were asked to complete after Session 13. Patients review their *relapse prevention plans* and family members review their *family member relapse prevention support plans* (see Chapter 17, Boxes 17.2 and 17.3). The R4R therapists encourage patients to discuss specific triggers and internal/external cues of these triggers, as well as concrete strategies and support needed from family members to maintain recovery. The therapists encourage family members to identify what they can do to offer support in a dolphin or St. Bernard caregiving style in response to high-risk situations identified by the patients. Family members are also asked to consider how AN may try to obstruct their efforts, how they will cope with AN's attempts to promote interpersonal disconnections, and the supports they need to engage in self-care in order to be emotionally available to their loved ones and promote mutuality and motivation for recovery. The therapists circulate through the room during this small group exercise to offer support and encouragement and positively reinforce group member communication.

The R4R therapists then reconvene the larger MFTG group. They ask patients and family members to share what they discovered about patient high risk times, triggers, external and internal cues indicative of the triggers, needed support, and possible relapse prevention strategies. (Group members can also be referred to their Session 13 handout regarding relapse prevention strategies as needed; see Chapter 17, Box 17.4). The therapists also ask family members to share how they will provide the needed support in dolphin- and St. Bernard-informed caregiving ways, despite AN's attempts to obstruct their efforts. Each family is given an opportunity to share what they discovered during the small group work. The therapists begin by promoting universality and connection and noting that there are likely a number of high-risk situations and caregiving challenges commonly experienced by all patients and families, while acknowledging that each patient and family are also unique with differing needs during recovery.

During or following the large group discussion (about 30 minutes) the therapists find an opportunity to specifically note several common challenges in recovery that can potentially lead to relapse including body image dissatisfaction/distortion, perfectionism, and social eating. For example, the R4R therapists can discuss how body image takes time to change and that it is often the slowest to change during recovery. The eating disorder knows this and will find opportunities to amplify body dissatisfaction or distortion such as when patients are clothes shopping (especially in isolation from others), engaging in new social situations with worries about others' perceptions of them and their body, and when they are involved in particular activities like wearing a bathing suit during a visit to the beach.

AN can also take advantage of patient vulnerabilities, e.g., perfectionism, and use them to create anxiety and other intense emotions related to the disparity patients experience between "good enough," realistic self-expectations and perfectionistic demands. Additionally, AN can take advantage of patients' strengths and twist these strengths in a way that works against them. For example, it will capitalize on patient perseverance and attention to detail in a way that is at the expense of seeing the big picture. This situation leaves the patient compelled to focus, for example, on the sour cream on her plate, but forget that she is eating it because she wants to return to college. Or AN will encourage the patient to focus on the one negative thing he thought he heard his partner say and not allow him to hear the three positive things she verbalized to him.

AN can increase patient anxiety in the face of eating with family, friends, and others. Patients are reminded that self-care in the form of food is essential in recovery, as this allows our brains to more fully benefit from therapy, make recovery-oriented decisions and goals, and generalize learning to everyday life. The patients are asked to involve others in supporting them to grocery shop, meal plan, and eat meals/snacks. If they need the help of a registered dietitian, this is also encouraged.

Therapists talk with the group about how patients can also create and implement an exposure therapy plan to address fears of social eating. While this exposure work is not done during R4R, patients are encouraged to work with their individual/family therapists to develop a list of mildly feared to highly feared social eating situations and to share these with their family members, so they can assist with graduated exposure to these situations. (If the patients have not already developed a fear food list with their individual or family therapist or dietitian, they are encouraged to construct this list too, and do the related exposure work with these team members.) Patients are directed to start with exposing themselves to the least frightening social eating scenario and to note their level of distress on a scale from 0 to 100 before and after they expose themselves to the scenario. They are encouraged to practice each scenario one at a time with a trusted family member or friend (supportive of their recovery) until their post-exposure subjective rating of distress is down to a 20 or 30 on a scale of 0 to 100 (Wolpe, 1969). They can then move onto exposing themselves to the next more challenging scenario. The therapists emphasize that the patients should not engage in AN symptoms following their exposures, as this obstructs them from practicing emotion regulation and living through the anxiety associated with each scenario. The brain cannot create a new pathway that leads to more adaptive self-care and coping strategies, if AN blocks this by tempting the patient to use it as a way to decrease anxiety.

It is ideal if the patient can practice these exposures first by mentally putting themselves in the feared scenario (through the use of imagery) and conducting the distress rating pre- and post-exposure and then move onto actually exposing themselves to the situation in real life. Ideally, over time, the patient should be able to move from practicing exposures with a therapist in the office and with close others in the community, to doing them on their own (e.g., having a drink or snack at a coffeehouse). An example of a list of feared social eating situations can be seen in Box 18.1. The R4R therapists are available to consult with the patients' individual/family therapists regarding this exposure work as needed.

The R4R therapists aim to "inoculate" patients by initiating discussion of common triggers for relapse (e.g., body dissatisfaction, perfectionism, and social eating) and soliciting feedback about how these triggers may apply to each patient and family. The therapists encourage dialogue about the earliest signs of these triggering situations and encourage discussion regarding how patients and family members will work together and respond in ways that foster ongoing recovery. The therapists emphasize the importance of planning ahead for how to handle triggering situations, especially as patients have difficulty with cognitive flexibility and experience high anxiety in the face of uncertainty, ambiguity, and unpredictability. The following vignette shows how the R4R therapist facilitated group discussion about social eating as it applies to Beth, a 25-year-old middle school teacher. The therapist enlists the aid of the group to help Beth and her family navigate how to respond to her triggering lunch-time situation at work.

Box 18.1 Feared Social Eating Situations

- Having to change my restaurant order at the last minute and eat something unplanned because the restaurant does not have what I initially ordered
- Having a meal at a buffet in a restaurant in the community
- Eating in the college cafeteria
- Eating with extended family during holidays
- Eating with co-workers in the break room at work
- Eating alone in the break room at work
- Eating something with a friend who is supposed to be in recovery but is having a tough time eating anything
- Eating with two of my cousins who talk about dieting and exercise at the table
- Eating a meal with my aunt who keeps asking me questions about my recovery
- Eating a meal with my grandmother (who has dementia)

260 *Mary Tantillo, Jennifer Sanftner McGraw, and Daniel Le Grange*

- Eating a snack or meal with my closest friends out at a restaurant
- Eating a snack or meal with my closest friends in one of our homes
- Having a drink or snack with my partner at a new coffee shop
- Having a drink or snack with my partner at a familiar coffee shop

Note: Situations are listed bottom to top from least to most frightening social eating scenarios.

Beth:	*I know the lunch-time situation at work is triggering, but I don't know what to do about it. I can't control what my co-workers talk about, and I don't feel comfortable telling everybody that I am in recovery.*
Therapist:	*Well, this is a great situation for us to discuss together. I am sure you are not the only person who has felt challenged by this scenario. When you were discussing your relapse prevention plan with your family, were you able to identify the earliest signs that indicate you feel triggered?*
Beth:	*Well, just thinking about having lunch in the faculty lunchroom is stressful. I have been out of work for the last few months and plan to go back soon. So, I need to figure out what to do, so I don't skip lunch. That starts me down the wrong road for the rest of the day.*
Therapist:	*And when you start thinking about having lunch in the faculty lunchroom, what are you experiencing inside? Do you know what bodily sensations you experience and what feelings you are having?*
Beth:	*I guess my earliest bodily sign is a sick feeling in my stomach and my heart starts racing. It is probably anxiety, and I worry about what people will think of me while I eat. And I worry about getting caught up in watching what others are or are not eating. A number of other faculty members are pretty thin, and some of them eat very little or nothing at all at lunch. I think one of them has an eating disorder, but she won't admit it. The faculty also tend to talk about weight loss and their latest diet and exercise plans.*
Therapist:	*So that is a challenging situation because it unfortunately is common practice for many people in our society to focus on weight loss and dieting. It does not mean you can't take care of yourself though. Can you share what you and your family discussed about ways to respond to this situation?*
Beth:	*Well, we weren't totally sure. My mom and sister offered to drive over to school and have lunch with me in my classroom, but I am not sure that is the best solution. It will draw attention to me if my mom or sister are always there, and people will wonder why I am not coming to the lunchroom. I feel like I just have to force myself to go into the lunchroom and deal with it somehow.*
Tammie:	*(Beth's mother) I just wanted her to know that I would be happy to do that if it seemed helpful in some way. I am trying not to be a kangaroo (group members chuckle), but I just want to be available to her that way, if she needs me.*
April:	*(Beth's 19-year-old sister) Me too. We didn't want her to isolate herself from everyone and skip lunch. It sounds like that can be pretty tempting.*

Relapse Prevention & Preparing for Termination 261

John: (Beth's father) I know Beth does not want to tell anyone about her eating disorder right now, but I was wondering if there was just one faculty member she trusted. Maybe that person could eat with her. She seemed stressed when I asked her that though.

Therapist: Beth, is dad correct? Were you stressed about that option or were you experiencing something different?

Beth: I just feel so overwhelmed going back and the thought of telling someone about my challenges at lunch feels awkward. Like I am 25 and should be able to come up with a plan for how to do this without having to involve another faculty member.

Therapist: So, you feel awkward. Any other feelings?

Beth: I guess vulnerable, like I am not sure I want another person to know. And I also feel like a burden. It is hard enough to let my family help me. Involving another faculty member is an additional stress.

Therapist: I am wondering what other group members are thinking and feeling about this?

Donna: (Another 25-year-old patient) I can understand why Beth feels this way. I felt nervous for her as she spoke about the lunchroom. That can feel overwhelming. There is a lot going on in there that could be triggering—having to eat your own lunch, watching others not eat theirs, and hearing the conversation about diets. I am wondering if there is a way she can gradually work her way back into the lunchroom.

Lori: (Another 19-year-old patient) Yes, I agree. It seems like too much to just show up for lunch when you get back. I would feel super anxious. It is probably better to ease into it if possible. What your dad said might be helpful if you have one faculty member you trust.

Peter: (Lori's father) Beth, your dad probably suggested it because he wanted you to have an advocate in case the eating disorder tries to take advantage of you during lunch. Someone in your corner so you aren't alone. Is there anyone you trust at school who you could confide in about your recovery?

Beth: Well, there is one faculty member I feel closer to—Sharon. She asked me if I was OK several times before I took medical leave. She told me she was worried about me. I think her sister had an eating disorder too. She seemed genuinely interested in how I was doing. I never told her directly what was going on with me, but I think she knew. She left a voice mail for me again the other day, asking how I was doing.

Therapist: So how do you feel about sharing your concerns regarding the lunchroom with her and involving her in a plan to help you with it?

Beth: I am worried about it, but I guess I could try.

Therapist: And what is the best way to approach this do you think?

Beth: I am not sure. I can't just walk back into school and mention it then. Probably in advance is better. I am not sure how to start the conversation.

Donna: Well, you said your co-worker has expressed interest in how you are doing. Can you call her back or at least text her or email her and thank her for expressing interest and caring for you and ease into the conversation that way?

Lori: And if you are too nervous to do this alone, could you do it with your individual therapist helping you? Like maybe you could call her from your therapist's office

262 *Mary Tantillo, Jennifer Sanftner McGraw, and Daniel Le Grange*

	or invite her to a therapy session if you need support to do it. I have done that with my best friend in the past. It was helpful.
Beth:	I could tell my therapist that I was doing this so she knows, but I think I could start out by texting or emailing Sharon. Then, based on her response, I could call her or visit face to face with her to say more. I think I could do that on my own, but I guess I could ask her to a therapy appointment if I needed help.
Therapist:	And Beth if it helps to role play how you would like to talk with Sharon, we can do that with you too. If we think really concretely about your plans, how do you think Sharon might be able to help you ease back into the lunchroom?
Beth:	I don't know. Maybe she could eat with me in my classroom for a few weeks and then we could eventually go together to the lunchroom.
Therapist:	That sounds like a good idea. I wonder what others think about this idea?
Donna:	That sounds like a good plan because if she had an understanding of what you felt triggered about, she could anticipate those things and try to redirect the conversation or use distraction so you could be more at ease socializing and eating your lunch.
Lori:	You could even come up with a code word or a certain look to signal that you are feeling triggered. Then you would at least have one other person there to support you. And if worse came to worse, Sharon could come up with a reason for why the two of you needed to leave the table to go to a meeting or something.
Beth:	I guess that would be helpful. I will think about what to text or email her tonight.
Therapist:	(Turning to Beth's family members) How are you guys feeling about the plan?
John:	I am glad Beth feels she can trust Sharon somewhat and confide in her. What Peter said is true. I wanted someone to be in her corner. I know at 25 we don't always want our parents involved in things. So, knowing she has a friend to advocate for her and support her is great.
Therapist:	Mom, you were trying not to be a kangaroo in response to Beth's lunchroom challenge (the therapist smiles). How are you feeling now?
Tammie:	I feel less nervous for her. Beth, I am so glad you will consider talking to Sharon. And if for any reason Sharon is not at school and you need a back-up plan, you know you can always call us for support at lunchtime. I don't mean to be a kangaroo. I just want you to know that I am a dolphin and willing to swim alongside of you if that is helpful.
Beth:	I know, mom.
Therapist:	And mom and dad and April, did you write down on your relapse prevention support plan what you need to take care of yourselves, so you can keep responding to Beth like dolphins and St. Bernards?
John:	I just need to know that I can touch base with Beth every so often to hear how she is doing, and I need to remind myself that she will come to me if she is in trouble. She promised this, and I have to allow her to follow through with the promise.
Tammie:	I need to take some time out to do self-care like do one good thing for myself at least once a week, try to get seven hours of sleep, and see my friends more. These things give me energy and help me worry less about Beth. When I am less stressed, I am less kangarooey.

Relapse Prevention & Preparing for Termination 263

April:	*Knowing I can spend some time with my sister at least every couple weeks helps me feel connected with her. Then I don't feel so worried about her.*
Therapist:	*OK, great work helping Beth figure out next steps. It is common for patients to experience some stress eating with others, especially at the start of recovery. What other relapse prevention strategies have folks used or what could we use in the face of feeling triggered when eating with others?*

In this vignette the therapist promotes universality, connection, and validation while helping Beth, her family and group members think about how to respond to the triggering lunch-time scenario. She purposefully begins with Beth by exploring her early signs of feeling triggered and problem-solving possible solutions to the lunch-time challenge. The therapist calls upon other group members when Beth needs help clarifying her needs and problem-solving potential relapse prevention strategies. She also checks back with family members about how they feel about the plan that Beth has formulated with the help of her father and other group members. She wants to assess whether the family will be able to respond in a mutually empathic and empowering way that will reinforce Beth's plan. She asks the family members what they need to respond like dolphins and St. Bernards in order to move ahead with Beth in her recovery.

As Session 14 draws to a close, the R4R therapists encourage members to continue planning for coordinated and continuous treatment after discharge from the group. For example, they ask members to consider next steps related to what is required to help patients successfully return to college or work or to move out on their own. These issues will be addressed more explicitly during the last two group sessions. Additionally, the R4R therapists encourage group members to continue to identify supports who foster patient and family resilience and recovery. The therapist helps members to discern whether available supports are mutual (i.e., promote mutuality and motivation) versus non-mutual (i.e., enable illness and foster relapse). For example, friends who struggle with eating disorders and are not in treatment may not be able to promote recovery. The therapist may have group members identify the characteristics of supports who do promote mutuality and motivation (e.g., those who actively listen, validate, are warm, empathic, nonjudgmental, encourage accountability and autonomy while offering support, and positively reinforce recovery efforts). Patients and family members need these kinds of supports in their lives and if they do not have them yet, then that is a primary discharge goal. This goal should be explicitly discussed in the following two sessions and beginning steps outlined regarding how to initiate relationships with at least one new support (for patients and family members).

Finally, during Session 14 the R4R therapists are attentive to themes related to termination and begin to name and respond to these as they reveal themselves. The therapists validate the concerns and feelings (e.g., anxiety, sadness, frustration) inherent in ending the group, while reminding members that group will end in eight weeks (i.e., after the next two monthly sessions). Being able to express emotions about what has been gained in connection

264 *Mary Tantillo, Jennifer Sanftner McGraw, and Daniel Le Grange*

with one another, while also grieving the loss of the group can assist members in the grief work related to other issues in their lives.

Session 14 goals, materials, and handouts reinforcing relapse prevention, ongoing recovery, and beginning discussion about termination themes are outlined in Box 18.2. The information obtained during Sessions 14–16 regarding patient and family member strengths, relapse prevention challenges, and discharge needs should be shared with other treatment team members (e.g., individual and/or family therapist and dietitian) to promote continuity of care post-MFTG.

Box 18.2   Session 14: Relapse Prevention (Continued) and Maintaining Good Connection

Goals

- Identify triggers, early internal/external cues including emotions, and relapse prevention strategies. (This includes ways the ED tries to use the patient's strengths against the patient, e.g., turning attention to detail and "getting it right" into paralyzing perfectionism.)
- Identify relapse prevention strategies targeting common difficulties including body image dissatisfaction/distortion, perfectionism, and social eating. Include discussion about exposure to feared social eating scenarios.
- Identify ways loved ones can respond effectively in the face of possible relapse signs. (How they can respond as dolphins and St. Bernards.)
- Identify supports who will foster recovery and help patients and family members discern if these connections promote perceived mutuality vs enable illness. Concretely plan how patients and family members can initiate relationships with new supports if this is an issue.
- If themes related to termination are raised, incorporate this into discussion. Validate that the group's end is coming and the different feelings that may accompany this. Being able to express emotions about the loss of group can also assist with grieving other things.

Exercise

- Review peaks and valleys
- Divide into family groups to review homework. Compare what patients wrote down on their Patient *Relapse Prevention Plans* and what family/friends wrote on their Family Member Relapse Prevention *Support Plans*. Encourage members to discuss triggers and internal/external cues of these triggers, as well as concrete strategies to help the patient. Reinforce dolphin/St. Bernard caregiving styles.

Handouts

- Review *Patient Relapse Prevention Plans* and *Family Member Relapse Prevention Support Plans* (encourage dolphin and St. Bernard strategies). Review *Relapse Prevention Strategies* for concrete suggestions that they do not identify when discussing ways to promote relapse prevention.

Reference

*No DOI

*Wolpe, J. (1969). *The practice of behavior therapy.* Pergamon Press.

19 Session 15: Relapse Prevention (Continued), Termination, and Next Steps for Continued Connections in Recovery

Mary Tantillo, Jennifer Sanftner McGraw, and Daniel Le Grange

The last two sessions of R4R focus on how to promote continued recovery, accomplishments, future goals, and termination. In Session 15 the R4R therapist aims to help patients and families:

- Identify and work through points of tension and disconnections that threaten recovery
- Continue practicing emotional and relational skills learned in the group
- Address meanings and feelings related to termination from the group
- Identify supports, strengths, accomplishments, next steps, and future goals

Session 15 begins with the review of patient peaks and valleys over the past four weeks. The R4R therapists use the information obtained from this review to celebrate successes and identify and work through points of tension and disconnections that threatened recovery over the past month. When patients note successes, the therapists should help them explicitly identify what they did (differently) to create these successes (as opposed to thinking the successes just happened to them). This intervention reminds patients of the power they have to make good decisions and take action in recovery, and that they are not just passive recipients of good fortune or misfortune. For example, if a patient reports that they were finally able to try a new fear food or expose themself to a new anxiety-provoking social situation, the therapists can remind them that it is tempting to think that their success "just happened" to them because of luck or because of what others did. They should remind patients that their attaining a goal usually relates to something *they* have done differently. The therapists can ask the following:

- What did you do differently that allowed you to accomplish this work?
- Did you ask for support during this time? If yes, who was that and what was it about the interaction with the person that helped you accomplish what you did?

Session 15: Relapse Prevention 267

If patients note challenges to recovery in the form of symptom use or the urge to use symptoms, the R4R therapists again help patients and families engage in functional/behavioral chain analysis of the events leading to and following the symptoms or urge to engage in symptom behaviors. It is essential that the therapists and group members help patients identify the earliest biological, cognitive, affective, and/or behavioral signs of potential relapse. This work allows them to intervene with relapse prevention strategies as soon as possible, when they experience vulnerability to AN symptom use. Patients are helped to identify what purpose AN is serving in the moment and alternative ways to meet the needs AN is serving. The R4R therapists help patients and family members practice the emotional and relational skills learned during previous sessions in order to foster connection with self and others. These skills include identifying emotions and bodily states, implicit and explicit rules, strategies for moving out of disconnection to better connection, strategies for promoting mutuality and motivation, strategies for connection that don't include the eating disorder, coaching and mealtime support strategies, and dolphin and St. Bernard caregiving strategies. If there is a relapse prevention challenge that seems common across the patients (e.g., return to college), the therapists should note it, and extra time can be given to discussion of this challenge before the end of the first half of the group.

After about 30–40 minutes of the review of peaks and valleys and the follow-up conversation targeting various successes and points of tension/disconnections, the R4R therapists inquire what it was like to skip the group for a month and how members are feeling knowing that the last group session is next month. Thoughts and feelings about these issues may have already surfaced during the first half of group and can be further explored now. The group therapists should identify termination themes shared by group members and help them process feelings related to group termination. These themes and feelings often trigger memories of previous losses or thoughts about potential future losses. Helping members grieve the loss of the group while acknowledging what they have gained allows them to re-examine and grieve other losses. While the latter is not the focus of MFTG, it is a benefit of effective termination work.

Common termination themes and feelings include patient and family member sadness and/or frustration about losing routine contact with other individuals who understand eating disorders; anxiety about losing active MFTG treatment that routinely held members accountable to themselves and each other; worry about not being able to accomplish next steps in recovery without group support; missing routine contact with R4R therapists who have become part of everyone's family; a wish that the group could continue; and a desire for some form of contact with members after the group ends. The R4R therapists should promote universality and validation as they have when discussing other experiences common to many or all group members. They should help members make explicit their feelings, wishes, and fears in the face of termination. They remind members that AN will, of course, try to take

268   *Mary Tantillo, Jennifer Sanftner McGraw, and Daniel Le Grange*

advantage of any implicit/unspoken feelings, desires, and disappointments related to the group's ending. As noted in past groups, AN will try to amplify feelings of anxiety, frustration, and/or vulnerability and foster disconnection, then offer itself as a solution to this disconnection. The goal is to prevent this from happening and instead to be authentic about the meanings and feelings associated with termination of the group. The therapists also help members identify strengths they can use to maintain forward movement in recovery, despite the eating disorder's attempts to obstruct this movement. The following vignette shows how the R4R therapist can engage group members in discussion about termination issues.

Therapist:	*So, this has been an excellent discussion of peaks and valleys over the last month. We heard about a number of patient successes, as well as some challenges to recovery and what we can do in the face of those challenges. I am also wondering what it was like for folks to have gone a month, instead of two weeks in between our sessions? And I am wondering what it is like thinking about the end of group coming next session?*
Ann:	*(Mother of a patient, Theresa) I missed seeing everyone over the last four weeks. And I am sure that feeling is only going to increase as I think about ending group in another month. Coming here has been such a comfort to me. It has helped me keep going over the rough patches. Hearing what other patients and parents experience has helped me not feel alone. I think Theresa would say the same thing. (She looks at her daughter.)*
Theresa:	*Yes. It has helped to hear other patients say the things I have told my mom. Like they affirmed what I have been feeling and needing. It gives her ideas about how to help me. And I know being with the other parents helps my mom not feel alone.*
Therapist:	*Thank you, Ann and Theresa, for starting us off on this topic. So, mom says she missed seeing other group members, and Theresa you said you like the affirmation you felt from hearing other patients. I am wondering what feelings both of you specifically feel about group ending in a month. Can you tell what you are feeling about it?*
Ann:	*Well, I know I am sad about it for sure. And I guess if I was honest, I am somewhat frustrated because I wish the group could go on for another six months. We know each other better now and are all so connected and could keep giving one another support. It is hard to let go of that.*
Theresa:	*I am sad because goodbyes are sad, but I think I will be OK. The number of sessions is OK with me. I am more worried about my mom. She provides me the majority of the support for recovery. I hope she uses my aunt as a support after group too, like she promised.*
Therapist:	*Theresa, the beauty of group is that you can ask your mom directly because she is sitting next to you. You want to tell her how you feel and ask her?*
Theresa:	*Mom, I am worrying about you. Will you use Aunt Sarah to support you and me like you promised?*

Session 15: Relapse Prevention 269

Ann:	Yes, I will practice doing this. I just worry about how busy your aunt is, but I know that is my issue. She told me she wants to help. I know that if I want to be a dolphin or St. Bernard, I need to connect with another dolphin or St. Bernard like your aunt to help me.
Therapist:	Mom, I am thinking that while it is hard to end the group, this may also help you practice relying more on your sister. I know you made this a future goal for yourself.
Ann:	Yes. It kind of forces my hand, doesn't it? I will need to do what I promised myself and Theresa. It is just hard asking for help. I tell my daughter she needs to do that, so I guess I have to practice doing the same thing.
Therapist:	I am sure you are not the only two who are experiencing the feelings you are experiencing about the group's ending. I am wondering what others are feeling and thinking?
Sue (a patient):	I will miss being here, too, and am a little nervous about going forward without our routine meetings. I missed the group over the last four weeks. Michael (patient's partner) tells me how much clearer he is about what I am experiencing after we talk here. It has really helped him understand what is happening for me.
Michael:	I did not realize what Sue was experiencing when certain things were happening, like me being late for dinner. I just thought she could eat without me. I did not realize what a big deal this was for her. I understand that better now. I guess there will always be new situations we need to face, and we will need to practice doing that without the group meetings. I feel more confident about us doing that, but I am still a little concerned about maintaining our momentum without routine meetings.
Therapist:	Sounds like you are afraid the eating disorder will try to get in the way. I am sure there are others with a similar worry in the room. And yes, the eating disorder will try to get in the way. At the same time, do you know the strengths you two have that will help you keep going?
Michael:	Well, we keep talking, even when we initially experience disconnections from each other. We always eventually come back to the table to talk.
Therapist:	Exactly. That means a lot. It is harder for the eating disorder to get the upper hand when you guys are staying connected and communicating, even when this is tough. The eating disorder can't divide and conquer you then.
Sue:	(She looks at Michael.) Yes, that is true. It is hard to do sometimes. I just want to avoid conflict with him. But I guess we have gotten better about that over the last few months. It is easy to forget this when we get anxious or upset about things. But it is true.
Therapist:	Yes, and the eating disorder knows this and capitalizes on this whenever it can. That is why connecting with ourselves and one another is so essential in recovery. How about everyone else? What are others feeling about the month that has gone by in between sessions and about ending group next month? Are your feelings similar or different from what other group members have discussed so far?

270 *Mary Tantillo, Jennifer Sanftner McGraw, and Daniel Le Grange*

After about 30 minutes of termination work, the R4R therapists should inquire about post-discharge needs, next steps, and future goals. They should begin by asking each young adult patient to identify what they believe are next steps and future goals post-group. They start with the young adults to reinforce their personal power and responsibility related to future goals and steps. Family members can be brought into the conversation in response to what the young adults propose. The R4R therapists ask each patient and their respective family members what will be required to promote success with next steps and goals (e.g., return to college or work, independent living, establishing new peer relationships, committing to a romantic partner). Patients and families are encouraged again to identify additional supports in the community that may be needed to foster successful achievement of next steps and future goals. Identifying supports is a primary discharge goal, as connections in the community with a treatment team and other supports foster continued growth, healing, coordinated and continuous care, and ongoing recovery. Similar to work done in Session 14, R4R therapists ask patients and family members to examine whether their supports are mutual (i.e., they promote mutuality, motivation, and recovery and disable AN) or non-mutual (i.e., they promote disconnection from self or others, obstruct recovery, and enable AN) (see Chapter 3 and Sessions 1, 2, 5, and 6). By this time in the group cycle, each patient, and their respective family members should be able to identify at least one other supportive mutual relationship outside MFTG. If this is not the case, this goal should be a primary focus of discharge planning. These community supports can be professional team members, but ideally should include natural supports (e.g., family/extended family, friends, neighbors, classmates, co-workers, members of religious and faith communities, and/or members of clubs, or social and recreational organizations). In addition to helping patients and families identify community supports, the R4R therapists emphasize how the combination of patient and family member strengths (including completing MFTG) and the use of community supports will help propel them forward in recovery.

Before the end of Session 15, the R4R therapists will also help members problem-solve regarding appropriate follow-up treatment. Most members join MFTG already connected with an individual and/or family therapist. If this is not the case, then the therapists explore with the help of group members, which kind and level of care seems the most beneficial post-group. Most patients and families will return to outpatient care (at college or in the community), but some may need more intensive care. Sometimes engagement in MFTG allows patients to develop the trust, motivation, and commitment required to engage in needed intensive ambulatory (e.g., Intensive Outpatient Program or Partial Hospitalization) or residential programming post-group.

At the end of Session 15, the R4R therapists remind group members that they will see each other at the last group session the following month. If the group members have not yet developed a group member contact list (members may have already requested this earlier in the group cycle), they are told that this is an option. The therapists can offer to circulate and distribute a list

Session 15: Relapse Prevention 271

that asks for group member contact information from those desiring to be part of the list. Alternatively, they can allow the group to initiate this activity. A group member may offer to collect this information and share it with others in group. The therapists should be sure to normalize the idea that patients and families do not have to participate and emphasize the importance of patient and family privacy and comfort level. The R4R therapists end Session 15 by encouraging young adults and family members to review their relapse prevention and support plans as needed over the next month, encouraging them to add any additional relapse strategies that came from today's group discussion. They also ask members to independently complete the handout *Future Plans to Maintain Connections and Recovery* and to review their responses as a family before Session 16. This handout helps members identify group accomplishments, future goals, next steps, and any other follow-up plans that will maintain connections with self and others and foster continued recovery (see Box 19.1). Session 15 goals, materials, and handouts are outlined in Box 19.2.

Box 19.1   Future Plans to Maintain Connections and Recovery

1   What have you **accomplished** during group? Think back on the goals that you set at the start of group. What have you accomplished with regard to those goals?

2   What are your **future goals and next steps** in recovery?

3   What are other **follow-up plans** that will help you maintain connections with yourself and others and continue recovery?

Box 19.2   Session 15: Relapse Prevention (Continued), Termination, and Next Steps for Continued Recovery

Goals

- Discuss successes and points of tension/disconnections families experienced since the last meeting. Conduct functional/behavioral chain analysis to determine events leading to successes and challenges in recovery.

- Encourage and positively reinforce use of the emotional and relational skills learned in earlier group sessions, as well as the supports that patients and families have used to maintain their recovery work. Emphasize support strategies representative of St. Bernard and Dolphin caregiving styles. Help group members discern mutual from non-mutual supports.
- Raise the issue of termination and incorporate associated concerns, meanings and feelings into the group discussion.
- Help patients and families to identify their strengths, post-discharge needs, next steps, and future goals. Help them problem-solve plans for needed follow-up, e.g., level of care, identifying providers at college, etc.

Exercise

- Review peaks and valleys.

Handouts

- Encourage members to review patient relapse prevention plans and family member relapse prevention support plans (see Session 13) as needed over the next month. Encourage them to add relapse prevention strategies that come from tonight's discussion.

20 Session 16: Relapse Prevention (Continued), Termination, and Next Steps for Continued Connections in Recovery

Mary Tantillo, Jennifer Sanftner McGraw, and Daniel Le Grange

Session 16 is the final R4R session and the therapist's aims in this session are similar to those in Session 15:

- Identify and work through points of tension and disconnections that threaten recovery
- Continue practicing and positively reinforcing emotional and relational skills learned in the group
- Discuss meanings and feelings related to termination from the group
- Identify supports, strengths, accomplishments, next steps, and future goals

After reviewing peaks and valleys since the last session, the R4R therapists use material shared during this review to help patients identify points of tension/ disconnections that could obstruct continued recovery. They promote and positively reinforce practice of emotional and relational strategies for moving out of disconnection to new and better connection with self and others. They also emphasize the use of support strategies representative of St. Bernard and Dolphin caregiving styles and celebrate patient and family member successes.

Next, the R4R therapists remind members that today's session is the final one and engage them in continued discussion of associated meanings and feelings related to termination. These meanings and feelings may also relate to past or anticipated future losses, and while these cannot be explored more deeply in this ending session, it is important that members make these connections. The therapists encourage patients and family members to continue the important discussion about these connections in their individual and/or family therapy. It is important to provide time for each group member to describe their experience of group termination and help them practice previously learned emotional and re-lational strategies as needed (e.g., use the emotions sheet, note biological and behavioral signs of emotions, ask for support from other members to help name feelings, etc.). In the spirit of mutuality, the R4R therapists should also share their feelings and thoughts related to termination after hearing from members. Alternatively, they can verbalize these things earlier in the discussion as a way to encourage self-disclosure if members are having difficulty beginning this discussion.

After helping each group member discuss meanings and feelings related to termination, the R4R therapists ask each family to review their responses to the handout *Future Plans to Maintain Connections and Recovery*. This review helps them identify their accomplishments, as well as anything they feel they wanted to accomplish but did not yet. The R4R therapists encourage patients and families to reflect on their originally stated group goals and to note whether they achieved those goals. If not, then they can be asked if they need to modify them or if there are additional next steps that could help them meet these goals. There may be goals they met in addition to the originally identified ones, and these should also be solicited. The therapists may also notice accomplishments that members do not yet recognize, and they should identify these accomplishments. Since the therapists know the goals each patient and family originally developed, they can assist with goal review as needed and remind patients and families of their initial goals.

Review of the handout also facilitates discussion about future goals and problem solving about next steps, including any needed follow-up treatment (e.g., individual, family therapy, intensive outpatient, residential treatment) and referrals to various treatment team members (e.g., in the community or at college). The R4R therapists again solicit information from each patient (and family members as needed) about community supports. Group members can be called on to help members problem-solve additional community supports as needed. Again, it is important to help young adults evaluate whether their identified supports are mutual or non-mutual (see Chapter 3 and Sessions 1, 2, 5, 6, and 15).

Before ending Session 16, the R4R therapists will also provide some time for member evaluation of group. Detailed group feedback can be obtained by having members complete a discharge group evaluation questionnaire (see Appendix 20.1a and 20.1b for patient and family member questionnaires). Group members should be asked to comment on what was or was not helpful about the group and what else would enrich the group experience for future patients and families.

The therapists close the group by reminding members of the time, date, and location of any follow-up meetings. It is ideal to follow up with members six months after treatment to collect information on eating disorder, mood, quality of life, and relational outcomes. This follow-up is probably best done by phone if possible because it is more personalized, and the return rate may be more favorable than obtaining responses via an electronic or hard copy questionnaire.

After obtaining feedback about the group, the therapists say their goodbyes and distribute the discharge group evaluation questionnaires. The R4R therapists emphasize the importance of member feedback for quality improvement. It is ideal to have members complete the questionnaires at the end of group, but an alternative is to allow them to return the questionnaires after the group. The latter may lead to a less favorable return rate but provides them more time to reflect and provide feedback. Session 16 goals, materials, and handouts are outlined in Box 20.1.

Box 20.1 Session 16: Relapse Prevention (Continued), Termination, and Next Steps for Continued Connections in Recovery

Goals

- Discuss points of tension/disconnections families experienced since the last meeting. Promote and positively reinforce practice of emotional and relational strategies for moving out of disconnection to new and better connection with self and others. Emphasize support strategies representative of St. Bernard and Dolphin caregiving styles. Celebrate successes.
- Note this is the last group and raise the issue of termination. Incorporate associated meanings and feelings into the group discussion.
- Ask each family to review their responses to the handout *Future Plans to Maintain Connections and Recovery* and discuss their accomplishments, as well as anything they wanted to accomplish but did not yet. Discuss future goals and problem-solve next steps and plans including treatment options if needed (individual, family therapy work, identifying providers at college, etc.).
- Review what members felt was helpful or not helpful during group.
- If a six-month follow-up is planned, remind members about this date and time.
- Encourage members to complete the patient and family member group discharge evaluation questionnaires. Emphasize the importance of their feedback for quality improvement.
- Say goodbyes and collect completed discharge group evaluation questionnaires. (Alternatively, you can ask members to return discharge questionnaires after group.)

Exercise

- Review peaks and valleys.

Handouts

- *Future Plans to Maintain Connections and Recovery* (Distribute another copy if needed.)
- Refer to patient relapse prevention plans and loved one relapse prevention support plans they have developed. Encourage them to add strategies that come from tonight's discussion.
- R4R discharge group evaluation questionnaires.

Appendix 20.1a

Date: _____

RECONNECTING FOR RECOVERY (R4R) MULTIFAMILY THERAPY GROUP

PATIENT DISCHARGE EVALUATION QUESTIONNAIRE

<u>Please circle the number that best answers the following questions:</u>

How *suitable* do you think R4R Multifamily Therapy Group has been for the treatment of your eating disorder?

1	2	3	4	5	6	7	8	9	10

Not At all   Somewhat   Extremely

How *successful* do you think your treatment in R4R Multifamily Therapy Group has been?

1	2	3	4	5	6	7	8	9	10

Not At all   Somewhat   Extremely

The MOST helpful thing about group was:

The LEAST helpful thing about group was:

One thing I would have liked from group was:

Session 16: Relapse Prevention   277

Did you accomplish what you hoped to accomplish in R4R Multifamily Therapy Group?

Overall, how do you feel about your group experience?

How hopeful are you that group will help you and your loved ones move ahead in recovery?

Was understanding anorexia nervosa as a Disease of Disconnection and working through disconnections during group helpful or not?

Do you feel group improved your eating disorder symptoms? If yes, what helped the most? If no, what do you think prevented improvement in your symptoms?

What changes would you make in the group format and/or experience to improve its effectiveness for young adults and their family members (e.g., content, small and large group work, number and length of sessions, etc.)?

Other comments about the R4R Multifamily Therapy Group experience:

278 *Mary Tantillo, Jennifer Sanftner McGraw, and Daniel Le Grange*

Appendix 20.1b

Date: _____

RECONNECTING FOR RECOVERY (R4R) MULTIFAMILY THERAPY GROUP

FAMILY MEMBER DISCHARGE EVALUATION QUESTIONNAIRE

<u>Please circle the number that best answers the following questions:</u>

How *suitable* do you think R4R Multifamily Therapy Group has been in assisting you to help your loved one engage in treatment for her/his eating disorder?

1	2	3	4	5	6	7	8	9	10

Not   Somewhat   Extremely
At all

How *successful* do you think treatment in Multifamily Therapy Group has been?

1	2	3	4	5	6	7	8	9	10

Not   Somewhat   Extremely
At all

The MOST helpful thing about group was:

The LEAST helpful thing about group was:

One thing I would have liked from group was:

Session 16: Relapse Prevention 279

Did you accomplish what you hoped to accomplish in R4R Multifamily Therapy Group?

Overall, how do you feel about your group experience?

How hopeful are you that group will help you and your loved ones move ahead in recovery?

Was understanding anorexia nervosa as a Disease of Disconnection and working through disconnections during group helpful or not?

Do you feel group improved your loved one's eating disorder symptoms? If yes, what helped the most? If no, what do you think prevented improvement in symptoms?

What changes would you make in the group format and/or experience to improve its effectiveness for young adults and their family members (e.g., content, small and large group work, number and length of sessions, etc.)?

Other comments about the R4R Multifamily Therapy Group experience:

21 What Is Next? Training, Dissemination, Clinical Practice, and Research

Mary Tantillo, Jennifer Sanftner McGraw, and Daniel Le Grange

R4R MFTG offers a novel therapeutic approach to treatment of AN in young women and men. Because it draws from several different theoretical perspectives and addresses a difficult-to-treat population, there are necessarily a number of intersecting issues that need to be considered when conducting MFTG for AN. This chapter concludes the treatment manual with information about training, dissemination, implementation in clinical settings, financial challenges, therapist attitudes and experiences, and current challenges and future needs in terms of research.

Training

First and foremost, use of the R4R MFTG approach requires understanding the psychopathology and treatment of eating disorders, both at the individual level and in terms of the impact eating disorders can have on family relationships. Basic educational preparation as a general practitioner without specialization in eating disorders will not, in most cases, be enough to provide the content necessary to fully understand the psychopathology or treatment of AN. This is evident in research showing that many primary care and behavioral health clinicians, including college health providers, do not feel competent or confident to diagnose or treat eating disorders (Currin, Waller, & Schmidt, 2009; Jones, Saeidi, & Morgan, 2013; National Eating Disorders Association, 2013; Thompson-Brenner, Satir, Franko, & Herzog, 2012) and/or are no more knowledgeable about eating disorders than patients themselves or college students (Schmidt, Ali, Slone, Tiller, & Treasure, 1995). Moreover, lower clinician competence is associated with more negative attitudes toward patients with eating disorders, as well as poor clinical outcomes (Thompson-Brenner, Satir, Franko, & Herzog, 2012).

Another strongly recommended area of competence is exposure to some form of systems theory, along with experience with family and/or group psychotherapy. During R4R MFTG sessions, there are interactions happening at the level of the individual, between dyads within a family, with the family as a whole, and at the intergenerational level. Also, in terms of group process, there are dynamics occurring between group members (including the

R4R therapists), between families within the group, and in the group as a whole. There are potential sources of connection and disconnection related to the recovery from and maintenance of the eating disorder that need to be addressed at each of these levels, sometimes simultaneously. The R4R therapist's ability to leverage the complexity and richness of family and group relationships, multiplies the healing power of R4R. However, this potential for healing and recovery also comes with a cost of requiring appropriate training in a variety of treatment modalities. Although couples, family, and group psychotherapy approaches are taught as part of training in most psychiatry, psychology, social work, and psychiatric mental health nurse practitioner programs, at least in the USA (Weissman, Verdeli, Gameroff, Bledsoe, Betts, Mufson, Fitterling, & Wickramarante, 2006), it is unclear the extent to which this applies to training programs outside the USA. Also, while group-based approaches are required for accreditation of counseling programs, family-based approaches are not (Council for Accreditation of Counseling & Related Educational Programs, 2018). Even when training includes family or group treatment, it is unknown the extent to which these skills are being emphasized given the many other requirements or how commonly clinicians in training are being given the didactic information, time, and supervised experience necessary to master them. Additionally, it is unclear how routinely trainees are exposed to didactic information about multifamily group therapy in general and, specifically, to eating disorder multifamily therapy group. MFTG observation and clinical supervision likely occur in treatment centers where MFTGs already exist. In comparison to other eating disorder treatment modalities, MFTGs are much scarcer in number (see Chapter 2 for MFTGs across the globe).

Finally, training in Motivational Interviewing principles (Miller & Rollnick, 2013), Stages of Change Theory (Prochaska, Norcross & DiClemente, 1994) and Relational-Cultural Theory (R-CT) and Therapy (Jordan, 2018) are ideal for a practitioner who desires to conduct R4R. While Motivational Interviewing principles and Stages of Change Theory are often addressed in psychotherapy training programs across disciplines, the majority of practitioners who acquire training in R-CT and Therapy have not done so in their basic training programs, at least not in the USA. Instead, the majority of clinicians familiar with R-CT and Therapy have attended workshops or institutes sponsored previously by the Jean Baker Miller Training Institute at Wellesley College in Boston, Massachusetts, USA. The institute is now newly branded as the International Center for Growth and Connection (https://www.growthinconnection.org), and training opportunities continue to be available. Training in R-CT and Therapy is more common in the counseling field (Duffey & Somody, 2011; Duffey, 2008; Frey, 2013; Comstock, Hammer, Strentzsch, Cannon, Parsons, & Salazar, 2011), but is often absent in the curriculum of practitioners from other disciplines. Until more recently, R-CT was not included in conventional textbooks describing psychological theories of human development. With the growth of research supporting R-CT constructs and R-CT-informed clinical interventions (Frey, 2013; Lenz, 2016) and the availability of a primer (Jordan, 2018) and other texts describing an R-CT approach, training in R-CT and Therapy can more easily be added to coursework addressing evidence-based treatments.

Dissemination and Implementation in Clinical Settings

Historically, many MFTGs for adolescents and young adults with AN have been conducted within day treatment/partial hospitalization or inpatient settings, and the majority of MFTGs are outside the USA (Simic & Eisler, 2015; see Chapter 2). Some MFTGs are conducted in free-standing residential programs that place more emphasis on psychoeducation than the relational/group process. R4R occurs in the outpatient setting and includes psychoeducation, while emphasizing emotional and relational skills. Given this diversity of practice settings and the lack of or limited exposure to MFTG, a main question is: What is the best way to disseminate the information contained in this manual to practitioners in order to help them effectively implement R4R in their clinical settings? Previous research findings have revealed possible barriers to effective dissemination and implementation of treatments (Cooper & Bailey-Straebler, 2015; Fairburn & Cooper, 2011; Fairburn & Wilson, 2013; Lilienfeld, Ritschel, Lynn, Brown, Cautin, & Latzman, 2013; Simmons, Milnes, & Anderson, 2008; Tobin, Banker, Weisberg, & Bowers, 2007; von Ranson, Wallace, & Stevenson, 2013; Waller, Stringer, & Meyer, 2012):

a   Therapist perception of lack of generalizability of empirically supported treatment research findings to their patients
b   Therapist perceived rigidity of manualized treatment
c   Therapist perception of lack of emphasis on therapeutic alliance
d   Lack of clinical examples in the manualized treatment
e   Inconsistency with therapist theoretical perspective
f   Ease with which a treatment can be learned (including intensity of training, time required, and cost)
g   Accessibility to treatment approach information and mode of delivery

Engaging therapists in the use of a new treatment intervention is akin to engaging patients in a new therapy. It is essential to use a relational/motivational approach in both endeavors. There are greater chances of effective dissemination and implementation if one considers therapist values, goals, and concerns related to a new treatment. With regard to therapist concerns related to (a) through (d) above, dissemination of R4R should, from the start, include emphasis on how R4R was developed in partnership with patients and families (e.g., review of group evaluations, solicitation of formal and informal patient and family feedback on group development, and content analysis of alumni comments [Tantillo, McGraw, Hauenstein, & Groth, 2015]). Additionally, it will be helpful to note that research conducted on iterations of MFTG leading to the R4R approach described in this treatment manual were based on samples of program evaluation and research participants with few exclusion criteria.

It will also be important to emphasize with clinicians that there are clinical examples in the R4R treatment manual and that the mainstay of R4R is about leveraging relationships with others (including the therapist) to maximize healing and psychological growth. While R4R theoretical assumptions may not be consistent with every therapist's theoretical orientation (barrier [e]), in general, therapists are interested in strengthening the therapeutic alliance and promoting motivation and connection with patients and families. R4R emphasizes all of these elements.

In thinking through barriers (f) and (g) above, one possible way to maximize accessibility and increase the ease with which R4R can be learned may be to establish an institute, where learning is synchronous or asynchronous and either in-person or online. Project ECHO[R] (Extension for Community Healthcare Outcomes—https://echo.unm.edu/) is an example of an interprofessional educational institute that provides training in the ECHO[R] model, an innovative telementoring approach to training professionals about physical or mental health conditions (Arora et al., 2011; Zhou, Crawford, Serhal, Kurdyak, & Sockalingam, 2016). Project ECHO[R] builds a collaborative learning community comprised of geographically distant practitioners, decreases health care disparities, and "moves knowledge" as opposed to "moving patients" who often have no local access to specialty-based health care services. Project ECHO[R] telementoring clinics include use of didactic instruction, case-based presentations, live multidisciplinary team discussion, and videoconference-based supervision of cases. Such a model (Project ECHO[R] Eating Disorders Clinic; Tantillo, Starr, & Kreipe, 2019) already exists at the University of Rochester Medical Center to educate primary care, college health care, and behavioral health care practitioners about eating disorders in Western New York in the USA (http://www.nyeatingdisorders.org/echo.html).

A similar format could be developed to extend the reach of R4R MFTG to settings beyond the Rochester, New York, clinic where it is currently practiced. Advantages of a Project ECHO[R] telementoring clinic approach to R4R dissemination include the availability of free CME for participation, its resonance with adult learning due to a focus on case-based presentations, ease of accessibility with ZOOM videoconferencing via a laptop or hand-held electronic devices, and a sense of community with other practitioners committed to learning and implementing evidence-based best practices. Barriers to ECHO[R] telementoring clinics mainly include practitioner time to attend 60–90 minute monthly or biweekly sessions. This barrier can be overcome by also archiving sessions for practitioners who are unable to synchronously attend an ECHO[R] clinic session. There is no cost for participation in Project ECHO[R] telementoring clinics because they tend to be funded by public and private grants and/or other sources of government funding.

Preliminary program evaluation findings for Project ECHO[R] Eating Disorders Clinic revealed practitioner acceptability and a high level of satisfaction. Evaluation comment themes revealed that clinicians gained knowledge in the three domains emphasized by Project ECHO[R] Eating Disorders Clinic (i.e., interprofessional teamwork, specialty-based knowledge/skills, and early identification and intervention). Findings also indicated that clinicians intended to make practice changes related to screening. In order to examine whether Project ECHO® Eating Disorders Clinic or R4R ECHO® telementoring clinics translate into practice changes and improved patient outcomes, future better-controlled research and program evaluation studies need to assess practitioner learning, competence, performance, and patient health changes. Studies should also include follow-up measurement time points to assess sustainability.

An alternative to the use of Project ECHO® telementoring clinics would be to develop an evidence-based R4R asynchronous online training program similar to that developed by Maguire and colleagues (*The Essentials*; Maguire, Cunich, & Maloney, 2019) in Australia. *The Essentials* is comprised of five modules that provide comprehensive training in relation to the medical, psychological, and nutritional management of patients with eating disorders. A R4R corollary would provide a comprehensive review of R4R MFTG and, similar to *The Essentials*, would include video segments (expert clinicians and patient/family members), role-plays, interactive exercises and quizzes, and didactic instruction regarding skills and techniques required to implement R4R. Maguire and her colleagues (2019) have shown that participation in *The Essentials* was associated with increases in confidence, knowledge, skills, and attitudes. Future studies examining online training programs such as *The Essentials* or R4R need to be better controlled via randomization and use of a control or comparison group and need to include follow-up measurements to assess sustainability. Costs for an online R4R training program such as *The Essentials* could be covered by public or private grants or government funding sources. Alternatively, some of this cost could be covered by a fee from clinician registrants.

Regardless of whether future R4R dissemination occurs via Project ECHO® telementoring clinics or an online program similar to *The Essentials*, once a clinician begins using the R4R MFTG model, it is important for them to attend to fidelity and treatment adherence. Although the strengths and limitations of manualized treatments are well documented, their use has grown in recent years and they are generally well accepted and viewed as helpful by clinicians (Forbat, Black, & Dulgar, 2015; Strupp & Anderson, 1997). As with any manualized treatment approach, it is imperative that clinicians have competence in methods of psychotherapy beyond technical skills (Vakoch & Strupp, 2000; Wilson, 1998). Development of a positive therapeutic alliance, along with the ability to flexibly alter the approach in response to certain conditions (e.g., a challenging patient or family) is essential (Kendall, Chu, Gifford, Hayes, & Nauta, 1998; Kendall, Gosch, Furr, & Sood, 2008; Wilson, 1998). Thus, there is a healthy balance between adhering to the procedures and practices outlined in the manual and veering from them in response to situations that arise. As in life, detours are sometimes important, even therapeutic, as long as they do not lead the clinician to veer irrevocably off course. A clinician may adhere less rigidly to a manualized treatment if an intervention will foster the *spirit* of the treatment and promote the desired outcomes in the long run. A therapist can rigidly adhere to a manualized treatment and lose the patient and family in the process. Inasmuch as is possible, dissemination of R4R should include cues for the clinician about possible places where she/he may need to take a small detour to accomplish the overall goals of R4R. For example, if the group needs more time to process a group exercise, it may be unwise to derail this discussion because of other psychoeducational material that needs to be covered by the end of the session. Instead, it may be wiser to allow for continued discussion and processing of a particular issue, and in the context of the discussion, introduce psychoeducation concepts that were supposed to be covered by group's end. The therapist can use the process discussion to point out real life examples of these concepts. This intervention maintains group member empowerment and fosters adult learning because the therapist leverages something experiential to teach new material. This action brings a static psychoeducational concept alive for group members and, in the end, may be more engaging.

Financial Challenges

Depending on how a clinic or private practice is set up, and whether this is in a public health versus private health care environment, certain financial challenges may exist for practitioners wishing to provide R4R and patients and families wishing to receive it. Because R4R MFTG occurs in a group format, it can be charged at a group rate. This is a benefit if the clinical setting has an established fee structure for group therapy and if group members' insurance policies or government third party payers cover group treatment. Additionally, many private therapists in the USA, and elsewhere perhaps, do not participate on insurance panels, leaving patients and families to pay out of pocket for group therapy sessions.

Treatment cost considerations are important because the cost of care for AN is high and comparable with that for schizophrenia (Striegel-Moore, Leslie, Petrill, Garvin, & Rosenheck, 2000). Although comparative cost analysis data for eating disorders treatment is sparse (Weissman & Rosselli, 2017), some research has shown that MFTG for adolescents with AN may be a more cost-effective treatment option, either because it leads to faster weight gain than treatment as usual or because it shows similar outcomes to single family therapy, but for less fiscal investment (Gelin, Cook-Darzens, & Hendrick, 2017). It is also the case that R4R MFTG can be implemented in outpatient and day treatment/partial hospitalization settings, possibly serving as a step-down from and/or preventing the need for higher levels of care. By creating a community of caring, R4R MFTG may provide a safety net for patients and their family members, allowing them to move ahead in recovery with fewer relapses and a decreased need for more acute and costly treatment.

Therapist Attitudes about Treatment of Young Adults with AN and Their Families

It is important to consider what type of therapist will be best matched to the goals of the R4R MFTG approach. Clinicians who value family and/or group psychotherapy will be better able to develop the skills necessary to respond to five to seven families in the group room. Those who appreciate the benefit of process work, where dynamic systems are attended to as a way of furthering patient goals and recovery, will be best suited to the treatment.

The therapist's ability to incorporate a developmental framework into their understanding and treatment of eating disorders is also important in the delivery of R4R. One commonality that exists among family therapy approaches for AN with adolescents and adults is an emphasis on the common challenges of family developmental transitions. It is understood that rather than having caused the disorder, the family has reorganized itself around the disorder (Eisler, 2005). The illness is externalized, which helps family members view the symptoms as separate from the patient (i.e., the patient is not intentionally causing disruption and the illness is the source of the difficulties [Eisler, 2005]). Families are viewed as a resource for the patient to draw on rather than a dysfunctional system in need of repair (Eisler, Wallis, & Dodge, 2015). When the eating disorder is conceptualized in this way, emphasis can be placed on how it is affecting family functioning. This approach enables the therapist to focus on the common challenges of early adult development and family role transitions and ensures family members are not feeling blamed (by clinicians) for potentially causing the patient's disorder. Eating disorders are highly stigmatized conditions, even more so than schizophrenia, and both patients and families may feel blame; patients for having the disorder (Stewart, Keel, & Schiavo, 2006) and families for causing it (Coomber & King, 2013; Eisler, 2005). Framing treatment in terms of developmental challenges helps create an atmosphere of collaboration, reducing stigma and shame and diminishing guilt and defensiveness on the part of patients and families and increasing the likelihood they can work toward productive change.

In addition to valuing and using a developmental framework to understand and work with patients and families, the R4R therapist must also be comfortable with demystifying their role and working toward egalitarian relationships with group members. Family therapy for young adults with AN emphasizes helping patients and families build collaborative relationships with each other (Dimitropoulos, Lock, Le Grange, & Anderson, 2015). This collaborative stance is modeled by the clinician engaging with patients and families more as a guide or a consultant, rather than as an all-knowing person and involves de-emphasizing hierarchical relationships.

Knowledge about and Experience with Young Adult Development

The R4R MFTG is best administered by clinicians with a clear understanding of the developmental stages that all adolescents and young adults have to navigate. Emerging adults are thought to be exploring identity, developing autonomy, considering college and career options, and frequently changing residences and living situations (Arnett, 2015). When eating disorders develop during adolescence, they can inhibit growth such that young adults continue to struggle with accomplishing the milestones of typically developing adolescents, such as identity formation, platonic and romantic intimacy, independence, and autonomy (Christie & Viner, 2005). In working with families, therapists should respectfully convey the importance of helping patients catch up developmentally. They need to help family members carefully consider what a young adult is able to take on at any given time. Family members learn how to balance the need to be more directive in unsafe situations with efforts to foster problem solving and healthy autonomy. It is important that therapists meet patients where they are in this process. They need to communicate that despite the delayed emotional, relational and psychosocial development due to the eating disorder, nonetheless, patients are intellectually bright, capable and resilient. Moving away from a deficit model characterized by self-blame to one emphasizing strengths and self-compassion, wherein the patient is seen as being different from, as opposed to less than, is essential. Emphasis on biological and psychological traits in terms of how patients differ from peers (e.g., different wiring, different needs, different readiness to do things, different coping skills, different levels of anxiety, etc.) helps de-emphasize the disorder as a deficit and instead, empowers patients and families to rise to the challenges of growth. The supportive atmosphere created by R4R MFTG enables patients to face what frightens them, furthers their emotional development in connection with others, and improves their ability to use their strengths to successfully navigate recovery.

Research Directions

We have outlined existing research support for the R4R MFTG in Chapter 2. There is much need for additional quantitative and qualitative research in order to understand the way R4R may best be used to help patients and families. Young adults with AN and family members should be involved in these future research endeavors, not only as study participants but also as partners in developing research questions and offering feedback about methods and results. Their lived experience can enrich the research process and send us in new directions of inquiry.

Additionally, R4R alumni lived experience may also be capitalized upon by adding an alumnus or alumna individual in recovery or family member as an

R4R co-facilitator. We could then study the impact of this addition. Perhaps adding a well-recovered individual or veteran personal carer may quicken group member engagement and disclosure and/or improve motivation and outcomes. A parent peer mentor has historically participated in a short-term (eight-week) relational/motivational MFTG conducted by the first author in an eating disorder partial hospitalization program. The parent mentor promotes a sense of normalcy, universality, and cohesiveness and serves as a reminder that group can be helpful and recovery is possible. The R4R therapists can decide if they would like the R4R alumna/alumnus there each session or for selected sessions, e.g., at the start of group for welcoming and orientation purposes and/or the end of group as members are preparing for the transition out of group and considering next steps in treatment and life.

In terms of research directions, the following are some important research related issues and questions that will need to be addressed: (a) Randomized Controlled Trials are needed comparing R4R with treatment as usual for young adults with AN. Outcomes of various treatments need to be examined with consideration of patient and family resources, severity of the illness, and availability of other treatments (Kass, Koliko, & Wilfley, 2013). (b) Questions need to be addressed regarding the optimal way to integrate R4R into treatment settings. Does it have the greatest impact as part of a more intensive treatment model or as part of an outpatient treatment package, or is it best delivered as a stand-alone treatment? (c) Research can help inform us about the best treatment combinations for young adults with AN, i.e., can R4R be implemented with only primary care and/or nutritional counseling offered or is another form of psychotherapy (e.g., individual or single family) necessary? Does the optimal combination vary based on the age of the patient, severity or length of the illness, weight, or other factors? (d) Empirical work can also help us explore whether technology can be utilized to increase accessibility to R4R for patients or families who are geographically distant from specialized treatment programs and/or have limited resources for travel. Is videoconference participation in R4R as beneficial as face-to-face participation?

Finally, more research examining R4R mechanisms of change will be helpful. The first two authors (MT and JM) are currently developing a Connection Disconnection Processes Coding System to identify and track internal and interpersonal disconnections and connections characterizing R4R group member interactions. This narrative coding system (using R4R transcripts), adapted from Lynn Angus's *Narrative Process Coding System* (Angus, Levitt, & Hardtke, 1999), will help identify patterns indicative of "upstream" processes (e.g., the interplay of intrapersonal and interpersonal processes of disconnection and connection) in R4R that promote or inhibit "downstream" AN treatment outcomes (e.g., BMI, binge eating/purging, ED thoughts), healing, and recovery. This finer narrative coding measurement allows examination of the specific therapeutic actions that promote better connection to self and the immediate effect of better connection to self on the patient's interaction with others. Identification of these processes may provide additional and potentially more effective targets for intervention,

What Is Next? 289

leading to R4R enhancements and other new and innovative family-centered treatments for young adults with AN.

Conclusion: Forging the Future Together

In looking toward the future, it is critical to increase awareness and decrease the stigma and shame that often accompany eating disorders. Through education, skills-building, compassion, and guidance, R4R MFTG can promote the healing and empowerment necessary for recovery. R4R MFTG creates a diverse, abundant, and sustainable therapeutic community that capitalizes on and maximizes the strengths, resources, and adaptive coping strategies of its members (Tantillo, 2006; Tantillo, McGraw, Hauenstein, & Groth, 2015; Tantillo, McGraw, Lavigne, Brasch, & Le Grange, 2019; Tantillo, Sanftner, & Hauenstein, 2013). AN works against these efforts, hoping to isolate young adult patients and leave them feeling deficient and disconnected from themselves and others.

Without a community surrounding us, we lack the growth-fostering connections that help us more fully become who we really are. R4R provides this community, allowing young adults and their families to name their fears and disconnections and focus on the abundance of gifts and strengths they have to navigate recovery. In making patient and family gifts and sorrows explicit, R4R makes them available for sharing (McKnight & Block, 2012). This sharing feeds back into our relationships with one another, further strengthening connectedness with oneself and others and increasing young adults' resolve to reclaim their health and their lives. When patients with AN are able to be in their bodies and in the world more comfortably, they become more active participants in their communities. Without the overwhelming preoccupation with food and their bodies, which serve to disconnect them from themselves and others, they are able to achieve developmental milestones and contribute their unique skills and abilities to the world around them. They are empowered to find their purpose, live out their passions, and make a difference in our world that AN tries to thwart. We end this treatment manual with a reminder from McKnight and Block (2012) about the importance of connections in recovery and life:

> "All of these people have gifts we need for a really strong community. And many of them desperately need to be asked to join and contribute. Their only real deficiency is the lack of connection to the rest of us.... We have often ignored or even feared them. And yet their gifts are our greatest undiscovered treasure!".... Therefore ... [we] need to pay special attention to the people at the edge, the people with the names that describe their empty half rather than their gifted full half.... For the strength of our [community] is greatest when we all give all our gifts. (McKnight & Block, 2012, p. 138).

References

Angus, L., Levitt, H., & Hardtke, K. (1999). The Narrative Process Coding System: Research applications and implications for psychotherapy practice. *Journal of Clinical Psychology, 55*(10), 1255–1270. https://dx.doi.org/10.1002/(SICI)1097-4679(199910)55:10<1255::AID-JCLP7>3.0.CO;2-F.

Arnett, J. J. (2015). *Emerging adulthood: The winding road from the late teens through the twenties* (2nd ed.). Oxford University Press.

Arora, S., Thornton, K., Murata, G., Deming, P., Kalishman, S., Dion, D., Parish, B., Burke, T., Pak, W., Dunkelberg, J., Kistin, M., Brown, J., Jenkusky, S., Komaromy, K., & Qualls, C. (2011). Outcomes of treatment for Hepatitis C virus infection by primary care providers. *New England Journal of Medicine, 364,* 2199–2207. https://dx.doi.org/10.1056/NEJMoa1009370.

Christie, D., & Viner, R. (2005). ABC of adolescence: Adolescent development. *BMJ: British Medical Journal, 330,* 301–304. https://dx.doi.org/10.1136/bmj.330.7486.301.

Coomber, K., & King, R. M. (2013). A longitudinal examination of burden and psychological distress in carers of people with an eating disorder. *Social Psychiatry and Psychiatric Epidemiology, 48,* 163–171. https://dx.doi.org/10.1007/s00127-012-0524-7.

Cooper, Z., & Bailey-Straebler, S. (2015). Disseminating evidence-based psychological treatments for eating disorders. *Current Psychiatry Reports, 17,* 12. https://dx.doi.org/10.1007/s11920-015-0551-7.

Comstock, D. L., Hammer, T. R., Strentzsch, J., Cannon, K., Parsons, J., & Salazar, G. (2011). Relational-cultural theory: A framework for bridging relational, multicultural, and social justice competencies. *Journal of Counseling and Development, 86*(3), 279–287. https://dx.doi.org/10.1002/j.1556-6678.2008.tb00510.x.

Council for Accreditation of Counseling & Related Educational Programs (2018). *Section 2: Professional Counseling Identity.* https://www.cacrep.org/section-2-professional-counseling-identity/.

Currin, L., Waller, G., & Schmidt, U. (2009). Primary care physicians' knowledge of and attitudes toward the eating disorders: Do they affect clinical actions? *International Journal of Eating Disorders, 42*(5), 453–458. https://dx.doi.org/10.1002/eat.20636.

Dimitropoulos, G., Lock, J., Le Grange, D., & Anderson, K. (2015). Family therapy for transition youth. In K. Loeb, D. Le Grange, & J. Lock (Eds.), *Family therapy for adolescent eating and weight disorders: New applications* (pp. 230–255). Routledge/Taylor & Francis Group.

Duffey, T. (2008). Promoting relational competencies and in counselor education through creativity and relational-cultural theory. *Journal of Creativity in Mental Health, 2*(1), 47–59. https://dx.doi.org/10.1300/J456v02n01_05.

Duffey, T., & Somody, C. (2011). The role of relational-cultural therapy in mental health counseling. *Journal of Mental Health Counseling, 33*(3), 223–242. https://dx.doi.org/10.17744/mehc.33.3.c10410226u275647.

Eisler, I. (2005). The empirical and theoretical base of family therapy and multiple family day therapy for adolescent anorexia nervosa. *Journal of Family Therapy, 27,* 104–131. https://dx.doi.org/10.1111/j.1467-6427.2005.00303.x.

Eisler, I., Wallis, A. & Dodge, E. (2015). What's new is old and what's old is new: The origins and evolution of eating disorders family therapy. In K. Loeb, D. Le Grange, & J. Lock (Eds.), *Family Therapy for Adolescent Eating and Weight Disorders: New Applications* (pp. 6–42). Taylor and Francis Inc. https://dx.doi.org/10.4324/9781315882444.

Fairburn, C. G., & Cooper, Z. (2011). Therapist competence, therapy quality, and therapist training. *Behavior Research and Therapy, 49*(6–7), 373–378. https://dx.doi.org/10.1016/j.brat.2011.03.005.

Fairburn, C. G., & Wilson, G. T. (2013). The dissemination and implementation of psychological treatments: Problems and solutions. *International Journal of Eating Disorders, 46*(5), 516–521. https://dx.doi.org/10.1002/eat.22110.

Forbat, L., Black, L., & Dulgar, K. (2015). What clinicians think of manualized psychotherapy interventions: Findings from a systematic review. *Journal of Family therapy, 37*, 409–428. https://dx.doi.org/10.1111/1467-6427.12036.

Frey, L. L. (2013). Relational-cultural therapy: Theory, research, and application to counseling competencies. *Professional Psychology: Research and Practice, 44*(3), 177–185. https://dx.doi.org/10.1037/a0033121.

Gelin, Z., Cook-Darzens, S., & Hendrick, S. (2017). The evidence base for multiple family therapy in psychiatric disorders: A review (part 1). *Journal of Family Therapy, 40*(3), 302–325. https://dx.doi.org/10.1111/1467-6427.12178.

Jones, W. R., Saeidi, S., & Morgan, J. F. (2013). Knowledge and attitudes of psychiatrists towards eating disorders. *European Eating Disorders Review, 21*, 84–88. https://dx.doi.org/10.1002/erv.2155.

Jordan, J. (2018). *Relational-cultural therapy* (2nd ed.). American Psychological Association. https://dx.doi.org/10.1037/0000063-001.

Kass, A. E., Koliko, R. P., & Wilfley, D. E. (2013). Psychological treatments for eating disorders. *Current Opinion in Psychiatry, 26*(6), 549–555. https://dx.doi.org/10.1097/YCO.0b013e328365a30e.

Kendall, P. C., Chu, B., Gifford, A., Hayes, C., & Nauta, M. (1998). Breathing life into a manual: Flexibility and creativity with manual-based treatments. *Cognitive and Behavioral Practice, 5*, 177–198. https://dx.doi.org/10.1016/S1077-7229(98)80004-7.

Kendall, P. C., Gosch, E., Furr, J. M., & Sood, E. (2008). Flexibility within fidelity. *Journal of the American Academy of Child & Adolescent Psychiatry, 47*(9), 987–993. https://dx.doi.org/10.1097/CHI.0b013e31817eed2f.

Lenz, A. S. (2016). Relational-cultural theory: Fostering the growth of a paradigm through empirical research. *Journal of Counseling & Development, 94*(4), 415–428. https://dx.doi.org/10.1002/jcad.12100.

Lilienfeld, S. O., Ritschel, L. A., Lynn, S. J., Brown, A. P., Cautin, R. L., & Latzman, R. D. (2013). The research-practice gap: Bridging the schism between eating disorder researchers and practitioners. *International Journal of Eating Disorders, 46*(5), 386–394. https://dx.doi.org/10.1002/eat.22090.

Maguire, S., Cunich, M., & Maloney, D. (2019). Evaluating the effectiveness of an evidence-based online training program for health professionals in eating disorders. *Journal of Eating Disorders, 7*, 14. https://dx.doi.org/10.1186/s40337-019-0243-5.

McKnight, J., & Block, P. (2012). *Abundant community: Awakening the power of families and neighborhoods*. Berrett-Koehler Publishers, Inc.

Miller, W. R., & Rollnick, S. (2013). *Motivational interviewing: Helping people change* (3rd ed.). The Guilford Press.

National Eating Disorders Association (2013). *Eating disorders on college campus: A national survey of programs and resources*. New York, NY. https://www.nationaleatingdisorders.org/sites/default/files/CollegeSurvey/CollegiateSurveyProject.pdf.

Prochaska, J. O., Norcross, J. C., DiClemente, C. C. (1994). *Changing for good: A revolutionary six-stage program for overcoming bad habits and moving your life positively forward*. William Morrow.

Schmidt, U., Ali, S., Slone, G., Tiller, J., & Treasure, J. (1995). The Eating Disorders Awareness Test: A new instrument for the assessment of the effectiveness of psychoeducational approaches to the treatment of eating disorders. *European Eating Disorders Review, 3*(2), 103–110. https://dx.doi.org/10.1002/erv.2400030206.

Simic, M., & Eisler, I. (2015). Multi-family therapy. In I. Eisler, A. Wallis, E. Dodge, K. L. Loeb, D. Le Grange, & J. Lock (Eds.), *Family Therapy for Adolescent Eating and Weight Disorders* (pp. 110–138). Routledge.

Simmons, A. M., Milnes, S. M., & Anderson, D. A. (2008). Factors influencing the utilization of empirically supported treatments for eating disorders. *Eating Disorders: The Journal of Treatment and Prevention, 16*(4), 342–354. https://dx.doi.org/10.1080/10640260802116017.

Stewart, M., Keel, P. K., & Schiavo, R. S. (2006). Stigmatization of anorexia nervosa. *International Journal of Eating Disorders, 39*(4), 320–325. https://dx.doi.org/10.1002/eat.20262.

Striegel-Moore, R. H., Leslie, D., Petrill, S. A., Garvin, V., & Rosenheck, R. A. (2000). One-year use and cost of inpatient and outpatient services among female and male patients with an eating disorder: Evidence from a national database of health insurance claims. *International Journal of Eating Disorders, 27*, 381–389. https://dx.doi.org/10.1002/(SICI)1098-108X(200005)27:4<381::AID-EAT2>3.0.CO;2-U.

Strupp, H. H., & Anderson, T. (1997). On the limitations of therapy manuals. *Clinical Psychology: Science and Practice, 4*(1), 76–82. https://dx.doi.org/10.1111/j.1468-2850.1997.tb00101.x.

Tantillo, M. (2006). A relational approach to eating disorders multifamily therapy group: Moving from difference and disconnection to mutual connection. *Families, Systems, & Health, 23*(1), 82–102. https://dx.doi.org/10.1037/1091-7527.24.1.82.

Tantillo, M., McGraw, J. S., Hauenstein, E., & Groth, S. W. (2015). Partnering with patients and families to develop an innovative multifamily therapy group treatment for adults with anorexia nervosa. *Advances in Eating Disorders: Theory, Research, and Practice, 3*(3), 269–287. https://dx.doi.org/10.1080/21662630.2015.1048478.

Tantillo, M., McGraw, J. S., Lavigne, H. M., Brasch, J., & Le Grange, D. (2019). A pilot study of multifamily therapy group for young adults with anorexia nervosa: Reconnecting for recovery. *International Journal of Eating Disorders, 52*(8), 950–955. https://dx.doi.org/10.1002/eat.23097.

Tantillo, M., Sanftner, J. L., & Hauenstein, E. (2013). Restoring connection in the face of disconnection: An integrative approach to understanding and treating anorexia nervosa. *Advances in Eating Disorders: Theory, Research, and Practice, 1*, 21–38. https://dx.doi.org/10.1080/21662630.2013.742980.

Tantillo, M., Starr, T., & Kreipe, R. E. (2019). Recruitment and acceptability of a Project ECHO® eating disorders clinic: A pilot study of telementoring for primary medical and behavioral health care practitioners. *Eating Disorders: The Journal of Treatment and Prevention, 4*, 1–26. https://doi.org/10.1080/10640266.2019.1580125.

Thompson-Brenner, H., Satir, D. A., Franko, D. L., & Herzog, D. B. (2012). Clinician reactions to patients with eating disorders: A review of the literature. *Psychiatric Services, 63*(1), 73–78. https://dx.doi.org/10.1176/appi.ps.201100050.

Tobin, D. L., Banker, J. D., Weisberg, L., & Bowers, W. (2007). I know what you did last summer (and it was not CBT): A factor analytic model of international psychotherapeutic practice in the eating disorders. *International Journal of Eating Disorders, 40*(8), 754–757. https://dx.doi.org/10.1002/eat.20426.

Vakoch, D. A., & Strupp, H. H. (2000). The evolution of psychotherapy training: Reflections on manual-based learning and future alternatives. *Journal of Clinical Psychology*, *56*(3), 309–318. https://dx.doi.org/10.1002/(SICI)1097-4679(200003)56:3<309::AID-JCLP7>3.0.CO;2-7.

Von Ranson, K. M., Wallace, L. M., & Stevenson, A. (2013). Psychotherapies provided for eating disorders by community clinicians: Infrequent use of evidence-based treatment. *Psychotherapy Research*, *23*(3), 333–343. https://dx.doi.org/10.1080/10503307.2012.735377.

Waller, G. I., Stringer, H., & Meyer, C. (2012). What cognitive behavioral techniques to therapists report using when delivering cognitive behavioral therapy for the eating disorders? *Journal of Consulting and Clinical Psychology*, *80*(1), 171–175. https://dx.doi.org/10.1037/a0026559.

Weissman, R., & Rosselli, F. (2017). Reducing the burden of suffering from eating disorders: Unmet treatment needs, cost of illness, and the quest for cost-effectiveness. *Behaviour Research and Therapy*, *88*, 49–64. https://dx.doi.org/10.1016/j.brat.2016.09.006.

Weissman, M. M., Verdeli, H., Gameroff, M. J., Bledsoe, S. E., Betts, K., Mufson, L., Fitterling, H., & Wickramarante, P. (2006). National survey of psychotherapy training in psychiatry, psychology, and social work. *Archives of General Psychiatry*, *63*, 925–934. https://dx.doi.org/10.1001/archpsyc.63.8.925.

Wilson, G. T. (1998). Manual-based treatment and clinical practice. *Clinical Psychology: Science and Practice*, *5*(3), 363–374. https://dx.doi.org/10.1111/j.1468-2850.1998.tb00156.x.

Zhou, C., Crawford, A., Serhal, E., Kurdyak, P., & Sockalingam, S. (2016). The impact of project ECHO on participant and patient outcomes: A systematic review. *Academic Medicine*, *91*(10), 1439–1461. https://dx.doi.org/10.1097/ACM.0000000000001328.

Index

action 107
adolescents with AN: Multifamily Therapy Group (MFTG) 26–8
advanced practice psychiatric nurse, role of 123
American Psychiatric Association (APA): AN clinical practice guidelines 9
animal caregiver styles 78, *79*, 80
animal metaphors 235–52, **242–7**
anorexia nervosa (AN) 158–71; age of onset 4; cognitive and cognitive behavioral models 7; family context 158–71; lifetime prevalence 4; models incorporating biology and environment 8–9; mortality rate 4; neurobiological models 7–8; overview 4–5; psychotropic medication 9–10; risk factors 5–6; sociocultural theories 6; treatment in young adults 9–13
APA (American Psychiatric Association): AN clinical practice guidelines 9
argumentation, avoiding 104, 106

care manager, role of 123
change, processes of 109–10, **110**; commitment 109, **110**; consciousness-raising 109, **110**; countering 109, **110**; emotional arousal 109, **110**; environmental control 109, **110**; helping relationships 109, **110**; reward 109, **110**; self-reevaluation 109, **110**; social liberation 109, **110**
change, stages of 107–8, 115–18; action 107; contemplation 107; maintenance 107; precontemplation 107; preparation 107; termination 107
coaching and mealtime assistance **189**
co-facilitation 62

cognitive and cognitive behavioral models of AN 7
Cognitive-Interpersonal Model 8–9
commitment 109, **110**
comorbid conditions 4–5, 132–3
connection, strategies to promote 152–7
consciousness-raising 109, **110**
contemplation 107
countering 109, **110**

disconnection *43*, 45–6, 69–70, *69–70*; forces that perpetuate interpersonal disconnections and AN 195, *195*; four levels created by AN 99–103; interventions to process and repair 118–22; intrapersonal and interpersonal processes of 2, 46, 126–30, **127–8**; moving through disconnection to better connection 182, **183–5**; transforming into stronger connections 208–9
discrepancy, developing 103–4, 106
disease of disconnection (AN) 45
dissemination and implementation in clinical settings 282–5

eating disorder (ED) behavior traps 145–6
emotional arousal 109, **110**
empathy, expressing 103, 106
environmental control 109, **110**
epigenome 131–2
explicit and implicit rules 158, 161–2, **164–5**

family-based treatment (FBT) 11–12; for transition age youth (FBT-TAY) 12
family context of AN 158–71, **170**; implicit and explicit rules 161–2,

164–5; recovery rules 162; relationship rules 162–3; strategies to promote mutual connections and recovery **159–60**
family member assessments 80–4
family member discharge evaluation questionnaire 278–9
family member relapse prevention support plan 253
family therapy 10–12; principles of 25
feared social eating situations 259–60
financial challenges 285
five good things 73, 77, *77*
Frank, Jerome 27
functional analysis 145–6, **147–9**, 149
future goals and problem solving about next steps 274
future plans to maintain connections and recovery 271

genetic vulnerability 131–2
getting ready: co-facilitation 62; group structure 62; medical follow-up 66; phone screening 62, **63–4**; psychiatric evaluation 66; recruitment 62–4, **63–4**
good conflict 207–16; overview 216; reviewing peaks and valleys 207; transforming disconnections into stronger connections 208–9
good things, five 73, 77, *77*
group structure 62
group therapeutic factors that promote change 24

helping relationships 109, **110**

implicit and explicit rules 158, 161–2, **164–5**
internal disconnections: family members' perception of patient internal disconnections 80–1; from self and one's body 76
interpersonal disconnections 76, 80–1

licensed clinical social worker (LCSW), role of 123
life coach, role of 124

maintenance 107
marriage and family therapist, role of 123
Maudsley Child and Adolescent Eating Disorders Service (London) 11, 27

mealtime guidelines and support strategies for recovery 185, **186–9**
medical follow-up 66
motivational principles 45, 103–6; avoid argumentation 104, 106; develop discrepancy 103–4, 106; express empathy 103, 106; roll with resistance 105–6; support self-efficacy 105–7
Multifamily Therapy Group (MFTG): adolescents with AN (MFT-AN) 26–8; nature, origins, and outcomes 22–6; Reconnecting for Recovery (R4R) MFTG approach *see* Reconnecting for Recovery (R4R) MFTG approach; young adults with AN 28–31
mutual connections and recovery, strategies to promote **159–60**
mutuality and motivation during recovery, strategies to promote 221–3
mutual relationships 73–5, *74*

National Institute for Health and Care Excellence, United Kingdom (NICE): AN clinical practice guidelines 9–10
Negative relational image and meaning 139–45, *140*
neurobiological models of AN 7–8
nourishing and empowering the "we" 196–7

parent peer mentor, role of 124
patient assessments 75–80
patient discharge evaluation questionnaire 276–7
patient relapse prevention plan 252
patient reticence to share about points of tension/disconnections 220
peaks and valleys 207
peer mentor, role of 124
Persuasion and Healing (Frank) 27
phone screening 62, **64–5**
precontemplation 107
preparation 107
primary care provider, role of 122
professional treatment team member roles 122–4
Project ECHO (Extension for Community Healthcare Outcomes) 283
psychiatric evaluation 66
psychiatrist, role of 122
psychologist, role of 122

296 *Index*

Reconnecting for Recovery (R4R) 1–13; anorexia nervosa *see* anorexia nervosa; goals **55**; introduction 1–4; outline of group sessions **56**
Reconnecting for Recovery (R4R) MFTG approach: conclusions about 289; development of 41–4; difference from other multifamily therapy groups 44–53; dissemination and implementation in clinical settings 282–5; financial challenges 285; getting ready *see* getting ready; knowledge about and experience with 287; outline of group sessions **56**, **95**; research directions 287–9; sessions *see* specific session numbers (session 1, session 2, etc.); therapist attitudes 286; training 280–2; treatment manual 53–4; working with other health care team members 54–5
recovery: promoting continued recovery 266
recovery, challenges to 267
recovery plate diagram *192*
recovery process 102–3
recovery rules 162
recruitment 62–3, **64–5**
reframing biopsychosocial factors 130–2
reframing eating disorders as diseases of disconnection *69–70*, 69–73
registered dietitian, role of 123
relapse prevention 235–55; animal metaphors 235–52, **242–7**; challenges to recovery 267; family member discharge evaluation questionnaire 278–9; family member relapse prevention support plan 253; future goals and problem solving about next steps 274; future plans to maintain connections and recovery 271; meanings and feelings related to termination 273–4; overview 254–5, 271–2, 275; patient discharge evaluation questionnaire 276–7; patient relapse prevention plan 252; promoting continued recovery 266; relapse prevention strategies 253–4; termination themes, common 267–9
Relational-Cultural Theory (R-CT) 45, 62, 73
relational image and meaning: negative 139–45, *140*
relationship rules 162–3

research directions 287–9
resistance, rolling with 105–6
reward 109, **110**
rhinoceros and dolphin caregiver responses **147–8**
roll with resistance 105–6
Royal Australian and New Zealand College of Psychiatrists (RANZCP): AN clinical practice guidelines 9
R4R approach *See* Reconnecting for Recovery (R4R); Reconnecting for Recovery (R4R) MFTG approach

self-efficacy, supporting 105–7
self-reevaluation 109, **110**
session 1: engaging and evaluating young adults with AN and their families: assessment, joining and orientation 67–85; description of nature and goals of R4R MFTG 67–8; emphasizing importance of mutual relationships in recovery 73–5, *74*; family member assessments 80–4; overview 84–5; patient assessments 75–80; reframing eating disorders as diseases of disconnection *69–70*, 69–73; wrapping up session 1 84
session 2: engaging and evaluating young adults with AN and their families: assessment, joining, and orientation (continued) 87–97; complete orientation to R4R MFTG 94–7, *95*; establishing patient and family group goals 92–3; nature, rationale, and overall aim of session 2 87–92; overview 97
session 3: AN, a disease of disconnection: introduction, recovery process, motivational interviewing principles, and spiral of change 98–113; introduction 98–9; levels of disconnection 99–102; motivational principles 103–6; overview 112–13; recovery process 102–3; spiral of change 107–12, *108*, **110**, *111*
session 4: AN, a disease of disconnection: introduction, recovery process, motivational interviewing principles, and spiral of change (continued) 114–25; interventions to process and repair disconnections 118–22; overview 124–5; spiral of change 114–18; treatment team member roles 122–4

session 5: AN biopsychosocial factors and comorbidity 126–34; comorbid conditions 132–3; intrapersonal and interpersonal processes of disconnection 126–30, **127–8**; overview 133–4; reframing biopsychosocial factors 130–2

session 6: AN biopsychosocial factors (continued), disconnection and functional analysis skills 138–50; functional analysis 145–6, **147–9**, 149; negative relational image and meaning 139–45, *140*; overview 149–50

session 7: strategies to promote mutual connection 152–7; overview 156–7

session 8: AN and the family context 158–71; implicit and explicit rules 161–2, **164–5**; overview **170**, 171; recovery rules 162; relationship rules 162–3; strategies to promote mutual connections and recovery **159–60**

session 9: identifying points of tension and disconnections related to AN, recovery, and relationships 173–93; coaching and mealtime assistance **189**; mealtime guidelines and support strategies for recovery 185, **186–9**; moving through disconnection to better connection 182, **183–5**; overview **175**, 190–1; recovery plate diagram *192*

session 10: nourishing and empowering the "we" in relationships 194–206; forces that perpetuate interpersonal disconnections and AN 195, *195*; nourishing and empowering the "we" 196–7; overview 205–6

session 11: waging good conflict in connection 207–16; overview 216; reviewing peaks and valleys 207; transforming disconnections into stronger connections 208–9

session 12: moving from disconnection to connection 217–33; challenges 219–21, 227; conducting first half of session 217–23; conducting second half of session 223–32; overview 233–4; patient reticence to share about points of tension/disconnections 220; strategies for promoting mutuality and motivation during recovery 221–3; talking about thoughts versus feelings 219–20; therapist statements that foster general discussion

of points of tension/disconnections 218–19; transitioning from adolescence to young adulthood 223–6; the whole group becomes quiet 220–1

session 13: relapse prevention and maintaining good connection 235–55; animal metaphors 235–52, **242–7**; family member relapse prevention support plan 253; overview 254–5; patient relapse prevention plan 252; relapse prevention strategies 253–4

session 14: relapse prevention (continued) and preparing for termination 256–65; feared social eating situations 259–60; overview 264–5

session 15: relapse prevention (continued), termination, and next steps for continued connections in recovery 266–72; challenges to recovery 267; future plans to maintain connections and recovery 271; overview 271–2; promoting continued recovery 266; termination themes, common 267–9

session 16: relapse prevention (continued), termination, and next steps for continued connections in recovery 273–9; family member discharge evaluation questionnaire 278–9; future goals and problem solving about next steps 274; meanings and feelings related to termination 273–4; overview 275; patient discharge evaluation questionnaire 276–7

social eating situations 259–60

social liberation 109, **110**

social worker, role of 123

sociocultural theories about AN 6

spiral of change 107–12, *108*, **110**, *111*, 114–18

Stages of Change Theory 45

strategies for connection 152–7

strategies for promoting mutuality and motivation during recovery 221–3

strategies to promote mutual connections and recovery **159–60**

support self-efficacy 105–7

termination 107; meanings and feelings related to 273–4; themes 267–9

therapist attitudes 286

therapist self-disclosure in R4R group 47–52

298   *Index*

therapist statements that foster general discussion of points of tension/disconnections 218–19
thoughts versus feelings, talking about 219–20
toxic Western sociocultural values 153
training 280–2
transitioning from adolescence to young adulthood 223–6
treatment manual 53–4
treatment team member roles 122–4

"we" in relationships, nourishing and empowering 194–206
whole group becomes quiet 220–1
working with other health care team members 54–5

young adults with AN: Multifamily Therapy Group (MFTG) 28–31

Zest 73
ZOOM videoconferencing 283

Printed in the United States
By Bookmasters